GENDER IN
PSYCHOANALYTIC SPACE

CONTEMPORARY THEORY SERIES

GENDER IN PSYCHOANALYTIC SPACE

BETWEEN CLINIC AND CULTURE

EDITED BY

MURIEL DIMEN

and

VIRGINIA GOLDNER

OTHER

Other Press
New York

Copyright © 2002 Muriel Dimen and Virginia Goldner

Production Editor: Robert D. Hack

This book was set in 11 pt. Berkeley by Alpha Design & Composition of Pittsfield, NH.

First softcover printing 2010
ISBN 978-1-59051-472-6

10 9 8 7 6 5 4 3 2 1

Library of Congress Cataloging-in-Publication Data

Gender in psychoanalytic space : between clinic and culture / Muriel Dimen & Virginia Goldner, eds.
    p. cm.
  Includes bibliographical references and index.
  ISBN 1-892746-84-0
  1. Sex (Psychology) 2. Psychoanalysis. 3. Postmodernism. I. Dimen, Muriel. II. Goldner, Virginia.
  BF175.5.S48 G46 2001
  155.3—dc21   2001037506

To feminism, for having given us our starting point as subjects and actors; for still being there, sustaining community and critical engagement; and for having provided us with a torch to pass on.

Contents

Acknowledgments

First, we wish to acknowledge Jessica Benjamin and Adrienne Harris, colleagues, comrades, and intimates, with whom we conducted the Seminar on Psychoanalysis and Sexual Difference at the New York Institute for the Humanities at New York University. Those ten years, 1986–1996, as well as the preceding decade, were formative in ways we could not know then. Freud says you can see the unconscious only as though seated backwards in a train, so that you glimpse the landscape just as you have passed it. So, midway through that decade, around 1991, we saw, looking back, that a new way of thinking about gender in mind, body, and culture had fused in the crucible of our collaborative work. This spontaneous combustion, the moment of theory inspiring this book, took us by surprise. Having worked for many years in several distinct idioms—feminism, social criticism, and relational psychoanalysis—we found that, unbeknownst to each other, we had put these theories together in separate essays in the form of what we now call psychoanalytic gender theory, the system of thought and practice that marks the spot where clinical psychoanalysis, feminism, and postmodernism meet.

Second, we wish to recognize the late Stephen A. Mitchell's generative contribution to this enterprise. It was in the very first year (1991) of *Psychoanalytic Dialogues: A Journal of Relational Perspectives*, which he founded, that gender was positioned at the core of relational psychoanalysis. There, in Volume 1, Issues 2 and 3, the moment of theory burst into form. The invitation and challenge of writing for an audience of psychoanalysts moved us to bring the politics of feminism and the theory of postmodernism into dialogue with the lived experience of clinical psychoanalysis.

Third, we want to thank Maureen Magrogan, editor extraordinaire, whose critical instincts about writing at the intersection of the disciplines and postmodernism first brought this project into being.

And finally, we want to acknowledge each other and our mutual ability to sustain friendship and collegiality in the inevitably tortuous process of editing a volume. Maureen warned us that friendships can break up on the co-editorial shoals, but we want to report that ours has survived, alive and kicking and living downtown.

Contributors

Lewis Aron, Ph.D., A.B.P.P., is Director, Postdoctoral Program in Psychotherapy and Psychoanalysis. He has written *A Meeting of Minds: Mutuality in Psychoanalysis* and has co-edited *The Legacy of Sándor Ferenczi, Relational Perspectives on the Body,* and *Relational Psychoanalysis: The Emergence of a Tradition.* An Associate Editor of *Psychoanalytic Dialogues,* he is in private practice in Manhattan and Port Washington, New York.

Donna Bassin, Ph.D, is Member and Faculty at the Institute of Psychoanalytic Training and Research where she serves as chair of The Women's Center at the I.P.T.A.R Clinical Center. In addition to her many papers and reviews she has co-edited *Representations of Motherhood* and edited *Female Sexuality: Contemporary Engagements.* Her private practice is in Manhattan.

Jessica Benjamin, Ph.D., is the author of *The Bonds of Love, Like Subjects, Love Objects,* and *Shadow of the Other.* A faculty member of the Postdoctoral Psychology Program in Psychotherapy and Psychoanalysis, New York University, and the Graduate Faculty, New School University, Program in Psychoanalysis, and associate editor of *Studies in Gender and Sexuality*, she practices privately in Manhattan.

Judith Butler, Ph.D., Maxine Elliot Professor in the Departments of Rhetoric and Comparative Literature, University of California, Berkeley, wrote *Subjects of Desire*, *Gender Trouble*, *Bodies That Matter*, *The Psyc¹ ic Life of Power*, and *Excitable Speech*, as well as numerous articles and contributions on philosophy, psychoanalysis, and feminist and queer theory. She is currently completing a manuscript on Antigone and the politics of kinship.

Nancy J. Chodorow, Ph.D., is Member and Faculty, San Francisco Psychoanalytic Institute, and is in private practice in Berkeley. Professor of Sociology and Clinical Professor of Psychology, University of California, Berkeley, she has written *The Power of Feelings*; *Femininities, Masculinities, Sexualities*; *Feminism and Psychoanalytic Theory*; and *The Reproduction of Mothering*.

Ken Corbett, Ph.D., Co-editor of *Studies in Gender and Sexuality*, is a member of The New York University Psychoanalytic Society of the Postdoctoral Program in Psychotherapy and Psychoanalysis.

Muriel Dimen, Ph.D., Associate Editor of *Psychoanalytic Dialogues* and *Studies in Gender and Sexuality*, is Clinical Professor of Psychology, Postdoctoral Program in Psychotherapy and Psychoanalysis, New York University, and Faculty and Supervisor, Adelphi University Derner Institute in Psychotherapy and Psychoanalysis. She wrote *Surviving Sexual Contradictions* and *The Anthropological Imagination*, and is in private practice in Manhattan.

Virginia Goldner, Ph.D., is co-editor of *Studies in Gender and Sexuality* and is on the Editorial Board of *Psychoanalytic Dialogues*. She is also Senior Faculty, Ackerman Institute for the Family. Her practices in psychoanalysis and family therapy are in Manhattan.

Adrienne Harris, Ph.D., faculty member at the Postdoctoral Program in Psychotherapy and Psychoanalysis, New York University, is an Associate Editor of *Psychoanalytic Dialogues* and *Studies in Gender and Sexuality*. She co-edited (with Lewis Aron) *The Legacy of Sándor Ferenczi* and (with Muriel Dimen) *Storms in Her Head*, and is completing work on *Softly Assembled Gender*.

Lilia Labidi, Ph.D., is a Tunisian anthropologist and psychoanalyst, and Professor of Psychology at the University of Tunis. Her books include *La génération des années trente, la mémoire vivante des sujets de l'histoire, Les origines des mouvements feministes en Tunisie, Çabra Hachma, sexualité et tradition*, and *Deuil impossible*.

Lynne Layton, Ph.D., Assistant Clinical Professor of Psychology, Harvard Medical School, Beth Israel-Deaconess Medical Center, teaches at the Massachusetts Institute for Psychoanalysis. An associate editor of *Journal for the Psychoanalysis of Culture and Society* and on the Editorial Board of *Studies in Gender and Sexuality*, she wrote *Who's That Girl? Who's That Boy?: Clinical Practice Meets Postmodern Gender Theory*.

Kimberlyn Leary, Ph.D., is Associate Director and Adjunct Assistant Professor of Psychology, University of Michigan Psychological Clinic, and candidate at the Michigan Psychoanalytic Institute. A Visiting Scholar at the Program on Negotiation at Harvard Law School, she has written several essays on race and difference in dynamic treatment and on the impact of postmodern perspectives on clinical psychoanalytic practice.

Maggie Magee, M.S.W., Member and Faculty of the Los Angeles Institute and Society for Psychoanalytic Studies, is co-author (with Diana C. Miller) of *Lesbian Lives: Psychoanalytic Narratives Old and New*. Ms. Magee is on the clinical consulting faculty of the California Institute of Clinical Social Work and is in private practice in Los Angeles, California.

Diana C. Miller, M.D., Member and Faculty of the Los Angeles Institute and Society for Psychoanalytic Studies, has co-authored (with Maggie Magee) *Lesbian Lives: Psychoanalytic Narratives Old and New*. Dr. Miller is on the clinical faculty of UCLA/NPI, a faculty affiliate of the UCLA Center for the Study of Women, and in private practice in Los Angeles.

Margo Rivera, Ph.D., is Professor of Psychiatry in the faculty of medicine at Queen's University in Kingston, Ontario, Canada, and co-director of the Personality Disorders Service at Kingston Psychiatric Hospital. She edited *Fragment By Fragment: Feminist Perspectives on Memory and Child Sexual Abuse* and wrote *More Alike Than Different: Treating Severely Dissociative Trauma Survivors*.

Introduction

MURIEL DIMEN AND VIRGINIA GOLDNER

This book captures a moment in the ongoing project of theory-making in psychoanalytic gender studies. No moment stays put, of course. New ideas take hold, age, engender critique, beget elaborations. The new ideas in this volume emerged at an intersection, a site on an intellectual map, a unique moment in our intellectual history—the point where clinical psychoanalysis first joined the systematic dialogue, already in progress, among postmodernism, feminism, and psychoanalytic theory.

Critical work in feminism has always been concerned with the deconstruction of gender, even before we had the term. In unfolding gender's discontinuities, gaps, and creativities, feminist thinkers made great use of psychoanalytic theory, particularly its founding Freudian texts. Historically, however, the academic use of text-as-theory-and-evidence had neglected a central source of psychoanalytic insight: the clinical situation. This omission was a critical lapse, since postmodernism, especially Foucauldian thought, had long established the insight that bodies of knowledge not only contain and purvey content, they also function as socially regulatory practices, sometimes even reproducing the very patterns of domination (such as heterosexism) they aim to critique. Psychoanalysis has been an emblematic case in point, since it is a site of cultural transmission as well as a formal theory of mind.

This collection remedies that absence in the literature, bringing together essays that were turning points in the development of a far more complex framework. The authors (with the exception of the distinguished Judith Butler) are all working clinicians, equally versed in psychoanalytic theory, gender critique, and postmodernism. Like all first-rate psychoanalytic writing, their essays address subtle and complex aspects of the psychoanalytic process, and many of them advance theories of clinical technique. At the same time, all these clinically grounded pieces are unique in their critique of gender and of psychoanalytic theory, as informed by postmodernism and the strategy of deconstruction.

These essays concern themselves with and occupy many tensions that produce useful paradoxes, such as the one between modernism and postmodernism. In the modernist vision, gender constitutes a foundational and transhistorical category of mind and culture, while in postmodern terms, gender is a fluid and variable social construction. Significantly, these categories emerged in tandem in psychoanalysis, such that at the very moment when gender was being revived as a crucial subject of interest and as a category of psychoanalytic thought, it also began to fall apart critically and creatively, losing both its philosophical and experiential coherence.

In the current context, modernist and postmodernist visions of gender cohabit in an unstable, uneasy, yet immensely productive form of synergy. This critical tension, which some of our contributors—Donna Bassin, Jessica Benjamin, and Lynne Layton—argue we must preserve, has been captured in three closely related metaphors crafted by members of our cottage industry of gender ironists. Adrienne Harris, following Jacques Lacan, writes of gender as a "necessary fiction"; Benjamin appropriates the Marxist metaphor of gender as a "real appearance"; and Virginia Goldner proposes that we conceive of gender as a "false truth." Each of these phrases condenses the art of the double take, ensuring that we neither essentialize gender nor dematerialize it—one of the core tropes that preoccupies all the authors in this volume.

If 1970s feminism may be said to have asked, "Gender, what is it?," these essays pose a more basic question, "Gender, is it?" When gender's meaning is inspected, its coherence is now most often ascribed to social construction—to the practices of language, culture, and psyche. Any given gender identity is no longer a self-evident psychic structure. Indeed, gender's multiplicity of significance can be deconstructed, as Muriel Dimen contends here, into a power matrix of difference(s). In one example of this radical way of thinking, Ken Corbett shows how the binary passive/active is implicated in the construction of masculinity, revealing how *different* masculinities exist within and between individuals and sexual practices and across life spans. Margot Rivera's contemporary classic documents the mutual constitution of gender and self-identity in the action of psychic coherence, splitting, and its extreme form, multiple personality disorder.

Judith Butler, whose *Gender Trouble* (1990) is a benchmark for many of the essays in this volume, has demonstrated how gender is both constituted by, and constitutive of, sexuality. She argues here that the mutual construction of binary gender and oppositional homo/heterosexuality make the homoerotic love objects of childhood (same-sexed parents) lost objects whose very loss is disavowed ("I never loved so I never lost him/her"), infusing heterosexual ideology and practice with a pervasive melancholy. In collegial critique, Lynne Layton endorses this deconstructive strategy, but makes the case that it scotomizes agency, a lapse Butler herself has tried increasingly to remedy (1993).

In articulating the multiple processes through which gender and subjectivity inform one another, these essays trace out gender's paradoxical circuitry. For example, while gender is demonstrably a psychic identity category through which one's subjectivity is constituted (beginning before birth), psychic experience is not always or necessarily "gender-saturated," as is illustrated by the clinical case material recounted by Dimen and Harris. Put another way, a paradox of gender is that while it is not an identity or essence to be found in the core of the person, it still constitutes a core experience of identity.

As a result of the feminist deconstruction project, we seem ready to see through gender, to know it is "everywhere and nowhere" (Bourdieu and Eagleton 1992, p. 115), indeed that it is not anything at all, but rather, as Dimen proposes, a "force-field of dualisms," and thus, as both Harris and Goldner have suggested, "a site and state of contradiction." Crucial to this moment of intellectual history were two theoretical interventions. Benjamin (1988) strategically deployed the conceptual remains of the polarity "masculinity/femininity" into profound questions about the underlying "either/or, subject/object" logic of the gender binary itself, while Butler (1990) shifted theoretical attention from the reified "body" to the creation of "embodiment," as for example, in her influential view of gender as a "melancholic masquerade."

As gender decomposed under the bright lights of postmodernism, psychoanalytic clinicians began to look for deconstructive strategies to address gender's psychic action. Lewis Aron, addressing the classic concept of the primal scene, argues for the possibility of both gender fluidity and stability. Bassin and Benjamin rework and critique, but also retain, psychosexual developmental categories. Benjamin proposes a postoedipal stage beyond the binary of "gender complementarity" that reconfigures preoedipal gender fluidity. Bassin, building on Benjamin, proposes that the psychic capacity for symbolization would support a postoedipal sensibility in which psychic femininity and masculinity can be played as a jazz musician riffs and improvises on musical themes.

In one way or another, all of these essays deal with the two-sided process through which discourses (cultural or theoretical) construct identities and subjectivities, while individual subjects locate themselves in some (but not in other) stories of the self. They thereby bridge a gap. Traditionally, feminist political theory absorbed itself with the first set of concerns, while feminist psychoanalytic theory focused on the second. This volume, in contrast, takes up the interimplication of the so-called psychic and social in the construction of gender and sexual subjectivity. Chodorow highlights the relationship between the psychological formation of personal gender and the cultural tropes through which gender takes shape. In a related vein, Magee and Miller focus on the multiplicity of sexual identities and the psychic and ideological pressures to simplify such complexity.

The intersection of psychoanalysis, feminism, and postmodernism is located, finally, in the space between clinic and culture. If power is knowledge, then psychoanalytic power lies in clinical treatment as well as in psychoanalytic writing. At the same time, psychoanalysis, like any regulatory practice, is subject to disruption and critique. There are a variety of ways to disrupt. Gender theory finds contradictions in psychoanalytic thought by examining gaps in the text where the central disciplinary terms of femininity and masculinity can be re-created and transformed. Clinical psychoanalysis proceeds in counterpoint. In the intimacy of the consulting room, it locates disjunctures in the associative process and intersubjective field that reveal what is unspeakable about gender. Kimberlyn Leary begins a crucial deconstruction of race in the clinical encounter, using some of the conceptual strategies that the feminist theorists and clinicians in this volume have brought to bear on gender. Lilia Labidi brings a distinct voice to this collection. The moment of theory represented in this book had its psychoanalytic genesis principally in the Anglo-American relational school (Mitchell and Aron 1999), while its postmodernist attitude owes much to Michel Foucault (1978) and Jacques Lacan (1977, Mitchell and Rose 1982). Labidi's essay, written entirely in the Lacanian vocabulary, deploys the three registers of Symbolic, Imaginary, and the Real to splice the construction and deconstruction of gender in psyche and politics, clinic and culture, body and language.

Insofar as gender is a ubiquitous category, we simply cannot see through it on our own, no matter how evolved our capacity for symbolization. Gender becomes visible as a cultural imperative only through the work of critical deconstruction—political, psychoanalytic, academic—which is the work of this book.

REFERENCES

Benjamin, J. (1988). *The Bonds of Love*. New York: Pantheon.

Bourdieu, P., and Eagleton, T. (1992). Doxa and common life. *New Left Review* 191:111–121.

Butler, J. (1990). *Gender Trouble*. New York: Routledge.

_____ (1993). *Bodies That Matter*. New York: Routledge.

Foucault, M. (1978). *The History of Sexuality, Vol. I*. New York: Vintage.

Lacan, J. (1977). *Ecrits*. New York: Norton.

Mitchell, J., and Rose, J. (1982). *Feminine sexuality: Jacques Lacan and the École Freudienne*, tr. J. Rose. New York: Pantheon.

Mitchell, S., and Aron, L. (1999). *Relational Psychoanalysis: The Emergence of a Tradition*. Hillsdale, NJ: The Analytic Press.

I

A Moment of Theory: Gender Deconstructed

Melancholy Gender-Refused Identification[1]

JUDITH BUTLER

> "In mourning it is the world which has become poor and empty; in melancholia it is the ego itself."
>
> [Freud, 1917]

> "How is it then that in melancholia the super-ego can become a kind of gathering-place for the death instincts?"
>
> [Freud, 1923]

It may at first seem strange to think of gender as a kind of melancholy, or as one of melancholy's effects, but let us remember that in *The Ego and the Id* Freud (1923) himself acknowledged that melancholy, the unfinished processs of grieving, is central to the formation of those identifications that form the ego itself. Indeed, those identifications that are formed from unfinished grief are the modes in which the lost object is incorporated and phantasmatically preserved in and as the ego. Consider in conjunction with this insight Freud's further remark that "the ego is first and foremost a bodily ego" (p. 26), not merely a surface, but "the projection of a surface." And, further, this bodily ego will assume a gendered morphology, so that we might well claim that the bodily ego is at once a gendered ego. What I hope, first, to explain is the sense in which a melancholic identification is central to that process whereby

---

1. Originally published in *Psychoanalytic Dialogues* 5:165–180. Reprinted with permission from The Analytic Press.

the gendered character of the ego is assumed. Second, I want to explore how this analysis of the melancholic formation of gender sheds
light on the cultural predicament of living within a culture that can
mourn the loss of homosexual attachment only with great difficulty.

Reflecting on his speculations in "Mourning and Melancholia,"
Freud (1923) writes that in the earlier essay he supposed that

> an object which was lost has been set up again inside the ego—
> that is, that an object-cathexis has been replaced by an identi-
> fication. At that time, however, we did not appreciate the full
> significance of this process and did not know how common and
> how typical it is. Since then we have come to understand that
> this kind of substitution has a great share in determining the
> form taken by the ego and that it makes an essential contribu-
> tion toward building up what is called its "character." [p. 28]

Slightly later in this same text, Freud expands this view:
"When it happens that a person has to give up a sexual object, there
quite often ensues an alteration of his ego which can only be described as a setting up of the object inside the ego, as it occurs in
melancholia" (p. 29). He concludes this discussion with the speculation that "it may be that this identification is the sole condition
under which the id can give up its objects. . . . it makes it possible
to suppose that the character of the ego is a precipitate of abandoned object-cathexes and that it contains the history of those
object-choices" (p. 29). What Freud here calls the "character of
the ego" appears to be the sedimentation of those objects loved and
lost, the archaeological remainder, as it were, of unresolved grief.

But what is perhaps most striking about his formulation here
is the way in which it reverses his position in "Mourning and Melancholia" on what it means to resolve grief. In the earlier essay,
Freud (1917) appears to have assumed that grief could be resolved
through a decathexis, a breaking of attachment, as well as the subsequent making of new attachments. In *The Ego and the Id*, however, Freud (1923) makes room for the notion that melancholic
identification may be a *prerequisite* for letting the object go. And
yet, by claiming this, he changes what it means to "let an object

go." For there is no final breaking of the attachment; there is, rather, the incorporation of the attachment *as* identification, where identification becomes a magical, a psychic, form of preserving the object. And, insofar as identification is the psychic preserve of the object and such identifications come to form the ego, then the lost object continues to haunt and inhabit the ego as one of its constitutive identifications and is, in that sense, made coextensive with the ego itself. Indeed, one might conclude that melancholic identification permits the loss of the object in the external world precisely because it provides a way to *preserve* the object as part of the ego itself and, hence, to avert the loss as a complete loss. Here we see that letting the object go means, paradoxically, that there is no full abandonment of the object, only a transferring of the status of the object from external to internal; giving up the object becomes possible only on condition of a melancholic internalization or, what might for our purposes turn out to be even more important, a melancholic *incorporation.*

If, in melancholia, a loss is refused, it is not for that reason abolished. Indeed, internalization is the way in which loss is preserved in the psyche. Or, put perhaps more precisely, the internalization of loss is part of the mechanism of its refusal. If the object can no longer exist in the external world, it will then exist internally, and that internalization will also be a way to disavow that loss, to keep it at bay, to stay or postpone the recognition and suffering of loss.

Is there a way in which *gender* identifications or, rather, those identifications that become central to the formation of gender, are produced through melancholic identification? More particularly, it seems clear that the positions of "masculine" and "feminine," which Freud (1905) understood as the effects of laborious and uncertain accomplishment, are established in part through prohibitions that *demand the loss* of certain sexual attachments and demand as well that those losses *not* be avowed and *not* be grieved. If the assumption of femininity and the assumption of masculinity proceed through the accomplishment of an always tenuous heterosexuality, we might understand the force of this accomplishment as the mandating of the abandonment of homosexual attachments or, perhaps more trenchantly, the *preemption* of the possibility of homosexual attachment, a certain foreclosure of possibility that produces a domain of homosexuality understood as unlivable passion and ungrievable loss. This heterosexuality is produced not only by implementing the prohibition on incest but, prior to that, by enforcing the prohibition on homosexuality. The oedipal conflict presumes that heterosexual desire has already been *accomplished*, that the distinction between heterosexual and homosexual has been enforced (a distinction that, after all, has no necessity); in this sense, the prohibition on incest presupposes the prohibition on homosexuality, for it presumes the heterosexualization of desire.

Indeed, to accept this view we must begin with the presupposition that masculine and feminine are not dispositions, as Freud sometimes argues, but accomplishments, ones that emerge in tandem with the achievement of heterosexuality. Here Freud articulates a cultural logic whereby gender is achieved and stabilized through the accomplishment of heterosexual positioning and where the threats to heterosexuality thus become threats to gender itself. The prevalence of this heterosexual matrix in the construction of gender emerges not only in Freud's text, but also in those cultural forms of life that have absorbed this matrix and are inhabited by everyday forms of gender anxiety. Hence, the fear of homosexual desire in a woman may induce a panic that she is losing her femininity; that she is not a woman, that she is no longer a proper woman; that, if she is not quite a man, she is like one and hence monstrous in some way. Or, in a man, the terror over homosexual desire may well lead to a terror over being construed as feminine, femininized; of no longer being properly a man or of being a "failed" man; or of being in some sense a figure of monstrosity or abjection.

Now, I would argue that phenomenologically there are indeed all sorts of ways of experiencing gender and sexuality that do not reduce to this equation, that do not presume that gender is stabilized through the installation of a firm heterosexuality. But, for the moment, I want to invoke this stark and hyperbolic construction of the relation between gender and sexuality in order to try to think through the question of ungrieved and ungrievable loss in the formation of what we might call the gendered character of the ego.

Consider that gender is acquired at least in part through the repudiation of homosexual attachments: the girl becomes a girl by being subject to a prohibition that bars the mother as an object of desire and installs that barred object as a part of the ego, indeed, as a melancholic identification. Thus, the identification contains within it both the prohibition and the desire and so embodies the ungrieved loss of the homosexual cathexis. If one is a girl to the extent that one does not want a girl, then wanting a girl will bring being a girl into question; within this matrix, homosexual desire thus panics gender.

Heterosexuality is cultivated through prohibitions, where these prohibitions take as one of their objects homosexual attachments, thereby forcing the loss of those attachments.[2] For it seems clear that, if the girl is to transfer the love from her father to a substitute object, she must first renounce the love for her mother and renounce it in such a way that both the aim and the object are foreclosed. Hence, it will not be a matter of transferring that homosexual love onto a substitute feminine figure, but of renouncing the possibility of homosexual attachment itself. Only on this condition does a heterosexual aim become established as what some call a sexual orientation. Only on the condition of this foreclosure of homosexuality can the scene emerge in which it is the father and, hence, the substitutes for him who become the objects of desire, and the mother who becomes the uneasy site of identification.

Becoming a "man" within this logic requires not only a repudiation of femininity, but also a repudiation that becomes a precondition for the heterosexualization of sexual desire and, thus perhaps also, its fundamental ambivalence. If a man becomes heterosexual through the repudiation of the feminine, then where does that repudiation live except in an identification that his hetero-

---

2. Presumably, sexuality must be trained away from things, animals, parts of all of the above, and narcissistic attachments of various kinds.

sexual career seeks to deny? Indeed, the desire for the feminine is marked by that repudiation: he wants the woman he would never be. Indeed, he wouldn't be caught dead being her; thus, he wants her. She is at once his repudiated identification, a repudiation he sustains as identification and the object of his desires. One of the most anxious aims of his desire will be to elaborate the difference between him and her, and he will seek to discover and install that proof. This will be a wanting haunted by a dread of being what it wants, a wanting that will also always be a kind of dread; and, precisely because what is repudiated and hence lost is preserved as a repudiated identification, this desire will be an attempt to overcome an identification that can never be complete.

Indeed, he will not identify with her, and he will not desire another man, and so that refusal to desire, that sacrifice of desire under the force of prohibition, will incorporate that homosexuality as an identification with masculinity. But this masculinity will be haunted by the love it cannot grieve. Before I suggest how this might be true, I'd like to situate the kind of writing that I have been offering as a certain cultural engagement with psychoanalytic theory that belongs neither to the fields of psychology nor to psychoanalysis, but that nevertheless seeks to establish an intellectual relationship to those enterprises.

This has so far been something like an exegesis of a certain psychoanalytic logic, one that appears in some psychoanalytic texts but that is also contested sometimes in those same texts and sometimes in others; this is, of course, not an empirical set of claims nor even an account of the current scholarship in psychoanalysis on gender, sexuality, or melancholy. These enterprises are not ones that I am equipped to take on. Trained in philosophy but working now in a field of cultural criticism that draws from psychoanalysis but also moves between literary theory and the emergent discourses of feminist and gay cultural practices, I want merely to suggest what I take to be some productive convergences between Freud's thinking on ungrieved and ungrievable loss and the cultural predicament of living within a culture that can mourn the loss of homosexual attachment only with great difficulty. This problem is made all the more acute when we consider the ravages of AIDS and the task of finding a public occasion and language in which to grieve this seemingly endless number of deaths. But more generally, this problem makes itself felt in the uncertainty with which homosexual love and loss is regarded: Is this regarded as a "true" love, a "true" loss, a love and loss worthy or capable of being grieved and, in that sense, worthy or capable of ever having been lived? Or is this a love and a loss haunted by the specter of a certain unreality, a certain unthinkability, the double disavowal of "I never loved her, and I never lost her," uttered by a woman; the "I never loved him, I never lost him," uttered by a man? Is this the "never-never" that supports the naturalized surface of heterosexual life as well as its pervasive melancholia? Is this the disavowal of loss by which sexual formation, including gay sexual formation, proceeds?

For if we accept the notion that the prohibition on homosexuality operates throughout a largely heterosexual culture as one of its defining operations, then it appears that the loss of homosexual objects and aims (not simply this person of the same gender, but *any* person of that same gender) will be foreclosed from the start. I use the word "foreclosed" to suggest that this is a preemptive loss, a mourning for unlived possibilities; for if this is a love that is from the start out of the question, then it cannot happen and, if it does, it certainly did not; if it does, it happens only under the official sign of its prohibition and disavowal.[3] When certain kinds of losses are compelled by a set of culturally prevalent prohibitions, then we may well expect a culturally prevalent form of melancholia, one that signals the internalization of the ungrieved and ungrievable homosexual cathexis. And where there is no public recognition or discourse through which such a loss might be named and mourned, then melancholia takes on cultural dimensions of contemporary consequence. Of course, it comes as no surprise that the more

---

3. The notion of foreclosure has become Lacanian terminology for Freud's notion of *Verwerfung*. Distinguished from repression, understood as an action by an already formed subject, foreclosure is an act of negation that founds and forms the subject itself. See Laplanche and Pontalis, 1967, pp. 163–167.

hyperbolic and defensive a masculine identification, the more fierce the ungrieved homosexual cathexis, and in this sense we might understand both "masculinity" and "femininity" as formed and consolidated through identifications that are composed in part of disavowed grief.

If we accept the notion that heterosexuality naturalizes itself by insisting on the radical otherness of homosexuality, then heterosexual identity is purchased through a melancholic incorporation of the love that it disavows: the man who insists on the coherence of his heterosexuality will claim that he never loved another man and thus never lost another man. And that love, that attachment, becomes subject to a double disavowal: a never-having-loved, and a never-having-lost. This "never-never" thus founds the heterosexual subject, as it were; this is an identity based on the refusal to avow an attachment and, hence, the refusal to grieve.

But there is perhaps a more culturally instructive way of describing this scenario, for it is not simply a matter of an individual's unwillingness to avow and to grieve homosexual attachments. When the prohibition against homosexuality is culturally pervasive, then the "loss" of homosexual love is precipitated through a prohibition that is repeated and ritualized throughout the culture. What ensues is a culture of gender melancholy in which masculinity and femininity emerge as the traces of an ungrieved and ungrievable love—indeed, where masculinity and femininity within the heterosexual matrix are strengthened through the repudiations that they perform. In opposition to a conception of sexuality that is said to "express" a gender, gender itself is here understood to be composed of precisely what remains inarticulate in sexuality.

If we understand gender melancholy in this way, then perhaps we can make sense of the peculiar phenomenon whereby homosexual desire becomes a source of guilt. Freud (1917) argues that melancholy is marked by the experience of self-beratement. He writes:

> If one listens patiently to a melancholic's many and various self-accusations, one cannot in the end avoid the impression that

often the most violent of them are hardly at all applicable to
the patient himself, but that with insignificant modifications
they do fit someone else, some person whom the patient loves
or has loved or should love. . . . the self-reproaches are re-
proaches against a loved object which have been shifted on
to the patient's own ego. [p. 248]

Freud goes on to conjecture that the conflict with the other
that remains unresolved at the time the other is lost reemerges in
the psyche as a way of continuing the quarrel. Indeed, the anger at
the other is doubtless exacerbated by the death or departure that
constitutes the occasion for the loss. But this anger is turned inward and becomes the substance of self-beratement.

Freud (1914) links the experience of guilt to the turning back
into the ego of homosexual libido. Putting aside the question of
whether libido can be homosexual or heterosexual, we might re-
phrase Freud and consider guilt as the turning back into the ego of
homosexual attachment. If the loss becomes a renewed scene of
conflict, and if the aggression that follows from that loss cannot be
articulated or externalized, then it rebounds upon the ego itself,
in the form of a superego. This will eventually lead Freud (1923)
to link melancholic identification with the agency of the superego,
but already in "On Narcissism" (Freud 1914) we have some sense
of how guilt is wrought from ungrievable homosexuality.

The ego is said to become impoverished in melancholia, but it
appears as poor precisely through the workings of self-beratement.
The ego ideal, what Freud calls the "measure" against which the ego
is judged by the superego, is precisely the ideal of social rectitude
defined over and against homosexuality. Freud writes that

this ideal has a social side; it is also the common ideal of a family, a class or a nation. It binds not only narcissistic libido, but
also a considerable amount of his homosexual libido, which is
in this way turned back into the ego. The want of satisfaction
that arises from the non-fulfillment of this ideal liberates homosexual libido, is transformed into a sense of guilt and this is
social anxiety. [pp. 101–102]

But the movement of this "transformation" is not altogether clear. After all, Freud (1930) will argue that these social ideals are transformed into a sense of guilt through a kind of internalization that is not, ultimately, mimetic. It is not that one treats oneself only as harshly as one was treated but, rather, that the aggression toward the ideal and its unfulfillability is turned inward, and this self-aggression becomes the primary structure of conscience: "by means of identification [the child] takes the unattackable authority into himself" (p. 129).

In this sense, in melancholia the superego can become a "gathering place" for the death instincts. The superego is figured as a site where the death instincts gather, but it is not necessarily the same as those instincts or their effect. In this way, melancholia attracts the death instincts to the superego, where they are understood as a regressive striving toward organic equilibrium, and the self-beratement of the superego is understood to make use of that regressive striving for its own purposes. Where melancholy is the refusal of grief, it is also always the incorporation of loss, the miming of the death it cannot mourn. In this sense, the incorporation of death draws on the death instincts such that we might well wonder whether the two are separable from one another, either analytically or phenomenologically.

The prohibition on homosexuality preempts the process of grief and prompts a melancholic identification that effectively turns homosexual desire back onto itself. This turning back onto itself is precisely the action of self-beratement and guilt. Significantly, homosexuality is *not* abolished, but preserved, and yet the site where homosexuality is preserved will be precisely in the prohibition on homosexuality. Freud (1930) makes clear that conscience requires the continuous sacrifice or renunciation of instinct to produce that peculiar satisfaction that conscience requires; conscience is never assuaged by renunciation but, paradoxically, is strengthened (renunciation breeds intolerance) (p. 128). For renunciation does not abolish the instinct; it deploys the instinct for its own purposes, such that prohibition, and the lived experience of prohibition as repeated renunciation, is nourished precisely by the instinct that it renounces. In this scenario, renunciation requires the very homosexuality that it condemns, not as its external object, but as its own most treasured source of sustenance. The act of renouncing homosexuality thus paradoxically strengthens homosexuality, but it strengthens homosexuality precisely *as* the power of renunciation. Renunciation becomes the aim and vehicle of satisfaction. And it is, we might conjecture, precisely the fear of setting loose homosexuality from this circuit of renunciation that so terrifies the guardians of masculinity in the United States military. For what would masculinity "be" if it were not for this aggressive circuit of renunciation from which it is wrought? Gays in the military threaten to undo masculinity only because this is a masculinity made of repudiated homosexuality.

Although I have been attempting to describe a melancholy that is produced through the compulsory production of heterosexuality and, so, a heterosexual melancholy that one might read in the workings of gender itself, I want now to turn this analysis in a slightly different direction in order to suggest that rigid forms of gender and sexual identification, whether homosexual or heterosexual, appear to spawn forms of melancholy as their consequence. I would like to reconsider first the theory of gender as performative that I elaborated in *Gender Trouble* (Butler 1990) and then to turn to the question of gay melancholia and the political consequences of ungrievable loss.

I argued that gender was performative, and by that I meant that there is no gender that is "expressed" by actions, gestures, or speech, but that the performance of gender was precisely that which produced retroactively the illusion that there was an inner gender core. Indeed, the performance of gender might be said retroactively to produce the effect of some true or abiding feminine essence or disposition, such that one could not use an expressive model for thinking about gender. Moreover, I argued that gender is produced as a ritualized repetition of conventions and that this ritual is socially compelled in part by the force of a compulsory heterosexuality. I used the example of the drag performance to illustrate what I meant, and the subsequent reception of my work unfortunately took that example to be exemplary of what I meant by performativity. In this context, I would like to return to the question of drag to explain in clearer terms how I understand psychoanalysis to be linked with gender performativity and how I take performativity to be linked with melancholia.

It would not be enough to say that gender is only performed or that the meaning of gender can be derived from its performance, whether or not one wants to rethink performance as a compulsory social ritual. For there clearly are workings of gender that do not "show" in what is performed as gender, and the reduction of the psychic workings of gender to the literal performance of gender would be a mistake. Psychoanalysis insists that the opacity of the unconscious sets limits to the exteriorization of the psyche. It also argues, rightly I think, that what is exteriorized or performed can be understood only through reference to what is barred from the performance, what cannot or will not be performed.

The relation between drag performances and gender performativity in *Gender Trouble* went something like this: when it is a man performing drag as a woman, the "imitation" that drag is said to be is taken as an "imitation" of femininity—the "femininity" that is imitated is not itself understood as being an imitation at all. And yet, if one considers that gender is acquired, that it is assumed in relation to ideals that are never quite inhabited by anyone, then femininity is an ideal that anyone always and only "imitates." Thus, drag imitates the imitative structure of gender, revealing gender itself as an imitation. However playful and attractive this formulation may have seemed at the time, it did not address the question of how it is that certain forms of disavowal and repudiation come to organize the performance of gender. How is the phenomenon of gender melancholia to be related to the practice of gender performativity?

Moreover, given the iconographic figure of the melancholic drag queen, one might ask whether there is not a dissatisfied longing in the mimetic incorporation of gender that is drag. Here one might ask also after the disavowal that occasions the performance and which performance might be said to enact, where performance engages "acting out" in the psychoanalytic sense.[4] If melancholia in Freud's sense is the effect of an ungrieved loss,[5] it may be that performance, understood as "acting out," is essentially related to the problem of unacknowledged loss. Where there is an ungrieved loss in drag performance, perhaps it is a loss that is refused and incorporated in the performed identification, one that reiterates a gendered idealization and its radical uninhabitability. This is, then, neither a territorialization of the feminine by the masculine nor a sign of the essential plasticity of gender. What it does suggest is that the performance allegorizes a loss it cannot grieve, allegorizes the incorporative fantasy of melancholia whereby an object is phantasmatically taken in or on as a way of refusing to let it go. Gender itself might be understood in part as the "acting out" of unresolved grief.

The foregoing analysis is a risky one because it suggests that, for a "man" performing femininity or for a "woman" performing masculinity (the latter is always, in effect, to perform a little less, given that femininity is cast as the spectacular gender), there is an attachment to—and a loss and refusal of—the figure of femininity by the man or the figure of masculinity by the woman. Thus, it is important to underscore that drag is an effort to negotiate cross-gendered identification, but that cross-gendered identification is not the paradigm for thinking about homosexuality, although it may well be one among others. In this sense, drag allegorizes some set of melancholic incorporative fantasies that stabilize *gender*. Not only are a vast number of drag performers straight, but it would be

---

4. I thank Laura Mulvey for asking me to consider the relation between performativity and disavowal, and Wendy Brown for encouraging me to think about the relation between melancholia and drag and for asking whether the denaturalization of gender norms is the same as their subversion. I also thank Mandy Merck for numerous enlightening questions that led to these speculations, including the suggestion that if disavowal conditions performativity, then perhaps gender itself might be understood on the model of the fetish.

5. See "Freud and the Melancholia of Gender" in Butler 1990.

a mistake to think that homosexuality is best explained through the performativity that is drag. What does seem useful in this analysis, however, is that drag exposes or allegorizes the mundane psychic and performative practices by which heterosexualized genders form themselves through the renunciation of the *possibility* of homosexuality, a foreclosure that produces a field of heterosexual objects at the same time as it produces a domain of those whom it would be impossible to love. Drag thus allegorizes *heterosexual melancholy*, the melancholy by which a masculine gender is formed from the refusal to grieve the masculine as a possibility of love; a feminine gender is formed (taken on, assumed) through the incorporative fantasy by which the feminine is excluded as a possible object of love, an exclusion never grieved, but "preserved" through the heightening of feminine identification itself. In this sense, the "truest" lesbian melancholic is the strictly straight woman, and the "truest" gay male melancholic is the strictly straight man.

What drag does expose, however, is that in the "normal" constitution of gender presentation the gender that is performed is constituted by a set of disavowed attachments, identifications that constitute a different domain of the "unperformable." Indeed, it may be, but need not be, that what constitutes the *sexually* unperformable is performed instead as *gender identification*.[6] To the extent that homosexual attachments remain unacknowledged within normative heterosexuality, they are not merely constituted as desires that emerge and subsequently become prohibited; rather, these are desires proscribed from the start. And when they do emerge on the far side of the censor, they may well carry that mark of impossibility with them, performing, as it were, as the impossible within the possible. As such, they will not be attachments that can be openly grieved. This is, then, less *the refusal* to grieve (the

---

6. This is not to suggest that an exclusionary matrix rigorously distinguishes between how one identifies and how one desires; it is quite possible to have overlapping identification and desire in heterosexual or homosexual exchange or in a bisexual history of sexual practice. Further, "masculinity" and "femininity" do not exhaust the terms for either eroticized identification or desire.

Mitscherlich formulation that accents the choice involved) than a preemption of grief performed by the absence of cultural conventions for avowing the loss of homosexual love. And it is this absence that produces a culture of heterosexual melancholy, one that can be read in the hyperbolic identifications by which mundane heterosexual masculinity and femininity confirm themselves. The straight man *becomes* (mimes, cites, appropriates, assumes the status of) the man he "never" loved and "never" grieved; the straight woman *becomes* the woman she "never" loved and "never" grieved. It is in this sense, then, that what is most apparently performed as gender is the sign and symptom of a pervasive disavowal.

Moreover, it is precisely to counter this pervasive cultural risk of gay melancholia (what the newspapers generalize as "depression") that there has been an insistent publicization and politicization of grief over those who have died from AIDS; the NAMES Project Quilt is exemplary, ritualizing and repeating the name itself as a way of publicly avowing the limitless loss (see Crimp 1989).

Insofar as the grief remains unspeakable (some part of grief is perhaps always unspeakable), the rage over the loss can redouble by virtue of remaining unavowed. And if that very rage over loss is publicly proscribed, the melancholic effects of such a proscription can achieve suicidal proportions. The emergence of collective institutions for grieving is thus crucial to survival, to the reassembling of community, the rearticulation of kinship, the reweaving of sustaining relations. And insofar as they involve the publicization and dramatization of death—as in the case of "die-ins" by Queer Nation—they call to be read as life-affirming rejoinders to the dire psychic consequences of a grieving process culturally thwarted and proscribed.

Melancholy can work, however, within homosexuality in specific ways that call to be rethought. Within the formation of gay and lesbian identity, there may be an effort to disavow a constitutive relationship to heterosexuality. When this disavowal is understood as a political necessity in order to *specify* gay and lesbian identity over and against its ostensible opposite, heterosexuality, that cultural practice culminates paradoxically in a weakening of the very constituency it is meant to unite. Not only does such a strategy attribute a false monolithic status to heterosexuality, but it misses the political opportunity to work the weakness in hetero-sexual subjectivation and to refute the logic of mutual exclusion by which heterosexism proceeds. Moreover, a full-scale denial of that interrelationship can constitute a rejection of heterosexuality that is to some degree an identification *with* a rejected heterosexu-ality. Important to this economy, however, is the refusal to recog-nize this identification, which is, as it were, already made, a refusal that absently designates the domain of a specifically gay melancho-lia, a loss that cannot be recognized and hence cannot be mourned. For a gay or lesbian identity-position to sustain its appearance as coherent, heterosexuality must remain in that rejected and repu-diated place. Paradoxically, its heterosexual *remains* must be *sus-tained* precisely through the insistence on the seamless coherence of a specifically gay identity. Here it should become clear that a radical refusal to identify suggests that, on some level, an identifi-cation has already taken place, an identification that is made and disavowed, whose symptomatic appearance is the insistence, the overdetermination, of the identification that is, as it were, worn on the body that shows.

This raises the political question of the cost of articulating a coherent identity-position if that coherence is produced through the production, exclusion, and repudiation of a domain of abjected specters that threaten the arbitrarily closed domain of subject posi-tions. Indeed, it may be that only by risking the *incoherence* of iden-tity that connection is possible, a political point that correlates with Bersani's (1986) insight that only the decentered subject is avail-able to desire. For what cannot be avowed as a constitutive identi-fication of any given subject-position runs the risk not only of becoming externalized in a degraded form but of being repeatedly repudiated and subject to a policy of disavowal.

The logic of repudiation that I have charted here is in some ways a hyperbolic theory, a logic in drag, as it were, that overstates the case, but overstates it for a reason. For there is no necessary reason for identification to oppose desire, or for desire to be fueled through repudiation. And this remains true for heterosexuality and homosexuality alike, and for forms of bisexuality that take themselves to be composite forms of each. Indeed, we are made all the more fragile under the pressure of such rules, and all the more mobile when ambivalence and loss are given a dramatic language in which to do their acting out.

REFERENCES

Bersani, L. (1986). *The Freudian Body*. New York: Columbia University Press.
Butler, J. (1990). *Gender Trouble*. New York: Routledge.
——— (1993). *Bodies That Matter*. New York: Routledge.
Crimp, D. (1989). Mourning and militancy. *October* 51:97–107.
Freud, S. (1905). Three essays on the theory of sexuality. *Standard Edition* 7:125–243.
——— (1914). On narcissism: an introduction. *Standard Edition* 14:73–102.
——— (1917). Mourning and melancholia. *Standard Edition* 14:243–258.
——— (1923). The ego and the id. *Standard Edition* 19:12–59.
——— (1930). Civilization and its discontents. *Standard Edition* 21:64–145.
Laplanche, J., and Pontalis, J.-B. (1967). *Vocabulaire de la psychanalyse*. Paris: Presses Universitaires de France.

2

The Mystery of Homosexuality[1]

KEN CORBETT

After fifteen years of frequent reflection on homosexuality, Freud (1920) was induced to characterize the relationship between a homosexual's gender experience and mode of sexual satisfaction (active or passive) as "the mystery of homosexuality" (p. 170). For homosexuals, maleness did not necessarily correspond to the activity Freud associated with masculinity, nor did femaleness necessarily correspond to the passivity he linked with femininity. Freud saw the homosexual's gender experience as a kind of category crisis: What gender do we assign these mysterious individuals?

In keeping with the narrative quality of mysteries (which are essentially stories of explanation), psychoanalysts have looked upon the homosexual as the suspect/subject who must be explained. Explanatory narratives about homosexuals have been a cornerstone of the psychoanalytic discourse on gender and sexuality. One con-

1. This chapter is an expanded version of a paper originally published in *Psychoanalytic Psychology* 10(3):345–358. Reprinted with permission from Lawrence Erlbaum Associates.

sistent feature of these narratives is the way in which the homosexual's gender experience has been looked upon as threatening
a known certainty—the binary (masculine/feminine) heterosexual
gender arrangement. Reflecting the manner in which solutions to
mysteries are sought in an effort to restore certainty, analysts have
repeatedly attempted to (dis)locate homosexuals within a theory
of gender that rests upon essential distinctions between what is
feminine and what is masculine. Perhaps the best illustration of
this (dis)location is the manner in which the male homosexual has
been regarded as feminine.

This homosexual male/heterosexual female gender conver-
gence has largely been based on what analysts saw as a similarity
between the passive mode of sexual satisfaction desired by both
homosexual men and heterosexual women. Such theorizing has led
to the following equation: male homosexuality = passivity = femininity = trauma.[2] Male homosexuals are thereby removed from the
realm of masculinity and recast as counterfeit women. As Freud
(1910) stated in describing Leonardo da Vinci's homosexuality,
"[Leonardo) was robbed of a part of his masculinity" (p. 117) and
left "to play the part of women" (p. 86).

Rather than draw upon the homosexual's experience to open
up the categories of gender, analysts have restricted the possibilities of gender to the conventional heterosexual masculine/feminine
binary. For example, Freud (1910) categorized da Vinci as feminine (albeit imitation feminine), as opposed to considering his
experience as illustrative of the vicissitudes and variance of gender. Through such categorizing, analysts have upheld the hetero-

---

2. This trauma equation has been given voice through a variety of psychoanalytic schools, ranging from Freud's classicism to the separation and individuation theory of Socarides (1978) to the object relations theory of Winnicott (1971)
to the modern French classicism of Chasseguet-Smirgel (1984), to name a few.

Further, this trauma equation points to the manner in which femininity is
often a stigmatized category. If a man is seen as effeminate, the implication is
that he is feeble, enervated, and unbecomingly delicate. Addressing this phenomenon, Garber (1992) has suggested that "in expressing condemnation of various
types of men, it is always women who are scapegoated" (p. 138).

sexual genders as a priori and natural, along with supporting the inevitability of a cultural order established through such reasoning. But as the homosexual's experience exemplifies, such logic is both the product and the progenitor of a sanctioned cultural order that does not adequately capture nature or sufficiently problematize the experience of gender. Calling gay men feminine does not go very far toward understanding them; it simply displaces them. Making counterfeit women of male homosexuals obscures the vicissitudes of gender instead of addressing the way in which homosexual gender experience challenges the conventional heterosexual masculine/feminine binary.

Consequently, I propose within this chapter to return to the mystery of homosexuality not only that we may learn more about homosexuality, but also that we might learn more about gender. Specifically, I focus on the gay man's experience of gender.[3] Most homosexual and heterosexual men readily identify themselves as male; however, many (if not most) gay men describe their gender experience as mixed. Neither masculinity nor femininity (nor nonmasculinity nor counterfeit femininity) adequately captures the experience of gender otherness many gay men describe. I suggest that this mixed gender identity rests, in part, on the gay man's experience of passivity in relationship to another man.

Turning toward the ways in which the gay man's gender experience may unfold within the course of a psychoanalysis, I argue, following on Isay (1986, 1989, 1991) and Lewes (1988), that the psychoanalyst's countertransference difficulties with male pas-

---

3. I recognize that by focusing solely on the gay male experience I am participating in the overestimation of the male homosexual in the psychoanalytic literature, in contrast to the underestimation of the female homosexual. I recognize the limits inherent in solely focusing on male homosexuality, along with the way in which this exclusivity could be seen as symptomatic of the phallocentrism, or perhaps more precisely, the gynophobia, that characterizes so much of the psychoanalytic developmental literature. But I must also recognize the limits of my own clinical experience, which does not at this time include extensive treatment of gay women. I look forward to analyses of homosexuality that address the similarities and differences in the gay male and female experience.

sivity have fostered misconceptions regarding male homosexual development. I believe that within the analyst's inability to tolerate male passivity is embedded the inability to comprehend and tolerate the gay man's experience of gender. This lack of comprehension, frequently accompanied by a lack of empathic positive regard, sets the stage for what I call "the father's censure."[4] The analyst (as father), via an unconscious exploitation of transference wishes (the son's wish to be like the father and disavow passive longings), seeks along with the patient (as son) to subjugate and repudiate the patient's experience of gender and sexual difference.

I argue that the father's censure and the son's repression rest on a distorted theory of masculine development that emphasizes the reproduction of fathering, the repudiation of passivity, the disregard of preoedipal contributions to adult sexuality, and the suppression of oedipal variation—in particular, the boy's oedipal desire for his father. The boy's desire for his father is but one thread within the complex strand of homosexuality. I cannot begin here to do justice to such complexity; I can only note that I am artificially pulling on this one thread, knowing all the while that it is not the whole strand. Clearly, a boy's desire for his father may be complicated or even contradicted by other oedipal and/or preoedipal dynamics, along with other factors that influence the family dynamic, as well as influences outside the family.

I focus on the transference reenactment of the boy's wish for the father, and the difficulties experienced by the gay male patient in allowing such a transference reenactment to emerge. Specifically, I contend that it is vitally important in the treatment of gay men to empathically recognize their fears of retribution for their experi-

---

4. It would be more precise to speak of the parents' censure as opposed to the father's censure. Clearly, this manner of censuring can also occur between a mother and son, as a result of a mother's wish that her son be either more like his father, or that he disavow passivity as she may feel she has done. I am focusing on the father–son dynamic in an effort to tease out this one thread of homosexual development, as I discuss at greater length below.

ence of gender difference, and to assist them in clarifying their distinct gender identity.

THE ACTIVE/PASSIVE BINARY

First, I define what I mean by passivity. As with all conventional binaries, passivity can exist only in reference to its dialectical opposite, activity. Given the nature of this dialectic, one could reasonably question whether passivity exists at all. However, opposites that are held in a dialectical tension are not negated through such tension. They may contradict one another. They may fold into one another, as passivity may fold into activity, and thereby be transformed. But contradiction and transformation do not neutralize the dialectical poles; rather they hold them in a qualified tension. I believe that as long as one is aware of the manner in which activity and passivity are qualified through this dialectical tension, passive and active wishes can be identified. Moreover, I maintain that identifying these wishes is both clinically relevant and significant.[5]

I am defining male homosexual passivity as manifested by a variety of wishes and behaviors, ranging from the object relational wish to be cared for by another man to the sexual wish to have one's erotogenic zones touched or filled by another man. Conversely, I am defining male homosexual activity as manifested by wishes and behaviors that range from the wish to care for another man to the wish to touch or fill the erotogenic zones of another man. For example, passivity can be expressed through the wish to be held by

---

5. Given my expressed intent to look at how homosexual gender challenges the conventional heterosexual gender binary, one could question my reliance on a vocabulary that is most often employed to convey a gender distinction. I can sympathize with the wish to step away from this vocabulary, but I cannot reasonably trust that a new vocabulary will not result in the same hierarchies it set out to deconstruct. Instead, I have chosen to stay within this contested vocabulary. As Fuss (1991) has suggested, "Change may well happen by working on the insides of our inherited sexual vocabularies and turning them inside out, giving them a new face" (p. 7).

another man. A gay male patient of mine speaks of his pleasure in "sleeping like spoons" cradled in his lover's arms. He especially enjoys the sense of his lover as being "bigger and stronger, and able to envelop" him. Passive desire is also expressed through the pleasure gay men experience in anal intercourse. Describing a fantasy of loving merger, a gay male patient stated, "When Alex is in me, it's like I feel filled up with him. Like his cock reaches all the way through to mine, as though we are one." Both of these examples illustrate a central feature of passivity—a temporary losing sight of the self through a merging surrender with another. Merging through activity, on the other hand, would mean temporarily losing sight of the self through a merging insertion into another.

Passive wishes do not negate the possibility of coexisting active wishes. Most gay men interchange activity and passivity in sexual relations. Moreover, many sexual practices such as mutual fellatio suggest that an individual could simultaneously experience activity and passivity, although it is the fantasy that underlies the practice that should guide us in this respect (Arlow 1969, Freud 1905). For example, while a particular sexual practice may appear passive, the underlying fantasy may actually be active.

My assertions as to the role of passivity in male homosexuality are also not meant to negate the fact that many gay men maintain an exclusively active role in object seeking and sexual relations. Homosexual phallic activity has consistently been either ignored or interpreted throughout analytic literature as sadistic intrusion, devoid of object love. The domain of love and the expression of loving merger wishes through phallic activity have been reserved for heterosexual men through analysts' continued idealization of heterosexual masculinity. I look forward to a reexamination of male homosexual activity. Nevertheless, I am arguing that there is a distinctly passive aspect that informs both the sexual fantasies and the practices of many gay men which, in turn, bears on the gay man's experience of gender.

I have found that passive longings stem, in part, from the manner in which a homosexual boy's choice of love object is modeled upon his parents, leading to the boy's wish to have his eroto-genic zones touched or filled by either the father or mother, or, more precisely, some amalgam of the two. I focus here on one thread of this complex strand: the boy's desire for the father. The fantasy of being loved by the father is essentially an expression of passive longing. However, like all sexual desire, this passive longing is coupled with a simultaneous and seemingly contradictory active impulse to appropriate and identify with the father. In other words, in choosing his father as his object the boy also identifies with his father's genital activity.

Herein lies the heart of the mystery: gay men move between passive and active sexual aims that do not reflect the kind of binary tension falsely associated with heterosexual masculine activity and feminine passivity. Instead, homosexual activity and passivity stem, in part, from the boy's simultaneous desire for and identi-fication with his father. Further, homosexual gender is not struc-tured according to differences between the sexes, and the gay man's experience of gender does not rest on a binary tension modeled upon heterosexual masculinity and femininity. The deconstruction of this binary tension not only speaks to the mystery of homo-sexuality, but to the mystery of sexuality—the ways in which all sexualities are informed by the push and pull of activity and passivity, along with the multiple threads of preoedipal and oedipal desires and identifications.

Finally, I have chosen to focus on the gay man's passive longings not because such longings solely constitute homosexual desire. Rather, I focus on them because I have found that the gay man's integration of such longings and the impact they have on his experience of gender are often the source of considerable con-flict and defense. Moreover, even though I believe that gender is discovered along with sexual identity, most gay men report an early conscious awareness of gender difference prior to conscious aware-ness of their homosexuality. Hence, a crucial step in the treatment of many gay men is the recognition of their early experience of gender and how that experience is knit into the fabric of their sexual identity.

THE FATHER'S CENSURE

As opposed to clarifying the developmental challenge faced by the homosexual boy as he attempts to integrate his experience of gender difference, analysts have leveled warnings such as that proffered by Chasseguet-Smirgel (1976, p. 349) that too much access to femininity can lead to "psychic death" for a boy. In fact, all psychoanalytic "cures" of homosexuality are based on the belief that one can assist the gay man in recovering his so-called lost masculinity and thereby return him to his natural heterosexuality (e.g., Socarides 1978). The underlying assumption is that homosexuality can be cured by an infusion of normative masculinity. This method bears a striking resemblance to parents' efforts to eradicate or ameliorate mixed or cross-gendered features of a child's subjectivity. What the anxious parent and theorists such as Socarides (1978) and more recently Nicolosi (1991) have failed to grasp is that homosexuality is not devoid of masculinity; it is, rather, a differently structured gender.

This failure of empathy and understanding is underscored by the belief that masculinity follows upon the reproduction of fathering, which rests in turn upon the repudiation of passivity. This belief is given voice in a variety of ways throughout the psychoanalytic discourse on masculinity, but perhaps it is nowhere more salient than in Freud's (1909) depiction of Little Hans's masculine development. Throughout the case study, Freud made passing references to Hans's "aggressive, masculine and arrogant way" (p. 16), and was particularly delighted when "in spite of his accesses of homosexuality, little Hans bore himself like a *true man*" (p. 17, italics added). This passage captures the manner in which a son is seen and reflected through a father's eyes; recall that Freud undertook Hans's "analysis" by speaking through Hans's father. Freud, as the proud shadow-father, illustrates his belief that a son's task, as he strives toward true masculinity, is to triumph over passivity to cocky aggressivity.

Beginning with Freud, analysts have maintained that it is through identification with the same-sex parent that gender identity and sexuality evolve. The boy identifies with his father's phallic activity, and thereby begins his struggle to represent the phallus. Regarding this belief that activity and phallic strength underlie masculine development, Person (1986) has pointed out that "the fundamental sexual problem for boys is the struggle to achieve phallic strength and power vis-à-vis other men" (p. 72). Phallic narcissism (by way of a false assumption that links phallic strength with activity) must be maintained and passivity repudiated. In particular, passive desire for another man is to be denied. Indeed, Freud (1937) suggested that a man's denial of passive longings for another man, which is partially maintained via "masculine protest," represents the "bedrock" of masculinity (p. 252). Equating biology with bedrock, Freud went so far as to posit that the biology of masculinity was expressed via such psychological protest:

> We often have the impression that with . . . masculine protest we have penetrated through all the psychological strata and have reached bedrock, and that thus our activities are at an end. This is probably true, since, for the psychical field, the biological field does in fact play the part of the underlying bedrock. [1937, p. 252]

According to Freud (1909), Little Hans illustrated this masculine bedrock as he triumphed over passivity through his arrogant and aggressive masculine protest. This accomplishment was greeted with much pleasure and acknowledgment by Hans's father and Freud. Hans had joined the ranks (Freud 1909, p. 89):

Hans's Father: "You'd like to be Daddy yourself."
Hans: "Oh yes!"

The telos of masculine development is succession to the role of father; the apogee of masculine biology is reproduction. Masculinity ultimately rests on the boy's reproduction of heterosexual fathering, thereby revealing analysts' reliance upon a teleology of reproductive function. Analysts have consistently proposed that the reality principle coincides with the recognition of this paternalism and its accompanying laws of sexual and generational difference (Chasseguet-Smirgel 1985, Erikson 1950, Freud 1911, Winnicott 1986). Through his theory of psychosexual development, Freud outlined the struggle between pleasure and reality. By interweaving the "suppression of the pleasure principle by the reality principle" (1911, p. 222) into his theory of psychosexual development, Freud united desire and reality. He, and the majority of analysts who were to follow, assumed there is a correspondence between reality and a form of sexuality that is subordinate to the reproductive function.[6]

However, is it logically consistent to equate reality with subordination of desire to reproduction? Does structuring a theory of human development around the nodal phenomenon of procreation adequately capture nature? Or does it collapse the normative into the natural? Linking sexual development with procreation and calling it reality ignores another reality—the vicissitudes of oedipal resolution along with the variations in gender and sexual identity that evolve from assorted oedipal desires and outcomes. Clearly, sexuality arises from overdetermined and various pathways. By not entertaining the vicissitudes of preoedipal contributions and oedipal resolutions, thinking about sexual development has become simplified and schematized. This is nowhere more evident than in the psychoanalytic literature on male homosexuality. For example, until the work of Isay (1989) and Lewes (1988), the possibility that a boy may take his father as his oedipal object has been either ignored or marginalized. As Isay (1989) pointed out, the fact that fathers do not figure more prominently in the developmental theories of male homosexuality underscores both analysts' fears in examining same-sex desire and analysts' reluctance to entertain the variation and ambiguity inherent in the ontogeny of male sexuality.

---

6. By this assertion I am not overlooking the contradiction in Freud's work between his proposing a course for normative sexual development and his simultaneous efforts to deconstruct such a course. Nor am I overlooking those theorists who have taken up Freud's deconstructive project. But all things considered, the volume of the normative chorus all but drowns out those theorists who seek to deconstruct normative sexuality and sexual development.

Analysts have been equally reluctant to examine the male experience of passivity or, for that matter, to examine passivity at all. Following on Freud (1937), male passivity has been looked upon as a turning away from true masculine destiny/biology.[7] Male passivity is seen as indicating a feminine identification and a corresponding resignation from masculinity. It is further assumed that this feminine identification is achieved via the abdication of phallic activity, the enactment of castration, and the fantasized experience of the anus as vagina. Through my clinical and research experience with more than 100 gay men, I have not found these assumptions to be accurate. Gay men experience a variety of fluid (projected and introjected) identifications during sex, including feminine identifications. However, I have not encountered a gay patient who fixedly fantasized his anus to be a vagina, or fixedly imagined himself to be a woman. Likewise, I have not found that passive experience is consistently linked with castration. In fact, as opposed to the expression of passive sexual fantasies and behaviors, I have found that the consistent embodiment of castration is accompanied by a shutdown of sexual fantasies and behaviors. The conflation of passivity and castration confuses the *aim* of passivity with the *aimlessness* of castration.

For most gay men the experience of being anally penetrated results in phallic arousal and erection (if not already achieved through foreplay). The erection and corresponding phallic pleasure leading to orgasm are focal, accentuated by the pleasure of penetration. For the man who is simultaneously penetrated and erect, orgasm is generally achieved following manipulation of his penis by his partner; this behavior is underscored by the wish for his partner to see and manipulate the penis, not to deny it. Though orgasm is not achieved as the result of active penetration, the erection and the experience of passive phallic arousal are fundamental to both the sexual behavior and fantasy. Through their reluctance

---

7. Christiansen (1993) reverses this fundamental psychoanalytic assertion by arguing that "an active masculinity originates as a defense against the pleasure of a passive and hysterically unpleasurable femininity."

to imagine a male body that is simultaneously penetrated and erect, analysts have conflated passive phallic arousal with castration. Indeed, the phenomenon of passive phallic arousal is virtually ignored within the psychoanalytic literature. Phallic arousal is exclusively alloyed with activity which, in turn, is coded as integrity and strength.

Along with the assumptions regarding fantasies and enactments of castration, it is assumed that masculinity is forsaken via the gay man's wish for anal erotism. To be penetrated is to abdicate masculinity and forgo the reproduction of fathering. As Foucault (1985) noted with reference to the history of sexuality, the only "honorable" male sexual behavior "consists in being active, in dominating, in penetrating, and in thereby exercising one's authority" (p. 154). To be penetrated is to relinquish power. To wish for the pleasure of passivity with another man is to break rank and crack the "bedrock" of masculinity. It follows that such desire comes under the attack of "masculine protest." One need only look at the manner in which young boys heap both verbal and physical abuse upon a gender variant boy to recognize their need to displace and subjugate their own repressed passivity.

Male homosexual passivity subverts the absolutism of heterosexual masculine activity and authority. Without such absolutism the culture's assumptions about normative gender are destabilized. As Bersani (1989) argued, passivity has the "terrifying appeal of a loss of the ego" and this "losing sight of the self" serves not only to confront notions of normative gender but also normative developmental theory (p. 220). Indeed, the teleological argument of the "Three Essays" and the developmental theories of most of Freud's followers rest upon the necessity of activity to the exclusion of developmental considerations of passivity. This history of denial relative to the developmental value of passivity has resulted in a skewed psychoanalytic canon: the development of heterosexual men is overestimated and overvalued. The development of heterosexual women and homosexual men is underestimated and undervalued, while their supposed pathologies are overestimated. And the development of homosexual women is glaringly underestimated, through the virtual lack of any representation within the psychoanalytic canon. This biased representation is upheld through normative assumptions about both biology and psyche—assumptions that negate the great sexual variability in the human species. The developmental actuality and value of passivity, especially male homosexual passivity, will continue to be denied until psychoanalysts begin to responsibly reconsider the fundamental constructs upon which they have based their understanding of human biology and psyche.

THE SON'S REPRESSION

It is not only psychoanalysts who are made uneasy by homosexual gender variance. Gay men frequently harbor the belief that their gender experience is flawed, especially in comparison to normative heterosexual masculinity. Recognizing the inherent dilemma in such experience, a gay male patient of mine commented, "There was this sense of otherness. You know, not being the norm—not the normal boy." Growing frustrated with his difficulty in describing his experience other than by reference to what he was not, he exclaimed, "But I don't know, I feel like civilization has robbed me of the words to describe this." This experience of simultaneously being located through and dislocated by normative masculinity is echoed by many of my gay male patients. In particular, I have found that they feel their fathers (less often, their mothers)[8] did not comprehend their early gender experience. This lack of comprehension is often experienced by the son as signaling the father's disappointment. Without exception, my gay male patients present themselves as having disappointed their parents, with greater emphasis generally placed on the disappointment of their fathers. They were not the sons for whom their fathers wished.

---

8. This observation may correspond with the consistent finding that fathers are more concerned than mothers that their children exhibit gender-appropriate behaviors.

Counter to the boisterous pride shared by Little Hans and his father, many homosexual boys feel humiliation and guilt in being seen by their fathers. This alienation is further compounded by the defeat they feel in the face of the condemnation/masculine protest of their male peers. I have found that a similar dynamic of alienation and withdrawal can color the transference within the early phase of therapy with gay male patients. Recognizing gay patients' expectation of repudiation in light of their early experience affords the opportunity to begin examining the defensive nature of their withdrawal. The recognition of repudiation for early gender experience brings back into the open not only early defensive adaptations but also the repressed desire for the father, and passive longings linked with that desire. The treatment course with a young gay man illustrates how this interplay between early gender experience and desire for the father can be expressed through the transference.

Luke entered therapy complaining of pervasive anxiety, coupled with feelings of loneliness and despair at not being able to form a relationship with another man. Though he expressed considerable anger at what he perceived to be men's lack of desire for him, he secretly concurred with what he felt to be their low estimation of him. Saying things like "I have good qualities, but those are not enough," he would consistently express his belief that he was not what men were looking for. Luke expressed a strong sense of alienation, believing he could not garner admiration from either his peers or his parents. Likewise, within the treatment, Luke was wary that I would judge him and find him lacking. He speculated that I was part of an exclusive crowd of gay men who were more accomplished and attractive than he. Looking on with envy, he bitterly assumed that my supposed friends and I would not allow him to join us. Luke felt that not only would I find him unattractive, but that I would go so far as to humiliate him. Specifically, I would call him a "fat sissy." This transference reflection led to considerable material about Luke's experience of humiliation and rejection by his male peers throughout his boyhood. But perhaps more importantly, Luke expressed painful feelings of deficiency in feeling unattractive to his father.

As treatment progressed and Luke's defenses abated, he reported a dream in which he was giving a small boy a bath. He and the boy were having a great deal of fun and Luke felt very tender toward the child. Luke became aware that the bathroom door was open, and that there were adults in the adjoining room. Fearing that the adults would think something illicit was taking place between Luke and the boy, Luke closed the door. The scene then changed to his parents' bedroom. He was in the bedroom as a teenager with another teenage boy. The other boy began to undress, but suddenly stopped. The dream ended with Luke feeling disappointed and angry. In associating to the dream, he spoke of a child patient of mine whom he had seen on occasion in the waiting room. Luke wondered what I did with such a small boy, and expressed his belief that I had to be more giving to a child, because a child would demand more. He felt that, most likely, I even held this boy. He remembered having seen this same child with his father on the street outside my office. Luke saw the father as handsome and as very attentive to the boy. Taking note of his associations, he indicated that he felt the little boy in the dream was himself, and that the dream expressed a wish for care, most likely from his father but also from me.

Luke went on to say that whereas the first half of the dream was a wish, the second half was a fear—his fear that if he let me know of his desire to be close and sexual, I would become disgusted and stop the therapy. As I inquired further, Luke anxiously revealed that he was aware of harboring a fantasy that I would take him into the playroom that adjoins my office, and there we would have sex. With great difficulty and disgust he expressed his interest in being passive—his wish to have me hold him, undress him, and suck his penis.[9]

---

9. Another aspect of the dream was to become important during a later phase of the therapy: Luke's feeling of frustration and anger at the end of the dream. His relationships with men were often colored by considerable feelings of anger and frustration at what he experienced as the men's inability to understand and appreciate him. Identifying this dynamic within the transference and recognizing how it reflected Luke's feelings with his father was central to this treatment. In turn, recognizing how Luke re-created this dynamic with other men allowed him to begin to develop closer relationships with his peers.

During the next hour, Luke recalled going as a young boy to a birthday party for a female cousin. At one point, his cousin climbed into his father's lap. Luke attempted to join them, but was pushed aside by his father, who indicated that such behavior was inappropriate for a boy. I commented that it seemed Luke wanted what he felt only a girl should have. He expressed discomfort with such a thought, but recognized that his disgust in the prior hour was due to his association of passive longings with "not being enough of a man and being too much like a woman." For a number of sessions thereafter, Luke returned to the subject of his childhood identification with girls. He characterized his friendships with girls as "strained allegiances." Though he recalled a sincere sense of friendship, he also remembered feeling that he was apart from them. He laughed as he said, "I didn't belong in either camp!" But his tone changed to sadness as he said, "What's so weird is how it was known and never spoken."

Luke's feeling in this regard points to what I believe to be a salient distinction between (a) a homosexual boy's experience of gender difference and (b) gender identity disorder: feminine identification for homosexual boys is not so much an expression of a wish to be a girl, but rather an avenue to passive experience and wish fulfillment. Passive longings and feminine identification reside alongside a masculine identification, often creating a puzzling gender experience for the homosexual boy. For example, a patient stated, "I know that my father wanted me to be a man, and I knew that I was not being a man like him. I was not being a woman, but I was not being a man within his definition of it." He rather aptly expresses the paradox of the homosexual boy's experience of gender: he did not feel himself to be a woman, yet he did not feel himself to be a man as defined by his father. He did not wish to grow up to be a woman, nor did he deny his male body. He did have girl friends, and enjoyed participating in games and pastimes with girls more than most boys. However, such pleasure did not constitute a preoccupation with femininity, and he did not engage only in stereotypically female activities. In fact,

in contrast to the characterization of homosexual boys as exhib-
iting heightened femininity, I have found that many homosexual
boys strive to repress their experience of gender difference. Following upon such repression is a boyhood depression, characterized by a partial shutdown of affective life and marked interpersonal alienation. One patient aptly reflected on such withdrawal
as his attempt to "neuter" himself (see Corbett, 1996 and 1997
for further discussion of these matters).

Working with gay male patients in an effort to help them speak
about and clarify their own distinct gender experience provides
them with access to a new vantage point from which they can re-
assess and revalue their development. Luke's ability to see his
wishes as variant as opposed to deviant conferred new possibility
on his sexual identity. He began to connect his passive wishes with
early erotic desire for his father (as well as for his mother, at other
points in this treatment), and his anxiety about his homosexuality
lessened. He was able to form a relationship with another young
man, and began to appreciate and resist the effect of discrimination on homosexual development. With increased tolerance for his
own identity, he was able to reestablish ties to his family and work
with them to understand his sexual difference.

Just as psychotherapy can promote the widening of ego boundaries and thereby allow a patient to form a more realistically tem-
pered system of values and ideals, we too as psychoanalysts must
begin to formulate a theory of gender and sexual development
that casts a wider net. I am not proposing that we need a theory
of gender and sexual development that is unbounded or that does
not offer us a means to reason about limits. Likewise, it would be
delusionary to ignore the necessity of a cultural order within
which any subject is sexed. But it is incumbent upon us to distinguish the normative from the natural, and to begin to present
the vicissitudes of gender. Likewise, it is incumbent upon us to
develop a theory that respects variation in human development
more than the desire to create a falsely symmetrical metaphysics
of gender.

REFERENCES

Arlow, J. (1969). Unconscious fantasy and distortions of conscious experience. *Psychoanalytic Quarterly* 50:67–76.

Bersani, L. (1989). Is the rectum a grave? In *AIDS: Cultural Analysis/Cultural Activism*, ed. D. Crimp, pp. 197–222. Cambridge, MA: MIT Press.

Chasseguet-Smirgel, J. (1976). Some thoughts on the ego ideal. *Psychoanalytic Quarterly* July, 345–373.

—— (1984). *Creativity and Perversion*. New York: Norton.

—— (1985). *The Ego Ideal*. New York: Norton.

Christiansen, A. (1993). *Masculinity and its vicissitudes*. Paper presented at the Seminar on Psychoanalysis and Sexual Difference, Institute for the Humanities, New York.

Corbett, K. (1989). *Interpreting male homosexual development*. Unpublished doctoral dissertation, Columbia University.

—— (1996). Homosexual boyhood: notes on girlyboys. *Gender and Psychoanalysis* 1(4):429–462.

—— (1997). Speaking Queer. *Gender and Psychoanalysis* 2(4):495–514.

Erikson, E. (1950). *Childhood and Society*. New York: Norton.

Foucault, M. (1985). *The Use of Pleasure*. New York: Pantheon.

Freud, S. (1905). Three essays on the theory of sexuality. *Standard Edition* 7:125–244.

—— (1909). Analysis of a phobia in a five-year-old boy. *Standard Edition* 10:1–149.

—— (1910). Leonardo da Vinci and a memory of his childhood. *Standard Edition* 11:57–137.

—— (1911). Formulations on the two principles of mental functioning. *Standard Edition* 12:213–226.

—— (1920). The psychogenesis of a case of homosexuality in a woman. *Standard Edition* 18:145–172.

—— (1937). Analysis terminable and interminable. *Standard Edition* 23:209–253.

Fuss, D., ed. (1991). *Inside/Out*. New York: Routledge.

Garber, M. (1992). *Vested Interests*. New York: Routledge.

Isay, R. (1986). The development of sexual identity in homosexual men. *Psychoanalytic Study of the Child* 41:467–489. New Haven, CT: Yale University Press.

—— (1989). *Being Homosexual*. New York: Farrar, Straus & Giroux.

———— (1991). The homosexual analyst. *Psychoanalytic Study of the Child* 46:199–216. New Haven, CT: Yale University Press.

Lewes, K. (1988). *The Psychoanalytic Theory of Male Homosexuality*. New York: Simon & Schuster.

Nicolosi, J. (1991). *Reparative Therapy of Male Homosexuality*. Northvale, NJ: Jason Aronson.

Person, E. (1986). The omni-available women and lesbian sex: two fantasy themes and their relationship to the male developmental experience. In *The Psychology of Men*, ed. K. Fogel, F. Lane, and R. Liebert, pp. 71–94. New York: Basic Books.

Socarides, C. (1978). *Homosexuality*. New York: Jason Aronson.

Winnicott, D. W. (1971). *Therapeutic Consultations in Child Psychiatry*. London: Hogarth.

———— (1986). *Home Is Where We Start From*. New York: Norton.

3

Deconstructing Difference: Gender, Splitting, and Transitional Space*

MURIEL DIMEN

In an early session, Elizabeth, then 43 years old, held back her tears because, she said, "I don't want to cry on your shoulder." When I questioned her reluctance, she replied that the danger lay in the shoulder, not in the crying: she would cry only on a man's shoulder; she was not interested in women.

I want to understand Elizabeth's reply by thinking about gender not as an essence but as a set of relations (May 1986) and to propose that at the heart of gender is not "masculinity" or "femininity" but the difference between them. My thinking is located in two intersecting contexts: feminist and psychoanalytic. The first may be described as the critique of gender, a phrase whose ambiguity is deliberate. I mean to suggest, simultaneously, gender as critiqued and gender as critique, gender as a concept that not only requires scrutiny but can itself illuminate other matters. Recipro-

*Originally published in *Psychoanalytic Dialogues* 1(3):335–352. Reprinted with permission from The Analytic Press.

cally, understanding gender depends on the second, psychoanalytic context of this chapter, framed here in terms of splitting and transitional space, concepts themselves capable of furthering the clinical relevance of the critique of gender. I am using the concept of splitting loosely (Benjamin 1988), signifying in its psychoanalytic sense both splitting of the ego and splitting of the object (Laplanche and Pontalis 1973) and in its cultural sense the many dichotomies and dualisms paradigmatic in Western thinking since Descartes and of critical relevance to feminist discourse. The doubled critique of gender I am proposing can, by defamiliarizing the emotion- and value-laden notions of femininity and masculinity, help to peel away what we think gender is (and believe it ought to be) from what it might be. When I speak thus of gender's possibility, I refer to the present, not the future. Deconstructing gender in our minds can help us stretch our clinical imagination about what our patients' inner worlds are like and, indeed, could be like.

GENDER AND SELF

Because the category of sex seems plain enough, the concept of gender likewise appears unproblematic, even though, in fact, it requires clarification or, better, deconstruction. Conventionally, gender denotes the psychological and social dimensions of the biological category of sex. This characterization sounds like a clear enough division of epistemological labor. But it is not. What gender seems to denote is one thing; what it actually connotes is another. Indeed, the connotations of gender are so complex as to generate an enormous indeterminacy, which Scott (1988), a feminist historian, phrases thus:

> [O]ften in patriarchal discourse, sexual difference (the contrast masculine/feminine) serves to encode or establish meanings that are literally unrelated to gender or the body. In that way, the meanings of gender become tied to many kinds of cultural representations, and these in turn establish terms by

which relations between women and men are organized and understood. [p. 37]

In other words, the category of sex is not transparent but is itself a dense weave of cultural significance, and the contrast masculine/feminine, as the representation of what psychoanalysts commonly refer to as "the anatomical difference," addresses a variety of matters, not all of which are germane to sex, gender, or the genitals. This slippage from sex to culture not only provides us with our understandings of gender as personally experienced but informs gender as a social institution.

Another elision, equivalent in power to that from sex to culture, informs what we might term the mutual definition of selfhood and gender identity, such that problems of self may come to be coded in terms of gender, and those of gender, in terms of self. Self and gender identity inhabit one another so intimately that questions such as these become familiar: If I feel womanly, am I at my most feminine? Or am I feeling most fully myself? When I do feel like myself, does that feeling have anything to do with my female identity? If I feel, by contrast and perhaps more pertinently, unwomanly, am I feeling somehow not myself? If I am not myself, is gender identity somehow also, and more secretly, involved? And so on.

The overriding question is, Would these puzzles even arise if selfhood and gender identity were not already in problematic relation? In other words, though selfhood and gender identity are structurally different, their contemporaneous crystallization in development makes them seem, indeed feel, joined at the heart, and leaves their relationship simultaneously unquestioned and questionable. The intrapsychic proximity of sense of self to sense of gender identity often obscures, not to say deepens, the complexities of gender representation generated. At the same time, the contrast masculine/feminine, by collapsing many representations of selfhood *that are unrelated to gender*, can disguise, and even create, dilemmas of self as well.

Sometimes the mutual coding of gender and self is directly translatable. For example, the conventional split between masculine and feminine in psychology and culture, that is, the contrast masculine/feminine, speaks also to pleasure, activity, and passivity. Pleasure in activity is wont to carry the valence of masculinity, while pleasure in passivity is charged with femininity, a split aligned with the traditional dichotomy in sex roles. As this splitting has been challenged socially, it is more often questioned in the clinical situation, where one may suspect, for example, that women's sense of activity may be gender-dystonic and therefore anxiety-inducing, just as men's fantasies of passivity may express a fear of being homosexual, itself often the code for the fear of being feminine.

This example seems straightforward enough. But the plot thickens. For example, gender identity, normatively defined as watertight, may normally be porous. We do not always feel in gender, and when we do not, we feel anxiety, which makes us less likely to remember that sometimes one's gender resembles an ill-fitting garment. When I asked a friend who had lost a tennis match how he felt during the game, he replied, "Like a girl"; he had had trouble wielding the racket. Clearly, "feeling like a girl" was not a pleasant experience for him. Still, was he anxious because he felt out of gender? Or out of gender because he was anxious about something else? Or both? Why was losing incompatible with masculinity? Is losing the same as castration? Does not losing also make us feel small? Could this man have been feeling like a child as well as like a girl? Does "feeling like a girl" represent a narcissistic wound (Shapiro, S. 1988, personal communication)? By way of comparison and contrast, another friend, who has always seen herself as nonathletic, represents her successful attempt to play squash by drawing a yapping, rushing Pekingese, which she reluctantly identifies as male. We might say that in her activity, she first and consciously experiences herself as not herself, as Other and, only second, unconsciously, and more painfully, as out-of-gender, as a junior, ridiculous male. If my woman friend experienced the narcissistic wound ultimately as gender loss, could my man friend have represented it finally by loss of self, by an encounter with the second-sex Otherness that femininity represents?

GENDER AS A SET OF RELATIONS

Let me review what has happened here, so as to make my main conceptual point. I began by critiquing the alignment of femininity with passivity and of masculinity with activity. In so doing, I came upon a whirl of dualisms orbiting in relation to the contrast masculine/feminine and to each other as well—self/other, preoedipal/oedipal, infancy/adulthood, autonomy/dependency, superiority/inferiority, heterosexuality/homosexuality. In this process, gender appears to be less a determinate category than something resembling a force field. Much like the atom, once thought of as substance but now construed as a set of interacting forces, so gender looks to consist not of essences but of complex and shifting relations among multiple contrasts or differences. Sometimes these contrasts remain distinct, at other times they intersect, and at still other times they fuse and exchange identities.

As a way of turning to how problems of self and gender may encode one another, let us focus for a moment more on activity and passivity and their relation to sexual difference. Recognizing the force field that marries the inherently unrelated contrasts masculine/feminine, self/other, and active/passive to one another permits us to understand, for example, that women's anxiety in activity may be equally a problem of gender as of self. On the other hand, this recognition also lets us understand that gender-neutral qualities of self, such as activity and passivity, can reciprocally organize and thereby evoke sexual and gendered splits. I have alluded, for example, to the fact that, for men, passivity may represent both homosexuality and femininity.

An analogous, although not identical, slippage among activity state, object choice, and gender identity shows up in the experience of Elizabeth, whose refusal to cry on a woman's shoulder now emerges as a negotiation among dangerous polarities. Her response to my inquiry implied that she was neither a dependent child nor a lesbian but an autonomous, heterosexual woman, and as such, her need for comfort was not a danger. To have admitted being a woman who wanted a woman's shoulder to cry on would have revealed what crying on a man's shoulder concealed, that sometimes she still felt like a child. The idea of leaning on a man defended against dependency longings because, in culture and psyche alike, heterosexuality lines up with, and symbolizes, adulthood and autonomy.

SEX, GENDER, AND SPLITTING

Heterosexuality, even though it is classically (though not always in Freud) the object choice of choice, can and does serve to conceal and express splits in the self. Nominally heterosexual, Elizabeth had not been sexually active in fifteen years, with the exception of masturbation (which she acknowledged but refused to discuss). Having had one homosexual encounter in junior college, she later married a mainly impotent man twenty years her senior with whom she had intercourse perhaps half a dozen times before a heart attack killed him three months after the wedding. Later, she had three major but short-lived love affairs; the last breakup so bereaved her that she resolved never to let anyone get close again.

These facts of her life, and those to be recounted, emerged slowly and painfully over the course of our work together. Contemplating our shared history now, I feel as I did then—dismayed, conscious of both reluctance and helplessness to grasp the full damage. Not untouched, I still was sensible of her wish that I not touch her uninvited, that I respect the cocoon of privacy protecting her most secret self. Shielding her was her obesity, which, she believed, distanced men in particular. In her fat, she was like a great big baby, reminding me of no one so much as Ralph Kramden. The gender ambiguity in my association reflects Elizabeth's sexual ambiguity. Elizabeth's attachment to a suspended heterosexuality masking childhood longings was a powerful means to disremember the sexual abuse that, from ages 3 to 5, she experienced with her adored brother, nine years older than she. Almost daily, Johnnie would masturbate before her in the parlor at quarter to five in the afternoon, while they listened to a favorite radio program and their mother prepared dinner in the kitchen, which happened to be the next room. Torn between feelings of specialness and betrayal, Elizabeth never revealed these encounters; she always believed that if she told her mother, she, not Johnnie, would be punished; when she was older and thought about taking the story to confession (the family was Catholic), she would somehow forget.

Not only her flesh but her words protected her. I was both moved and often made to feel helpless by the verbal fence Elizabeth planted around her private self. When, one time, she said, by way of explanation, "Johnnie set me up too early," she sounded like a forlorn child prostitute turned out by her lover-turned-pimp, a child now homeless but denying the despair of her psychic bondage to him. Yet, even as Elizabeth's speech (she often used clichés, for example) deftly dispatched emotion to some unreachable part of the galaxy, it served to consolidate her personal universe. Shattered, she wrapped the wounds of her amputated feeling in tried-and-true language that normalized her tragedy. At the same time, Johnnie's betrayal of her trust disrupted not only the consolidation of her selfhood but the emergence of her sexuality and gender identity, and left her caught between identification with and desire for men. Was she female or male? While watching his performance, was she watching and desiring her idol or identifying with him? It was not clear. The only way she found relief was not to choose, not to be either gender (a dilemma identified by Harris, this volume).

Here, in summary fashion, is the sequence as it appears to me in retrospect, for it was not one she could have constructed herself. The cessation of the incest coincided with the birth of her younger sister (the last of five children) and the start of school, a traumatic concatenation of events that resulted in the tantrums for which she was punished after she started school. At the age of 5, she wanted to drown her newborn younger sister "because she wasn't a boy." She remembered stimulating her clitoris when she was 8. Between the ages of 9 and 10, she frequently wore one of her father's cast-off ties, which she hoped would transform her into a boy. During her eleventh year (when, after Johnnie's return from the army, the incest recurred briefly until she put a stop to it), she began her avid consumption of novels and was at the time equally drawn to stories of swashbuckling pirates and tales of lascivious sultans.

She was disappointed that menstruation was not a one-time-only event yet was humiliated that her first brassiere was her oldest sister's yellowed cast-off, delivered, to her embarrassment, by Johnnie as a present at a holiday dinner. By adolescence, she had come to feel that boys were dangerous. As an adult, she had come to hold what she regarded as the prejudiced opinion that boys should not be allowed to babysit. Finally, she feared sexually assertive men and preferred those who were shy and a bit unsure.

Frozen between femininity and masculinity, on guard against painful affect, and just out of others' reach, she came, in her adult life, to be cleft between body and mind, a cleavage that was apparently odd but, down deep, a source and sign of shame. Trained in physical therapy, by which she was supporting herself, she was finishing a scholarly doctorate, was already becoming known in her field, and had friends who were liberal, intellectual, and sophisticated. Yet she resided alone in her suburban family home next door to her oldest sister's household; the culture of her family and hometown friends was lower middle class, anti-urban, and politically conservative. Her work life was also polarized. Her specialty within her field relied more on concrete data than on speculation, while the theoretical abstraction found in other sectors of her discipline made her very anxious. She preferred gothic and horror genres for extracurricular reading but generally found the news media too distressing to witness.

Her major symptoms were consistent with splitting—not only obesity but myriad physical ailments and a dependence on an oral hypnotic; dissociation in sessions and amnesia between them; a sometimes dogged, sometimes mischievous balking at interpretations of her unconscious. Although she always remembered the facts of the incest and the sense of privilege she derived from it, she was, until a year and a half before we terminated, unconscious of her anger about it. At that time, Elizabeth began to follow the increasing media coverage of the sexual abuse of children, because she had just learned that there had been more sexual abuse in her own family. Johnnie, who had died in a freak accident at the age of 26, had left behind a wife and two children. His widow later married a man who, it turned out, molested both his stepdaughter and his stepson's daughter, that is, Johnnie's own daughter and granddaughter. Elizabeth's subsequent outrage on behalf of her niece and her grandniece allowed us to probe her rage about what had happened to her.

As Elizabeth recovered her anger and sense of betrayal about the incest, her splitting generally lessened, and her drug and nicotine dependencies disappeared. Nevertheless, the obesity, about which she was unhappy, and her resistance to unconscious interpretation, which did not interest her, held fast all the way to the end. As I write this, I can now link this tenacity to a splitting in the transference/countertransference configuration, in which Elizabeth embraced the manifest, the literal, the body, and I embraced the latent, the symbolic, the mind. Nor is it surprising that this split intersected gender as well. During one session, when she was in deep distress about her family's inability or refusal to appreciate her work, she spoke of her "inquiring mind." Together, we then discovered that, of her parents, brother, and three sisters, the only other person in her family who could also be so described was her father. If, therefore, her mind inquired, then it followed that she could not be female. For reasons to which I will return, we were unable to explore the paradox that women, too, could have inquiring minds.

DESIRE IN THE SPACE OF DIFFERENCE

Let me sum up what I have said so far. Taking a deconstructionist tack, I have said that the core of gender is difference, not essence, the relation between masculinity and femininity as culturally conceived, interpersonally negotiated, and intrapsychically experienced. To put this view in developmental terms, one becomes gendered not by learning "a one-dimensional message that [one is] either male or female"; rather, one "absorb[s] the *contrast* between male and female" (Dimen 1986, p. 8). In theoretical terms, looking at either masculinity or femininity without looking at the contrast between them encourages us to imagine fixed essences, hard-and-fast polarities. If, however, we enter the space occupied by their difference, we can see more clearly other differences that, though not necessarily related to sex, in fact secretly construct gender (Scott 1988). What I have done in that space is examine the gender dualism as it shiftingly intersects other dualisms, any pole of which, rigidly clung to, may also signal splits in the self. I have also suggested, via a clinical example, that gender identity as we know it can organize and disguise such splitting, and I have implied that a focus on the space between the poles can reveal and help to dismantle these splits.

So far, then, the axis of my discussion has been splitting and its interface with the gender polarity. Other, crosscutting axes introduce other considerations. Take, for example, desire. It, too, is dualistically organized, such that desire is gender-syntonic for men, dystonic for women. Let me quote myself (Dimen 1986) again (but cf. Benjamin 1989, pp. 85–133): "Our culture has two patterns for desire, one for males and another for females. The first pattern honors, masculinizes, and makes adult the felt experience of 'I want.' The second demeans, feminizes, and infantilizes the state of being wanted, the felt experience of 'I want to be wanted'" (p. 7). This dualism between wanting and wanting-to-be-wanted intersects not only the contrast masculine/feminine but that between subject and object and results in a primary contradiction that I have termed the "Subject-as-Object" (1986, p. 3). Subjects, in our cultural and intrapsychic representations, are men. The subject says, "I want." The subject, "Man," desires. Since men represent authorship, agency, and adulthood, women as adults are expected to be subjects too. At the same time, through splitting that occurs equally on cultural and psychological levels, women are also expected to be objects ("object" here meaning not the intrapsychic representation of persons, as psychoanalysis uses the term, but "thing," as the vernacular has it). As inanimate things, women are represented to be without desire, to be the targets of the subject's desire. If subjects want, objects are there to be wanted.

Women, then, are expected to be both the subject and the object. The development of femininity is, therefore, a compromise, almost, you might say, a compromise formation. It is the process of learning to be both, to take yourself as an object and to expect others to do so too, and all the while you know that you are a subject. Elizabeth's case is an extreme version of this common dilemma, an embodiment of a primary sexual contradiction. On the one hand, as a woman, you would want to be a woman, not a child or a man; unwilling to weep on my shoulder, Elizabeth pronounces herself a woman. On the other hand, if being a woman means being both the subject of your own desires and the object of others' and therefore torn or suspended between these two positions like Elizabeth, who, as a little girl, feared she would have been held responsible for her brother's sexual incursions, then perhaps you would not want to be feminine after all. So Elizabeth stopped time when the incest ceased; often feeling like a 5-year-old girl, she walks with the rolling gait of a sailor, identifies as a heterosexual woman, and generally keeps clear of sexual intimacy.

HIERARCHY AND AGGRESSION BETWEEN WOMEN

Examining the gendering of desire and the contrast subject/object or, better, subjectivity/objectification returns us to gender as critiqued, because it introduces the particularly critical notion of hierarchy. The contrast power/weakness intersects all the others considered so far. As literary critic Armstrong (1988) describes the ambiguities of the gender hierarchy, "gender refers not only to a polarity within a field of cultural information but also to the asymmetry between the two poles of that opposition" (p. 2). Or, to put it less formally and more whimsically, all genders are created equal, but some are more equal than others.

The contrast masculine/feminine, then, interfaces not only with inherently gender-neutral and a-hierarchical polarities but also, via the gender hierarchy characterized variously as male dominance, patriarchy, and sexism, with the duality of domination and subordination as well, as indeed do all polarities, since, according to postmodernism, "binary oppositions are inseparable from implicit or explicit hierarchies" (Flax 1990, p. 101). Without, however, recapitulating what the last quarter-century of gender politics has had to say about the effects of gender hierarchy on women, I would like to consider how this new contrast, power/weakness, can illuminate masculinity as well.

That femininity is not essentially, but only contingently, a compromise between subjectivity and objectification is revealed when we understand that men, too, can be the subject-as-object. In fact, this contradiction is what they, like women in the workplace, enter every Monday morning. On the job, most men have to follow someone else's orders with the same alacrity as though they had thought of them themselves. There, they too must be subject-as-object. They escape this contradiction only when they leave; even then, if they are Third World or in some other way stigmatized, they are not safely free of this sort of domination until they return to their own communities or homes. The difference for women is that hierarchy follows them everywhere they go; most men are "feminized" at work, but most women are stigmatized not only at home but in the community and on the street, because they wear the contradiction of subject-as-object on their bodies. It may be, indeed, that the only time they are safe is when they are with other women. Even then, not only the social hierarchies women inhabit but the relational structures of domination and subordination govern them almost as surely.

Indeed, hierarchy between women may have kept Elizabeth's treatment from going further than it did. I had hoped that before she terminated, we would have been able to negotiate the paradox that she, a woman of an active intellectuality, was in a room with me, a woman of like mind, a woman on whose shoulder she could finally permit herself to cry without any threat to her gender, sexual identity, and sense of maturity. There were barriers, however, to the mutual recognition of our common engagement with the dilemma of being the subject-as-object. Although all women are created equal, some, particularly "archaic" mothers (Chasseguet-Smirgel 1986, Dinnerstein 1999), are more equal than others. As Shapiro and I (Dimen and Shapiro n.d.) have argued elsewhere, trouble arises between women in the analytic situation because

> the juncture of caring and authority in one member of the dyad, that is, the analyst, painfully juxtaposes the most primitive dimensions of the mother/daughter relationship to the complications of femininity's social construction. The profound longing for maternal nurturance conflicts with an equally deep repudiation of women's subjectivity and authority, itself rooted in, simultaneously, infantile love and hate, gender-identity formation, and conventional sexual stereotyping. [p. 15]

Sometimes, in consequence, "a collusive pretense to a sisterly, mutually nurturant relationship" emerges to deny "competition, contempt, envy, and devaluation" (p. 15). In particular, the anxiety that comes with aggression between women evokes the dangers of preoedipal maternal destructiveness, dangers that, in turn, incline women to excise aggression from their intimacy and replace it with pseudomutuality. This excision not only prevents them from understanding the creative potential of aggression in politics and in analysis (Harris 1989) but can also threaten them with merging, a common solution to which is splitting (Lindenbaum 1985).

Interestingly, countertransference anxiety was less of a problem when my superiority to Elizabeth depended on my not being a woman. When I was the actively probing, thinking, and sometimes bullying father to her passively resisting, vegetating, and sometimes helpless daughter, my interpretations permitted her to engage her rage and therefore her ambivalent identification with her father. When I was superior as a woman, however, I became far more dangerous. Neither I nor Elizabeth could give words to the fact that, so often, I seemed to be the better woman: not only could I think, but I was thin. As winner of both contests, of minds and of bodies, I became the omnipotent preoedipal mother with a monopoly on power and desire. I therefore remained, in Elizabeth's belief, incapable of understanding the shame, despair, and neediness she felt inside her fat. Instead, I was the mother who heaped her children's plates and insisted they eat everything, even when, as an adolescent, Elizabeth begged to be allowed to diet.

To some extent, Elizabeth was right. Like so many women who think of themselves as fat even though they are not, I could, indeed, imagine her anguish, but I could not cathect my empathy with her despair and self-hate. Unable to own my ruthless triumph in being the thin, thinking winner, I could neither enter into her feeling of humiliation nor use my aggression in the service of recognizing her own desire to be the woman warrior. Unreleased, my competitiveness, instead, became contempt, which only now finds expression in my likening of Elizabeth to Jackie Gleason's brilliant television creation, that gentle blowhard, the lower-middle-class bus driver, Ralph Kramden. It is, in retrospect, no wonder that Elizabeth presented as a split her plan to terminate her eight-year, once-a-week treatment; now that she no longer had to commute to Manhattan for therapy, she would have time to work on her obesity with a self-help group in the suburbs.

DIFFERENCE AND TRANSITIONAL SPACE

I would like to end with some remarks about the transitional, paradoxical space between apparent opposites, the space in which I have been playing throughout this chapter. Although the idea of a creative and pleasurable tension within dualisms is an increasingly familiar one in feminist theory, its most useful psychoanalytic expression is, I believe, Benjamin's (1989). The answer to splitting is never simply the recall of the forgotten pole of any split but, in her phrase, the tension of holding "the paradox of simultaneity." This paradox is essential to both development and treatment and is one that is potentially pleasurable, as it represents the Winnicottian transitional space where play occurs. Indeed, this pleasurable play was rare for Elizabeth and me, play being laborious when splitting dominates (Winnicott 1971), when the "inability to 'play with reality' . . . result[s] in using reality as a defense against fantasy" (Bassin n.d., p. 13).

The pleasure of the tension is, then, intrapsychic as well as intersubjective. Consider what Greenberg and Mitchell (1983) say about Jacobson's redefinition of the constancy principle: "Rather than operating in the service of keeping the level of tension as low as possible, it is the function of the constancy principle as redefined [by Jacobson], to establish and maintain a constant axis of tension and a certain margin for the biological vacillations around it" (p. 321). As Greenberg and Mitchell suggest, pleasure paradoxically inheres in the cycle of tension, in its oscillating reduction and increase, not in its reduction alone. Cyclicity, in turn, implies the oscillation between two positions, not an unvarying habitation of one. The pleasure of play, for example, lies in the repeated oscillation between reality and fantasy; indeed, play loses its piquancy when it settles into either reality or fantasy, when, for example, "the nip becomes a bite," to quote Bateson's (1972) famous insight. To my mind, one way to describe Elizabeth's sexuality is in terms of a frightened and pleasureless holding to one position, an asexual attachment to a heterosexual identity that is never played out, with or against, because it serves to defend against an inner world in which nips are bites and, as such, too terrifying to enter.

Within desire, this pleasurable oscillation takes place between want and need. Desire is conventionally defined as wish, emergent in the psyche, and is thereby absolutely distinguished from need, rooted in the drives (Laplanche and Pontalis 1973). I regard this definition, however, as a false dichotomy that intensifies polarization instead of illuminating experience. In contrast, I see the longing that characterizes desire as engaged with both want and need. As I (Dimen 1989) have written elsewhere:

> Merged in infancy as different aspects of desire, need and want
> separate out as development proceeds. Although they continue
> unconsciously to be kin to one another, they appear culturally

as unequal strangers. Wanting, associated with adulthood, active will, and masculinity, is better than need, linked to infancy, passive dependency, and femininity. [Need is, furthermore, frightening, recalling as it does unconscious memories of help-less, total dependence on others for love and care.] Adults therefore try to distance their dependency needs by regard-ing their longings for love, tenderness, and care as weak, childish, "womanish." [pp. 41–42]

In other words, adults split. Via the intersection of the contrast want/need with adulthood/infancy, activity/passivity, and mascu-linity/femininity, they effect what I have termed the gendered divorce of want from need, with undeniable, serious consequences for their own well-being. As they try to want and not to need, they inevitably diminish what they try to preserve, any appetite for living. Although, then, mental health is normally defined by the triumph of desire—defined as want—over need, I would propose a neces-sary, creative tension in the space between want and need. How else, for example, might we negotiate Fairbairn's (1952) paradox of "mature dependence" than to feel both want and need for the other?

Difference, as I have been speaking of it here, is a paradoxical space that selfhood itself inhabits. Autonomy and dependence, activity and passivity, heterosexuality and homosexuality, body and mind, selfness and otherness, subjectivity and objectification, superiority and inferiority, want and need, and I could go on: these apparent polarities are but different moments of the self, the pas-sage between which might be regarded as pleasurable, even though when we leave the preferred polarity—when, for example, we tran-sit from want to need—we are, as things now stand, extraordinar-ily uncomfortable. To repeat, the solution to the problem of split-ting is not merely remembering the other pole but being able to inhabit the space between them, to tolerate and even enjoy the paradox of simultaneity.

What, then, of masculinity and femininity, which do not ap-pear on this increasingly long list of contrasts? I might have said that they, too, are but different moments of the self. But I am not sure that they are because, in fact, I am not sure *what* they are. I am not arguing, as I once did, that, since masculinity and femininity are less determinate than conventionally thought, gender need not exist (Dimen 1982). On the other hand, even though the ethnographic evidence for the predominance of dual-gender systems is very persuasive (Cucchiari 1981), the content of gender or the number of genders in any given system remains cross-culturally variable (Gailey 1988), suggesting the desirability of further investigation. I would still make the same case for the possibility and pleasures of gender multiplicity (Dimen 1982; see also Goldner, this volume).

Perhaps, then, it would be better to restate this position as a question: If masculinity and femininity were to be regarded as different moments of the self, what would each moment mean to a particular self? What is masculinity? What is femininity? In other words, I question these terms because, although we can name everything we think they are, on examination their meanings become uncertain. Therefore, I have used this uncertainty epistemologically; if, this chapter is asking, we assume nothing about gender other than that it is a socially and psychologically meaningful term, what meanings can we find for it?

At the same time, I do not take the deconstructionist train all the way to its nihilist last stop of saying that things are only what texts say they are, that there is no ontology. I believe in the reality of gender-identity experience and of gender as an organizer in the psyche; as such, gender is variably meaningful, a variability that generates uncertainty, invites inquiry, and offers richness. This "diagnosis" of uncertainty should not, however, be regarded as a failure of method or theory. Instead, it is *sign* of what gender is. Gender, as an internally varied experience, is sometimes central and definitive, sometimes marginal and contingent. Consequently, it is fundamentally and inalterably paradoxical (Goldner, this volume). Harris's (this volume) phrasing expresses well a conceptualization of gender's ambiguity and complexity, with which I agree:

> [g]ender is neither reified nor simply liminal and evanescent. Rather, in any one person's experience, gender may occupy both

positions. Gender may in some contexts be thick and reified, as plausibly real as anything in our character. At other moments, gender may seem porous and insubstantial. Furthermore, there may be multiple genders or embodied selves. For some individuals these gendered experiences may feel integrated, ego-syntonic. For others, the gender contradictions and alternatives seem dangerous and frightening and so are maintained as splits in the self, dissociated part-objects. [p. 212]

To put it more figuratively, if life is a sea, then gender is an island. Sometimes people drown in the sea, sometimes they are stranded on land. I am arguing that we need the sea as much as we need the land, and, to push this Winnicottian metaphor further, we also need the seashore, where land and water merge (Winnicott 1971).

In other words, I am suggesting that the notion of transitional space can help us comprehend what our theory has heretofore been able to handle only by splitting. Gender identity, born in the space of difference between masculinity and femininity, always retains the marks of its birth. Therefore, although gender identity has come to be seen in developmental theory as finalizing differentiation, I would suggest, counterintuitively, that it does more: at one and the same time gender identity seals the package of self and preserves all the self must lose. It serves to bridge the archaic depths, the Impossible that underlies human creativity (McDougall 1985), and the self, the psychic agency that authors creation. Not only, as Fast (1984) has it, does gender identity incline us to look for what we are not in the opposite-sexed other, alternatingly definitive and liminal, gender identity also permits us to find in ourselves the overinclusiveness we have had to renounce so that we can also recognize it in the other, of whatever gender. This view of gender tracks the progress Fast charts from "gender differentiation" to "overinclusiveness" to gender identity, conceptualizes how access to the overinclusive depths of the self might be conserved even as renunciation entails their loss, and addresses "the capacity to identify with the opposite sex as a fundamental element in the mobilization of sexual desire" (McDougall 1980, pp. 149–150).

I am ending, then, where I began, on a moment of ambiguity, because the space of paradox is where psychoanalysis works (Boris 1986). There are many instances of paradox in the clinical situation. At any given moment, for instance, countertransference may be complementary and/or concordant (Racker 1985). Gender's habitation of transitional space is another instance. The analyst may be a good mother and/or a bad one; a preoedipal and an oedipal father; sometimes a sister, a transference Elizabeth and I explored, and sometimes a brother, a transference that, unfortunately, we did not examine and that did not occur to me at the time. Imprisoned not only within my own gender but within a sense of femininity that splits aggression from nurturing, I could not imagine then what seems likely now, that my inquiry may have represented to Elizabeth the early violation she suffered at her brother's hands.

There is, as well, a final instance of ambiguity: we are not always gendered; sometimes, as the orthodox position traditionally has it, the analyst's gender is irrelevant. Analysts dwell not only in the paradox of being sometimes female, sometimes male, but also in that of feeling and being construed as variably gendered and gender-free. Thus we enter the countertransferential counterpart of our patients' experience, a paradox captured by Boris's (1986) exemplification of Bion's approach: "If the 10:00 [a.m.] patient is one we know to be a married man in his thirties, we know too much, for how are we to attend the four-year-old girl who has just walked in?" (p. 177).

REFERENCES

Armstrong, N. (1988). The gender bind: women and the disciplines. *Genders* 3:1–23.

Bassin, D. (n.d.). *Toward the reconciliation of the masculine and feminine in the genital stage.* Unpublished manuscript.

Bateson, G. (1972). A theory of play and fantasy. In *Steps Toward an Ecology of Mind*, pp. 177–193. New York: Ballantine.

Benjamin, J. (1988). *Elements of intersubjectivity: recognition and destruction.* Presented at Relational Track Colloquium, New York University Postdoctoral Program, December.

———— (1988). *The Bonds of Love*. New York: Pantheon.

Boris, H. N. (l986). Bion revisited. *Contemporary Psychoanalysis* 22:159–184.

Chasseguet-Smirgel, J. (1986). Freud and female sexuality: the consideration of some blind spots in the exploration of the "Dark Continent." In *Sexuality and Mind*, ed. J. Chasseguet-Smirgel, pp. 1–28. NewYork: New York University Press.

Cucchiari, S. (1981). The gender revolution and the transition from bisexual horde to patrilocal band: the origins of gender hierarchy. In *Sexual Meanings*, ed. S. B. Ortner and H. Whitehead, pp. 31–79. Cambridge: Cambridge University Press.

Dimen, M. (1982). Notes for the reconstruction of sexuality. *Social Text* 6:22–30.

———— (1986). *Surviving Sexual Contradictions*. New York: Macmillan.

———— (1989). Power, sexuality and intimacy. In *Gender/Body/Knowledge*, ed. A. Jaggar and S. Bordo, pp. 34–51. New Brunswick, NJ: Rutgers University Press.

Dimen, M., and Shapiro, S. (n.d). *Trouble between women*. Unpublished manuscript.

Dinnerstein, D. (1999). *The Mermaid and The Minotaur*. New York: Other Press.

Fairbairn, W. R. D. (1952). *Psychoanalytic Studies of the Personality*. London: Routledge & Kegan Paul.

Fast, I. (1984). *Gender Identity*. Hillsdale, NJ: Lawrence Erlbaum.

Flax, J. (1990). *Thinking Fragments*. Berkeley: University of California Press.

Gailey, C. (1988). Evolutionary perspectives on gender hierarchy. In *Analyzing Gender*, ed. B. Hess and M. Ferree, chap. 1. Newbury Park, CA: Sage.

Greenberg, J., and Mitchell, S. A. (1983). *Object Relations in Psychoanalytic Theory*. Cambridge, MA: Harvard University Press.

Harris, A. (1989). Bringing Artemis to life: a plea for militance and aggression in feminist peace politics. In *Rocking the Ship of State*, ed. A. Harris and Y. King, pp. 93–114. Boulder, CO: Westview.

Laplanche, J., and Pontalis, J.-B. (1973). *The Language of Psycho-Analysis*, trans. D. N. Smith. New York: Norton.

Lindenbaum, J. (1985). The shattering of an illusion: the problem of competition in lesbian relationships. *Feminist Studies* 11(1):85–103.

May, R. (1986). Concerning a psychoanalytic view of maleness. *Psychoanalytic Review* 73:179–194.

McDougall, J. (1980). *Plea for a Measure of Abnormality*. New York: International Universities Press.

———— (1985). *Theatres of the Mind: Illusion and Truth on the Psychoanalytic Stage*. New York: Basic Books.

Racker, H. (1985). *Transference and Countertransference*. London: Maresfield Library.

Scott, J. W. (1988). Deconstructing equality-versus-difference: or, the uses of post-structuralist theory for feminism. *Feminist Studies* 14:33–50.

Winnicott, D. W. (1971). *Playing and Reality*. New York: Penguin.

4

Toward a Critical Relational Theory of Gender[*]

VIRGINIA GOLDNER

Contemporary psychoanalytic thinking about gender has resulted in a profound critique of Freud's phallocentric theories of male and female development. While there is no simple consensus among the many competing perspectives now being developed, most are rooted in an empirically based, modern theory of gender identity development (e.g., Benjamin 1988, Chodorow 1978, Coates 1990, Fast 1984, Money and Ehrhardt 1972, Person and Ovesey 1983, Stoller 1975). This collective body of work challenges Freud's view of women as the second, inadequate sex (his notion of femininity as thwarted masculinity). Indeed, in Stoller's upended version of Freud's gender theory, it is masculinity that is the makeshift construction, with femininity, not penis envy, representing "bedrock" (Stoller 1975).

While Freud's ideas make gender crudely derivative of the anatomical difference between the sexes, contemporary gender-

*Originally published in *Psychoanalytic Dialogues* 1(3):249–272. Reprinted with permission from The Analytic Press.

identity theorists utilize ego psychology and object relations theory to people the psychological space in which gender and sexual development coevolve. Thus, without sacrificing the body, modern psychoanalytic theories of gender emphasize the particular and the symbolic over the generic givens of biology.

While these developments lift the psychoanalytic view of gender out of its biologism and either/or dichotomies, gender identity theory remains a problematic solution to classical orthodoxy. As May (1986) has trenchantly argued, the very notion of identity, "can imply a sense of self too final, smooth, and conflict-free to do justice to our clinical (or personal) experience" (p. 181). Indeed, from a truly analytic perspective, the idea of a unified gender identity makes sense only as "a resistance in terms of treatment and an impoverishment in terms of character (p. 188).

This essay takes up the challenge of May's critique and attempts to look through or beyond the construct of gender. The arguments to be developed here challenge the presumption that an internally consistent gender identity is possible or even desirable. Instead, social and philosophical readings of gender derived from feminist theory, as well as revisionist psychoanalytic formulations, form the basis of a deconstructionist critique of our dominant gender-identity paradigm.

This perspective opposes the reification of gender as a coherent essence or entity and argues, instead, that gender is fundamentally and paradoxically indeterminant, both as a psychological experience and as a cultural category. Indeed, I will argue, in an elaboration of some earlier collaborative work (Goldner et al. 1990), that the normal process of "gendering" generates (psycho)logical paradoxes analogous to those Bateson and his coinvestigators (1956) considered to be characteristic of a double bind.

My argument is situated among many contemporary attempts, particularly, although not exclusively, by feminists, to lift Freud's radically disruptive method and beliefs ("I bring you the plague") out from their embeddedness in his naively misogynistic, normative presumptions. Indeed, the story of the transformation of psychoanalysis from an uncompromising, radical inquiry into human psychology and culture to a domesticated, medicalized "conformist psychology" has achieved the status of a cautionary tale.

At the same time, as a "postmodern tide of uncertainty" (Benjamin, this issue) undermines the intellectual status and truth claims of virtually all academic disciplines, there has been an extraordinary resurgence of scholarly interest in psychoanalysis as the discipline most practiced in the art of uncertainty. This is because the analytic stance fosters skepticism about the knower and the known by illuminating the motivational structures underlying ideas, actions, and systems of knowledge (including itself). Moreover, the analytic method of inquiry and interpretation defines itself in terms of the elaboration of multiple-layered meanings, as opposed to a "final truth."

Rescuing this subversive method and content from the normative, socially conformist uses to which psychoanalysis has been put has now become an intellectual cottage industry. Chodorow (1989), acknowledging her debt to Schafer's (1974) early classic, "Problems in Freud's Psychology of Women," captures the common strategy of these revisionist critics in a witty one-liner: "[T]here is a method to Freud's misogyny, and this method can be used against him" (p. 173). She continues:

> He goes wrong, when he undercuts his own psychoanalytic methodology and findings. . . . [P]sychoanalysis is founded on Freud's discoveries that there is nothing inevitable about the development of sexual object choice, mode, or aim. . . . The theory becomes coercive, when a functionalist teleology [conceptualizes] gender differentiation [as necessary] for the purposes of procreative [i.e., heterosexual] sex. [pp. 172–173]

Given that there is now generalized agreement, even within important sectors of the psychoanalytic mainstream, that Freud's gender-conventionalized functionalism is not inherent to psychoanalysis but actually runs counter to it (Grossman and Kaplan 1988, Kaplan 1990, Person and Ovesey 1983, Schafer 1974), we might ask, as Person (1990) has done, "why reformulations of female development seem to have lagged unduly [in the face of] considerable countervailing data and the serious critiques of early formulations" (p. 307).

While a fully comprehensive response to this critical question lies beyond the scope of this chapter, a partial answer, imported from feminist theory, will provide a necessary conceptual bridge for my own contribution to a revised gender paradigm.

The feminist scholar de Lauretis (1990) has observed that in virtually all knowledge systems, "gender or sexual division is either not visible, in the manner of a blind spot, or taken for granted, in the manner of an a priori" (p. 130). She goes on, in a play on Rousseau's "social contract," to suggest the metaphor of a "heterosexual or Oedipal social contract": an implicit (unconscious) "agreement between modern epistemologies not to question the a priori of gender" (p. 148; Wittig 1980).

While this view may read as rhetorical overstatement, it is a remarkable description of the silences in psychoanalysis. Given that psychoanalytic theory is preoccupied with sex and gender and that Freud was in an explicit debate about the character of femininity, not only with opponents from within but with the feminist ideas of his time, it is striking to consider how rarely, if at all, in the long and fitful history of these debates, any of the protagonists paused to question the universal polarity of gender categories.

Since Freud collapsed the distinctions between biological sex, sexuality, and gender, deriving, in sequence, heterosexuality and gender polarity from the anatomical difference, certain kinds of questions could not be asked of the theory because they could not be seen. As long as gender was derived from sexuality, which, while bisexual in essence, was "ordained by Nature" to express itself heterosexually, the terms of the debate were restricted to a revolt against the intolerable and implausible inferences about femininity that he derived from this schema.

Reasoning backward, we can say that there were three interrelated elements to Freud's thesis: the derogation of femininity, the normative dominance of heterosexuality, and the dichotomous, complementary division of gender. While the first was the focus of heated debates early on, and the second, although inadequately interrogated, was nonetheless always a subject of analytic interest and speculation, the third, the binary division of gender, remained, in de Lauretis's terms, "invisible."

Given the constraints the original model imposed on the critical tradition it provoked, it would make sense to assume that with the emergence in the 1960s of a more complex gender-identity paradigm, one that untangled gender from sex and sexuality, the presumptive dichotomizing of gender would be made visible and, thus, subject to question. Yet, even now, within the American psychoanalytic mainstream, it remains practically impossible to find an explicit instance in which the a priori status of oppositional gender categories is questioned. (An exception that proves the rule is Person and Ovesey's [1983] one-line remark embedded in a footnote and repeated with similar brevity in a separate publication, "The question is really why only two gender possibilities exist" [p. 221].) Thus, within the terms of conventional psychoanalytic discourse, except for the Freudian retreat into evolutionary biologism, the questioning of gender as a binary system is still fundamentally repressed.

By contrast, it would not be an exaggeration to characterize feminist theory as obsessed with the question of gender polarities. Indeed, mapping the trajectory of ideas on this single issue from De Beauvoir (1949) to the current controversies would, of necessity, be a précis of the essential papers and moments in the intellectual history of the field.

For our purposes, the central argument can be found in the anthropologist Gayle Rubin's (1975) classic essay "The Traffic in Women." In this theoretical tour de force, Rubin constructs a system of analytic coordinates to describe what she calls the "sex/gender system: that set of arrangements by which a society transforms biological sexuality into culturally sanctioned systems of sexual expression" (p. 159).

Her work is relevant here, because the thesis turns on an innovative reading of Freud and Claude Lévi-Strauss, whose "oeuvres," she argued,

show a deep recognition of the place of sexuality in society, and
. . . [although they] would not see the implicit critique their
work could generate when subjected to a feminist eye, [their
thinking reflects] upon the profound differences between the
social experiences of men and women. [pp. 159–160]

Since Rubin moves from analyzing the explicit content of the
texts to deconstructing their interrelated, underlying logic and presuppositions, her "freely interpretive exegesis" (p. 159) potentiates
critical ideas that are available but repressed under the strictures of
Freud's biologism. For example, while Freud seems unconscious of
his presumptive leap from the necessity for procreative (i.e., heterosexual) sexuality to the oppositional status of gender, Rubin considers these "givens" as questions to be investigated.

The idea that men and women are two mutually exclusive categories must arise out of something other than a nonexistent
"natural" opposition. Far from being an expression of natural
differences, exclusive gender identity is *suppression of natural
similarities.* [pp. 179–180, italics added]

In an attempt to connect this arbitrary bifurcation of gender to
the culturally normative dominance of heterosexuality, Rubin first
deconstructs the conventional interpretation of the incest taboo. By
emphasizing that its subject is the "prohibition against *some* heterosexual unions," she argues that this "presupposes a prior, less articulate taboo against *non*-heterosexual unions" (p. 180).

Extending the reach of the construct of "taboo," Rubin now
makes a conceptual bridge between the normative oppositional
categories of gender and sexuality:

The division of labor by sex can . . . be seen as a taboo against
sexual arrangements other than those containing at least one
man and one woman, thereby [enforcing the primacy] of heterosexual [bonding]. . . . Gender is [therefore] not only an identification with one sex, but also entails that sexual desire be
directed [at the "opposite" sex]. . . . [Thus] gender can be seen
as a socially imposed division of the sexes, a taboo which exag-

gerates the . . . differences between the sexes. . . . Male and
female it creates them, and it creates them heterosexual. [p. 178]

Thus, the binary system of gender and the obligatory status of heterosexuality are linked, not as the inevitable consequences of evolutionary imperatives but as complementary psychocultural processes that require and imply each other.

From this perspective, the analytic construct of gender identity reads not only as a psychic defense, as May has so cogently
argued, but as a socially instituted normative ideal. The cultural
matrix that sustains the illusion of two coherent gender identities
prohibits and pathologizes any gender-incongruent act, state, impulse, or mood, as well as any identity structure in which gender
or sexuality is not congruent with biological sex. Thus, those gender and sexual identities that fail to conform to norms of cultural
intelligibility appear only as developmental failures or logical im-
possibilities (Butler 1990).

The social regulation of this cultural insistence on gender
polarity has been documented in a remarkable study of medical
decision-making practices in cases of "intersexed" infants: babies
born neither male nor female (Kessler 1990). Based on interviews
with surgeons and endocrinologists, Kessler's study documents the
technological applications of a rigid gender ideology designed to
ensure physical conformity with the two-gender system and with
heterosexual practices.

Despite the formal sophistication with which these physicians
discuss gender and genital ambiguity (all were steeped in Money's
gender-identity theories), Kessler's close and subtle interviews reveal that "even in the face of apparently incontrovertible physical
evidence to the contrary, they held an incorrigible belief in, and
insistence upon, female and male as the only 'natural' options"
(p. 4). Moreover, cultural assumptions about (hetero)sexuality—
the importance of a "good-sized" penis or a vagina large enough to
receive the "average" penis—seemed to constitute the dominant
criteria for gender assignment. In the opinion of one team of clinicians, for example, the most serious mistake in gender assignment

is to create "an individual unable to engage in genital [heterosexual] sex" (p. 20).

Remarkably, despite their professional knowledge that the medical task was to *construct* anatomically consistent gender where it did not exist (as in the quote above), Kessler shows how the language and imagery that the doctors used suggested an implicit fantasy that they were *uncovering* a gender that was anatomically hidden. This magical distortion translates into the notion that it is not the gender of the child that is ambiguous, but the genitals, as in the statement that "the [baby's genital] development isn't complete, so we'll need to do a blood test to determine what the *actual* sex is" (p. 16). This medicalistic ideology promotes the fantasy that "the real gender will be determined/proven by elaborate testing and the bad (i.e., confusing) genitals will be repaired and completed" (p. 16). Hence, a technocratic illusion masks the cultural mandate that informs the "medical mission": "to keep individual concrete genders as clear and uncontaminated as the notions of female and male are in the abstract" (p. 23).

Kessler's analysis of the primitive fantasy structure underlying these highly esteemed medical practices is a particularly convincing illustration of the ways in which the construction of gender and of gender difference is a social practice that permeates contemporary cultural life. Indeed, the "rule" of the two-gender system can be construed as a universal principle, manifesting itself in the individual psyche, the symbolic framework, and the social practices of a society (Young 1984). In this sense, gender can be understood as a basic metaphysical category that, as Rubin demonstrates, prescribes an artificial division of the world into masculine and feminine.

For our purposes, therefore, we might think of gender as a transcendent social category whose truth, though false, remains central to thought; indeed, it constructs the very analytic categories we would use to *de*construct it. Because psychoanalysis has been slow to recognize the epistemological paradox of gender, it has been slow to recognize how it remains trapped in its circularity.

Thus, it is not surprising, given the cultural taboo against gender similarity and the dread of the collapse of gender difference, that classical psychoanalysis organized itself in terms of gender dichotomies and that even its modernizers retain a belief in the necessity of the gender divide. For example, in a recent collection of psychoanalytic essays whose stated purpose was "to present the best current psychoanalytic thinking on male psychology . . . in which psychoanalytic theory itself [would] be reassessed and reformulated" (Fogel et al. p. 5), the following assertion is to be found in the introductory chapter: "The inevitability and universal importance of the sexual distinction . . . and the necessity for every man to come to terms with [it] . . . [is] central here" (p. 120).

Thus, it appears that American psychoanalysts still subscribe to the cultural rule of a binary gender system. Yet, interestingly, they do not explicitly argue for it on psychoanalytic grounds. Indeed, if the chapters in this collection are any guide, the two-gender system is taken as a priori in De Lauretis's sense, and the promised analytic "reformulations" of gender theory begin "after the fact" [sic], with discussions of its complex meanings, psychic consequences, and "stages of development."

By contrast, in France, even such creative revisionists of Freud's gender theories as Chasseguet-Smirgel and McDougall virtually take the position that the elimination of gender differences would lead to psychosis (Baruch and Serran 1988). The French analysts' insistence on gender as a psychologically essential opposition can be derived from their idea that the recognition and acceptance of gender difference is necessary to preserve the distinction between self and other (Dimen, in Baruch and Serrano 1988) and, more generally, to maintain *all* necessary separations and distinctions. Arguing, for example, that perversion is the attempt to "homogenize" difference, Chasseguet-Smirgel (1983) writes, "The man who does not respect the law of differentiation challenges God, [by] creat[ing] new combinations of new shapes and new kinds" (p. 298).

Since it is not immediately self-evident, from our American way of thinking, that closing or denying the gender gap is tantamount to a sacrilegious or psychotic denial of all forms of difference, the French position makes it easier to see the way in which the gender dichotomy can be made to carry other profound polarities. Indeed, many feminist scholars have called attention to the way in which oppositions such as self and other, as well as culture and nature, mind and body, reason and unreason, subject and object, and, of course, active and passive, are coded in gender terms, with masculinity appropriating the first term, which is highly valued, while femininity is left to absorb the devalued, complementary pole, as in Freud's blunt aphorism, "What we call strong and active is male, what is weak and passive, female."

This uncritical, unformulated relationship to what Foucault (1980) has called the "regulatory practices of culture" accounts for the contradictory readings of gender in Freud's work. While critics demonstrate how the theory is riddled with abstract, gendered dichotomies that betray phallic idealization and the derogation of femininity, critical admirers find the theory riddled with radical ambivalences about normative assumptions, which surface in his idea that, gender and sexuality cannot be taken as givens but must be seen as complex accomplishments that are inherently fragmentary and labile, like all other mental structures (Grossman and Kaplan 1988, Harris 1991, Kaplan 1990).

My essay attempts to extend and deepen these radical trends in the analytic canon by proposing a way to formulate gender that does not succumb to, but reflects on, the problem of reification. This perspective is informed by the contemporary critical tradition of feminist postmodernism. As a consequence, my thinking insists upon the deconstructive commitments of psychoanalysis and emphasizes a fundamental skepticism toward essences and stable meanings and an analytic rather than submissive posture with regard to the ideological pressures of gender coherence, consistency, conformity, and identity.

Indeed, I argue that consolidating a stable gender identity is a developmental accomplishment that *requires* the activation of pathological processes, insofar as any gender-incongruent thought, act, impulse, mood, or trait would have to be disowned, displaced, (mis)placed (as in projective identification), split off, or, as Dimen suggests (this volume), renamed via symbolic slippage. In this regard, a critical appropriation of Fast's (1984) work would emphasize her reference to the intense feelings of narcissistic injury and loss that accompany the child's realization that she or he must abandon gender-discrepant self-representations and would argue, as May (1986) does, that such losses are never abandoned but are merely sent underground via a panoply of defensive operations.

From this perspective, it could be argued that even our most advanced conceptualizations of gender-identity formation and of gender pathologies remain compromised by a subtle kind of naturalism insofar as they implicitly support the fiction that there is a psychic safe haven from a universal pathogenic situation. If there is a developmental, theoretical, or cultural goal toward which to aspire, why should it be the "hegemony of one, consciously coherent, sex-appropriate view of oneself" (May 1986, p. 183), as opposed to the capacity to "tolerate the ambiguity and instability of these profoundly personal and ideologically charged categories of experience"? (Harris 1991, p. 205).

By not questioning the cultural rule that gender is a binary system and by conceiving of gender as an identity structure, the theory, despite itself, carries, rather than critiques, the underlying essentialism of gender categories (as in the universal acceptance of Stoller's metaphor of a gender core).

It has already been argued that the construct of identity, in any form, is problematic because it denotes and privileges a unity of experience. The issue, however, is not merely that "unity" is an implausible analytic category but that any schematic rendering of gender acquisition masks the extent to which the illusion of a singular, personal identity is *established* via gender designations. In our two-gender system, "persons only become intelligible through becoming gendered in conformity with recognizable standards of gender intelligibility" (Butler 1990, p. 16). Since gender is a psychic and cultural designation of the self that "cleanses" itself of opposing tendencies, it is, by definition, a universal, false-self system generated in compliance with the rule of the two-gender system.

Given the cultural ubiquity and hierarchical ordering of the dichotomous categories male and female, we might, then, conceptualize gender (in an elaboration of Person and Ovesey's [1983] ego-psychological construct of "gender role identity") as an ide-alized "presence" and prohibition in the mind, to which each of us maintains a dynamically motivated, constantly shifting rela-tionship. In this sense, a gender experience is not necessarily a self-*state*, but a complex, evaluatively structured self-*representa-tion*, which is then measured against an idealized, abstract, di-chotomous gender category. The dominant psychic metaphor shaping this evaluative process concretizes gender as if it were a substance of which one could have too much or too little (every man's anxiety that he is not man enough or, reciprocally, a woman's fear that she is too manly).

This primitive, narcissistic reification effectively obscures the cultural practices and relational arrangements that construct and enforce dichotomous genders. Moreover, as our discussion of Rubin's work has shown, these very practices and the ideology that supports them can serve to promote another illusion: the presump-tion that sexual desire is *normally* (not normatively) heterosexual, as if it were brought "into being" as Butler (1990) suggests, through an oppositional relation to that other gender it desires. In other words, the internal coherence of reciprocal genders requires and implies a stable and oppositional heterosexuality, and, in reverse, a coherent heterosexuality requires and implies oppositional, bi-nary genders (Butler 1990).

Thus, by not questioning the rule of dichotomous genders, psychoanalysis still glosses the question of compulsory heterosexu-ality. Although in contemporary theorizing, gender, sex, and sexu-ality are conceptualized as separate developmental lines that re-ciprocally influence each other at multiple levels of reorganization (Coates 1990), Freud's slippery slope of inferences still shadows current theory. We now recognize that sexual fantasies and acts reflect, express, and can be used to consolidate (or defy) gender identity (Bassin 1990, Chasseguet-Smirgel 1983, Goldner 1989, Ovesey and Person 1973, Ross 1986, Stoller 1975). We have yet, however, to consider if and how gender conformity props up and privileges heterosexual object choice. Minus this critical edge, psy-choanalytic theorizing does not constitute a challenge to the culturally obligatory status of heterosexuality; indeed, by its omissions it can be said to aid in its legitimation.

TOWARD A DECENTERED GENDER PARADIGM

In the balance of this chapter, I argue that dichotomous gender categories, precisely because they are essentialized, mutually exclusive, and unequally valued, can be used for magical ends in the psyche, in the family, and, as we have already seen, in the culture to carry, solve, or exploit existential oppositions and dilemmas. By examining the use of gender in the relational dynamics of family life and in the psychic representation of those dynamics as internalized self-object ties, I hope to make a further contribution to a psychodynamic and critical reading of gender.

In the family, gender can set the terms of relationships, alliances, and coalitions, just as in the internal world, it can function magically to split off mental states and to establish, regain, or deny attachments. Looking first at the denial of attachment, think, for example, of Greenson's (1968) now familiar construct of *disidentification* and of Abelin's (1980) formulation of preoedipal triangulation. In Greenson's somewhat sketchy account, masculine gender identity required both a disidentification from the "security-giving" mother and the establishment of a new identification with the "less-accessible" father. Abelin's complex and suggestive use of Mahler's work postulated a psychic mechanism for this process. In his view, the male toddler imitates his father's perceived gender in sensorimotor fashion, and enacts the masculinity that would distinguish and separate him from mother.

Psychoanalytic feminists have critically reworked Greenson's and Abelin's material and emphasized the psychic and cultural consequences of their implicit endorsements of maternal repudiation. For our purposes, however, what is important is the explication of the defensive use of gender as a difference marker. In all these formulations, the "normal" boy (with mother's help) solves the separation crisis of rapprochement by *exaggerating* the importance and meaning of the sex difference between mother and son. By exploiting a negative identification ("I am not like my mother, I am not female"), the boy constructs an identity out of a "not-me" experience of difference, and thus, in Benjamin's (1988) terms, he invents a magical solution to the profound human crisis of interdependence: a strategy for separating without feelings of loss.

At the other end of the spectrum, we can look at Coates's (1990) profoundly moving and theoretically elegant work with gender-identity–disordered boys. Following Greenson, she suggests that such boys utilize the *denial* of gender difference to solve the problem of severe separation anxiety. They confuse being like mommy with having her available, and invent the magical solution of cross-gender behavior, as if by imitating mommy they can reclaim her presence.

In a third variant on this theme, Chodorow (1978) discusses the identificatory dilemmas boys face with regard to their fathers. Calling attention to the cultural prohibitions and social practices that keep fathers distant from their children, she speculates that boys utilize their common gender to make a bond with father symbolically, since they are deprived of a real relationship with him. In other words, in Greenson's terms, instead of "being with" father, the boy must settle for "being like" him. In place of a paternal relationship, he can substitute only a paternal identification.

Chodorow considers the substitution of gender identification for the real experience of a relationship to be a fairly universal consequence of the asymmetrical parenting characteristic of what she calls "patriarchal, father-absent families." To this extent, what she describes as "positional" as opposed to "personal" identification is a virtually normative aspect of male identity formation. Since father is typically only marginally present, the boy identifies with an image or abstraction, such as the father's social role or position, or, as I argue, he forms an identificatory relationship with the symbolic category of "masculinity."

This passionate transference to, and false-self identification with, the phallic imagery of masculinity eventuates in a familiar hypermasculine stance, a version of manhood that Ross (1986) eloquently critiques as "a screen, a sheath, an artificially aggressivized, brittle, cardboard creation . . . [pointing toward] the unavailability early on of the father as a *libidinal* object and figure for internalization and identification" (p. 54).

These examples provide dramatic illustrations of the ways in which gender can be used as a vehicle to establish, maintain, or deny crucial attachments. Thus, gender can be said to provide a deus ex machina for the relational dilemmas of development. Conceptualizing gender in these terms highlights the ways in which personhood, gender identity, and relationship structures develop together, coevolving and codetermining each other. From such a relational perspective, it is not useful to think of gender as being "acquired" by the child at all; rather, the symbolic structure of gender shapes and organizes the conflict-laden layering of internalized self-representations and object ties that become the child.

BEYOND A TWO-PERSON PSYCHOLOGY

This narrative of development, while not succumbing to the problems of reification inherent in the idea of a self that acquires a singular gender, is still, however, insufficient for our purposes. Since we have established that gender is not a substance, entity, or identity but a set of (polar) relations, a theory that is not systematic about the relational matrix that constructs, polarizes, and contains gender is ultimately hobbled. Since gender develops in and through relationships with gendered others, especially parents and siblings, its meaning and dynamics must be located, minimally, in a three- or four-person psychology that can make room for the interplay between different minds, each with an independent center of gravity.

While this way of formulating psychic processes has become increasingly central to the relational perspective in psychoanalysis, it is typically conceptualized dyadically, as in the characterization of the analytic situation as a field of intersection between two subjectivities (Stolorow 1988). This realm of experience and theory has also, however, been mapped by systems thinkers such as Gregory Bateson, R. D. Laing, and Jay Haley, whose work, beginning in the late fifties, can be said to have anticipated many of the central concerns of relational theory. In the discussion to follow, I import and adapt ideas from the systemic tradition because its radical emphasis on the relational matrix and its early and enduring contributions to the "perspectivist epistemological paradigm" that Hoffman (1991) and others have argued for can be useful to the philosophical elaboration of relational theory.

Bateson, for example, captured the radical potential of the relational perspective with his idea that a relationship is the product of a "double description." Using the analogy of binocular vision, he argued that the two parties to an interaction could be conceived as two eyes, each giving a monocular view of the process, but together making a binocular view, which, in keeping with the visual analogy, would make it possible to see in depth. Condensing this idea in what would now be called social constructivist terms (Gergen 1985, Hoffman 1991), Bateson (1979) said, "The double view *is* the relationship."

While the binocular metaphor is, by design, an evocation of the nature of subjectivity in a two-person system, Bateson was always thinking about more complex relational patterns, in particular, about the superimposition of "view upon alternative view." Indeed, anticipating contemporary postmodern theories of knowledge, he argued that the combination of such multiple perspectives was necessary for any "increment of knowing" (p. 77).

Laing (1972a) was also, early on, developing a theoretical vocabulary for an intersubjective view of mind and relationships. Like Bateson, he argued that a "spiral of reciprocal perspectives" constituted the core of the interpersonal process, which, he suggested, was then internalized "as a whole" rather than as isolated elements ("What is internalized are not objects as such, but patterns of relationship"):

> The family as a *system* is internalized. . . . Relations between elements and sets of elements [such as] persons, things, or part-objects are internalized, not elements in isolation. . . . Mother

and father may be merged as a sort of fused parental matrix [in relation to self], or be broken down into segments that transect the usual personal partitions. . . . Members of a family may feel more or less "in" or "out" of any part or whole of the family, according to how they feel themselves to have the family inside them, and to be inside the set of relations characterizing the "internal family" of other family members. . . . The family [is thus] an introjected object . . . which may be felt to be alive, dying or dead . . . a protective or destructive container. [It is also] an introjected set of relations . . . with partitions the self is in, together with others who have it in them. [pp. 2–4]

Theorizing gender as it is mediated through the enactment and internalization of family relations that have been so richly described can clearly produce "an increment of knowing," as in the following:

The internal group may condition . . . a person's relationship to him [or her] self. Triadic relations are collapsed into self-self relations. An adult feels like a child trying to reconcile two "sides" of him [or her] self that pull in opposite directions, experienced perhaps as good or bad, male or female. . . . [He or she] tries to put ideas together but an internal third party intervenes, and so on. [Laing 1972a, p. 8]

These ideas not only are compatible with contemporary relational formulations of internalization (Aron 1991, May 1986, Mitchell 1991), but they add important layers of complexity to the two-person psychology of intersubjective theory because they offer a framework to describe the kaleidescopic, coalitional patterns of family relationships that provide the passionate context for the development of mind and gender.

Insofar as gender relations are power relations, contextualizing gender in this fashion can illuminate the mechanisms by which gender not only organizes mind and relationships but organizes them hierarchically (with men and masculinity in the elevated position). Interestingly, although Laing and his contemporaries were "gender blind" in their theoretical and clinical formulations, Laing's interest in relational contexts and their internalization was animated by existential and ethical concerns very similar to those informing Benjamin's (1988, 1990) feminist work. Her morally profound, psychoanalytic emphasis on the psychological necessity for mutual recognition, such that "where objects were, subjects must be," is foreshadowed in this passage from Laing (1965).

> [I]n order to recognize persons and not simply objects, one must realize that the other human being is not only another object in space, but another center of orientation to the objective world. It is just this recognition of each other as different centers of orientation; that is, as persons, that is in such short supply. [p. 203]

While Laing was not thinking about objectification as a gendered phenomenon, his work, like that of Bateson and Haley, can be used to deconstruct the intimate politics of gender, in much the same way as revisionist readings of Freud and Lévi-Strauss have been used to rework gender theory in psychoanalysis.

For example, Bateson's aphorism that "every message is both a report and a command" is useful here because it emphasizes how communication controls. By deconstructing the "influential" aspects of a communicative process and attending especially to whether these control mechanisms are conscious, acknowledged, denied, or mystified, one can decode the processes that are set in motion by the inevitable pursuit of power and recognition between men and women, boys and girls.

This kind of naming is crucial for the development of what Levenson (1983) calls "semiotic competence," the ability to know "what's going on around here." In a cogent distillation of an analytic process organized around answering this question, Levenson, acknowledging his debt to Bateson, writes, "We go from asking what has been done to the patient to asking what has been the communicational nexus of which he [sic] was a part" (p. 161).

While Levenson's clinical approach to this question hinges on an innovative reworking of the meaning and technical implementation of transference/countertransference material, another way of addressing these issues is to be found in the technique of circular questioning, a clinical translation of Bateson's notion of double description. Although this form of interviewing is not necessarily assimilable to the analytic situation, it illustrates how an emphasis on the perception of pattern can clarify the relational politics of gender and promote therapeutic change.

In this variant of what Sullivan would have called a "detailed inquiry," the questions themselves are designed to decenter the subject by orienting the respondent toward seeing himself or herself in a relational context and toward seeing that context from the perspectives of the other interacting participants. For example, the therapist might ask, "How would your mother have characterized your father's relationship with your brother, if she had felt free to speak with you about it?" Such a question is structured so that one cannot *not* give a relational description as an answer. Moreover, the inquiry insists on the recognition of the mother's subjectivity, since even if she did not have a *voice* in the family conversation, the question constructs her as having a *mind*, which can then be "voiced" by the patient in an act of empathic imagination. At such a moment, mother must be granted an "otherness that survives" the infantocentric categories of "not-me" or "part of me." In Levenson's terms, this way of thinking "widens the patient's perspective" and makes "him better equipped . . . to live in the real world [as opposed to] the neat, contained, nursery world of hermeneutic doctrine" (p. 164).

GENDER AS A PARADOXICAL INJUNCTION

From the systemic, relational perspective we have been developing, the gendering process can now be conceptualized as immanent in the communicative matrix of family relations. As the psychologist Jerome Bruner puts it:

> It is in the act of relating oneself to others . . . initially in the microculture of the family . . . via the process of communication, that the self is formed in a fashion to relate to the demands

of one's culture. . . . It is in the negotiation of intended meaning that the self is formed. [Bruner, in Levenson 1983, p. 37]

Since the self that culture forms is gendered, we might refine
Bruner's thesis to focus on the specific "negotiations of intended
meanings" that produce and maintain discrete, polarized genders.
In other words, can we articulate the processes whereby gender
premises (ideas about how to be male or female) are not only being
internalized but also being enacted as part of the family drama?

As has been argued earlier, the either/or structure of the gender paradigm can provide an ideological and psychic frame for
splitting, both in the internal world and in the relational matrix of
the family. Thus, by exploiting and amplifying gender distinctions,
we can organize, simplify, and rationalize relational conflicts and
dilemmas in terms of gender categories and hierarchies.

Just as gender dichotomies dictate that one psychic state cannot include the other, gender categories also lend themselves to
divisive family processes that dictate that one kind of love must
preclude another. As a consequence, relationships come to be defined as mutually exclusive, so that complex attachments must be
renounced for a Hobson's choice of loyalties organized in terms of
gender.

These relationship patterns and the injunctions that surround
them are always in negotiation, since establishing how relationships
are to be defined and who is to control their definition is central to
the interpersonal process (Haley 1963). Such "negotiations," which
are rarely explicit and never final, are embedded in a communicative exchange of messages that convey, by implication, how each
person wishes to define the terms of the relationships in which he
or she participates.

Although every relational arrangement, along with the meta-
communicative context of meanings and injunctions that surrounds
it, is a unique subculture, it is also a product of culture, and in that
sense, it is socially patterned and symbolically structured in terms
of normative gender categories. Thus, fundamental expectations
about how spouses, parents, and children should feel and behave

toward one another are shaped by cultural fantasies about masculinity and femininity. For example, who should be in charge, and of what? Who should be taken care of, and when? How are power and privilege to be distributed? Which relationships should have primacy over others (for example, should mother put husband or children first?), and Who should decide who should decide?

In difficult and ambiguous relationships, people cannot reach agreement on a mutual definition of their respective positions with regard to such issues, and as a consequence, every exchange becomes a politicized medium through which their struggle for control of the relationship is enacted. Even in stable relationships definitional agreements are problematic because conventionalized gender assumptions dictate psychic terms that simultaneously require compliance and provoke resistance: men can never be needy, women must never put themselves first, masculinity is to be elevated and envied, femininity is to be devalued and repudiated, "male" and "female" must remain uncontaminated oppositional categories, and so on.

Since these gender injunctions can neither be carried out nor openly defied, all intimate relationships take on a peculiar, paradoxical cast. For example, if father "teaches" mother how to be his equal, he is actually retaining, rather than sharing, control of the relationship. Similarly, if mother induces father to take care of her by being needy, she may appear to be his subordinate; but since she has induced him to submit to *her* definition of the relationship, she is actually in the superior position.

These paradoxical gender configurations are also enacted between the generations as children take up their positions in the family drama. For example, one woman's story reads: "Mom didn't stand up to Dad, and she was always silently angry and depressed. But whenever I was argumentative, she would say I was too masculine and no man would ever want me." From a man's story, here is the message that he felt his mother was sending: "Be strong like your father so that you will be able to protect women like me from men like him." From a powerful father to his favored, outspoken daughter: "The reason I have to beat your mother is that she makes me do it [by having a mind of her own]." From father to son: "Men should not have to talk to make their wishes known, so be aware that your mother is the vehicle through which I speak, although she disagrees with me" (Goldner 1985, Goldner et al. 1990).

The contradictions inherent in the conflicting logic of these gender constructions generate paradoxes at all levels of psychic and familial organization. Not only does the child absorb these mystifying presentations of filial gender arrangements, but since these descriptions are commands as well as reports, they create an injunctive context that is double-binding. In other words, at some level the child is being given an implicit paradoxical instruction, one that if correctly executed, is disobeyed.

Since people feel pain and confusion when they are put in the wrong for acting in ways they have understood to be right, such a message is inherently damaging. As Laing (1976) has argued, this kind of communicative context is pathogenic not necessarily because it activates psychic conflict but because it generates confusion, muddle, or doubt, often unrecognized as such. Without realizing it, or understanding why, a person may feel intensely, but vaguely, in an untenable position. Think of the metaphor of the tourniquet that is always liable to be tightened by a further twist in response to an attempt to wriggle free.

Moreover, with regard to gender injunctions, the child is being put in an untenable position merely because of his or her *sex*. Since it is the arbitrary fact of the child's sex, not anything particular to the child's person, that prompts the parent to demand or expect compliance and understanding, gender is being infused with powerful, polarizing, relational meanings that the child, perforce, internalizes into his or her identity structure. Indeed, in my view, it is these overdetermined, internally contradictory, deeply embedded relationship premises that are always at risk of collapsing under their own weight that constitute the pathogenic, wobbly bedrock of gender.

Psychoanalytically speaking, we can say that these "gender-saturated" (Dimen, this volume) relational paradoxes are internalized as mutually contradictory self–object ties, which generate psychic splits with gendered connotations. This split internal world is the outcome of contradictory parental injunctions organized around gender, such that different parts of the self or ways of being are prohibited by one parent, while being encouraged by the other.

Since complying with contradictory gender injunctions and reifications is tied to sustaining the child's primary object relations, the child must accommodate to these impossible terms by performing acts of internal violence on the self. In so doing, the relational complexity of the internal world fragments, and ambivalence devolves into splitting and false-self operations.

As Laing (1972b) has written:

> If [parental] attributions are inconsistent or mutually exclusive . . . [one will] not be able to be father's child and mother's child simultaneously. . . . To try to "fit in" with two dissonant definitions at once, [one] will feel . . . without knowing why, suffocated, oppressed, stifled, hemmed in. [pp. 87–88]

For example, for the boy to follow his mother's injunction that he grow up to be "strong like his father in order to protect women like mother from men like father," he would have to construct a hypermasculine, false self out of loyalty to mother's need to defeat father. But such an identity requires *identifying* with father, a process that, as Benjamin (this volume) points out, is not merely an internal process but is a kind of relationship itself. Thus, in identifying with father, the boy is expressing paternal object love, which, in this polarized family, would constitute a betrayal of his mother. Moreover, even if father is unavailable to the boy, he will still, in Ross's (1986) terms, identify with father's phallic narcissism. In other words, he will, by default, identify with what I would call the symbolic category of masculinity. Since such an identification includes the incorporation of male misogyny, the boy would have to deny his own femininity and therefore repudiate his identification with his mother. Thus, in being a loyal son to mother, by attempting to protect her as she has instructed him, the boy will have, in fact, become a traitor to her cause.

The effect of having to accommodate to conflicting, polarized messages has been powerfully described and evoked by Nachmani (1987) in his description of the family history of female incest survivors:

> Their parental introjects, and later their parental object representations, were multiply split experiences. . . . There was much false-self compliance . . . as part of their ordinary family experience, long before the incestuous relationship began. . . . If a child has to act and feel one way with one parent, and another way with another parent, mystifications, confusions, and a conspicuous lack of validated constancies, will undermine . . . [psychic] development. . . . What the child calls anger or tenderness toward mommy has rules and conditions which do not apply when it has similar experiences with daddy. Self experiences vary considerably from parent to parent, validations are lacking consistency, and [as a result, psychic integration] does not occur. [pp. 626–627]

Although this description of relational splitting and its consequences is taken from the developmental history of abused women, I think it can be generalized to capture the psychic consequences of gender development in a two-gender system, in which only one sex mothers. By arguing that gender itself is pathogenic, I am, finally, arguing against a deeply embedded foundational premise of psychoanalytic ideology. In this regard, I do believe that psychoanalysis, with its complex and subtle methodology for the deconstruction of symptoms, has been used to inscribe the dividing practices that Foucault (1980) has described, rather than to undermine them, as Freud originally intended.

If we were, however, to shift our social location, the radical insights and attitudes of psychoanalysis could be used to critique the subtly coercive processes that dictate gender conformity. For example, now that gender-identity disorder has achieved the status of a diagnosis, Coates's work could provide the criteria for the conceptualization of a more universal pathogenic syndrome, a gender paradigm, in which splitting is a central feature. From this perspective, normative masculinity, with its repudiation of feminity, would be viewed as psychically problematic if not eventually diagnosed. Similarly, Ovesey and Person's (1973) elegant deconstruction of the psychic conflicts and symptom strategies that underlie the gender and sexual "psychopathology" of homosexuals could be as effectively applied to "normal" and normative heterosexual and gender configurations.

Once gender comes to be read as a problem as well as a solution, and as a defensive inhibition as well as an accomplishment, the dilemmas of masculinity and femininity can, once again, provide the dramatic raison d'être for psychoanalysis as a critical tradition. Such a tradition could promote resistance to the normative construction of gender polarities and hierarchies by documenting how the exploitation of gender distinctions in the inevitable struggle for power in society and in domestic life produces untenable relationship binds and unbridgeable psychic splits, which damage the human spirit in all of us and in the next generation.

REFERENCES

Abelin, E. (1980). Triangulation, the role of the father, and the origins of core gender identity during the rapprochement subphase. In *Rapprochement*, ed. R. Lax, S. Bach, and J. Burland, pp. 151–170. New York: Jason Aronson.

Aron, L. (1991). Working through the past, working toward the future. *Contemporary Psychoanalysis* 27:81–109.

Baruch, E., and Serrano, L. (1988). *Women Analyze Women*. New York: New York University Press.

Bassin, D. (1990). *Towards the reconciliation of the masculine and feminine in the genital stage: transitionality in body ego states*. Presented at the meeting of the American Psychological Association, Division of Psychoanalysis, New York City, April.

Bateson, G. (1979). *Mind and Nature*. New York: Dutton.

Bateson, G., Jackson, D., Haley, J., and Weakland, J. (1956). Toward a theory of schizophrenia. *Behavioral Science* 1:251–264.

Benjamin, J. (1988). *The Bonds of Love*. New York: Pantheon.

——— (1990). An outline of intersubjectivity: the development of recognition. *Psychoanalytic Psychology* 7(suppl.):33–46.

Butler, J. (1990). *Gender Trouble*. New York: Routledge.

Chasseguet-Smirgel, J. (1983). Perversion and the universal law. *International Review of Psycho-Analysis* 10:293–301.

Chodorow, N. (1978). *The Reproduction of Mothering*. Berkeley: University of California Press.

——— (1989). *Feminism and Psychoanalytic Theory*. New Haven, CT: Yale University Press.

Coates, S. (1990). Ontogenesis of boyhood gender identity disorder. *Journal of American Psychoanalysis* 18:414–438.

De Beauvoir, S. (1949). *The Second Sex*. New York: Vintage.

de Lauretis, T. (1990). Eccentric subjects: feminist theory and historical consciousness. *Feminist Studies* 1:115–150.

Fast, I. (1984). *Gender Identity*. Hillsdale, NJ: Lawrence Erlbaum.

Foucault, M. (1980). *The History of Sexuality*, vol. 1. New York: Vintage.

Fogel, G., Lane, F., and Liebert, R. (1986). *The Pschology of Men*. New York: Basic Books.

Gergen, K. (1985). The social constructionist movement in modern psychology. *American Psychologist* 40:266–275.

Goldner, V. (1985). Feminism and family therapy. *Family Process* 24:31–47.

——— (1989). Sex, power and gender: the politics of passion. In *Intimate Environments*, ed. D. Kantor and B. Okun, pp. 28–54. New York: Guilford.

Goldner, V., Penn, P., Sheinberg, M., and Walker, G. (1990). Love and violence: gender paradoxes in volatile relationships. *Family Process* 29:343–364.

Greenson, R. (1968). Dis-identifying from mother: its special importance for the boy. *International Journal of Psycho-Analysis* 49:370–374.

Grossman, W., and Kaplan, D. (1988). Three commentaries on gender in Freud's thought: a prologue to "The Psychoanalytic Theory of Sexuality." In *Fantasy, Myth, and Reality*, ed. H. Blum, Y. Kramer, A. Richards, and A. Richards, pp. 339–370. Madison, CT: International Universities Press.

Haley, J. (1963). *Strategies of Psychotherapy*. New York: Grune & Stratton.

Harris, A. (1991). Gender as contradiction. *Psychoanalytic Dialogues* 1:197–224.

Hoffman, I. (1991). Toward a social constructivist view of the psychoanalytic situation. *Psychoanalytic Dialogues* 1:74–105.

Kaplan, D. (1990). Some theoretical and technical aspects of gender and social reality. *Psychoanalytic Study of the Child* 45:3–24. New Haven, CT: Yale University Press.

Kessler, S. (1990). The medical construction of gender. *Signs* 16:3–26.

Laing, R. D. (1965). Mystification, confusion and conflict. In *Double Bind*, ed. C. Sluski and D. Ransom, pp. 129–219. New York: Grune & Stratton, 1976.

———— (1972a). *The Politics of the Family*. New York: Vintage.

———— (1972b). *Self and Others*. New York: Pelican.

Levenson, E. (1983). *The Ambiguity of Change*. New York: Basic Books.

May, R. (1986). Concerning a psychoanalytic view of maleness. *Psycho-Analytic Review* 73:175–193.

Mitchell, S. (1991). Contemporary perspectives on self: toward an integration. *Psychoanalytic Dialogues* 1:121–147.

Money, J., and Ehrhardt, A. A. (1972). *Man and Woman; Boy and Girl*. Baltimore: Johns Hopkins University Press.

Nachmani, G. (1987). Fathers who mistake their daughters for their mothers. *Contemporary Psychoanalysis* 24:621–630.

Ovesey, L., and Person, E. (1973). Gender identity and sexual psychopathology in men. *Journal of the American Academy of Psychoanalysis* 1:53–72.

Person, E. (1990). The influence of values in psychoanalysis: the case of female psychology. In *Essential Papers on the Psychology of Women*, ed. C. Zanardi, pp. 305–331. New York: New York University Press.

Person, E., and Ovesey, L. (1983). Psychoanalytic theories of gender identity. *Journal of the American Academy of Psychoanalysis* 11:203–226.

Ross, J. (1986). Beyond the phallic illusion: notes on man's heterosexuality. In *The Psychology of Men*, ed. C. Fogel, F. Lane, and R. Liebert, pp. 49–71. New York: Basic Books.

Rubin, G. (1975). The traffic in women: notes on the "political economy" of sex. In *Toward an Anthropology of Women*, ed. R. Reiter, pp. 157–211. New York: Monthly Review Press.

Schafer, R. (1974). Problems in Freud's psychology of women. *Journal of the American Psychoanalytic Association* 22:459–485.

Stoller, R. (1975). *Perversion: The Erotic Form of Hatred.* New York: Pantheon.

Stolorow, R. (1988). Intersubjectivity, psychoanalytic knowing, and reality. *Contemporary Psychoanalysis* 24:331–338.

Wittig, M. (1980). The straight mind. *Feminist Issues* 1:103–110.

Young, I. (1984). Is male gender identity the cause of male domination? In *Mothering*, ed. J. Treblicot, pp. 129–147. Totowa, NJ: Rowman & Allanheld.

5

Gender as Contradiction*

ADRIENNE HARRIS

Gender is one of the most contested concepts in contemporary social thought and social life. It has provided an organizing principle for social movements and critical analyses. In some contexts, it has been seen as an inalienable fact of life and biology. Gender has also been viewed as a troublesome set of shackles, best broken off and discarded. In the last three decades, our understanding of gender experience has undergone profound critique and reframing within psychoanalytic thought and practice (Benjamin 1988, Chodorow 1976, Dinnerstein 1976, Mitchell 1975).

This chapter makes a contribution to these ongoing debates by considering gender as a point of paradox. Gender can be as core and coherent an experience as any structure of self and subjectivity. But gender can also mutate, dissolve, and prove irrelevant or insubstantial. In short, gender can be as fragile, as unreliable, or as tenacious as any structure of defense or layer of the self.

---

*A longer version of this paper originally published in *Psychoanalytic Dialogues* 1:197–224. Reprinted with permission of The Analytic Press.

"SHE WAS IN FACT A FEMINIST."

This is Freud's (1924) summary judgment of a young girl sent to him by her father. The father is determined to disrupt the passionate attachment formed by his daughter for an older, disreputable woman. But this young girl is not ill, has no symptoms, and has no noticeable motivation to give up her lover. She has, however, in the throes of conflict with her father and the older woman, made a serious suicide attempt.

Rounding up the usual suspects, Freud summarizes his patient's "masculinity complex":

> A spirited girl, always ready for romping and fighting, she was not at all prepared to be second to her slightly older brother; after inspecting his genital organs she had developed a pronounced envy of the penis and the thoughts derived from this envy still continued to fill her mind. She was in fact a feminist. [p. 169]

If "she was in fact a feminist," she was a feminist quite without the protection and support of feminism. Through recent work in psychoanalytic feminism, the widening theory of transference and countertransference (inherent in relational perspectives) and through a semiotics-based mode of reading psychoanalytic narratives, I want to recuperate and position the woman in this case. For she is not positioned. Strikingly, the woman Freud treated and mistreated in this case has been almost completely effaced. Eclipsed under the generic terms given in the title, a "case of homosexuality in a woman," she is denied her real name on the grounds of medical discretion, but also, inexplicably, denied a metaphoric displacement into pseudonym. Without even the luxury of disguise, this woman is relegated to object status. Introduced descriptively as "a beautiful and clever girl of eighteen," she remains throughout the essay nameless and virtually speechless. In the course of an extended discussion of sexual object choice, the patient loses not only her name, but even her gender in the slippage, midparagraph, to the masculine pronoun:

Further unfavorable features in the present case were the facts
that the girl herself was not in any way ill (she did not suffer
from anything in herself) . . . thus restoring *his* bisexuality.
After that it lay with *him* to choose whether *he* wished to abandon the path that is banned by society and in some cases *he* has
done so. [pp. 150–151, italics added]

If we cannot encounter her subjectivity, can we come closer
to her desire? Again, Freud's language relegates this desire to the
margins. The particular love object of our nameless, subjectless
heroine is also barred from subjectivity by Freud's language. The
lover is variously described by Freud as *cocotte* or *demimondaine*
or, contemptuously, "society lady," in quotes. Freud uses these
quotation marks as a kind of linguistic semaphore signaling instruc-
tions on how to read this term so that we get its ironic twist. This
lady, who is no lady, is Other who slips perversely in a degraded
circuit of sexuality—with men, with women, in a social space outside the realm of bourgeois security and family. Like Dora's gov-
erness, or the beautiful white body of Frau K, this is a love outside
legitimacy. The sexual woman, the object of homosexual desire and
the subject of bisexual sexuality, is marginal and degraded. Even
the young girl's longings for this woman are rendered in another
language: "*Che poco spera e nulla chiede*" (p. 160). The *cocotte*
enbodies an illicit, free-ranging desire. A woman's desire is presented paradoxically as exotic, dangerous, and degraded.

In this reading of Freud, I want to set contradiction center
stage. Published in 1920, the essay depends on the core ideas of
the "Three Essays" (Freud 1905), glances laterally though enigmatically at "The Interpretation of Dreams" (Freud 1900), and prefig-
ures the later essays on femininity and female sexuality. It has a
crucial and underestimated place in the development of Freud's
thought and holds some of the subtlest writing on sexuality and
identity that exists in Freud's canon.

In this essay, Freud both perpetuates and breaks with the
conventional patriarchal thinking on homosexuality and femininity. His contradictions are embodied in the very circumstances of
agreeing to undertake the analysis. As with Dora, he has responded

to a father's insistence that a daughter be brought to heel, This father, "an earnest, worthy man, at bottom very tenderhearted," actually reacts to his daughter's homosexual tendencies with "rage,"
"threats," and "bitterness." Should psychoanalysis fail, the father's
fallback position is "a speedy marriage. . . . to awaken the natural
instincts of the girl and stifle her unnatural tendencies" (p. 149).
Tracking the voice of patriarchy through this essay, we hear the
outraged voice of the father of a disobedient, rebellious girl. Freud's
alliance and, I would suggest, his identification with this father,
thus undermine his theoretical claims for the constructed and complex dynamics in all forms of sexuality and identity.

This essay exemplifies a historically new censorious attention
to female friendship. The girl's relationship to her love object, so
disagreeable to her father, is characterized as an instance of the de-
votion of friendship taken to excess. Carol Smith-Rosenberg (1985)
identifies a shift late in the nineteenth century when female friendship, which had formerly enjoyed much social and moral approval,
became problematic and pathological. Freud's essay shows the un-
mistakable signs of a cautionary tale on the forms and fate of female
friendship, on the potentially dangerous connections between
women. This narrative of danger is one theoretical move through
which deviance can be constructed. Empowered scientific discourse
simultaneously lights up female desire and problematizes it.

Yet Freud places so many cool and rigorously argued ideas
before the reader. Following the radical insight of the "Three
Essays," he traces out the view that sexuality and identity can never
be simply some hard-wired, constitutionally driven forms but,
rather, that the formation of sex and identity operates like the rules
of grammar. As Chomsky (1965) demonstrated formally in the case
of language, any given sentence has no inherent linkages or simple
linear connections. His theory of generative grammar demonstrates
that all human language creatively combines elements according
to a set of special combinatorial rules, which permit many optional
selections and arrangements. If we extend this analogy to the sphere
of sexuality, any human experience of sexuality and identity is built
on a unique and particular sexual sentence in which the elements

of subjectivity, action, and object are never inherent or inevitable. Unlinking aim from object and allowing the play of sexual forms and symbolic meanings for bodies, selves, and acts are the radical core of Freud's theory of desire and gender.

The theoretical revolution Freud (1924) proposes is set within an essay whose opening paragraph enigmatically invokes the law and whose closing paragraph evokes gender surgeons and a rather horrible prefiguring of fascist medicine: "the remarkable transformations that Steinach has effected in some cases by his operations" (p. 171).

We can track the contradictions in the tonal variations in Freud's voice and stance in regard to this patient. A Foucaultian twinning of science and power sets a doomy beginning to the essay. A hitherto hidden practice, homosexuality in women, ignored by the law and neglected by psychoanalysis, is to be excavated to make "a claim" on our attention. At the very beginning, the patient is brought into Freud's sight-lines. All the exits seem closed off. "It is possible to trace [the origin of this case] in complete certainty and almost without a gap" (1924, p. 147). But later, Freud likens treatment to a train ride (though which of Freud's trains is not so clear). "An analysis falls into two clearly distinguishable phases" (p. 152). In the first the analyst does the explaining, and in the second "the patient himself gets hold of the material put before him" (p. 152). The analyst is then a powerless passenger, sitting passively with ticket in hand until the patient-engineer agrees to start the journey. Ticket and seat offer up only the right and the possibility of voyage, never the necessity. But perhaps what was in sight here was "a journey to another country," the preoedipal home of femininity. Freud (1931) wrote his own Baedeker to this country in his essay on femininity by sketching out the trip into that terrain of womanhood as a place of gaps and silences, a place without certainty, a "pre-Minoan-Mycenaean civilization" whose tourism Freud left finally to the women analysts.

Late in the essay and late in the short-lived treatment. Freud must acknowledge that gaps yawn open in the "hypocritical dreams" in which revenge and the wish to please are reverberating transforms of each other, played out in respect to Freud and to the father.

> Warned through some slight impression or other, I told her one
> day that I did not believe these dreams, that I regarded them as
> false or hypocritical, and that she intended to deceive me just
> as she habitually deceived her father. I was right: after I had
> made this clear, this kind of dream ceased. [p. 165]

Freud's harshness and the sermonizing admonitions in his commentary to the patient about her wish to distort and deceive her
analyst are stunning. Then the tone shifts, and in a more wonder-
ing, open register, so different from the imperious voice of his
conclusions about this patient, Freud speculates on how little we
know of whom and why we love. "It would seem that the information received by our consciousness about our erotic life is especially liable to be incomplete, full of gaps, or falsified" (pp. 166–
167). These unsettled and unsettling moments in the essay are its
golden possibilities.

"HER FACIAL FEATURES WERE SHARP"

Within the body of this essay, Freud (1924) establishes his commitment to the independence of physical constitution, mental traits,
and love object choice. The idea that sexual object choice is necessarily fixed and immutable is undermined in various ways. In the
discussion of situational homosexuality, the power of setting to
shape drive and counter inhibition is considered. In the discussions
of motives for accepting treatment, the person's youth, vulnerability, and commitment to family and object ties are all proposed as
elements in the shaping of sexuality. Indeed, in the very term *choice*,
the role of consciousness and the multiplicity of options, decisions,
and reflections are all raised in regard to experiences that are often
considered to be immutable. Paradoxically, Freud also describes
the entrenched resistance of sexual object choice.

Freud seems to speak here against two different literary and
scientific traditions. In regard to one, medical psychiatry, with its
commitment to taxonomies and the rigid alignment of constitu-

tion and sexuality, Freud marks his great revolutionary stance, the disjunction of body and culture. But in repudiating the idea of a "third sex," he also speaks against a politicizing polemic of the nineteenth century that sought to carve out a psychic and social space for homosexual persons (see Weeks 1979 for an analysis of these historical developments). It is interesting that psychoanalysis is still poised against both these traditions, though they themselves are so implacably oppositional.

Political works in gay liberation have often refused any account of sexuality as a developmental achievement and have considered that a constitution-based sexual identity offered safer and securer ground for a politics and a life-style organized around sexual object choice and homosexual identity. This politicized stance served another important function, namely to protect gay people from institutional practices that privilege one gender (male) and one object choice (heterosexual) as unremarkable and thus unquestioned, while homosexuality becomes a developmental dilemma that needs to be understood. Gender identity and sexuality can perhaps be freely investigated only in a social, institutional, and therefore political situation in which everything may be put in question and nothing is fixed or "natural." This utopian possibility was sketched in Freud's theory of sexuality and was at the heart of his method in the technique of "free" association. This hope for a freedom to question, this radical skepticism is also psychoanalytic feminism's deepest utopian vision.

There is a magisterial flow to the final section of the essay. Sexual object choice is achieved, not given. Any individual contains and, in some forms, retains multiple sexual needs and objectives. Only a reflective, psychoanalytically based study of an individual's history yields some understanding of the relative potency of homosexual and heterosexual libido. Femininity is connected to maternal attachment. The oedipal moment is a developmental hinge for boy and girl in which each must give up the mother, though with differing symbolic meanings attached to each repudiation. But, as Freud always insisted, nothing is ever fully given up, merely displaced.

Yet how curious the final paragraph. Freud makes a pitch for a hermeneutic method for psychoanalysis as opposed to prescriptive and predictive scientism. Then enigmatically he speaks of a masculinity that fades into activity and a femininity that fades into passivity. And, finally, he counterposes powerful surgery against a puny, feminized, castrated psychology. As against the more phallic, surgical interventions of Steinach, Freud presents psychoanalysis in rather the same way as he presents the female genital: "When one compares the extent to which we can influence it with the remarkable transformations that Steinach has effected in some cases by his operations, it does not make a very imposing impression" (p. 170).

Even more curious is the final sentence: "A woman who has felt herself a man and has loved in masculine fashion, will hardly let herself be forced into playing the part of a woman, when she must pay for this transformation, which is not in every way advantageous, by renouncing all hope of motherhood" (p. 172). If a woman homosexual were to give up her hermaphroditic organs, she would be one sex but would be deprived of motherhood. She would be doubly punished through a loss of masculinity and a loss of that phallic possibility offered to femininity, the birth of a child. From the high ground of theory, the writing drifts into enigma and defeated retreat. This movement has continued to operate within psychoanalysis. Lacan (1977) initially sought to recuperate Freud's notion of a complex and fragmentary sexuality but ends in a position that displaces women, conflates them with the place of the Other, and mystifies social power by a reified treatment of language's relation to subjectivity. Chasseguet-Smirgel (1966, 1986) critiques phallic monism but puts in its place biologically based feminine and masculine drives.

It is tempting to ask whether, within psychoanalysis, there are two genders or one. As in comparable debates about a one-person or a two-person psychology, we can inquire whether psychoanalysis makes a commitment to a one-gender (male) or two-gender system. Could gender fluctuate like any system of meaning? But if we insist on the symbolic meaning of the body, can we, in our practice and our theories, tolerate the ambiguity and instability of these profoundly personal and ideologically charged categories of experience?

In Freud's treatment of this patient his own insights fail him. He tells us that this sharp-featured, tall girl has a body that evokes that of her father and a mind that echoes this body: sharp, imperious, tough. Constitution as an explanation for homosexual identity and object choice is rejected in theory but sneaks in the back door of practice and countertransference.

"SHE CHANGED INTO A MAN"

As Freud sets out the case, he puts into play a fascinating set of possibilities, a complexity of attachments and identifications. The girl faces a set of relational problematics to which sexual object choice could offer a resolution. First, there is the girl's relation to her mother, an attractive young woman who Freud thinks may be content with a daughter who refuses to compete with her.

One strand of explanation woven throughout the case material is that the primary object choice for the girl, the mother, is never fully given up but transferred to other mothers and finally to the lady love. In this way, the patient continues a "masculine protest," which for Freud never quite attains the legitimacy of male identification.

We can take a moment to look at the Freudian position on the differences between male identification and masculine protest. The former is thought to rise wholesomely from libido and desire; the latter is thought to be a more unsavory outcome of aggression. This position only restates the valuative judgment and double standard in different terms. The problem still remains. Why would a girl's identification with her father arise solely from envy and aggression? Benjamin (1988) addresses this question by proposing a legitimate role for a girl's identificatory love for her father and examining the conflicts and inhibitions that arise for women when this process of loving identification is thwarted.

Alternatively, a feminine object choice is the resentful consolation prize after an oedipal defeat. In this case, mother gets father's boy baby (when the girl is 5 or 6 and again in adolescence), and the daughter spurned gives up men altogether and "changes into a man." The spoiling of her chances for a love object lead, in extreme form, to an abandonment of gender identity. The changeling now enacts the conventions of male love.

This interpretation allows us to see the contradictions in the theory of normative male heterosexual choice that Freud brings to bear on the case of this young girl. He lays out the unconscious dynamic of masculine love, both in its oedipal and its narcissistic components. Certain men choose an idealized yet degraded woman lover. Freud (1920) understands this choice as an aspect of masculine idealized love operating as a defensive distortion within the Oedipus complex. This scene goes as follows. An idealized pure love develops for a degraded creature who is really a stand-in for mother. In the boy's fantasy, mother stays with father only for protection and convenience; her sexual love for father is degraded and bad, and she saves her purity for the devoted son. The boy loves a pure mother and will save her from the degradation of heterosexuality.

There is also the narcissistic element in mature male object choice. The man defers to the pleasure and the narcissistic preoccupations of the lover: "the humility and the sublime overvaluation of the sexual object . . . the renunciation of all narcissistic satisfaction and the preference for being the lover rather than the beloved" (p. 154). This position is somewhat of a theoretical double standard. A man's love of women is cast in the language of submission and deferral, of living through the narcissism and pleasure of the Other. A comparable construction in a woman would have been tagged with the epithet of masochism. This aspect of male love of women, perhaps the theoretical twin of penis envy in a woman, has none of that construct's negative play. The central point to extricate from this piece of theory that Freud produces is the feature of distortion and defense in normal heterosexual development that is nonetheless not introduced as a "problem."

Freud's interpretive solution to this patient's problem is a relational solution: sexuality and desire are at the mercy of object relations. Choosing a woman or rechoosing a woman comes after a defeat and a disappointment in respect to her longing for her father. She seems then, to Freud, to have jumped tracks from a positive to a negative oedipal complex, changed into a man, taken on a rebellious struggle with her father (surely a version of the oedipal identificatory struggles of father and son), and fallen in love with a mother substitute, whom symbolically she will win back from the degraded sexuality of heterosexual life.

I want to take up first the fate and form of Freud's patient's primary love object, her mother, who consistently deserts her for men, for father, and for flirtations and male attention. The most crucial abandonments were for a male baby sibling when she was 5 or 6 and at yet another crucial developmental juncture, adolescence. The trauma of these narcissistic injuries might well be measured in the girl's obliteration of any thought that these births were psychically disruptive. But perhaps the trauma resurfaces, disguised, in an attempted solution when she begins to play with a 3-year-old boy. Freud connects this play to maternal and feminine identification. But it is also possible that the identification is with the rapprochement boy, an alter ego who represents her child self before the narcissistic (and obviously also oedipal) disaster. If she is a little boy, she retains the exclusivity of her mother. There is not yet a new baby boy. Also if she retains "boyness," the discovery and despairing loss associated with femininity are warded off. Did she change into a man or simply always stay one, imagining within her family that to be loved by mother you have to be a boy? As a mother's boy, she looks for an adored love object and seeks to love an ego ideal that Chasseguet-Smirgel (1985) has always connected to the longing for narcissistic healing and reunion with the preoedipal mother.

At the same time, many factors (father and culture) prevent her from occupying the privileged position of adult masculinity. Perhaps one compromise solution is to be a rebellious "boy" in a failed relation to a heterosexual woman. Loving the "cocotte" serves multiple functions. It symbolically plays out the oedipal defeat and the preoedipal possibilities and hope, also finally defeated. The suicide attempt signals the futility, not merely the oedipal enactment of the wish for father's baby. Rather, we are back at the railroad as the girl, fallen on the tracks, symbolically expresses having nowhere to go, and is caught in a preoedipal and oedipal no person's land. Her chastity then arises from confusion and a double inhibition. This enactment of futility could also preserve the elements Freud sees in the suicide attempt, its mixture of hate and excitement. Stasis and refusal remain the fundamental stance, hidden behind a mask of compliance and interest.

One poignant dilemma for this girl is the contradiction between the preoedipal and the oedipal mother, the mother of longed-for exclusivity and the mother who rivalrously reserves the ground of femininity for herself. We cannot know, in this woman's case, whether she chooses masculine identity as a solution to defeat at mother's hands, at father's, or at both. We know more, I suspect, of the creative resolution of her object choice as it preserves the complexity of her sexuality.

Freud suggests that the patient's love object is a complex solution, a fusion of male and female object choice, the expression of homosexual and heterosexual libido. An object choice ideally represents a world of multiple sexualities and the preserving of all prior forms of loving. The love object technically must be one gender or another, that is, formally either female or male, but unconsciously and symbolically, this object choice is a multilayered, multisexed creation. It is not, of course, that the gender identity of the lover is unimportant, but that it both expresses a powerful resolution of conflicting aims and preserves all elements of the conflict.

In formal identity terms, the patient makes a homosexual object choice. But in the more subtle terms of identity and unconscious meaning, I read this patient's love relation as a heterosexual object choice in which a fictive "boy" chooses a mother to idealize and save from an oedipal father. Despite Freud's reading of the girl's disappointment in respect to her father, the transference–

countertransference deadlock suggests this oedipal battle has not been conceded. The mother's body and feelings are still contested zones.

"RUSSIAN TACTICS" BY THE PATIENT, SO THE ANALYST "BREAKS IT OFF"

Like an Escher engraving, the question of who drives and who buys a train ticket and sits waiting on this treatment journey is constantly fluctuating. "In the case of our patient, it was not doubt but the affective factor of revenge against her father that made her cool reserve possible. . . . As soon as I recognized the girl's attitude to her father, I broke off treatment" (p. 164). Freud claims to see, through the false self-analysis and the subterfuge, a repetition of tactics with the father. He sees that envy and defeat are the real project, refuses the charade, and stops the work.

In another enactment, Freud's response to the dream reports is to make a transference interpretation, not a dream interpretation. The reporting of dreams of marriage and heterosexual happiness is given transference meaning as an enactment of the wish to deceive the father by presenting him with "hypocritical" dreams. Although he uses the judgmental term *hypocritical* in the footnoted section in "The Interpretation of Dreams" (1900), he simply presents the dual level, manifest and latent, in any dream and notes that dreams disguise just as they express.

The enactment of silenced, disowned countertransference in this treatment is the story of father–son rivalry. Freud plays out the struggle of father versus girl-who-is-really-a-boy and consistently relates to the patient both as a ridiculous rival for male terrain and as a girl refusing to give up the position of masculine protest and accept and internalize the analyst's interpretations. I would say it is less clear that she wants these interpretations (for Freud the symbolic equivalent of the father's babies) than that she wishes to be the boy to mother and thus comes into a situation of difficult rivalry with her father and then with Freud.

Freud interprets the patient's single quoted comment in the essay, "How very interesting," as an intellectualized defense. Yes, but also a masculinized one. We are two colleagues sitting here discussing a patient we have in common, who happens to be me. How very interesting. This patient practices, as Freud suggests, a Russian tactic: an entrenched, defensive resistance against which penetration must fail. Freud notes with some exasperation the mildly interested attention the girl gives to the analytic work. He sees resistance, certainly. But perhaps she is calm because he was so obviously off target. Freud presses on as if he were treating a young girl who is vengeful because she was betrayed by her father. One thinks of Winnicott (1971) glimpsing one gender masked behind another. In the daring move Winnicott makes in making the acquaintance of the "girl" in his male patient, the treatment lights up and moves.

To summarize this reading of the case, I hope to suggest some advantages to reading gender identity as a complex, multiply figured, and fluid experience. This view is in contradiction to work on core gender identity, such as that of Fast (1984), but it does not preclude experiences of the sort Coates (1991) has written about in which young boys feel profoundly in opposition to their gender. In fact, Coates's interpretation of gender identity disorder in boys, in which a disruption in gender coincides with a disruption in separation experience and self-structure, rather supports this view that gender can become heavily freighted with meaning and can be put to the service of crucial psychic work.

The position I am suggesting is one in which gender is neither reified nor simply liminal and evanescent. Rather, in any one person's experience, gender may occupy both positions. Gender may in some contexts be as thick and reified, as plausibly real, as anything in our character. At other moments, gender may seem porous and insubstantial. Furthermore, there may be multiple genders or embodied selves. For some individuals these gendered experiences may feel integrated, ego syntonic. For others, the gender contradictions and alternatives seem dangerous and frightening and so are maintained as splits in the self, dissociated part-objects. Any view of sex, object choice, or gender that grounds these phenomena as categories of biology or "the real" misses the heart of Freud's radical intervention in our understanding of personality. Biologically determined theories keep such experiences as gender and sexuality outside the system of meaning itself. To be meaningful, these experiences must be understood as symbolizable. Gender, then, and the relation of gender to love object can be understood only by acts of interpretation. In that way the density of their unconscious and conscious elaborations is brought into the realm of language. Only with the reflective narratives on which psychoanalysis depends can we know the complex meaning of "masculine," "feminine," "boy," "girl," "same," "different."

In the remainder of this chapter I want to begin to translate this perspective into clinical work and refuse any monolithic, single-determinant, and single-dynamic theory of homosexuality or gender. In considering two contemporary clinical examples in the light of Freud's work, I will keep formal gender identity as a point of comparison. I consider the consciously experienced totality of being a male or female person, as Lacan (1977) noted, a necessary fiction. I will therefore write about my work with two women who use love objects as points of identification as well as desire. The symbolic meaning of these loves undermines the surface meanings of their choices.

I have also chosen to highlight women's problem of masculine or father identification as well as the complexity of conscious and unconscious gender meanings. These two women are preoccupied with and conflicted over the meaning and symbols of masculinity as internal aspects of ego functioning and of self-structure. As gender identity and sexual choice become more complex, so the constructs of maternal and paternal imagoes become more complexly figured as they appear, develop, and alter in the patients' internal worlds as aspects of gender identity and self.

"I DON'T LIKE TO BE ENCUMBERED"

This statement is my patient Hannah's explanation of a routine of daily workouts at the gym and her refusal to risk weight gain by giving up smoking. For Hannah, flesh itself symbolizes encumbrance, the entangling encumbrance of need and desire. A beautiful and delicate young woman, an aspiring performer, always freshly turned out, she seems the platonic form of the lovely, contemporary urban girl. As her mother wryly observed, in a town where girls cannot find a date, Hannah always has a line of suitors. At first glance, then, not an obvious case of masculine identity.

Each life arena in which aggression, activity, and mobility may hold sway has been excruciatingly difficult for Hannah to occupy. She is torn and enraged with frustration over her career and her possibilities; she is furious in the knowledge that she must thwart herself from having the success and contentment she longs for; she is furious that she cannot seem to stop her mind from turning on itself and destroying any sense of ampleness or possibility. The prohibition on action touches many spheres of life, both fundamental and trivial. The capacity for sexual pleasure, learning to drive and securing a license, serving at tennis, succeeding at intellectual projects at a university, being hired by an employer—each of these experiences, which entail accepting one's own power and wish, has been powerfully forbidden, and only grudgingly have the rights and access been won.

The daughter of a seductive and intrusive father, she spent many early confusing years (her parents divorced when she was an infant) listening to her father bind her to him in complex identifications against the maternal family and against society. This father kept his daughter in a folie à deux of outsiders and oddballs. Later in her adolescence he treated her as his perfect feminine object. In a kind of seductive initiation into exhibitionism, she would be told in any public setting that all eyes were on her, that everyone wanted her. The unspoken implication was that she, the one wanted, was Daddy's. Yet this understanding has given way to a deeper and more unsettling possibility, for Hannah had always sensed her father's investment in attracting the interest of young men. One of her favorite dramatic monologues is the scene from *Suddenly Last Summer* in which a beautiful young girl discovers she has been bait for her male homosexual companion's interest in young men. This scene reappears in fantasy in many guises, a sort of disabling myth. Hannah's father's feminine identification and homosexual desires disrupt her own possibilities for display and power, that is, not only must she deal with her own fantasies of grandiose display and exhibitionism, the delight in being seen and admired, but she must also struggle with the complex projections of her father's exhibitionist and homosexual desires, which contaminate her fantasy life.

Identification and attachment to her mother have become problematic in another way. In the marital dynamic, the mother ruled, and the father was defeated and castrated. So her mother, in the world of work and in her interactions with Hannah's father, embodies phallic power and hegemony. Her mother's understanding of her own life connects efficacy, ambition, and power to her liberation from men altogether. One of the tasks of Hannah's adolescence was to begin to integrate and manage the meaning for herself of her mother's lesbian identification and its correlation with greater happiness and power for her mother. There is one other feature of this confusing family dynamic— the preoedipal mother. For Hannah, this relation is split between her mother and grandmother. Her memories of the mother of her early childhood are terrifying. An angry, unhappy woman, furious at any evidence of need in a child, corrosively contemptuous of weakness or dependency, her mother discovered a capacity to parent and love a child only upon the birth of Hannah's younger brother, when Hannah was 6. This injury to narcissism has been excruciating for Hannah to acknowledge.

Where is masculinity? Primarily, in Hannah's relation to her body, which is experienced and maintained as a place of phallic triumph. She lifts weights, works out, monitors appetite, eats sensibly if somewhat obsessively, and contains in her own body the fusion of masculine and feminine ideals. To draw on Bertram Lewin's (1933) idea of the body concretizing as a phallic object, we can say that Hannah at the gym is pure phallus, pure object; she embodies the male desire, but as its object, and is thus usually rendered powerless to act in any personal way on her own authority.

Second, there is her relationship to men. She is never without a boyfriend for very long and always chooses handsome, aggressive men. What is powerfully clear in these relationships is that they are founded as much on processes of identification as on processes of desire. She wants to be with these men and to be like them. What she enjoys is a life on male turf, hanging out at clubs, late night poker games. She prides herself on being able to outdo, outtalk, outdrink, and outplay any boyfriend and his coterie of male buddies. Her relations with men are a mixture of object choice and identification. In these heterosexual object relations, which she finds compelling and exciting, she is also working out masculine identification. An intriguing analysis of this process is found in Mikkel Botch-Jacobsen's *The Freudian Subject* (1988). Drawing on Freud's work on dream interpretation, he notes the placement or displacement of some wish or desire into being the one who possesses the desired object: if I cannot have something for myself, I will be like one who can or does. Hannah then encounters, in her wish to be subject like these hypermasculine men, the paradox that they themselves insist on highly conventional feminine attitudes in women.

Finally, she plays out in her analysis her idea and ideal of masculine identification. I am experienced as a version of her well-meaning, ineffectual grandmother—distanced, unskilled, impotent in regard to the treatment. Any insight she will have to develop for herself. She attends her analysis politely, dutifully, but without hope of her change or of my efficacy. She monitors and maintains all systems of control. She cannot know or experience any need for me. She can need analysis in some abstract sense, but her sessions with me are lined up with duty visits to grandmother and other burdensome obligations. To feel need in her analysis would to be give in to terrifying possibilities, to be, in her derisive words, "a betty," apparently a code word she uses to signify any dependent, weak girl. It is also a term her mother reserves for her girlfriends. She is depressed but bewildered whenever a separation from the analysis presents itself. Sessions are canceled for headaches and stomachaches, but if I question the absences, there are angry outbursts at the banality of my suggestions, at the ordeal of having to come for analysis that cannot help because she is hopeless. There is, above all, the terrible, degrading idea that if she needs her analyst, she is hopelessly female and I will become the triumphant, contemptuous, masculinized figure to whom she must submit.

"LOOK MA, NO CAVITIES"

A greeting at the beginning of a session. BK continues: "The good news is that I went to the dentist. No cavities. The bad news is that I went to the gynecologist." BK tells more than a medical history. The good news is that she could be a boy, my boy, teeth without holes, body without messy insides. The bad news is that it is not the whole truth; she is a girl with a long-standing relationship to gynecology and its ministrations. Perhaps the analyst can cast the deciding vote.

I have chosen this "homosexual" patient to challenge the idea of "homosexuality" as a monolithic, simple, transhistorical category. An important guide in this work has been Eisenbud's (1982) paper on lesbian identity. BK has her own form of ironic linguistic markers, humorous commentaries that embrace and transform conventional descriptions of lesbian identity. She uses the term "little butch" as a self-description but lives this identity in a social and personal space that is marked by feminism and by urban culture. Freud's patient was struggling with conflicts in male identification while simultaneously living within the conventions of respectability and bourgeois culture. BK experiences and expresses symbolically, through her body, a more frankly male identification but complexly set within a woman-based scene.

Male identification for BK works and does not work. In the urban world she inhabits, part subculture, part community, she has constructed a personal, social, and occupational world in which boyish style, feminist stance, and working-class identity all coexist. Her self structures mix and disrupt. Crew-cut, always in pants, shorts, or work suits, tattooed, she has fashioned a body ego and self-presentation that express her identification through the blurring of gender boundaries. Moreover, she has found a way to live in a social world in which this stance is unremarkable. She tailors her name to suit her particular notion of her gender and gives up a rather feminine name, first for androgynous nicknames and later for initials.

In work, she is socially permitted and has permitted herself to choose a working-class skilled trade and to live out an occupational life akin to her father's. But she cannot permit herself fully to thrive and succeed in this world. She thwarts herself, doubts that she can bear the "responsibility" of the full title of tradesman. She stays defensively at the level of "helper," occasionally having to defeat the practitioners of equal-opportunity programs by deliberately failing various exams. Her dream life is full of images of workmates driving cars while she is stuck in parking lots or is never quite in the driver's seat. Nothing can occur to disrupt the reign of the idealized father. Does fear of male retaliation play a role in her inhibition? Perhaps. But loyalty and love also play a role. And recently she has come upon the shadowy idea that she cannot have what she wants at work and also live a gay life-style. That idea, though certainly plausible at a social level, given cultural homophobia, runs against some reality on her job. A gay woman, BK's age, obtained a senior administrative position. The practical possibilities of advancement seem to make the psychic taboos against such successes even fiercer. BK tells me she cannot come to know this woman, and she avoids any contact. Indeed she assures me that this whole problem of work and success is impossible to think about, unknowable. To underscore this point, she brings in a dream in which she was decapitated.

BK is the daughter of an adored and idealized father, who ran a store. As he appears in her material, the father is warm, funny, big, and hairy (there are many gorilla dreams both scary and fun). He is seen as responsible, hardworking. Curiously, he is the only parent about whom any memories of feeding and sensory care remain. His store was the source of treats and food

Her mother, by contrast, was experienced as first absent, then horribly controlling, and later sick and frighteningly debilitated.

When BK was 2, a sister was born, and her mother simultaneously began the slow, inexorable slide to debility, a double loss experienced by BK because of the mother's preoccupation both with the new baby and with her mysterious and terrifying illness. What seems relevant here is that BK enters all relationships with the conviction that she cannot be interesting, that the other will be bored and drift away, and that a rival may at any moment exclude her. In a dream early in treatment she is at a cafe, and a waitress wants her to spoon cocaine over her Rice Krispies. She spies her former girlfriend buying coffee and rolls to go. BK reports a panicky feeling as she tries to see if the bag the lover is holding is "big enough to hold food for two." She is riven with jealousy.

In a striking and powerful way, BK has used sexual excitement and later drugs to regulate tension and to cover separation anxiety and depressive loss. Constant masturbation, a lifelong habit of thumb sucking, and, in her childhood, the frantic excitement of sports and sex play with boys were placed against the constriction and anxiety of school and home. BK was a child who could play hard and wildly but who often felt speechless at school. Outside, she felt alive and sure. Inside, she felt ashamed, silent, bored, and boring. In the wildness of outdoor play, she remembers pulling down boys' pants "to have a look." As an adolescent this frantic quest for identity and soothing emerged in an intense sexual and love relationship with a boy. Locked in combat with her mother over this relationship, she experienced in it a quality of absolute desperation, an obsessional and addictive tie later overlaid with drugs. The potency and power of this experience are a mix of desire and identity. At this time BK seemed most determined to inhabit and have pleasure in a homosexual space as one of the boys, freed from the maternal eye and control and looking for pleasure and freedom. I am terming "homosexual" her love of a young adolescent boy in that it is a choice of an object experienced as same-sexed, at least in unconscious fantasy.

This period coincided with the escalation of the mother's illness. In a dream that takes place in the street and back alley of her childhood, she is trying to escape on a bicycle as her mother comes toward her. But it is BK who is wearing the hospital gown, which is covered with shit. She is humiliated, carrying her mother's shame, the horror at physical collapse and loss of control.

Behind the memories of a shamed and damaged mother is a depressed and withholding mother, a silent mother who is longed for. An evocation of this mother partially inspires the lovers chosen in adulthood. Romantic enactment is always orchestrated around bringing a woman to life. For BK, as she says, pleasure for herself is "always second." Her relationships are primarily heterosexual in the sense that BK enacts symbolically the role of "boy/butch" courting mother. She is, in symbolic terms, not exactly the same sex as her love object. In making this claim, I am preserving Freud's insight into the distinction between biology and culture and Lacan's insistence on the fictive nature of sexuality and gender.

BK has a quality about her that has always puzzled me. For a person with such a florid and elaborate sexual history, the term *latency* does not exactly hold. Yet, stylistically, BK lives like a latency boy. Her apartment is full of toys, games, and projects. She builds rockets, takes craft classes, does handiwork for friends. In this way she is caught as boy, not able to inhabit adult masculinity, and this inhibition is sharply problematic to her in her work. "It's natural for them. They always knew how to do it." She is talking about her workmates, and if we hear penis envy here, we can think of Marie Torok's (1966) account of that structure as a defensive move against owning and inhibiting one's own life, body, and prospects. "In penis envy, there is a projection into the Other of some desire, deemed natural to that other and treated as fundamentally unavailable to the self" (p. 140).

CONCLUSION

Despite the shortcomings and contradictions in Freud's work with his patient, there is still an astonishing richness in his ideas of sexuality and gender. This complexity in the structure of anyone's gender and object choice now meets up with the analyses in feminism and in current deconstructionist and semiotic theory. These perspectives argue for a multiply figured and multiply determined model of gender, for the fluid and fragmentary nature of desire, and for the potency of culture to shape and construct both identity and desire.

What might be helpful is to maintain a contradictory model of gender in which it is a serious, fully lived, conscious experience of self, often core to one's being, and at the same time it can dissolve or transmute under our very gaze. Ann Snitow (1989) has recently argued for this approach as one that keeps in play the currently unresolvable conflicts within and around this category.

We might try to hold to a paradox. What is persistent is that gender and sexuality are fluid and unsettled and labile. What can be consistently addressed is the disruptive and complex and multiply determined developments that end up in adult identity and adult love. Giving up commitments to a bifurcation of normality and abnormality where object choice and identity are concerned means that other criteria can be watchfully considered.

Yet even with a revitalized vision of the complexity of gender structure and sexual choice, there is still the problem of politics, culture, and power. Freud's theory of the construction of the relation of sexual aim and object, of the free play of associations and symbolic meaning that arise for any child in regard to the body can sound remarkably idealistic. Our society marks some practices as wholesome and some as pathological, and these markings hold powerful meanings for all of us. Feminist and gay liberation texts have revalenced the degraded positions of homosexual practices and refused patriarchal culture hegemony. What is needed is a theory that recognizes the social power of categories like gender and sexuality in both conscious and unconscious experience but can also account for the way in which these categories, at certain moments, lose salience and become more porous. Benjamin's (1988) ground-breaking work holds that promise.

At this point historically, we need to understand the psychic costs of contesting for entry as a subject in the symbolic order, a privileged psychic space from which women are barred, both in unconscious fantasy as well as in social reality. We need a theory to encompass the complexity of rebellion in masculine and feminine character, its liberating potential and its painful costs. We need a theory of gender with room for both reified categories and fluid new forms of social and personal life. Psychoanalysis and Freud's radical model of sexuality as he theorized it in the essay on homosexuality in a woman, can be one crucial resource in such a project.

REFERENCES

Benjamin, J. (1988). *The Bonds of Love*. New York: Pantheon.

Borch-Jacobsen, M. (1988). *The Freudian Subject*. Stanford, CA: Stanford University Press.

Chasseguet-Smirgel, J. (1966). *Feminine Sexuality*. Ann Arbor: University of Michigan Press.

———— (1985). *The Ego Ideal*. New York: Norton.

———— (1986). *Sexuality and Mind*. New York: Basic Books.

Chodorow, N. (1976). *The Reproduction of Mothering*. Berkeley: University of California Press.

Chomsky, N. (1965). *Aspects of a Theory of Syntax*. Cambridge, MA: M.I.T. Press.

Coates, S., Friedman, R. C., and Wolfe, S. (1991). The etiology of boyhood gender identity disorders: a model for integrating temperament, development and psychodynamics. *Psychoanalytic Dialogues* 1(4): 481–523.

Dinnerstein, D. (1976). *The Mermaid and the Minotaur*. New York: Harper & Row.

Eisenbud, R. (1982). Early and later determinants of lesbian identity. *Psychoanalytic Review* 69:85–109.

Fast, I. (1984). *Gender Identity: A Differentiation Model*. Hillsdale, NJ: The Analytic Press.

Freud, S. (1900). The interpretation of dreams. *Standard Edition* 4 & 5.

———— (1905). Three essays on the theory of sexuality. *Standard Edition* 7:135–246.

———— (1920). Psychogenesis of a case of homosexuality in a woman. *Standard Edition* 18:145–174.

————— (1931). Female sexuality. *Standard Edition* 21:223–242.

Lacan, J. (1977). *Ecrits*. New York: Norton.

Lewin, B. (1933). The body as phallus. In *The Selected Writings of Bertram D. Lewin*, pp. 28–47. New York: Psychoanalytic Quarterly Press, 1973.

Mitchell, J. (1975). *Psychoanalysis and Feminism*. New York: Basic Books.

Smith-Rosenberg, C. (1985). *Disorderly Conduct*. New York: Knopf.

Snitow, A. (1989). A gender diary. In *Rocking the Ship of State: Towar , a Feminist Peace Politics*, ed. A. Harris and Y. King, pp. 35–74. Boulder, CO: Westview.

Torok, M. (1966). The significance of penis envy for a woman. In *Feminine Sexuality*, ed. J. Chasseguet-Smirgel, pp. 135–169. Ann Arbor, MI: University of Michigan Press.

Weeks, J. (1979). *Coming Out: A History of Homosexuality from the Nineteenth Century to the Present*. New York: Quartet Books.

Winnicott, D. W. (1971). *Playing and Reality*. London: Tavistock.

II

Critical Reconstructions:
Identity and Multiplicity

6

The Internalized Primal Scene[1]

LEWIS ARON

Psychoanalysis is a complex system of thought in which any one proposition is in some respect systematically related to all other propositions. One cannot tamper with one aspect of an integrated system without thinking through the effect of that change on the rest of the system. Clearly, at least for most of us, rethinking all of psychoanalysis is impossible. Nevertheless, I believe that it is only by allowing myself the grandiose phantasy that I can re-create psychoanalysis that I can begin to think through even the limited set of ideas involved in any one chapter. Of course, this first inspirational and manic phase of the creative process must lead to a second phase, more dominated by secondary process, judgment, and reality testing, in which I view the chapter more objectively and

1. A substantially expanded version of this chapter was previously published in *Psychoanalytic Dialogues* 5:195–238. This abbreviated version was edited by Johanna Tiemann. Special thanks to Muriel Dimen, whose clarity and insight into the very complex area of gender and postmodern feminist critique were invaluable. Reprinted with permission from The Analytic Press.

from the point of view of the audience. However, I emphasize that the first phase, which is dominated by primary process, grandiosity, and omnipotence, is just as important as the second phase, which seems so much more reasonable, healthy, and mature.

Conflicts relating to the regulation of grandiosity are often responsible for the difficulty that so many analysts have in writing papers. To control these narcissistic conflicts it is tempting to inhibit one's grandiosity, and in eliminating access to one's omnipotent and omniscient phantasies, people deprive themselves of an important prerequisite to the creative process (see Eigen 1993). We struggle to the realization that it is not necessary to overcome, give up, or abandon our omnipotent phantasies, but, rather, that we need to appreciate them, celebrate them, and integrate them into our overall sense of self. Yet this integration may be hard won, so compelling is the urge to ground our grandiose flights, wherever they might take us.

One grandiose phantasy in particular that, it has been argued, requires renunciation is the "bisexual" wish to be both sexes. Such a view was emphasized by Kubie (1974), who argued that the drive to become both sexes is one of the most self-destructive of human motives. I argue, in contrast, that the omnipotent wish "to have it all," to fulfill symbolically the phantasy of being both sexes, can be used constructively and needs to be appreciated as a valuable human motive. Just as the central importance of narcissism was recognized but for a long time viewed pejoratively, so too bisexuality, and particularly the grandiose, omnipotent wish to be both sexes, has long been acknowledged but underappreciated. I am proposing that our understanding of the pathogenic significance of narcissism and grandiosity and the attendant wish to be both sexes be supplemented by a more affirmative approach.

Further, I suggest that the concept of the primal scene and Klein's related notion of the combined parent figure, which have been regarded as a pathogenic event and phantasy, be recast in a more positive role as valuable organizing structures. The internalization of the primal scene is made possible by, and in turn permits, at increasingly higher levels of development, the capacity to hold two contrasting ideas in mind simultaneously. This psychic achievement becomes possible with, and contributes to, the capacity for symbolic thought, for sustaining ambiguity, and for creativity (Aron 1993, Britton 1989). I use Melanie Klein's (1929) notion of the combined parent figure and the classical concept of the primal scene as metaphors that illuminate the capacity to hold two contrasting ideas in mind at once without either fusing them or splitting them apart.

My intention is to play with the metaphors and images that I have found helpful in understanding psychic life. To that end, I disembed Kleinian clinical ideas from her metapsychology and reset her concepts into a frame of reference that is consistent with the relational-perspectivist epistemological stance that I advocate (see Aron 1992a,b). In particular, I use the concepts of the combined parent figure and the primal scene as a means for illuminating the contributions of aspects of psychic development to our experience of multiplicity, with an emphasis on the development of bisexual awareness.

PSYCHIC BISEXUALITY

Contemporary psychoanalytic, postmodernist, and feminist thinking regarding gender has led to a radical critique of Freud's theory of gender development: Freud's phallocentric and patriarchical bias has been attacked; postmodernist thought has destabilized the question of gender differences. Essentialist notions, such as that masculinity can be equated with activity and femininity with passivity, have been challenged. Gender is not seen as biologically given and immutable, but rather as constructed.

Moreover, the significance of a core or unitary gender identity, as presented by post-Freudian theory, has been challenged. In contrast, it is now being argued that exclusive and consistent gender identity is a result of the suppression of the natural similarities between men and women (Rubin 1975). The very construct of "gender identity" serves as a "socially instituted normative ideal" that "pathologizes any gender-incongruent act, state, impulse, or mood" (Goldner 1991, pp. 254–255). The current argument is that all characteristics can occur in all people regardless of sex, and that the repudiation of certain traits as incongruent with a person's sex causes a pathological outcome. Less radically, Benjamin (1988), while not arguing that the category of gender be eliminated, suggests that, along with a conviction of gender identity, people should be able to integrate and express both male and female aspects of self as these are culturally defined (p. 113).

Irene Fast's (1984, 1990) differentiation model of gender development proposes that children's primary identifications, both with their mothers and with their fathers, provide a developmental base for bisexuality. For Fast (1990), however, unlike for Freud, "the meanings of masculinity and femininity are not constitutionally determined, but are functions of children's experiences and their cognitive organizations" (p. 111). Fast proposes an early developmental period during which children maintain a narcissistic sense that all sex and gender possibilities are open to them. Only after the recognition of sex differences at about 18–24 months of life does the child renounce "early gender-indiscriminate aspects of self and gender inappropriate identifications" (Fast 1990, p. 111). Awareness of the differences between the sexes requires the recognition of limits that are associated with feelings of loss, denial, envy, and demands for restitution. The differentiation model suggests that the wish for "bisexual completeness" (Fast 1984, p. 146) occurs in both boys and girls. Not only do girls envy boys their penis, but boys envy girls the ability to bear babies.

Fast's term *bisexual completeness* is confusing because it conflates two different kinds of wishes: one, the wish to have both types of sex organs, vagina and breast and a penis, and two, the choice of love object, the wish to love both a man and a woman. It also may refer to the wish to have traits culturally associated with each sex; that is, it may refer to the wish to be both active and passive, penetrating and receptive. The lack of clarity in Fast's concept of bisexual completeness follows from the complex and confusing use of the term *bisexuality* in Freud's (1940) work. Throughout this chapter, I use the term *bisexual* in reference to the wish to have it all, both male and female organs, identifications, love objects, and culturally designated gender traits.

Fast (1984) puts forth a model that emphasizes the need to progress through developmental stages from undifferentiated states of narcissism and egocentricity to more differentiated states in which one renounces the wish for bisexual completeness, accepts limitations, and commits oneself to one's own sexual identity. She views a variety of pathological developments, including neurosis and perversion, as due in part to the failure to move beyond the early narcissistic stage.

The approach that I am advocating here considers narcissism, and particularly the illusion of bisexuality, not as something that needs to be overcome, abandoned, or renounced, but rather as something to be integrated with other, more differentiated positions. I believe that the phantasy of bisexuality continues to exist in everyone and plays a fundamental and constructive role in creativity and in our capacity to think and symbolize. The difference between Fast's position and mine is one of emphasis: she stresses the need to move beyond narcissism; I focus on the need to move toward an acceptance and celebration of multiplicity, to allow the masculine and feminine "sides" of our personalities to engage each other, to conjoin.

Of course, masculine and feminine can refer only to what culture construes as characteristic of each gender. We do not actually have male or female sides to our personality, any more than certain traits are essentially male or female. But there is a common, if not universal, phantasy, often consciously believed or even reified in theory, of aspects of ourselves as male or female. Here we come to a significant paradox: while we need a core gender identity to maintain the boundaries of our gender, we also need to preserve a multigendered self that preserves the fluidity of our multifarious identifications. Ogden (1989) concluded that "the development of a healthy gender identity is a reflection of the creation of a dialectical interplay between masculine and feminine identities. . . . in healthy masculinity and healthy femininity each depends upon, and is created by, the other" (pp. 138–139).

Postmodernist or poststructuralist thought has questioned the very existence of a unitary, cohesive, essentially unique identity. Poststructuralism deconstructs and decenters the human subject and insists that an individual is socially and historically constituted. It is from this postmodernist perspective that Dimen (1991) and Goldner (1991) have portrayed the notion of a unitary gender identity as a simplified version of a self from which opposing tendencies have been split off and repressed: "a universal, false-self system generated in compliance with the rule of the two-gender system" (Goldner 1991, p. 259). The postmodernists insist on each of our "multiplicities" and view our "identities" with suspicion. Sympathetic critics (Flax 1990), however, have argued that postmodernists have erred by not distinguishing between a "core self" and a "unitary self." Flax proposes that "those who celebrate or call for a decentered self seem self-deceptively naive and unaware of the basic cohesion within themselves that makes the fragmentation of experiences something other than a terrifying slide into psychosis" (pp. 218–219). Similarly, Rivera (1989) concluded that the idea of personality integration or unification is necessary but that personality integration prescribes not the silencing of different voices with different points of view, but the growing ability to call all those voices "I," to disidentify with any one of them as the whole story, and to recognize that the construction of personal identity is a complex continuing affair in which we are inscribed in culture in a myriad of contradictory ways.

I am suggesting, in agreement with Flax and Rivera, that instead of abandoning the notion of identity, as the postmodernists would have us do, we need both it and the idea of multiplicity. Postmodernism is correctly concerned with the way in which identity obscures differences within and between human beings. People need to accept, tolerate, and even enjoy confusion, contradiction, flux, lack of integration, and even chaos in their sense of who they are. Thus, rather than abandon identity, I am suggesting that we maintain both identity and multiplicity. In terms of gender identity, it seems to me, as it does to Benjamin (1988), that we need not eliminate gender as a category but rather recognize the need for both gender identity and "gender multiplicity" (Dimen 1991, p. 349) within each of us.

Whatever masculinity or femininity may mean to us personally, moments of masculinity, femininity, and moments that are gender free (see Dimen 1991, who raises and questions this idea) are modeled on our experience of each of our parents' own internal, multiple, phantastic male–female relationships. This relational experience is captured in the constellation of phantasies that constitute the primal scene. To understand the internal structure of the multigendered sense of self, we may understand the interaction between our various traits, characteristics, and identifications as patterned and structured on the basis of our internalizations of primal scene experience.

THE PRIMAL SCENE

Freud (1905) believed that the observation of parental intercourse could be traumatic and that the child inevitably interprets the sexual act as sadistic. The child's character is shaped on the basis of identifications formed with one or both participants in the primal scene. Freud (1918) argued that even if the child did not actually witness the primal scene, he or she would develop and elaborate primal phantasies of the scene derived from hereditary phylogenetic influences. The primal scene has been used more recently to refer to the child's mythology regarding human sexual relations (see especially Kaplan 1991, and McDougall 1980).

According to classical theory there are many reasons that the primal scene can be traumatic. One well-known cause is that, because of the child's immature cognition and because of the projection of jealous rage, the child imagines the sexual act as an aggressive and dangerous battle. Another explanation is that the primal scene is traumatic narcissistically because of the child's shame and humiliation at being excluded from the parental dyad. Further, inasmuch as both partners to the scene are seen as in the pursuit of pleasure, it is plausible for the oedipal witness to be inclined to identify with both parties to the scene, male and female. The confusion that results from the wish to identify with both parents can be traumatic, intensifying castration anxiety and penis envy and leading to the splitting or repression of bisexuality and the extreme stereotyping of identity along gender lines.[2]

In his review and reconsideration of the primal scene, Esman (1973) concluded that indeed, the primal scene is a universal element in mental life. However, he found no evidence to support the belief that observation of the primal scene is inevitably traumatic or pathogenic. Furthermore, he argued that conceiving of the primal scene as sadistic is not inevitable and seems to be based on other elements in the parents' behavior, such as their overt expression of violence and aggression.

The concept of the primal scene need not be interpreted as the child's literal viewing of sexual intercourse between the parents, or as pertaining specifically to the child's phantasies about his or her parents' sexual activity. It may be understood as the total of the child's experience, elaboration, and personal mythology of the interaction and relationship between the parents, which is often best symbolized by the child's image of the parents in sexual intercourse or in some form of pregenital sexual activity. From this perspective, the nature and quality of the primal scene fantasies reflect, in symbolized form, the child's perceptions, understandings, and experience of the parental relationship and interaction. This is consistent with the findings of Esman (1973).

Why would the relationship between the child's parents, which is so complex and multidimensional, be so universally symbolized by the phantasies of the combined parent figure and the primal scene? For classical drive theorists the answer is obvious, because for them experience is largely determined by libidinal phase dominance. Mitchell (1988), however, has explained the centrality of sexual experience for most people as being not a result of the in-

---

2. I am indebted to Donald Kaplan for this understanding of the traumatic effect of the primal scene.

ternal pressure of biological drives but, rather, an expression of interactive and relational meanings.

Mitchell suggests four reasons sexuality takes on centrality as an organizer of childhood experience. First, because bodily sensations dominate the child's early experience, they form the basis for the child's imaginative elaborations of the world and of the important people in it. Second, since sexuality involves both an interpenetration of bodies and contact with the bodies, boundaries and openings, it is ideally suited to represent longings, conflicts, and negotiations in the relations between self and others. Third, bodily, and especially sexual, experience entails powerful surges that are used to express the dynamics of conflict and interpersonally generated affect. Fourth, the very privacy, secrecy, and exclusion in one's experience of one's parents' sexuality make it perfectly designed to take on meanings concerning a division of interpersonal realms, the accessible vs. the inaccessible, the visible vs. the shadowy, surface vs. depth. Sexuality takes on all the intensity of passionate struggles to make contact, to engage, to overcome isolation and exclusion.

The meaning and function of the primal scene certainly concerns sexuality, but it also concerns much more. The primal scene is one of the primary psychic organizers linking narcissism and object relations (Ikonen and Rechardt 1984). The child's desire to participate in the world of adults represents both a wish for relationship with the parents (an object-relational need) and an attempt to maintain self-esteem (a narcissistic need). It is both a narcissistic injury to be excluded from the couple's activities and a relational deprivation in being cast out of the parents' interaction. If the primal scene phantasies are worked through in the context of a supportive family environment, then the primal scene does not inevitably have to be pathological or traumatic. Rather, the primal scene serves as an internal structure regulating both narcissism and object relations. As long ago as 1928, Margaret Mead suggested that even repeated primal scene exposure, under certain cultural conditions, might foster sexual and social development in the context of that culture. Analysts have generally rejected this idea, however, and at most they have conceded that an individual might master the primal scene trauma, thus making some "use of adversity" (Blum 1979). I suggest that we think of reactions to the primal scene as varying from the more malignant to the more benign.

In the classical psychoanalytic tradition, the primal scene is thought of as "the quintessential oedipal drama" (Blum 1979, p. 30), although the child may regressively experience the primal scene along preoedipal lines. Therefore, the primal scene is thought of as involving three people: the mother, the father, and the child in an interaction of three whole objects, and it is thought to involve genital sexuality. In contrast, for Klein (1928) the oedipal situation begins in relation to part-objects, and its content is pregenital. Klein's concept of the combined parent figure serves a transitional function emphasizing the continual interaction of oedipal and preoedipal issues, whole-object and part-object relations, and movements between the paranoid-schizoid and depressive positions.

THE COMBINED PARENT FIGURE

Kleinian theory holds that one of an infant's most profound experiences is the wish to penetrate the mother's body, to explore it, to take possession of the contents, and then to destroy the contents out of anger, frustration, and jealousy. These phantasies lead to the terror that the mother and the objects contained inside of her will retaliate. The child's earliest version of the primal scene entails the phantasy of the combined parent figure, in which the parents' sexual organs are locked together permanently in violent sexual intercourse. When frustrated, the infant feels that the father and mother enjoy all the desired pleasurable objects the infant feels deprived of. The intercourse is viewed in pregenital terms, as a constant sharing of good foods and good feces; an "everlasting mutual gratification of an oral, anal and genital nature" (Klein 1952b, p. 55).

Thus, the child's phantasy of the primal scene comes to include pregenital and genital formulations of the parents' ongoing feeding, beating, cutting up, biting to pieces, messing each other, penetrating, and controlling each other (Klein 1927; see also Hinshelwood 1989). Because of the continual operation of internalization, the infant establishes the combined parent figure inside of himself or herself. The combined parent figure may be symbolized by the young child as a monster, "the beast with two backs," and it is this terrifying figure that forms the core of children's fears of monsters, nightmares, and other terrifying delusions of persecution (Segal 1964).

In her more mature papers Klein (1957) emphasized that the strength of the combined parent figure was determined in large measure by the intensity of envy. In severe psychopathology, such as the psychoses, the inability to disentangle the relation to the father from the relation to the mother, owing to the intensity of the envy, plays an important role in generating confusional states. In pathology, the combined parent figure operates in a way that is detrimental to both object relations and sexual development. In contrast, in healthy development, the imago of the combined parent figure loses strength; there is a more realistic relation to the parents, who are now seen as separate whole-objects related to each other in a happy way (Klein 1952a). Even after the parents are more fully differentiated, however, jealousy and envy may lead the child to regress to the image of the combined parent figure as a defense. In this case, the combined parent figure serves to deny the relationship between the parents as separate individuals and also to deny the recognition of sexual intercourse (Segal 1964).

In outlining a theory of thinking, Bion (1962a,b) described how conceptions are born as a result of the mating or satisfying conjunction of preconceptions and realizations. In this lies the basis for the Kleinian view that thinking is modeled on sexual intercourse. Meltzer (1973) extended Bion's approach by describing creativity as a function of the further mating between previously formed conceptions. Thus, the personality is structured on the basis of the internalization of the parents in sexual intercourse. These internal copulating parents provide a sense of Godlike omnipotence, from which emerges the inspiration for constructive and creative activity. According to Meltzer, one of the essential developments of the depressive position is that the primitive part-object combined parent figure is reconstructed along more realistic lines in terms of whole objects of mother and father. Meltzer emphasizes that the reconstituted combined internal object becomes the basis for personal creativity. Creativity, in the realms of sexuality, the intellect, or aesthetics, is the product of identification with the internal whole-object parents in pleasurable and restorative sexual intercourse.

Meltzer's point is a radical one because for Klein the emphasis was always on the combined parent figure as frightening and dangerous. Meltzer's contribution expands on the idea, only hinted at by Klein (1952a, p. 79n), that the combined parent figure gradually develops and matures. For Meltzer, it evolves in the mind to encompass whole-objects; it is not seen as dangerous and destructive but, rather, as a model of a productive interaction. Although he does not directly refer to Klein's notion of the combined parent figure, Ogden (1989) has elaborated a point of view regarding the primal scene that is based on Kleinian theory. Ogden proposes that primal scene phantasies are pivotal organizers of internal and external object relations. He proposes a developmental line of primal scene phantasy in which there are early preoedipal phantasies of part-objects engaged in mysterious sexuality intermingled with battle and violence. For Ogden, these primitive primal scene phantasies operate in the paranoid-schizoid mode, and therefore the observing child has no reflective awareness. The child in this mode is unable to see himself or herself as the author or interpreter of his or her own experience, and therefore thoughts and feelings seem just to happen to the child, with symbols being experienced concretely.

Ogden contrasts this early version of the primal scene (which I believe is equivalent to Klein's concept of the combined parent figure) with the developmentally later and more differentiated version of the primal scene. The latter occurs in the context of the depressive position. In this mode, the child is aware of herself or himself as a separate subject in interaction with whole and external objects. The achievement of whole-object relations, and the concomitant establishment of the individual's subjectivity, allows for the experience of the primal scene on the oedipal level. Now the child is an interpreting subject in a world of whole-objects; the child can form identifications with each parent and also take each parent as a love object. In the depressive mode, the child can maintain awareness of his or her own subjectivity and of the separateness of the other; he or she maintains a symbolic relation with the primal scene and is therefore not threatened with merger and the loss of identity.

I am suggesting, then, that as children move from functioning predominantly in the paranoid-schizoid mode to functioning predominantly in the depressive mode, the internal imago of the combined parent figure becomes transformed into the image of their parents as separate whole-objects in a mutually gratifying interaction with each other. Now, with a sense of themselves as separate and with the capacity for symbolic thought, children can elaborate that group of phantasies that constitutes the primal scene. Insofar as the child is further along in psychosexual development, the primal scene takes on a more predominantly phallic-oedipal cast. Inasmuch as it is a transformation of earlier preoedipal phantasies, it will, however, forever be subject to interpretation along preoedipal lines.

Following Ogden's (1986, 1989) extension of Kleinian theory (especially as elaborated by Bion), I, however, view both the paranoid-schizoid and depressive modes each as being enduring and fundamental components of all psychological states. This is to say that the development of mind is not simply linear. Klein's positions, unlike stages, are not developmental phases, but "synchronic dimensions of experience" (Ogden 1989) or, as Ghent (1992) has put it, "paradoxical dimensions of experience." From this perspective, one never renounces, gives up, or abandons old positions (see Aron 1991a). Instead, there is a continual movement back and forth between the two positions, a "dialectical interplay of synchronic modes" (Ogden 1989, p. 18). Similarly, it is not as if the primal scene, with the implication of separate whole-object relations and an observing subject, replaces the earlier combined parent figure, with its implication of fused or undifferentiated object relations.

Rather, both the combined parent figure and the primal scene continue to operate synchronically as crucial dimensions of experience. Developmental research and theory (e.g., Stern 1985) suggests that infants have some sense of self and other much earlier than was previously thought. Therefore there are problems with positing relations with part-objects as earlier than relations with whole-objects. Instead of viewing the move from the combined parent figure to the primal scene as a progressive developmental sequence, it makes more sense to view them as two alternate phantasy systems, each of which has versions ranging from the more primitive to the more mature. The dialectical relationship between the paranoid-schizoid and depressive positions serves as a theoretical framework to highlight the necessity of maintaining a view of the person as both unified and multiple, stable and in flux, identical and different.

The internalization of the primal scene is central psychologically in that it regulates self and object relations as well as relations between our phantasies of masculine and feminine selves. However, it also requires, and enhances, the capacity to tolerate feelings of omnipotence and grandiosity. Furthermore, containing the primal scene requires the capacity to tolerate the manic excitement, chaos, and confusion of the highly charged scene, without attacking the parental imagoes or splitting them apart. One implication of this is that in order to hold two contrasting ideas in mind at once, to sustain the paradox that is necessary for the creative process and for higher level conceptualization, people need to be able to tolerate and even enjoy their own grandiosity without, of course, being carried away with these beliefs to the point of actual conviction.

I have one strong reservation regarding this formulation. Suggesting that the origins of thought and creativity can be traced back to an internalized model of the primal scene is appealing, for it suggests a phantasy that underlies sexuality both as procreation and as creativity. Creativity, however, has many other developmental sources and equally suitable metaphors. Bion's (1962a,b) focus on satisfying conjunctions giving birth to conceptions and Meltzer's

(1973) explanation of creativity as based on the model of sexual intercourse places heterosexual intercourse in too privileged a position. The Kleinian notion of the combined parent figure is useful precisely because it does not privilege heterosexual intercourse but rather allows for, and even suggests, all sorts of sexual and aggressive arrangements: heterosexual and homosexual combinations and also nongenital sexuality. Within the metaphor of the combined parent figure, the child has not yet sorted out the idea that fathers are men and have penises and mothers are women and have vaginas, and therefore the phantasies that constitute the combined parent figure are not exclusively heterosexual or genital. Thus, this is a better model to use as a basis for creativity and thought than the traditional primal scene.

The Kleinian tradition has, moreover, used the metaphor of the combined parent figure to highlight the continual importance of aggression in psychic life. It needs to be emphasized that as metaphors, the combined parent figure and the primal scene remind us of all kinds of sexuality and not only with whole separate objects but also with part-objects and confused objects. These metaphors evoke the dark side of sexuality—the power, the destructiveness—as well as the creativity. The dark side, all varieties of sexuality and aggression, plays a significant role in creativity, which should not be conceptualized as the exclusive result of mature, healthy, clean, procreative heterosexuality.[3] To continue to use the primal scene as a central metaphor in psychoanalytic theory and clinical practice, while benefiting from the advances made in social and critical theory, gender studies, and feminist thought, psychoanalysis needs to broaden the primal scene concept beyond the privileging of normative heterosexual genitality to include a whole range of pregenital polymorphous sensualities.

In my expanded vision, the primal scene becomes an example of pastiche, in which varying styles, often from different epochs,

---

3. Because I am trying to stress the affirmative side of the primal scene, I have not paid enough attention in this chapter to what happens when children observe a more destructive relationship between the parents.

are combined, although not integrated, with effects that are both shocking and fascinating, encouraging a plurality of perspectives and a fragmentation of experience. This revisioning of the primal scene evokes not so much stable heterosexuality as an unstable, chaotic process and flux, sameness, difference, and multiplicity.

THE COMBINED PARENT FIGURE AND
THE INTERNALIZATION OF RELATIONS

One of the most significant aspects of Klein's concept of the combined parent figure is the implication that the child internalizes not just the mother or the father, but also a representation of the perceived relationship between the parents. This emendation of psychoanalytic theory opens up the possibility that children internalize a complex network of perceived relationships. It implies that individuals internalize structures based on the field of forces by which they are surrounded. That patterns of relationship, rather than objects per se, are internalized is a view first proposed by R. D. Laing (1972).[4]

Prior to the oedipal stage, the child lives in a two-person world, maintaining separate and unique relationships with each parent. It is only with the oedipal stage of triadic object relations that the child perceives that he or she is part of a system that includes a separate relation between the parents from which the child is excluded. In discussing what I am calling the internalized primal scene, Britton (1989) suggests that it creates a "triangular space," which allows for the possibility of being a participant in a relationship and observed by a third person and of being an observer of a relationship between two other people. Thus, it is in the oedipal stage that the child first alternates between observation and participation. This fact is clinically important because the oscillating function becomes the basis on which a person can participate in an analysis.

---

4. I am indebted to Virginia Goldner (1991) for highlighting Laing's ideas on the internalization of relational systems.

I believe that the internalization of the primal scene and the creation of an internal "triangular space" is the basis for the integration of the sense of self as both a subject and an object (see Bach 1985) and therefore for the development of intersubjectivity. In the full development of the Oedipus complex and particularly in the drama of the primal scene, the child feels excluded from the intersubjective dyad (see Kaplan 1991, p. 62). Thus, in conceptualizing the later development of the primal scene, there is an assumed capacity for intersubjectivity. In reversing the configurations of the oedipal triangle, the child comes to identify the self-as-subject with the self-as-object and to identify the other-as-subject with the other-as-object. Children need to establish a sense of self as a center for action and thought, and they need to view this self in the context of other selves as an object among other objects (Bach 1985). Similarly, they need to establish a sense of the other as a separate center of subjectivity as well as a view of the other as the object of their own subjectivity (Benjamin 1988). These developments are of central importance to psychoanalysts since the analytic process consists of introspection and reflective self-awareness as well as of awareness of the self's interpersonal relations. The internalization of the primal scene facilitates this evolving capacity on increasingly higher levels.

With the internalization of the combined parents and the transformation of this imago into the primal scene, which occurs with the shift from the paranoid-schizoid to the depressive position, the individual consolidates a sense of self as bigendered, a self that is constituted by different, opposing, and contradictory self-representations, all of which exist in dynamic interaction with each other. When we say that the primal scene is traumatic, we mean that this consolidation of one's subjectivity with one's objectivity has been disrupted, that is, that one's cohesive sense of self has become unbound. Conversely, trauma may leave someone rigidly identified with a single sense of self, an identity that is incapable of change and flexibility. Trauma disrupts the capacity to maintain an ongoing dialectic between one's identity and one's multiplicity, including one's gendered identity and one's multigendered multiplicity. This view highlights the ways in which the paranoid-schizoid position and the depressive position each continue to exert a constructive force on mental life. The paranoid-schizoid position contributes the capacity that we each should have for multiplicity, difference, and discontinuity, while the depressive position contributes the capacity for integration and identity. Both are critical for development.[5]

Contemporary psychoanalytic theory needs to contain contradiction and to respect paradox in addressing issues of oedipal and preoedipal stages, part-objects and whole-objects, paranoid-schizoid modes and depressive modes, intrapsychic and intersubjective realms, phantasies of masculine and feminine selves, and sense of self and other, each viewed as both subject and object. Psychoanalytic theory and practice needs to avoid the dual errors, first, of condensing these realms or collapsing them one into another so that only one aspect is highlighted. This is the error of premature synthesis, modeled on the combined parent figure, which collapses what should be two distinct elements. It needs to avoid the other error of splitting off contradictions and ambiguities, separating them from each other so that they are thought to apply to different developmental stages or different diagnostic groups. This error is modeled on attacks on the primal scene, which attempt to separate the parents and keep them apart, away from interacting with each other.

FUSION, SPLITTING, AND INTEGRATION OF GENDER IN RELATION TO THE ANALYST

The relevance of the internalized primal scene for the clinical psychoanalytic situation was anticipated early on by Harold Searles (1966–1967), who wrote that

---

5. Ultimately, the necessity of and our capacity for unity, integration, cohesiveness or identity, as well as for multiplicity and difference, may be related to Freud's (1940) broadest dual-instinct theory of Eros and Thanatos as forces that bind together and undo connections.

the acceptance of the parents-in-intercourse marks an unpre-
cedentedly deep integration of the young person's identifications with his father on the one hand and with his mother on
the other hand. This landmark in identity development is seen
in projected form, in the context of the developing transference
relationship in analysis, in those rare but deeply significant
instances when the patient reacts to the analyst as being both
parents simultaneously, engaged in sexual intercourse with one
another. [p. 59]

An analyst may be experienced in the transference as a combined
parent figure or as representing both parents in the primal scene.
Therefore much of the analytic interaction may be viewed as representing attacks on the combined parents as represented by the
analyst.

Attacks on the analyst's mind and body, and especially the
splitting of the analyst's gender into male and female components,
is engaged in by patients and by analysts alike and is even embodied in our theories and metapsychologies. O'Shaughnessy (1989)
has described this form of splitting, which she refers to as "fracturing," as representing an attack on the heterosexual properties
of the parental couple. It is only by integrating or tolerating split-
off parts of ourselves, both in practice and in our theoretical constructions, specifically those elements that we phantasize to be male
and female, that we can function effectively and creatively as psychoanalysts. This requires both patient and analyst to function on the
basis of an internalized primal scene. The primal scene symbolizes
two contrasting ideas that can be held together in the mind, can
interact with each other, and do not become fused, on one hand
(as in the combined parent figure), or split apart or fractured, on
the other.

According to the Kleinian theory of part-object functions, at
the deepest levels of the mind the infant experiences each of the
mother's functions as if performed by separate objects. Thus feeding, cleaning, and holding give rise to the experience of separate
part-objects: the holding mother, the feeding mother, and so on.
So, too, in relation to the analyst, on the deepest and most uncon-

scious levels the patient regards each separate function of the analyst as a concretely separate part-object analyst. There may be a
feeding-breast analyst, an evacuating-breast analyst, a fecal-penis
penetrating analyst, and so forth (Meltzer 1973).

Thus (as described by Hinshelwood 1989), the analyst may
be experienced by the patient as empathic; and yet another aspect
of the analyst, for example a more firm and penetrating side, may
be split off and projected onto others or it may be introjected and
identified with (Lipton 1977). Frequently, such split aspects of the
analyst's mind are experienced in gender terms, as male or female
aspects of the analyst, and are equated with maternal and paternal
aspects of the analyst, which the patient then needs to keep separate. Conversely, a feeling and intuitive side of the analyst may be
felt to be missing if the analyst is seen as functioning through his
or her intellect. Integrating these parts of the analyst's mind may
be resisted and fiercely attacked by the patient and by the analyst
as well. A more confusing situation arises when, instead of splitting the two aspects of the analyst and keeping them apart, the
patient defensively fuses the disparate analytic functions. This fusion, modeled on the combined parent figure, results in frightening confusional states and a paranoid mistrust of the analyst. For
example, at these times the patient may see the analyst as perse-
cuting and loving simultaneously, not in rapid oscillation as in some
forms of splitting. During moments of the clinical encounter in
which this has occurred, I have understood the usefulness or affirmative aspects of splitting, which provides order and controls chaos
until such time as integration is possible.

Consider the following two-part scenario. In the first, the
patient realized that our time was almost up and that shortly we
would have to stop. He said to me, "Of course, you will end right
on time, you always do. That's because you always follow the rules.
You do whatever he says [pointing to a picture of Freud hanging
on my office wall]. You are more concerned with the rules than
you are with me." On another occasion, this patient struggled with
the sense of obligation he felt to say everything that came to his
mind. He again pointed to the Freud portrait and said, "He said

so," implying that Freud had ordered this harsh requirement. My sense was that I was being experienced as less demanding and more permissive. In this instance, my patient split his image of me in two. One side was identified with me, and the other was split off and projected onto Freud.

In the first scenario, I end the session because I love Freud and my profession, psychoanalysis, more than I love my patient and so I am ending the session on time because I love someone else more than I love him. Here, what might be viewed on a pre-oedipal level as a conflict between the patient and me about whether I would be seen as frustrating or gratifying is transformed into an oedipal scenario in which the conflict is among three of us: my patient, me, and Freud (or my profession). My patient experiences himself as excluded from my marriage to my profession, which he experiences concretely as my relationship with an internal object, Freud.

In the second scenario, the patient is more clear about his sense of my being in conflict. He has moved a bit closer to articulating his sense that my professional marriage is in trouble. Here he says that it is Freud who is stern and harsh and requires him to say everything. I am really more understanding and would be more permissive if I could. So, if he pushes hard enough, maybe he can get me to relax the rules, break with my passive submission to my lover, and side with my patient. Does he believe that I am in some conflict about requiring him to say everything? In fact I am. My patient is not projecting onto a blank screen. When he says to me, "He [Freud] says so," he is accurate that Freud, not I, said so. He has accurately picked up on something that I feel conflicted about.

One can see in this vignette how my patient sees me as united with my lover against him; we act in concert to exclude him. Or do we? Am I not really the good parent, who does not really want to abandon him at the end of the session or force him to speak? Is it not only because of my love for someone else that I betray him? And perhaps it is a particular type of love, a "passive-homosexual-love" (to use, for the moment, a classical, but highly problematic, category). Could it be that my patient experiences me as a wimp who submits passively to my lover's greater strength and authority? What does he imagine about my relationship with my spouse? What has he observed about me so far in the analysis that may give him clues about my relationships and my tendency to be bossed around or to submit? Indeed, he has picked up on one area where I have not submitted to Freud but where I have remained in some conflict. I believe that patients often do pick up on areas of conflict in the analyst. Patients are highly motivated to penetrate the analyst's inner world, and in doing so they are especially likely to be sensitive to the analyst's conflicts. This is a critical area of analytic inquiry inasmuch as it opens the door to the patient's experience of the analyst's subjectivity (Aron 1991b, 1992b) and offers an entrance to memories of the patient's experience of the parents' inner worlds or character structures. Furthermore, because the analyst represents both mother and father, the analysis of the patient's experience of the analyst's subjectivity also provides a window on the patient's experience of the relation between the parents, especially where they were in conflict.

Most commonly, the splitting of gender is followed by primitive idealization of one object, and denigration, devaluation, and contempt of the other. These positive and negative evaluations may or may not remain stable. For example, at one moment, the analyst's penetrating qualities may be admired and idealized. The patient feels that the analyst has "the tools" to break through his or her resistances and "uncover" the patient's secrets and "expose" the patient's weaknesses. At these times, the patient may devalue and ridicule anyone who is regarded as maternal, more understanding or empathic. The patient may dismiss a more understanding person as someone "who just takes a lot of crap" and who does not have the strength to stand up to abuse. This is the devaluation of what the Kleinians have called the "toilet-breast analyst." At other times, the patient may be contemptuous of the phallic qualities of the analyst and may express that the interpretations are worthless, irrelevant, or disgusting and that they reflect the analyst's own dirty mind. The analyst is seen as the devalued, denigrated, paternal fecal-phallus. At these times the patient may admire a friend who seems to have an analyst who is understanding, nurturant, empathic, and warm. The feeding-breast analyst at these times is idealized and longed for. My point is that to arbitrarily link a particular trait with one gender is to engage in a form of splitting. To believe that empathizing is feminine or that to be intellectually penetrating is masculine is to split off each of our complex and multiple capacities. Terms like "toilet-breast analyst" or "phallic-penetrating interpretations" should be used only to capture metaphorically the way in which certain functions are experienced unconsciously; they should not be taken to imply that we believe that these functions are intrinsically male or female.

Consider the way in which the dichotomy thought-affect is linked to male-female. The common isolation of thought and affect in patients can be thought of as a form of fracturing in which thought, which is often associated in our culture with masculinity, is kept separate from affect, which is more often connected to femininity. From this perspective, a typical obsessional defense is seen not simply as a psychic deficit, but also as an active keeping apart of mother and father because of the danger represented by their intercourse. Schafer (1983) illustrates this by describing a patient who, by keeping his thoughts and feelings apart, was unconsciously keeping his parents apart and saving himself "from the extreme violence of a primal scene involving parents at war with one another in the bedroom" (p. 201). In addition, Schafer points out that transference and resistance may be usefully viewed as enactments of primal scene voyeurism and exhibitionism. In my view, patient and analyst coparticipating in the transference–countertransference, resistance–counterresistance interactions may each alternate in identifications with the two parent imagoes. I need to stress, though, that it is not analytic theory (or at least it should not be) that claims that thinking is male and feeling is female; rather, in our culture this is a common conscious and unconscious belief, which itself needs to be subject to analysis.

PSYCHOANALYTIC SCHOOLS AND
THE SPLITTING OF GENDER

In the history of psychoanalysis there has been a significant shift in the functions and attributes assigned to the analyst, and this shift has taken place along the lines of gender. In its early days, the analyst was thought of as the fearless and adventurous male who seeks to expose and penetrate the feminine "unconscious." The analyst needs to be sharp and insightful, brave and intrepid, fearless in "his" pursuit. The idea of the analyst functioning as a penetrating, phallic instrument was reinforced by the one-sided emphasis within classical analysis on interpretation, rather than relationship, as the exclusive agent of structural change.

By contrast, much of contemporary psychoanalytic theory uses distinctively feminine imagery in its attempt to capture the functioning of the psychoanalyst. It was in the writings of Ferenczi (1932) and of Rank (1926) that psychoanalysts were first alerted to the importance of the mother–infant relationship and of the importance of the mother transference. Especially since the work of Melanie Klein and, following her, Winnicott (1971) in Britain and Kohut (1971) in America, analysts have shifted their gendered metaphors. Analysts now think in terms of "holding environments" and of "mirroring" their patients' affect states; of "containing" their thoughts through maternal-like "reverie" (Bion 1962a); of being "good-enough analysts" modeled on "good-enough mothers" (Winnicott 1971). Instead of thinking of themselves as penetrating, they think of themselves as reflecting. Instead of confronting, they think of empathizing. The imagery has generally shifted from the penetrating phallus to the relational matrix or womb.

Whole schools of psychoanalysis tend to be characterized, by their proponents as well as their opponents, along gender-stereotyped lines. For instance, the ongoing debates between Kernbergians and Kohutians have the quality of contrasts between the paternal and the maternal. To make my point briefly, I will oversimplify. For Kohutian enthusiasts, the maternal, empathic, holding qualities of the analyst are idealized and thought to be curative, whereas they view Kernberg's tough, firm, interpretive and confrontive approach as unnecessarily aggressive—the angry, phallic-aggressive father. For Kernberg-influenced analysts, these same stereotypically male functions are idealized. Thus, they see it as curative to be firm, confronting of primitive defenses, relentless in pursuing the interpretations of the meaning of interpretations. They are likely to disparage the self psychologists' maternalistic emphasis on reflection, mirroring, holding, and empathy. The extreme polarization of these two approaches represents the outcome of our tendency to split or fracture the interaction between masculinity and femininity. Of course, it is critical to keep in mind that viewing empathy as feminine and viewing assertiveness as masculine is itself a symptom of cultural splitting.

Another example of our tendency to polarize theory along gender lines can be seen in the work of some recent feminist therapists. I am referring to a trend within feminist theorizing arising out of and influenced by Gilligan (1982) and Miller (1987) and developed at The Stone Center, Wellesley College. The orientation being developed has been referred to as "self-in-relation" theory. Miller has highlighted the ways in which women are constituted by qualities of affiliativeness, relatedness, empathy, and nurturance, all of which are devalued in the dominant male culture. There is a tendency among these theorists toward a polarized view of male and female development. The danger here is that psychology can be fractured, split between the masculine and the feminine, such that men are seen as developing a sense of self-in-opposition and women a sense of self-in-relation. It is this splitting that leads Gilligan's and Miller's followers to idealize the "feminine" attributes of nurturance and empathy and to devalue "male" attributes such as agency, assertiveness, and boundedness.[6]

---

6. This critique of the "self-in-relation" school has developed in collaboration with Jessica Benjamin (see Benjamin 1992).

While it may be that, under present social-cultural arrangements in which women mother, girls are destined to be more relational and boys to strive for autonomy (Chodorow 1978, Dinnerstein 1999), nevertheless, this does not imply that relatedness is essentially female and autonomy male. As Hare-Mustin (1986) has persuasively argued, it may well be that women's concerns with relationship results from their having less power in our society rather than from any essential psychological difference between men and women. By conflating traits such as autonomy with masculinity and relatedness with femininity, theorists essentialize the differences between the sexes, construe these traits in mutually exclusive terms. By such stereotyping, they simplify human psychology and thus also privilege and essentialize heterosexuality since the two mutually exclusive genders then essentially need each other. In contrast, I am arguing that no trait is essentially, naturally, or specifically male or female but that under present social and cultural arrangements, they are thought to be so, consciously and especially unconsciously. Rather than split off aspects of ourselves that according to these dichotomies are gender incongruent, we need to find ways to integrate them or, perhaps better said, to contain these multiplicities within our identities.

In line with the postmodern emphasis on deconstructing dichotomies, this chapter has emphasized the deconstruction, or, rather, the psychoanalysis, of such polarized concepts as male-female, masculine-feminine, heterosexual-homosexual, father-mother, genital-pregenital, oedipal-preoedipal, identity-multiplicity, paranoid-schizoid depressive position, drive theory-relational theory, and even patient-analyst. Our tendency to split the world in these artificial ways is understandable and, as I have been arguing, is even useful and necessary, for it helps us to organize our experience until such time as we are ready for greater complexity. We cannot, however, afford to get stuck in either–or thinking; rather, we must value both splitting (either–or thinking) and integration (both–and thinking), making room for both identity and multiplicity.

REFERENCES

Aron, L. (1991a). Working through the past—working toward the future. *Contemporary Psychoanalysis* 27:81–109.

———— (1991b). The patient's experience of the analyst's subjectivity. *Psychoanalytic Dialogues* 1:29–51.

———— (1992a). From Ferenczi to Searles and contemporary relational approaches. *Psychoanalytic Dialogues* 2:181–190.

———— (1992b). Interpretation as expression of the analyst's subjectivity. *Psychoanalytic Dialogues* 2:475–507.

———— (1993). Working toward operational thought: Piagetian theory and psychoanalytic method. *Contemporary Psychoanalysis* 29:289–313.

Bach, S. (1985). *Narcissistic States and the Therapeutic Process*. New York: Jason Aronson.

Benjamin, J. (1988). *The Bonds of Love*. New York: Pantheon.

———— (1992). Discussion of Judith V. Jordan's "The Relational Self: A New Perspective for Understanding Women's Development." *Contemporary Psychotherapy Review* 7:82–96.

Bion, W. (1962a). *Learning From Experience*. New York: Basic Books.

———— (1962b). A theory of thinking. *International Journal of Psycho-Analysis* 43:306–310.

Blum, H. P. (1979). On the concept and consequences of the primal scene. *Psychoanalytic Quarterly* 48:27–47.

Britton, R. (1989). The missing link: parental sexuality in the Oedipus complex. In *The Oedipus Complex Today*, ed. J. Steiner, pp. 83–102. London: Karnac.

Chodorow, N. J. (1978). *The Reproduction of Mothering*. Berkeley: University of California Press.

———— (1989). *Feminism and Psychoanalytic Theory*. New Haven, CT: Yale University Press.

Dimen, M. (1991). Deconstructing difference: gender, splitting, and transitional space. *Psychoanalytic Dialogues* 1:335–352.

Dinnerstein, D. (1999). *The Mermaid and The Minotaur*. New York: Other Press.

Eigen, M. (1993). *The Electrified Tightrope*. Northvale, NJ: Jason Aronson.

Esman, A. H. (1973). The primal scene: a review and a reconsideration. *Psychoanalytic Study of the Child* 28:49–82. New Haven, CT: Yale University Press.

Fast, I. (1984). *Gender Identity*. Hillsdale, NJ: The Analytic Press.

——— (1990). Aspects of early gender development: toward a reformulation. *Psychoanalytic Psychology* 7:105–117.

Ferenczi, S. (1932). *The Clinical Diary of Sandor Ferenczi*, ed. J. Dupont. Cambridge, MA: Harvard University Press, 1988.

Flax, J. (1990). *Thinking Fragments*. Berkeley: University of California Press.

Freud, S. (1905). On the sexual theories of children. *Standard Edition* 9:205–226.

——— (1918). From the history of an infantile neurosis. *Standard Edition* 17:3–123.

——— (1940). An outline of psychoanalysis. *Standard Edition* 23:139–207.

Ghent, E. (1992). Paradox and process. *Psychoanalytic Dialogues* 2: 135–160.

Gilligan, C. (1982). *In a Different Voice*. Cambridge, MA: Harvard University Press.

Goldner, V. (1991). Toward a critical relational theory of gender. *Psychoanalytic Dialogues* 1:249–272.

Hare-Mustin, R. T. (1986). The problem of gender in family therapy. *Family Process* 26:15–27.

Hinshelwood, R. D. (1989). *A Dictionary of Kleinian Thought*. London: Free Association Books.

Ikonen, P., and Rechardt, E. (1984). On the universal nature of primal scene fantasies. *International Journal of Psycho-Analysis* 65:63–72.

Kaplan, L. J. (1991). *Female Perversions*. New York: Doubleday.

Klein, M. (1927). Criminal tendencies in normal children. In *Love, Guilt and Reparation and Other Works*, pp. 170–185. New York: Delacorte Press/Seymour Lawrence, 1975.

——— (1928). Early stages of the Oedipus conflict. In *Love, Guilt and Reparation and Other Works*, pp. 186–198. New York: Delacorte Press/ Seymour Lawrence, 1975.

——— (1929). Infantile anxiety situations reflected in a work of art and in the creative impulse. In *Love, Guilt and Reparation and Other Works*, pp. 210–218. New York: Delacorte Press/Seymour Lawrence, 1975.

——— (1952a). Some theoretical conclusions regarding the emotional life of the infant. In *Envy and Gratitude and Other Works*, pp. 61–93. New York: Delacorte Press/Seymour Lawrence, 1975.

——— (1952b). The origins of transference. In *Envy and Gratitude and Other Works*, pp. 48–56. New York: Delacorte Press/Seymour Lawrence, 1975.

———— (1957). Envy and gratitude. In *Envy and Gratitude and Other Works*, pp. 176–235. New York: Delacorte Press/Seymour Lawrence, 1975.

Kohut, H. (1971). *The Analysis of the Self*. New York: International Universities Press.

Kubie, L. S. (1974). The drive to become both sexes. *Psychoanalytic Quarterly* 43:349–426.

Laing, R. D. (1972). *The Politics of the Family*. New York: Vintage.

Lipton, S. D. (1977). Clinical observations on resistance to the transference. *International Journal of Psycho-Analysis* 58:463–472.

McDougall, J. (1980). *Plea for a Measure of Abnormality*. New York: International Universities Press.

Mead, M. (1928). *Coming of Age in Samoa*. New York: Dell.

Meltzer, D. (1973). *Sexual States of Mind*. Perthshire, Scotland: Clunie.

Miller, J. B. (1987). What do we mean by relationships. In *Works in Progress of the Stone Center*. Wellesley, MA: The Stone Center.

Mitchell, S. (1988). *Relational Concepts in Psychoanalysis*. Cambridge, MA: Harvard University Press.

Ogden, T. H. (1986). *The Matrix of the Mind*. Northvale, NJ: Jason Aronson.

———— (1989). *The Primitive Edge of Experience*. Northvale, NJ: Jason Aronson.

O'Shaughnessy, E. (1989). The invisible Oedipus complex. In *The Oedipus Complex Today*, ed. J. Steiner, pp. 129–150. London: Karnac.

Rank, O. (1926). The genesis of the object relations. In *The Psychoanalytic Vocation*, ed. P. Rudnytsky, pp. 171–179. New Haven: CT: Yale University Press.

Rivera, M. (1989). Linking the psychological and the social: feminism, poststructuralism, and multiple personality. *Dissociation* 2:24–31.

Rubin, G. (1975). The traffic in women: notes on the "political economy" of sex. In *Toward an Anthropology of Women*, ed. R. Reiter. pp. 157–211. New York: Monthly Review Press.

Schafer, R. (1983). *The Analytic Attitude*. New York: Basic Books.

Searles, H. F. (1966–1967). Concerning the development of an identity. In *Countertransference and Related Subjects*, pp. 45–70. New York: International Universities Press, 1979.

Segal, H. (1964). *Introduction to the Work of Melanie Klein*. New York: Basic Books.

Stern, D. (1985). *The Interpersonal World of the Infant*. New York: Basic Books.

Winnicott, D. W. (1971). *Playing and Reality*. London: Tavistock.

7

Beyond the He and the She: Toward the Reconciliation of Masculinity and Femininity in the Postoedipal Female Mind[1]

DONNA BASSIN

Fast (1984) speculated that the earliest experiences of girls and boys are undifferentiated and overinclusive as to gender. She pointed out, for example, the commonalities of organ actions, in which both girls and boys share similar action schemas (later transposed to a symbolic level). These organ actions, like Erikson's (1968) organ modes and Kestenberg's (1975) descriptions of organ-objects, are modes of relating or going at objects based on early body experiences, for example, grasping, receiving, and penetrating.[2] These

---

1. Originally published in *Journal of the American Psychoanalytic Association* 44(1996 Suppl.):157–190. Reprinted with permission from International Universities Press. This essay was written without the benefit of queer theory, from whose vantage point several incisive critiques have been made (Layton 2001, Schwartz 1998), which I lack the space to engage, having had to reduce the original version for this volume. Winnicott's observation, that an object must allow itself to be destroyed in order to be of use, seems applicable to our theoretical contributions and suggests the generative aspects of engaged critique.

2. Erikson, a transitional theorist, assumed a simultaneous contribution of psyche, soma, and culture in all experience, thereby bridging essentialisms with

organizers are experienced in the bodily world and get their underlying structure from the corporeality of the body, but they develop
into psychic metaphors that do not properly belong to either biological sex. They are transitions to symbolic behaviors, or flexible
sets of categories in which the mind experiences the body and organizes its making and perceiving systems.

Erikson argues that the infantile genital stage is dominated in
both sexes by combinations of intrusive and inclusive modes and
modalities that become differentiated only during puberty. Considering this differentiation, however, he asked the question that I
am concerned with: "What becomes, in either sex, of the countermodes?" (1982, p. 39).[3] I argue that these early bodily representations do not drop out or become totally eclipsed by later developments. Rather, as Rose (1980) demonstrated in his discussion of
the creation and appreciation of the arts (in particular, music and
dance), they may be "stored" and can be reconstituted or reexpe-
rienced. These early overinclusive structures or cross-sex representations, I suggest, are used not only metaphorically in the service
of self-definition in an adult female organization, but are necessary for the optimal transcendence of sexual polarities and rigid

---

social constructivism. His notion of organ modes linked psychosocial development with psychosexual development. According to Erikson (1950) each body
ego zone—oral-sensory, anal, and genital—can serve a number of social modalities or inter-actionable patterns of functioning (incorporative, retentive, elimi-
native, intrusive, and inclusive). His elaboration of the bisexual disposition con-
sisted of his observation that both sexes have a combination of all the modalities
at their disposal, and thus similar experiences regarding, for example, their locomotion, sexual activities, and mental and social intrusiveness. They differ only
in regard to genital equipment and their respective future roles in the reproductive cycle. So while genitals may come to represent, for example, intrusion or
penetration (following the associations of Miss A. later in this chapter) they are
in fact, modes from the common ground of other organ zones in addition to general motility and locomotion.

3. I have found aspects of Erikson and Fast to be useful, although I view
them as limited in their conventional conclusions that countermodes and overinclusive states must be subsumed for the sake of anatomical confluence and
gender identity. Fast relies on an epigenetic model implying a linear progression
of development.

gender identities. Overinclusive body-ego representations afford the raw material, or foundation, for the imaginative elaboration of the Other. Furthermore, this organization provides the female with the capacity to understand or conceive her male counterpoint, allowing her to see him as a subject and not a male object. With Fonagy (1991), I offer that understanding or conceiving the Other requires the ability to imagine temporarily that one is the Other and the capacity to distinguish between this pretense and reality.

Despite the rather politically radical and utopian flavor of Reich's declaration (see Bergman 1988) that "the genital character is not resigned, but rather rebellious to gender norms" (Reich 1929, p. 161), his comments provoke a reexamination of the organization of the mature female genital position in light of gender identity. In viewing the complexity of genital experience from a gender-neutral position, I am suggesting that the reconciliation of femininity and masculinity in the genital stage depends in part on the extent to which the self is able to generate a transitional space and to use true symbols of cross-sex representation. It is by means of symbols that early overinclusive body-ego states and cross-gendered representations can be reintegrated within a *predominantly* gendered self. These symbolic representations serve as a bridge between the dichotomies articulated as gender. Lasky (1989) suggested that the analyst's work requires an integration and acceptance of bisexual substrates; I argue that obtaining genitality requires them as well.[4]

The idea of bisexuality certainly assuages castration anxiety on both sides and provides, as Blos (1979, 1985) suggests, the idea of limitless possibilities. Yet within the context of a postoedipal differentiated self, the infantile fantasy of realizing a perfect gender completeness can be modified into what Blos (1985) called a tolerance of self-limitation and a push for self-determination and possibilities. Regarding Jacobson's (1964) resistance to the idea of the containment of development, we can conceive of this capacity

---

4. Schwartz's (1998) observation that my contribution rests on the assumption of a heterosexual orientation and parenting is certainly apparent here.

of the female mind as a process of potentiality, allowing for an ego that assimilates cross-sex representations simply for their value in internal and external mastery rather than based on anatomical possession. Essentially, these observations provide a way to separate Kubie's (1974) understanding of the pathological wish to be both sexes or the hermaphroditic omnipotence of classical Greek tales from the adaptive use of symbolic transcendence of gender differentiation. The task, then, might be to articulate a series of character types or organizations, ranging from phallic or vaginal characters to genital characters that would reflect mixtures of masculinity and femininity with varying abilities for symbolic and imaginative use. There is ultimately no normal psyche organization, only certain organizational types and certain paradoxes to be resolved. A series of possibilities in sexual organization would allow each type its own pleasures, anxieties, and resolutions.

Chodorow (1994) suggests that we should find a wide variety of heterosexuality (as well as homosexuality) clinically and that we should treat all sexualities as problematics that we need to account for. In this version of the female genital mind, the woman is tied to her core sexual identity yet is simultaneously able to draw on bisexual fantasies. She can symbolize relatively freely from overinclusive body-ego representations. Her integration of bisexual components in the psyche makes it possible for her to transcend normative, polarized sexual positions and gender conformity—an appropriate goal for psychoanalysis, which should aim not for normative behavior but for psychic health. This kind of female psychic organization allows for the symbolic integration of masculine strivings and body-ego representations and of cross-gender identifications, without recourse to a disturbed gender identity.[5]

Through the efforts of feminist psychoanalysts, psychoanalytic clinical theory has illuminated a phallocentric logic that affects the way we perceive gender, mature object relations, and heterosexu-

---

5. On the other hand, perhaps the reference to masculinity and femininity is too entrenched with heterosexist associations (see Butler 1994).

ality. According to this critique the word *phallic* and its erroneously literal tie to the male genital distract us from articulating the limitations of the phallic order for both sexes. Unduly privileging male gender, that order ignores the complex variability within the same sex and provides a fixed, normative, and rigid gender identity by polarization and repression. The resolution of the oedipal stage should mark an end to the division of the world into the phallic and the castrated, but this is rarely accomplished fully, thus giving normative male and female sexuality an unduly phallic cast. Lacan, as cited by Gallop (1982) suggests that the phallic order, the logic in which genitality has been conceived theoretically, represents "a failure to reach the Other" (p. 34).

Because the phallic order cannot account for femininity, it closes back on itself, and any real sexual relation between the sexes is doomed to failure. As Benjamin (1988) argues, where gender relations are organized around domination and polarity, gender splitting occurs and one part of the self disowns another part. As normatively construed within this psychosexual logic, heterosexuality is a sexual organization that knows only one active sexuality: a phallic one that refuses the vagina. Chodorow (1994) suggests that psychoanalysis has provided a normative story that ties heterosexuality to male dominance and sexuality to gender.

CLINICAL DATA

Miss A.

The patient, Miss A., a beautiful 28-year-old single woman, initially presented with anxieties about penetration during intercourse and an intense fear of driving a car. She was very much in love with a man; they were moving toward marriage, and yet she was distressed by her inability to enjoy intercourse. She felt close to her father and was aware of the guilt she experienced regarding her loyalty to another man. Miss A. felt anger over what she perceived to be her lover's invasion of her body and his penetration into her emotional life. She felt resentment and contempt toward the legitimate owner of the penis but also felt positive about her own sensuality and identity as a woman. She reported a history of good early body closeness with her mother, who supported Miss A.'s developing relationship with her own body. Despite having loving feelings for her fiancé and knowing that he cared deeply for her, she felt he was demanding too much of her, that he was impatient, selfish, and unwilling to take her needs into account. Although initially the sight of his erect penis excited her, Miss A.'s sexual excitement quickly abated at penetration and was replaced by an uncomfortable sense of floating. She felt safe in this floating state but frightened by a loss of sensations and an emotional emptiness. During those moments she could not relate to her lover; she felt detached and alienated. She experienced his penis as an inert object or an object that was "sticking itself into places where it did not belong."

While she found her work gratifying insofar as it called upon her ability to be generative, she reported moments of intense anxiety about not being able to come up with creative solutions to problems at her job. Moreover, her fear of losing control while driving and killing an innocent bystander interfered with the necessary independence and mobility she needed to develop her career.

Over time in the transference, Miss A. began to experience me, as her analyst, as an intrusive Other who was sticking my analytic structure into what she previously experienced as a warm, safe, comforting, and generative space. Manifestly, she began to disagree with the structure of the sessions, in particular, with their length, complaining that her free associations were being disrupted by my need to end the sessions at an appointed time. She objected to my bringing up her not paying me at a previously agreed upon time as an intrusion into her analytic session and claimed that I was disrupting and controlling the content of her sessions. During this period, Miss A. often met my questions and interpretations with sensations similar to those she had felt during intercourse. She would float off, much to her dismay, as she had during her orals for an honors Masters degree and as she occasionally did during problem-solving situations at work. She claimed that she liked the "old me" better, namely, when I let her free-associate and did not comment. She wanted to be left alone to float quietly away into the room, somehow held in space but free from the intrusive disruptions of my voice. The warm floating feelings were eventually transformed into feelings of immobilization whereby she could watch and listen but not act. She felt safe and protected, as when she had been held by her mother, from what she now experienced as demanding and intrusive. In addition, by floating away, untouched by my comments, she could render me helpless to touch her psychically. I told her that this was a way to castrate me as her analyst, just as she wished to do with her lover. Rendering us both impotent, she robbed me of my analyzing tools and her lover of his means of getting inside her.

Some months later, during another phase, seemingly triggered by a lengthy visit from her mother, Miss A. began to express an active preoccupation with my personal life. She had seen my male office mate and she wondered whether we got together between sessions. How did I feel about men, really? Did I still have an active sexual life? What were my sexual fantasies? Although she wanted me to respond because she thought my answers might be important for her progress, she was ambivalent. She felt they would be intrusive and dangerous. Miss A. saw her mother as a successful woman, still very sexy and beautiful, despite her age, and extremely competent as a mother. She felt that she was like her mother in many ways and that her mother had given her many gifts, including her creativity and warmth. She recalled childhood memories of sneaking to look through her mother's closet. The closet was filled with beautiful women's things, such as silky nightgowns and loungewear. The soft and pliable garments were saturated with her mother's perfume. She remembered many such visits to her mother's closet, touching the wonderful fabrics and stopping herself from trying on the garments. She had been frightened that she would be caught doing something or looking at something she was not supposed to.

Her wishes and fears regarding knowledge about me as a woman intensified. The comparison between her wish to know the inside of her analyst and her wishes to know about the inside of her mother's body/closet evoked a memory of being punished for her curiosity, for her intrusion into her mother's space. She thought that perhaps her mother had "slammed" or slapped her. Miss A. was shocked by this "memory"; she had never thought of her mother as physically hurting her. The memory of being slammed led to Miss A.'s recollection of her banging her head against her closet door when she was a child. The head banging was her response to frustration over not getting what she wanted; it felt powerful and it soothed her. At those times her mother would attempt to comfort her by sitting Miss A. on her lap. The slam-slap, as we reconstructed it, might have been her childhood distortion of a psychic narcissistic blow by her mother experienced as an assault on her body as well as a projection of her own frustrated aggression. Her head banging was an aggressive response to feeling shut out. Overdetermined, it represented her futile attempt to understand what went on inside a woman, her wishes to harm her mother for depriving her of softness, and reparation for her envy of the imagined intimacy between her parents.

The recall of memories of childhood head banging led us into the analysis of her fear of driving. Driving was associated with her father, who had taught her to drive and who had communicated his pleasure at her new mobility. It represented an oedipal victory over the mother, who had never learned to drive despite her husband's efforts to teach her. Miss A. remembered the sense of power and exhilaration of chauffeuring her father. Next came a fantasy wherein she would inadvertently press the gas pedal rather than the brake at a red light. Instead of stopping, in complying with traffic rules, she feared feeling overwhelmed by her wishes to push forward, to use the car as an expression of her power. She feared her driving would lead to her or someone else's death. The unconscious wish to thrust the car and smash into others was a derivative of her early frustrated intrusive mode for getting into her mother's body.

It seemed impossible for her to express the exhilaration and power of motion without hurting herself or others. Gradually, she was able to see the connection between her fear of penetration by her lover and her projection of her aggressiveness in wanting to penetrate her mother's and analyst's insides. In addition, penetration represented a mastery of facing things and knowing them from having been inside. She experienced her little-girl disappointment over her inability to get to know her mother as she imagined her father had as an inadequacy on her part and perhaps even as a punishment for her aggression. I suggested to her that she wanted to be free to stick her nose into my affairs, to penetrate my secrets, to find out how I felt, and to use her curiosity and aggression. Yet she hid behind her floaty softness for fear she was too intrusive and that she would hurt someone. An unconscious masturbation fantasy was eventually revealed in a series of dreams. Miss A. found the following dream significant:

> It was my head inside his body. I am making love to a woman,
> but it is really him. I can feel the sensation of penetration.
> I am myself, and then I am him. I have an erection, and it is
> obvious to him how I feel.

She felt joyful and liberated by this dream. Her associations to the dream, however, were initially block d by her concerns that I would misinterpret it and superficially interpret her sexual confusion. When I pressed her about her fantasy about my interpretation, she suggested that I might think that the problem she had had with her lover was based on some deep homosexual wishes, and furthermore, that her wishes to love a woman might mean that she really must wish to be a man. Was a woman who wished to be inside a male body not a woman? I asked. I then suggested that she could not imagine that I could understand her wishes to know what it was like to be a man inside a woman or a woman inside a man without denying her sexuality or identity as a woman. Further associations deepened the meaning of the dream. She recalled leafing through a book of poems by Anne Sexton. She said she wished in part that she could let herself have a breakdown as Sexton had. For Miss A., a breakdown was associated with an ability to lose control, to break out of the rules of behavior that were causing her to behave like a good girl—passive, disembodied, and floating around in her life. She claimed that following the rules of analysis was like conforming to what her father and mother wanted for her. She remembered discovering "rubbers" in her mother's closet, thinking about her parents having sex, her mother wanting her father and encouraging him with her beautiful nightwear. I suggested that finding the rubbers and understanding that her mother had a sexual desire for her father had made Miss A. feel she had violated their privacy with her excitement.

In later sessions there was a surge of oedipal material when the patient was a good, passive girl who followed rules. I suggested that her feelings must have been overwhelming in light of her felt attachment to her mother and her needing at that time to deny her active sexuality and be good. Going limp with her lover at the moment of penetration was to deny her own excitement and keep herself from remembering exciting, forbidden feelings and guilt, as had the child in her mother's closet. She experienced the choice she made between hiding the feelings and allowing herself the feelings as a defeat. In a sense, every aspect of her life had represented a loss of part of herself as a result of that choice. She felt she had to conceal those aspects of herself, that she wanted interpretations as she desired the penetration, even though it meant something forbidden, something she was not entitled to have.

Miss A. then revealed that the "he" in the dream was her lover; it was also her finger. It was her curiosity and her sexual power. It was a part of her, like the little unself-conscious girl who danced vigorously through the house. In her childhood fantasy she could enjoy those feelings and escape punishment. These aspects of Miss A., which enabled her to fulfill her desire—concretely, using her finger during masturbation, and symbolically, using her mind inside her lover's body in her dream—had been cast. Her denial of her own wishes led her to resent me, the male–female analyst, and her lover for being free to get into things and penetrate and to be sexually alive and cause her to be frustrated by rage. She feared that her mother, like her analyst, would either deny her, punish her, or not recognize her sexuality (telling her she was sexually confused) because of her wishes both to love and be like her father and know the inside of a female. Miss A. was striving to reclaim an aspect of herself, represented symptomatically by her childhood head banging and her more current fears of driving a car and being intrusive and too curious. She had found symbolic expression for her active sexual desire in her male lover's body and erection. She had described childhood wishes and physical attempts to penetrate her mother's closet, to get inside her mother's clothes/closet/body in order to be part of the sexually exciting experience that she imagined between her parents but felt was forbidden. Instead, she contented herself to sit passively on her mother's lap and on the analyst's couch.

The patient saw Sexton as a representation of her own defeated self but as someone with the tools to transcend her situation through imagination and creativity. Miss A.'s anger toward herself was comparable to her anger at Sexton for having killed herself rather than using her imagination and creativity to transcend difficulty. This anger was now available to be transformed into initiative. She could allow herself to put fantasies to imaginative use and to experience her pervasive need to be a woman in a male body temporarily, without feeling that she was a wolf in sheep's clothing. Erection for her had to do with her own tools. She could give them form, she suspected, through her lover's penis; perhaps it was something that could be shared.

Miss A. began to realize that her use of the penis in her dream was symbolic rather than the reflection of a wish for the anatomical part itself. With the assistance of the visible form of the penis and a borrowing of her lover's male body, Miss A. could imagine and represent her abilities to penetrate previously closed-off parts of her mind without having to negate her female experience. She began to understand the construction of sexuality as something to which she had given meaning rather than something given to or taken from her. Her envy of her lover and her contempt for him were gradually transformed into an appreciation of her somewhat aggressively tinged wishes to penetrate. The reclamation of her representations of penetration and thrusting promoted empathy for her lover and for his expression of desire rather than power and aggression. She understood both his vulnerability and his need for her and knew that she was not giving herself over to an image of herself as her own lover. As Segal (1991) suggests, "The symbol is the result of psychic work, and therefore the subject has the freedom of its use" (p. 96).

Miss B.

In my original essay Miss B. was extensively discussed to contrast with Miss A. Miss B. was not able to uncouple the concrete anatomical difference from psychic attributes and general bodily capacities. Most reductively, Miss B.'s "penis" was not utilized as a metaphor or as a playful appropriation of an aspect of her over-inclusive body ego, but as the real and only legitimate origin of activity, aggression, and penetrative wishes. Miss B.'s rather rigid gender identity and perception of gender structure was organized by the repudiation and splitting of the phallic-oedipal period.

WHAT CONSTITUTES THE NORMAL MIND?

Jones (1942) argues that the normal mind can be defined only in relation to specific cultural norms. The healthy mind, however, can be evaluated by its flexibility, its ability to frolic and roam, accommodating contradiction and conflict. Jones's conception of the healthy mind as one that accepts conflict without undue polarization or repression may be utopian, but it is nevertheless generative in its attempt to understand how we can transcend the norms of gender conformity. Both Jones and Winnicott (1966) refer to what Mitchell (1974) calls the "uneven relationship between the two sexual possibilities [of masculinity and femininity] within a person as well as between persons" (p. 45). For Mitchell, it was the exploration of this relationship that was Freud's true project.

As many researchers today note, much of the classical theory of female development is now interpreted as reflecting conformity to culturally normative gender roles, compliance with the biological needs of reproduction, or both. In the 1930s, Boehm (1930) argued that the goal of analysis was to free the male of his feminine wishes and the woman of her masculine ones. By the 1980s, Bergman (1988) suggested that the psychoanalyst had the dual goal not only of uncovering repressed countergendered wishes but also of increasing the superego's tolerance of these wishes. Our analytic commitment to understanding female sexual organization and our analytic responsibility of neutrality (which Poland [1984] defines as the "technical manifestation of respect for the essential otherness of the other" [p. 289]), require an ongoing push against the tide of conscious gendered ideals.

American culture, in some ways still in its adolescence in its intolerance of gradation, may reinforce society's restraints on the flexibility of gender roles. But the task of psychoanalysis, as Jones (1942) poetically described it and as Grossman and Kaplan (1988) and Kaplan (1990) have argued powerfully, is to treat gender roles and their normative values as manifest content.

The norms of conformity in gender-role behavior obscure the diverse sexual identities within the psyche and the admixture there of the active and passive, subject and object, and masculine and feminine. The limitations of our language force categorizations that level out the complexities of nonlinear experiences. As Wisdom (1983) suggested, "We have difficulty in specifying what a man is when he is part female and in specifying what a woman is when she is in part male" (p. 161).

There are alternatives to the female's acceptance of castration and to the repression or dissociation by both men and women of the limitless bisexual wish to be both sexes. These alternatives will be overlooked, however, unless we are able to elaborate a transitional resting space, a mastery mode in which the fact of castration and the differences between the sexes are not lost but transcended through true symbolization.

Analysts' increased attention to cross-gender identifications in the development of the transference—indeed, to their necessity there—(Bernstein 1991, Lasky 1989) makes further investigation of more flexible and elastic sexual identities a clinical essential.

TOWARD NEW MODELS OF ORGANIZATION AND INTEGRATION

New models of organization and integration are needed to assist in the arduous task of pushing forward content latent in the female narrative. Winnicott's (1971) appreciation of how the intermingling of fantasy and reality leads to an adaptive playing with reality and Loewald's (1988) refusal of a fixed, linear model of development provide the theoretical context for an integration and reconciliation of cross-sex representations. Ego states of transitionality and fluidity suggest conceptual structures within which the developmental progression of the female mind might be understood, not as a hierarchical stabilization of sexual component instincts, but as an integration and dynamic application of deep early ego states, in this case, the recuperation of early bisexuality in the context of a postoedipal differentiated self (see also Benjamin 1995).

Here, I believe, we have theoretical guides for understanding how each sex integrates components of the opposite sex into its psyche without compromising its core gender identity, which Person and Ovesey (1983) defined as a sense of belonging biologically to the male or female sex. One's core gender identity provides a frame for self-identity and self-continuity, but it can also drop into the background as the situation requires. The female's cross-sex identification with paternal figures, as well as her same-sex synthesis with maternal figures, is a significant dimension in her adult ego organization. Kestenberg (1968), McDougall (1980), Mendell (1988), Winnicott (1988), and Benjamin (1991) discussed the desirability of cross-sex identifications in the empathic understanding of the Other.

Classical theory has it that the Oedipus complex directs bisexuality into a clear dichotomy between masculinity and femininity. Alongside the classical view are other clinical narratives of the development of gender and of the female psyche. Contemporary gender theory continues to debate the place of the body and the impact of the Oedipus resolution in the construction of gender identity and fantasy. Freud's omission of a female body-ego organization skewed our understanding of sexual development. It did not allow for a specific elaboration of how the female's body affected her character other than her preoccupation with loss.

Counterbalancing the monistic view of the female as simply non-male, revised contributions have described a uniquely female body ego and an early, primary sense of femaleness for the girl child. This vision of a truly active female subjectivity, surfacing in part from the female body ego, was foreshadowed in the work of Horney (1926, 1933) and Jones (1935) and was theoretically detailed later by Bassin (1982), Bernstein (1983, 1990), Irigaray (1985), and Lord (1991). Bernstein's elaboration of a gender-specific body ego has illuminated a female subjectivity and has fostered clinical interventions that help the female subject understand her particular bodily interiority, anxiety, and modes of mastery.

In my earlier work (Bassin 1982) I explored the relation between woman's experience of inner space and her construction of a category of experience or metaphor that serves as a structure for knowing and creating the world. This symbolic organization, based on a uniquely female body-ego schema, provides a specific mode of activity, self-knowledge, organization, and subjectivity as a counterpoint to phallic modes. The illumination of symbolic possibilities for the female ideally provides interpretative alternatives or "conditions of possibility" (Foucault 1978) in the clinical narrative. Unfortunately it has also resulted in theoretical positions that have led to the creation of new norms of female development, or new versions of the essentialism that Freud strove to deconstruct. These new norms of female behavior, for example, "women's ways of knowing" or "self-in connection" may pose as great a threat to psychoanalytic work as did those of the fin-de-siècle (see Grossman and Kaplan 1988). A normative model of female behavior and fantasies that excludes the presence of masculine wishes and strivings may represent just another fantasy of gender consistency to normalize characteristics of interiority, relatedness, and connectedness at the psychic expense of competition, assertion, and aggression (Harris 1987).

Compelling experiences of gender overinclusiveness make distinct and invaluable contributions to the female mind. In my view, the apparent conflict between the narratives of the classical position, with its monistic body ego, and those of the revised theory, which posits a specifically female body ego, is reconcilable. The overlap of these two narratives might be seen as the "duality at the heart of the feminine" (Breen 1993, p. 36). Breen, in her extensive analysis of the Freud–Jones debates and the subsequent arguments for both sides, concluded that the narratives of a "positive femininity" and the experience of lack coexist in the female. These two aspects of femininity together present a paradox of sameness and difference within and between the sexes, or, as Dimen (1991) suggested, a gender multiplicity whereby the recuperation of split-off aspects of the self occupies a transitional space.

We can envision a body-ego experience, in other words, that is both differentiated and overinclusive. Two strands of development affect this female organization: one moves toward firm gender identity based on anatomy, identification with the same-sex parent, and resolution of the positive oedipal drama; simultaneously, another allows the psyche to move away from the comforting but containing limitations of gender based on early overinclusive body-ego experience with nongenitalized parents, identifications with opposite-sex parents, and resolution of the negative oedipal in adolescence. Thus we can understand the girl child simultaneously mapping a specifically female body ego while integrating multiplicity through memorial symbolization of an earlier, overinclusive body ego.

This paradoxical conception of a simultaneous identity and multiplicity (Aron 1991) of a self that is differentiated yet fluid and elastic has developmental support. First (1994), for example, detailed it empirically in her observation of cross-identifications in toddler play.

BODY EGO AS ORIGIN AND CONTAINER
FOR SYMBOLIZATION

Although the two contributions of the body ego cannot be divided functionally, I discuss the body ego first as an origin and generative source in the creation of metaphoric and symbolic representation and second as a container for experience to help us understand cross-sex representations in an adult female psyche. As an origin for the content of symbols, the contested relation between anatomy and sexuality has presented a thorny problem for the psychoanalytic claim that sexuality is not based on biology. What impact, if any, does the specificity of different bodies have on thought? Questions within cybernetic theory, such as is identity closer to an informational pattern or an embodied enaction, or what is the relationship between embodied and disembodied forms of subjectivity, may be useful to our psychoanalytic quest.

When Freud laid out his well-known arguments regarding the ego's development from the body in "The Ego and the Id" (1923), he suggested that the ego is first and foremost a *body ego*, a structure that represents its psychic activities as equivalents of bodily activities. The conception of the body ego as the *imaginative elaboration of the body* (Winnicott 1966) allows sufficient play for indeterminate contributions from both the body and the psyche that are elaborated in affect-laden object relations (for example, identifications from significant Others arising from separation-individuation, primal scene, and oedipal drama). The body ego has a symbolic and metaphoric relation to the body; we might say that what we have here is an imaginary anatomy (Lacan 1953). The radical disjunction between anatomy and sexuality rests in the fact that these representations are not veridical imitations or accurate representations of the body and its relations, but rather are interpretations based on object relations and representational abilities.

The body ego incorporates representations of sex and gender that are both differentiated (specifically related to anatomy) and undifferentiated (i.e., overinclusive). From the vantage point of symbolic processes, then, the body is actually elastic rather than "given." The body ego can shrink, expand, take parts of the outside world into itself, and give parts of itself to the outside world (Schilder 1935). It is this flexible entity that constitutes the self's elemental representations of experience. The body may be a significant origin of experience and a model through which other experiences are understood, but this model is not simply given. It requires interpretation and symbolic mediation. The body ego cannot be reduced to anatomy, nor can anatomy be seen as an obstacle to the imaginative elaboration of cross-sex representations. Body-ego organizers originating from the early, overinclusive stages contribute to the body ego's imaginative symbolic representations of the opposite sex and are ready for access when necessary. The physical impossibility of cross-sex behavior does not prevent the mind from playing with reality, creating imaginative elaborations of the Other, empathic identifications that serve as an internal bridge between gender polarities. The interaction of the body ego with the outer world provides for the development of a self that becomes firmer and fuller as it enriches itself through isomorphic structures. Also, the outside world takes on a sense of familiarity as it is processed through the self (Bassin 1982). Through this interactive process we build bridges from inside and out, enriching both realms of experience.

The containing function of the body ego in relation to significant others serves as a boundary for the self and not-self. It is crucial in the self's use of symbolization and differentiation of fantasy. A secure and activated body ego provides the space in which adaptive functions can thrive and good contents reside. As a containing structure, it is an organizer of drive activity. Instinctual experiences focus and organize infants' sense of themselves as authors of their experience (Winnicott 1966); their integration of body parts and libidinal zones, in part a function of the mastery of discharge, reflects the achievement of the container function of the body ego. The well-developed body ego allows children to recognize themselves as initiators of actions that have effects on the external world (Grand 1982). This in turn contributes to their development of intentionality, instrumentality, and self-competence.

From this perspective, both passivity and activity—unduly associated, respectively, with femininity and masculinity—have more to do with ego autonomy, specifically body-ego integrity, than with gender. White (1963) argued that the self's feelings of efficacy originate in the activity of the body, not just from the specific consequences of our actions, but from activity itself. Indeed, Benjamin (1988) argued that it is the ability to be a container of the drives and not the drives' direction per se that creates a feeling of subjectivity. Subjective self-experiences of passivity and activity need to be ferreted out from both those states as theoretical constructs related to the aims of instincts. During toilet training, for example, physical letting go can be experienced passively in regard to the body but actively in response to the mother's request.

In fantasy life, similarly, both the male and the female subject take the active and the passive position. On the one hand, the assumption that all the characters of the dream or fantasy are the dreamer reveals the oscillation between the active and the passive position within unconscious fantasy. On the other hand, the ideal of gender polarity, manifestly assuming exclusive predominance of active or passive aims toward the object masks this underlying oscillation. In fact, I postulate an interchangeability of positions within fantasy, which Freud (1915) discussed in "Instincts and Their Vicissitudes," as necessary for reconciliation of masculinity and femininity. Whatever the individual choice, the opposite aim is simultaneously being realized and gratified in the unconscious. What appear to be dichotomies are merely defensive surface splits.

SYMBOLS: LINKS BETWEEN POLARITIES
AND MEMORIALS TO LOST OBJECTS

Ogden's (1986, 1989) interpretation of Klein's depressive stage provides further clarification of the possibility of a differentiated adult female organization that transcends the rigidity of masculinity and femininity in adult life. For Ogden, psychic growth is not simply a result of the modification of unconscious psychological contents; it is a shift in the psychological matrix within which fantasy is experienced. As Segal (1991) argued, the great achievement of the depressive position is the individual's capacity to use symbols and to know that he or she is creating them to differentiate among the symbol, what is symbolized, and the interpreting sub-ject. As a clinical example of this, Chertoff (1989) suggested that although the patient's biological sex may influence the specifics of the transference fantasy, the patient's ego strength may allow him or her to let go of the analyst's biological sex in order to work through the cross-gender transference. This psychological matrix allows for the as-if relation that is necessary if the patient is to tran-scend the reality of the analyst's sex and thus tolerate a full range of parental transference.

It is the advent of the depressive position, with its experi-ence of separation and loss, that brings true symbolic represen-tation into play: symbols can now be used to overcome loss. Imagi-natively elaborated cross-sex representation may be seen, for example, as an elegiac emergence from the ashes of the earlier, overinclusive body ego, a kind of mourning of lost bisexuality. In opposition to the repression of gender-incompatible fantasies and images (a repudiation that inevitably leads to a return of the repressed in symptom formation or in love relationships in which incompatible polarities prevail), we can envision a mastery of loss that is accomplished through memorial symbolization. The penis, for example, a useful symbol of penetration, may be experienced not concretely but metaphorically and can link the female to her experience. This link, I believe, is what is restored in treatment and through true symbolization.

Older formulations of symbolization, as, for example, Jones's (1938) model, required repression between symbol and fantasy in which symbolization had a defensive cast. In Loewald's (1988) model, symbolization is part of ego development, without the traditional emphasis on defense. Here the creation of a symbol emphasizes a hidden linkage and restores the breach between primary and sec-ondary process. These memorial symbolizations are to be differen-tiated, then, from the fetish—another memorial to castration—in that they do not disguise what is symbolized. Kaplan (1991) suggested, for example, that the "fetishist brings a misperception of anatomical difference to the theme of absence and presence that belongs to early infancy" (p. 73).

CONTRIBUTION TO A FEMALE GENITALITY: TRANSITIONALITY OF MASCULINITY AND FEMININITY

The concept of genitality, which the classic psychoanalytic literature posits as the provocative and rather utopian culmination of psychosexual development, can be reexamined. Although the idea of a genital stage has largely been relegated to the archives of classical psychoanalytic thought, it can still help to deepen our understanding of adult femininity and to address the psychoanalytic problems of polarities, such as homosexuality and heterosexuality, and conformity.

As Benjamin (1988) suggested, we have come to realize that psychoanalytic theory's failure to elaborate a postoedipal stage is powerful testimony to the theory's limits. In addition, Chodorow argued for the necessity to articulate—as we have already done with the development of various homosexualities and perversions—a clinical and developmental account of the various heterosexualities. We have, in Chodorow's (1994) observations, been blind in theorizing about the variations and complexities in heterosexuality and have assumed masculine and feminine to be single rather than multiple, owing in part to the overarching division of sexual orientation in our culture.

The classical conception of the genital stage has always implied a postoedipal resolution of gender polarities and object love, but the idea has never been extensively developed. Novey (1955) argued that in Abraham's (1926) understanding of the capacity for postoedipal ambivalence, relatedness toward the partner was part and parcel of the psychoanalytic ideal of the genital character, but the lack of theoretical differentiation between heterosexual functioning and genitality (Hershey 1989, Ross 1970) has opened this sketchy aspect of psychoanalytic theory itself to infantile fantasies of a gendered polarity. Most relevant to this discussion are Ross's questions about the achievement of genital levels in the face of immature functioning in object relations and ego development. The impossibility of maintaining a true symbolic functioning, in which symbols are always differentiated from what is symbolized, is reflected in the difficulty that we have as theorists and clinicians in staying with the metaphoric and symbolic relation to the body in our writings and readings about the clinical data of our patients.

The rather sketchy classical model assumes that in the genital phase proper, cross-sex representations are conceded to the Other for gender consistency. It is thought that in many traditional heterosexual relationships, this loss of the bisexual fantasy is assuaged by the exchange of cross-gender and cross-sex behavior. Bergman (1988), for example, suggested that love could be seen as the benign outcome of the bisexual conflict: to find one's other half in the safety of a heterosexual relationship frees one from the need to repress countergender wishes. In addition, Kernberg (1991) has written extensively on the dynamics of the couple, suggesting that a function of coupling is an "attempt to overcome boundaries between the sexes" (p. 58) as well as a "repository of both partners' conscious and unconscious sexual fantasies and desires" (1993, p. 653). Yet the discovery of the repressed in the Other, while appearing to provide what one lacks oneself, can result in each partner's relating primarily to her or his projective identifications. Thus, neither person can understand the other's experience (Goldner 1991). In this normative mind, then, repudiation of opposite-sex characteristics within the psyche, while fueling the fire of erotic desire for the Other, also contributes to the antagonism of the interpersonal relationship between the sexes. The female's passive surrender of her masculine components to her male partner may result in an unconscious, coercive enlistment of the male lover to portray a role in her unconscious fantasy. As Lord (1991) eloquently stated, "Male libidinal objects [are asked] to perform what should be an inner symbolic function." The Other cannot really be imagined or loved as a subject if he or she is asked to provide a sense of the completeness of one's own self (Benjamin 1988, 1990, Goldner 1991).

The project of articulating a route to the transcendence or breakdown of gender polarities has been a major task of Benjamin (1988, 1990, 1991). In her understanding of intersubjectivity, the transcendence of opposites occurs through the reformation of the relation between them. Her deconstruction of the polarity between difference and Otherness with respect to identification has also illuminated the difficulties psychoanalytic theory has in understanding what allows us to love the Other not merely as an object but as a subject.

The endeavor to understand "difference without constituting an opposition" (Gallop 1982, p. 93) has led me to articulate a mature genital-stage female organization that is an alternative to the traditional heterosexual either-or of phallocentric logic. This organization posits transitionality as a central aspect of the female genital-stage psyche.

Gender polarity might usefully be seen as a stage-appropriate fantasy—a concept extrapolated from Grossman's (1982) notion of self as fantasy—necessary for the development of self-identity, object relations, and social requirements, but requiring transcendence later in development. Polar gender identity, perhaps even a rather rigid gender identity, as Lasky (1989) has discussed, has its functions in development, providing needed stability, consistency, and differentiation. Recalling Goldner's (1991) provocative description of gender as not only a solution but also a problem, however, we may clinically understand rigid gender identity in postadolescent life as a defensive character structure, an unfortunate fixed solution to a conflict.

GENDER AS CHARACTER

Baudry (1989) commented that when one approaches an understanding of the problems of masculine and feminine sexuality, one is close to understanding character. Identity, as May (1986) observed, can be a sustaining delusion when it is used as a protection against the various conflicting wishes and aspects of the self. Yet this protective identity, which may serve to smooth over contradictory inner wishes and fantasies, can also lead to shame and doubt. Kaplan (1991) argued that socially normative gender stereotypes serve to mask cross-gender wishes and desires. She further proposed that female perversions reflect distress in coming to terms with this underlying inconsistency. Character as a solution to conflict may situate itself primarily through modes typical of that organ on which they are organized. (Here we may apply, for example, Erikson's [1968] description of the female's receptive way of holding and of the forceful linearity of the male.) Yet heterosexual functioning that fixates on one organ mode or one gendered identification at the expense of the other can result in an impoverishment. Although culturally "normal," such rigid gender roles may involve a developmental arrest or a defensive character structure.

NOTES TOWARD A REFORMULATION OF A MALE GENITAL STAGE

I have focused on the female mind in this discussion, but the exploration of the relation between genitality and transitionality may be equally usefully applied to male development. Although one might suspect that playful cross-symbolization symmetrically applies to "normal" male gender identity as well, the parallel set of challenges for male development is beyond my supporting clinical data at this time. I can provide only a brief clinical illustration of its parallel potential in men.

A male patient who prided himself on female conquests, associated to being force-fed during a physical illness in childhood. Later in his treatment he recalled feelings of passivity, helplessness, and intrusion in relation to this event and his latest lover's ambivalence over his foreplay style. He had finally understood the difference between waiting for her to want him and forcing his way in. Thus, he was able to tell her that she should lead more during lovemaking. The availability of an experience of force-feeding, which he used as a model of a feminine experience that he needed to master, allowed him to empathize with his lover and to modify their lovemaking.

Many analysts have noted that female sexuality has greater latitude to accept masculine aspects than masculine sexuality has to accept female aspects (Blos 1979, 1985, Harris 1987, Wisdom 1983). Lacan's work suggested that the male, who has always been associated with "having it" (because of his penis), is in fact more susceptible to confabulating the literal and the symbolic. This would make his entrance into the symbolic use of cross-sex representations that much more difficult. Winnicott (1988) as well commented on how female sexuality calls upon pregenital aspects in a way that male sexuality does not. In light of the undue synonymity between genital organization and the male phallic stage, however, a fuller understanding of the symbolic integration of early bisexual representations in the male lies dormant in our limited theoretical organizers. Gallop (1982) postulated that phallic order suppresses not only femininity but masculinity, pointing to a footnote in Freud's writings (1923) in which he muses on how remarkable it was that a small child could be so uninterested in the other part of male genitals, the little sac and its contents. Subsequently, others, such as Bell (1968) and Kestenberg (1968), elaborated on the boy's interest in his scrotum and the elaboration of his feminine components in his psychic development. Stressing the differences that inner and outer genitals play in the development of male and female children, Kestenberg also implied that boys go through a feminine stage. The awareness of this inner genital stage is terminated by a repudiation of the inside, which Kestenberg argued is required for the phallic stage. Later in development, however, with the onset of male emissions, there is proof of the existence of an inner genital structure, and the opportunity for reintegration is possible.

CONCLUSION

The polarization between core gender identities, the biological sense of being female, and the ability to symbolize freely and draw upon cross-gender fantasies and representations do not signify obligatory choices. The physical impossibility of cross-sex behavior does not prevent the mind from playing with reality, symbolizing, and creating imaginative and empathic identifications. Symbols serve as intrapsychic bridges between rigid gender polarities, and help the self reconcile the dilemma of bisexuality and of fantasies of castration and other limitations without recourse to repression or perversion. The troublesome resolution of bisexuality as a rigid, one-sided sexual identity contributes to the phenomenology of gender as dualistic and based on repression, splitting, and projection. The alternative is the possibility of a more mobile, flexible sexuality under the control of a symbolizing ego.

Freedman (1985) proposed that the formation of symbols reflects a psychic structure in which antagonistic component wishes, previously held apart by splitting, are assimilated in a new context. When one side of a polarized conflict is not brought into awareness in symbolic form, or united through an image, projective identification occurs, such as the perception of the Other as castrated or as dominating phallus. In the model I am suggesting, however, it is crucial to understand that cross-sex representations are developed and facilitate the capacity to know the Other as a mutual subject.

Entrance into this female genital stage requires integration, acceptance, and symbolic elaboration of the body-ego genitals of both sexes within the psyche. To the extent that a woman cannot call upon her early overinclusive body-ego experiences and use them in playful symbolic representations, a vaginal world, her inner generative space, or an empty hole will dominate her. Finding herself surrounded only by this vaginal world, she forecloses a true object relationship with a man.

For the female, the wishes and activities of her male counterpart, such as the desire to penetrate, must be familiar desires. The tender feelings of mature relationships require temporary empathic identifications. Cross-sex representations assist in the construction of an inner image of the lover, an image like a flexible working hypothesis, open to amendment through feedback and observation. As Freedman (1985) remarked, the "familiar is found in the unfamiliar." The resolution, integration, and acceptance of physical impossibility need not impair the mind's ability to symbolize, to make imaginative elaborations and empathic identifications. Accepting biological reality does not preclude a transcendence of that reality in fantasy and play.

The mastery and symbolic use of cross-sex identifications contribute to the ability to play beyond gender-normative structures, as in the musician's ability to improvise after mastering the basic musical technique. In this context, one can know but can supersede the reality of one's gender-specific identifications and overinclusive body-ego representations, as a jazz musician can play on tempo and as a dancer must respect gravity and space but is not tied to them.

REFERENCES

Abraham, K. (1926). Character formation on the genital level of libido development. *International Journal of Psycho-Analysis* 7:214–232.

Aron, L. (1991). *The internalized primal scene*. Paper presented at the New York University Post-Doctoral colloquium, October.

Bassin, D. (1982). Woman's images of inner space: data towards expanded interpretive categories. *International Review of Psycho-Analysis* 9:191–203.

Baudry, F. (1989). Character, character type, and character organization. *Journal of the American Psychoanalytic Association* 37:655–686.

Bell, A. I. (1968). Significance of scrotal sac and testicles for prepuberty male. *Psychoanalytic Quarterly* 34:182–191.

Benjamin, J. (1988). *The Bonds of Love*. New York: Pantheon.

——— (1990). An outline of intersubjectivity: the development of recognition. *Psychoanalytic Psychology* 7(suppl.): 33–46.

——— (1991). Father and daughter: identification with difference—a contribution to gender heterodoxy. *Psychoanalytic Dialogues* 1:277–299.

——— (1995). *Like Subjects, Love Objects*. New Haven, CT: Yale University Press.

Bergman, M. (1988). Freud's three theories of love in the light of later developments. *Journal of the American Psychoanalytic Association* 36:653–672.

Bernstein, D. (1983). The female superego: a different perspective. *International Journal of Psycho-Analysis* 64:187–201.

———— (1990). Female genital anxieties, conflicts, and typical mastery modes. *International Journal of Psycho-Analysis* 71:151–165.

———— (1991). Gender specific dangers in the female/female dyad in treatment. *Psychoanalytic Review* 78:37–48.

Blos, P. (1979). The genealogy of the ego ideal. In *Adolescent Passage*, pp. 319–369. New York: International Universities Press.

———— (1985). *Son and Father: Before and Beyond the Oedipus Complex.* New York: Free Press.

Boehm, F. (1930). The femininity complex in men. *International Journal of Psycho-Analysis* 11:444–456.

Breen, D., ed. (1993). *The Gender Conundrum.* London: Routledge.

Butler, J. (1994). Against proper objects. *differences: A Journal of Feminist Cultural Studies* 6(2–3):1–26.

Chertoff, J. M. (1989). Negative oedipal transference of a male patient to his female analyst during the termination phase. *Journal of the American Psychoanalytic Association* 27:687–713.

Chodorow, N. (1994). *Femininities, Masculinities, Sexualities: Freud and Beyond.* The Blazer Lectures for 1990. Lexington: University Press of Kentucky.

Dimen, M. (1991). Deconstructing difference: gender, splitting, and transitional space. *Psychoanalytic Dialogues* 1:335–352.

Erikson, E. (1950). *Childhood and Society.* New York: Norton.

———— (1968). Womanhood and the inner space. In *Identity, Youth, and Crisis.* New York: Norton.

———— (1982). *The Life Cycle Completed.* New York: Norton.

Fast, I. (1984). *Gender Identity: A Differentiation Model.* Hillsdale, NJ: The Analytic Press.

Fonagy, P. (1991). Thinking about thinking: some clinical and theoretical considerations in the treatment of a borderline patient. *International Journal of Psycho-Analysis* 72:639–656.

Foucault, M. (1978). *History of Sexuality, Vol. I.* New York: Random House.

Freedman, N. (1985). The concept of transformation in psychoanalysis. *Psychoanalytic Psychology* 4:317–340.

Freud, S. (1915). Instincts and their vicissitudes. *Standard Edition* 14:109–140.

———— (1923). The ego and the id. *Standard Edition* 19:3–63.

Gallop, J. (1982). *The Daughter's Seduction: Feminism and Psychoanalysis.* Ithaca, NY: Cornell University Press.

Goldner, V. (1991). Toward a critical relational theory of gender. *Psycho-analytic Dialogues* 1:249–272.

Grand, S. (1982). The body and its boundaries: a psychoanalytic view of cognitive process disturbances in schizophrenia. *International Review of Psycho-Analysis* 9:327–342.

Grossman, W. I. (1982). The self as fantasy: fantasy as theory. *Journal of the American Psychoanalytic Association* 30:919–929.

Grossman, W. I., and Kaplan, D. (1988). Three commentaries on gender in Freud's thought: a prologue to the psychoanalytic theory of sexuality. In *Fantasy, Myth, and Reality*, ed. H. P. Blum, Y. Kramer, A. K. Richards, and A. D. Richards, pp. 339–370. New York: International Universities Press.

Harris, A. (1987). Women in relation to power and words. *Issues in Ego Psychology* 10:29–38.

Hershey, D. W. (1989). On a type of heterosexuality and the fluidity of object relations. *Journal of the American Psychoanalytic Association* 37:147–172.

Horney, K. (1926). The flight from womanhood. *International Journal of Psycho-Analysis* 7:324–339.

——— (1933). The denial of the vagina. *International Journal of Psycho-Analysis* 14:57–70.

Irigaray, L. (1985). *Speculum of the Other Women*, trans. G. C. Gill. Ithaca, NY: Cornell University Press.

Jacobson, E. (1964). *The Self and the Object World*. New York: International Universities Press.

Jones, E. (1935). Early female sexuality. *International Journal of Psycho-Analysis* 16:459–472.

——— (1938). Theory of symbolization. *Papers on Psychoanalysis*. Baltimore: William Wood.

——— (1942). The concept of a normal mind. *International Journal of Psycho-Analysis* 23:1–12.

Kaplan, D. (1990). Some theoretical and technical aspects of gender and social reality in clinical psychoanalysis. *Psychoanalytic Study of the Child* 45:3–24. New Haven, CT: Yale University Press.

Kaplan, L. J. (1991). *Female Perversions*. New York: Doubleday.

Kernberg, O. (1991). Aggression and love in the relationship of the couple. *Journal of the American Psychoanalytic Association* 39:45–70.

——— (1993). The couple's constructive and destructive superego functions. *Journal of the American Psychoanalytic Association* 41:653–678.

Kestenberg, J. (1968). Outside and inside, male and female. *Journal of the American Psychoanalytic Association* 16:457–519.

———— (1975). From organ-object imagery to self and object-representations. In *Children and Parents: Psychoanalytic Studies in Development*, pp. 215–283. New York: Jason Aronson.

Kubie, L. (1974). The drive to become both sexes. *Psychoanalytic Quarterly* 43:349–426.

Lacan, J. (1953). Some reflections on the ego. *International Journal of Psycho-Analysis* 34:11–22.

Lasky, R. (1989). Some determinants of the male analyst's capacity to identify with female patients. *International Journal of Psycho-Analysis* 70:405–418.

Layton, L. (2001). The psychopolitics of bisexuality. *Studies in Gender and Sexuality* 1:41–60.

Loewald, H. W. (1988). *Sublimation: Inquiries into Theoretical Psychoanalysis*. New Haven, CT: Yale University Press.

Lord, M. (1991). *Women's body, women's self: the contribution of genital representation to the woman's experience of identity*. Doris Bernstein Memorial Lecture, presented at the Institute of Psychoanalytic Research and Training, New York, January.

May, R. (1986). Concerning a psychoanalytic view of maleness. *Psychoanalytic Review* 73:175–193.

McDougall, J. (1980). *Plea for a Measure of Abnormality*. New York: International Universities Press.

Mendell, D. (1988). Early female development: from birth to latency. In *Critical Passages in the Life of a Woman: A Psychodynamic Perspective*, ed. J. Offerman-Zucherberg. New York: Plenum.

Mitchell, J. (1974). On Freud and the distinction between the sexes. In *Women and Analysis: Dialogues on Psychoanalytic Views of Femininity*, ed. J. Strouse, pp. 39–52. New York: Dell.

Novey, S. (1955). Philosophical speculations re: concept of genital character. *International Journal of Psycho-Analysis* 36:88–94.

Ogden, T. H. (1986). *The Matrix of the Mind*. Northvale, NJ: Jason Aronson.

———— (1989). *The Primitive Edge of Experience*. Northvale, NJ: Jason Aronson.

Person, E. S., and Ovesey, L. (1983). Psychological theories of gender identity. *Journal of the American Academy of Psychoanalysis* 11:203–226.

Poland, W. (1984). On the analyst's neutrality. *Journal of the American Psychoanalytic Association* 32:283–300.

Reich, W. (1929). The genital character and the neurotic character. In *The Psychoanalytic Reader*, ed. R. Fleiss, pp. 57–68. New York: International Universities Press, 1948.

Rose, G. (1980). The power of form. *Psychological Issues*. Monograph 49. New York: International Universities Press.

Ross, N. (1970). The primacy of genitality in the light of ego psychology. *Journal of the American Psychoanalytic Association* 18:267–284.

Schilder, P. (1935). *The Image and Appearance of the Human Body*. London: Kegan Paul, French, Trubner.

Schwartz, A. (1998). *Sexual Subjects: Lesbians, Gender, and Psychoanalysis*. New York and London: Routledge.

Segal, H. (1991). *Dream, Phantasy, and Art*. London: Routledge.

White, R. (1963). Ego and reality in psychoanalytic theory. *Psychological Issues* 3(2), monograph 11. New York: International Universities Press.

Winnicott, D. W. (1966). The split-off male and female elements to be found in men and women. In *Psychoanalytic Explorations*, ed. C. Winnicott, R. Shepherd, and M. Davis, pp. 168–182. Cambridge, MA: Harvard University Press.

——— (1971). *Playing and Reality*. London: Tavistock.

——— (1988). Inter-relationship of body disease and psychological disorder. In *Human Nature*, pp. 19–22. New York: Schocken, 1988.

Wisdom, J. O. (1983). Male and female. *International Journal of Psycho-Analysis* 64:159–168.

8

Sameness and Difference: An "Overinclusive" View of Gender Constitution[1]

JESSICA BENJAMIN

The idea of gender development has of necessity been linked to the notion of coming to terms with difference. What has changed in contemporary psychoanalysis is the meaning of sexual difference. Assimilating the meaning of sexual difference(s) and assuming a position in relation to it/them are no longer seen as being triggered by the discovery of anatomical facts. The way in which perceptions of anatomy and the body come to *figure* difference is now a matter for further exploration. Psychoanalytic assumptions about the character of gender difference, however, have not been wholly liberated from the naturalizing tendency in Freud's thought, although they exist in a more covert and subtle form: the tendency to view the realization of difference as if it were more significant than, and detached from, the realization of likeness. The implicit assumption in differentiation theory is that acknowledging difference has a higher

---

1. Originally published in *Like Subjects, Love Objects*, pp. 49–79. Reprinted with permission from Yale University Press.

value, is a later achievement, and is more difficult than recognizing likeness. The neglected point is that the difficulty lies in assimilating difference without repudiating likeness—that is, in straddling the space between the opposites. It is easy enough to give up one side of a polarity in order to oscillate toward the other side. What is difficult is to attain a notion of difference, being unlike, without giving up a sense of commonality, of being a "like" human being.

Some time ago Chodorow (1979) suggested that men characteristically overvalue difference and depreciate commonality because of their more precarious sense of masculinity and repudiation of the mother. To conceptualize a tension between sameness and difference, rather than a binary opposition that values one and depreciates the other, is thus part of the effort to critique the masculinist orientation of psychoanalysis. But to deconstruct that binary opposition between sameness and difference—rather than simply to critique the overvaluation of difference or to revalue sameness—requires us to address the problem of identity as well. For the term *identity* pertains in contemporary gender-differentiation theory inasmuch as it equates difference with the boundary between identities. That conception of difference has been criticized in recent feminist thought in favor of a notion of multiple differences and unstable identifications.

To move beyond a discourse of opposites requires the notion of something more plural, decentered, than is implied by the simple axis of sameness-difference, the idea of the one Difference. The notion of a singular Difference as a dividing line suggests that on either side of that line exists identity; everything on that side is homogeneous with everything else. By that logic identity is destiny, like has only to identify with like, and acknowledging difference means respecting the boundary between what one is and what one cannot be. The idea of gender identity implies an inevitability, a coherence, a singularity, and a uniformity that belies psychoanalytic notions of fantasy, sexuality, and the unconscious (Dimen 1991, Goldner 1991, May 1986).

Although I intend to use this critique of identity, I wish to first clarify an essential distinction between identity and identification.

In giving up the notion of identity, reified as thing, one need not (and should not) throw out the notion of identification, as internal psychic process. One need not assume that the process of identification always falls along one side of the axis of sameness-difference. To attend to the process of assimilating differences and of learning to know "the difference," it is not necessary to privilege Difference. To define that process as reflecting the work of culture—that is, as organized by discursive systems rather than by the innate, presocial imperatives of the psyche—does not in itself reveal the complexity of that work. To point out the reification of gender only confronts us with its mysterious persistence as a demarcation of psychic experience that is at once firm and resilient but highly volatile in its location and content (see Harris 1991); like bacteria, gender categories often seem able to mutate just enough to produce resistant strains.

To begin an investigation of identifications that takes the feminist critique into account, let us review some current psychoanalytic thinking about gender development. I will discuss some of the prominent positions in the contemporary theory, which can be traced from Stoller's work on gender identity to Fast's "differentiation model." I want both to make use of this theory and to critique it, at the same time preserving its notable observations and pushing it past the notion of identity. I will follow the axis of sameness-difference and highlight the changes in the contemporary view of the early development of gender identifications.

In presenting this outline, I recognize that feminist theory has raised as many objections to the notion of developmental order as to the idea of identity. But the developmental narrative to which these objections refer is an antiquated oedipal model (circa 1933) that is only one of the stories that inform current psychoanalytic practice. Before subjecting it to criticism, we ought to differentiate the contemporary narrative of gender development from Freud's, or even the later revisions by Stoller. Furthermore, as the category of identification continues to be central to all theorizing about gender, the contemporary narrative on how gender categories take hold in the psyche remains instructive. In the past decade or so, there have been some interesting insights into the formulation of sexual difference outside the oedipal structure. These insights enlarge our potential understanding of the many identifications and experiences, conscious and unconscious, that exceed the rigid notion of identity. And finally, it is necessary to retain a tie, however elastic, to the observational world in which, whatever we infer about the unconscious, it is apparent that children really do represent and assimilate some things before others, are preoccupied with certain conflicts at one time more than another, as the idea of phase suggests.[2] It is the normative use of this notion, as I shall discuss, that disparages earlier in favor of later. But this disparagement is not logically necessary, any more than is the disparagement of subjects and verbs because they are learned earlier than adverbs, of walking because it precedes skipping.

One previously undervalued, if not denied, aspect of gender development that I will highlight is the coming together of likeness with difference—in particular, the identification with the parent understood to be of a different sex. "Identification with difference," an intentionally paradoxical formulation, is meant to suggest an identification that crosses the line that demarks what we are supposedly like, the boundary that encloses the identical. Theorizing by Fast (1984) shows how children use cross-sex identifications to formulate important parts of their self-representations as well as to imaginatively elaborate their fantasies about erotic relations between the sexes. Fast's (1984) theory of gender differentiation argues that children are initially bisexual, reinterpreting the idea of bisexuality to mean not a constitutional, biological anlage but a position of identifying with both parents (1990). In the pre-

---

2. We may wish to exchange the idea of *phase* as a self-enclosed, exclusive geological layer for a sense that psychic events overlap and recur, are not merely successive but often coincident, are usually known retroactively through appearance rather than in "pure culture." Still, retaining a flexible idea of phase has the advantage of allowing a notion of complexes which, if they do not remain temporally organized after their initial introduction, still retain a structural connection. The idea of development has to be suspended and yet preserved—Lacan, who is often cited by feminist critics, did no less.

oedipal phase children are "overinclusive": they believe they can have or be everything. They do not yet recognize the exclusivity of the anatomical difference; they want what the other sex has, not *instead* of but in *addition* to what they have.

The premise of this differentiation perspective, as will be evident, is virtually the opposite of the position that genital difference is the motor of developing gender and sexual identity (see Roiphe and Galenson 1981). Rather, it embarks from the position, articulated clearly by Person and Ovesey (1983), according to which gender differentiation, evolving through separation conflicts, early losses, and identifications, defines and gives weight to the genital difference, which then assumes great (if not exclusive) symbolic significance in the representation of gender experience and relations. However, my scheme is "overinclusive," rereading critically and integrating many contributions of earlier psychosexual theory.

Stoller (1968), as we know, offered a new conceptualization of the earliest phase of gender development as the formation of core gender identity in the first year and a half of life: a felt conviction of being male or female, which later expands to the conviction of belonging to one or the other group. Rather than referring to this as identity, we might call it nominal gender identification. Perhaps because the conclusions of infancy research were not available to Stoller when he postulated his notion of core gender identity, he was not sure how to formulate a kind of "primordial representation" (Stoller 1973) appropriate to the first year of life. He thought that identification and incorporation were not appropriate categories, for he subscribed to the then-current view in which the mother was considered not yet outside or separate and therefore not able to be taken in. But since Daniel Stern (1985) presented his notions of an infant who begins differentiating mother almost from birth and of presymbolic interaction (representation of interactions generalized or RIGS; see also Beebe 1985, 1988), we can posit a process of nominal gender identification, rather than a product, core gender identity; we can picture this identification as developing through concrete representations of self-body and self-other body interactions, which are retroactively defined as gendered (Fast 1984).

Stoller (1973) by no means postulated core gender identity as a final achievement of masculinity or femininity. He acknowledged that the "sense of belonging to a sex becomes complicated" by later conflicts and fantasies, anxiety and defense, complications that render masculinity and femininity far more ambiguous than maleness and femaleness. Indeed, he argued that only if the male child separates from his mother in the separation-individuation phase—"disidentifies" in Greenson's term—can he develop that "non-core gender identity we call masculinity." He did not offer a full picture of the preoedipal period, however, and both he and Greenson used the notion of disidentification to imply that the male child fully gives up his identification with mother. I hold, rather, that at this point the child still identifies with both parents, who are only beginning to be partially, concretely differentiated. Given this persistence of multiple identifications, the idea that the self identifies as belonging to a sex should not be equated with the idea of an unambiguous and coherent identity. On the contrary, the core sense of belonging does not organize all gender experience. Core or nominal gender identification makes sense only if we conceptualize it as a background for future gender ambiguity and tension, a repetitive baseline against which all the other instruments play different, often conflicting or discordant, lines.[3]

Sometime in the second year of life, particularly with the advent of symbolic representation in the second half of the second year, the next phase of gender constitution begins, at the level of identifications. Person and Ovesey (1983) refer to this as gender

---

3. To make *core* and *nominal* equivalent is, I am aware, highly contradictory, for they are rooted in different metaphors, one geometrical, the other linguistic. Because this early identification figures as unknown quantity, I prefer the idea of "nominal"; but this early identification may, indeed, be central, so I do not wish to prematurely dismiss the notion of "core." Assignment or appellation, moreover, from which we derive the idea of "nominal," may at times be violently rejected as a "false" surface by those who experience their "core" to be other (transsexuals, e.g.)—a phenomenon too compelling to explain away, except to note that other identifications, other early experiences may be equally constitutive of the presymbolic "core."

role identity to distinguish it from core gender identity: masculine or feminine self-image rather than male and female designations. (Again, "gender role identification" would be a better term.) Gender role identity is defined as a psychological achievement occurring in the conflictual context of separation-individuation. Person and Ovesey disagree with Stoller's theorem that boys must separate more than girls, arguing rather that conflict around separation has a gender marker for boys. Coates's work on gender disorder (Coates et al. 1991) supports this critique of Stoller, disputing the notion that transsexuals have difficulty separating from maternal symbiosis. She finds, rather, that maternal withdrawal can inspire a profound melancholic identification, which is manifested as excessive femininity in boys as well as in girls. The upshot of this analysis is to emphasize dynamic issues like separation anxiety or envy rather than to see disidentification from mother as an inherently pathogenic process.

At this same point of early separation, I have proposed, we see before and alongside object love something we might call identificatory love, a love that has conventionally appeared first in the relationship to the rapprochement father (Benjamin 1986, 1988, 1991). Following Abelin (1980), I have stressed that in traditional gender arrangements the father (or other masculine representation) plays a crucial role in representing separation, agency, and desire in the rapprochement phase. In contrast to Abelin, though, I have argued that ideally children of both sexes continue to identify with both parents and that the rapprochement father is therefore as important for girls as for boys. In this phase, the parents begin to be differentiated in the child's mind, but the child continues to elaborate both identifications as aspects of self. Traditionally, the mother, the source of goodness, as Klein put it, is experienced as the complementary other, a precursor of the outside love object, whereas the father is sought as an object to be like. The mother has represented holding, attachment, and caretaking while the father has represented the outside world, exploration, freedom— a "knight in shining armor." This parental constellation has created a distinct structural position for the rapprochement father, a function that may be played by other figures who represent separate subjectivity. Indeed, I would argue that this position is so psychically and culturally important, so distinct from that of the oedipal father, that it persists despite variations in the role and gender of those who represent it.

The function of the father at this point, as Freud (1921, 1925) originally stated and as Blos (1984) and Tyson (1986) have restated, is dyadic, not triadic, that is to say, not rivalrous or forbidding, like the oedipal father. He does not so much represent the one who can exclusively love mother (as the child still imagines doing directly) as he embodies the desire for the exciting outside. What I wish to underscore is the importance of a second adult, not necessarily a male or a father, with whom the child can form a second dyad. The key feature of this person, or position, is not yet that this adult loves the mother and seals the triangle, but that he or she creates the second vector, which points outward and on which the triangle can be formed. Identification with a second other as a like subject makes the child imaginatively able to represent the desire for the outside world.

As a consequence of this representation of desire, the new feature associated with this phase, its legacy to adult erotic life, is identificatory love. Identificatory love remains associated with certain aspects of idealization and excitement throughout life.[4] This identification with the ideal has a defensive function, masking the

---

4. Identificatory love is related to what Freud (1914) referred to in distinguishing narcissistic from anaclitic object choice. Why not use that terminology? If identificatory love *is* love and is a relationship to an outside other, then it is arguably a less "narcissistic" relationship than the anaclitic relation, which "leans on" the ego instincts—that is, the original attachment figure, source of goodness, in Freud's words "the woman who feeds him" (p. 88). In other words, identificatory love first shows up in relation not to "the same" but to "the one who is different from the first." The point Freud got right here was that women engage in "narcissistic"—that is, identificatory—love when they love in a man the ideal self they would have wished to be. But, oddly, he failed to see that this might be less regressive, more exciting, more of an "object love," than loving the person who feeds you.

loss of control over mother that would otherwise be felt intensely at this point. It is a way of sustaining the practicing grandiosity that would otherwise be challenged. But it is not only defensive, insofar as the ideal father serves symbolically to represent longings that the child may one day hope to realize, as well as the freedom, agency, and contact with the outside world of other people that partially compensate for loss of control.

The idea that the child represents her or his own desire by identifying with an idealized figure who is imagined as the subject of desire has wider repercussions. It was on the basis of such a formulation—that the ego constitutes itself by taking the Other as its ideal—that Lacan (1949) argued that the ego is necessarily alienated. It misrecognizes itself in the ideal, in the image of the unified figure in the mirror; it takes the other or an imaginary construct for itself. In this sense the subject is produced, "subjected," at the very moment it imagines it is finding itself. I have suggested (Benjamin 1988) that, indeed, the identification of self with the ideal other constitutes the point of alienation in recognition. But the acts of creating the ideal, forming an identificatory bond, and actively pursuing the relationship with the beloved figure are, in effect, the subject's own. In the experience we call "subject of desire," the subject casts out the line of identification as well as reeling in the other at the end of the hook. It is the casting outward that constitutes desire, and the recognition that both I and the other can do this symmetrically that creates a shared identificatory bond, "like subjects." If the placing of the ideal in the other, a process meant to avoid the conflict of dependency, reinstalls dependency on otherness at the heart of the subject, that is problematic only if we understand the subject to be somehow originally independent, enclosed, and identical with itself. (Or, we could say, proof of this dependency is newsworthy only if one is still crusading against unresolved aspirations to independent identity.) If not, we accept that the activity of identification and identificatory love may give the lie to identity but make possible the position as a subject of desire.

Unlike Abelin (1980), Roiphe and Galenson (1981), and others who have emphasized girls' "castration reaction," I am convinced that identificatory love of the father (or the position of the "second") is important to the girl in her effort to define herself as a subject of desire. This idea is one illustration of the way that *identification with difference* is crucial. The girl, too, needs to use the fantasy of power to inspire efforts to attain a sense of autonomy over her own body and the ability to move into a wider world. Likewise, a girl's identification with so-called masculinity primarily reflects not a reaction to a sense of castration but love and admiration of father.

But the relationship to father has conventionally had a different meaning for boys and girls. Identificatory love of the father figure for boys not only supports separation but also confirms the achievement of masculinity as a naturalized "male destiny." This gives the relationship with father a desperate urgency, often visible in the analytic encounter, as if it were the bulwark of the boy's representation of gender as identity. In patriarchal convention, sons are not only oedipal rivals but are also more important to a father's narcissism. A stronger mutual attraction between father and son is often fostered by the father himself, and this promotes recognition through identification, a special erotic relationship. As I have written elsewhere, the practicing toddler's love affair with the world turns into a homoerotic love affair with the father, who represents the world. The boy is in love with his ideal. This homoerotic, identificatory love serves as the boy's vehicle of establishing masculinity, both defensively and creatively; it confirms his sense of himself as subject of desire. Of course, identificatory love must be reciprocated for identification to stick—it is not loss of love, not asymmetry, but mutuality that furthers this kind of identification. Its baseline is the father's own narcissistic pride, when he identifies with his son and says, "You can be like me," or when the validating mother says, "You are just like your dad."

I should make it clear that the rapprochement father is a kind of first love, but not the one and only paradigm of identificatory love, particularly for girls. Later on, for instance, adolescent girls often develop this sort of love for a woman who represents their ideal, a "second" mother. (Gail Goodwin's novel *The Finishing School* describes a girl's adolescent crush on a woman who represents independence and access to the world, who is meant to compensate for a sexually dependent mother.) And although identificatory love of the father figure, under traditional gender arrangements, has had this special representational meaning, of course the mother remains an important figure of identification for boys as well as girls. Furthermore, although girls know they are female like mother, it is an effort to become feminine like her. Insofar as the rapprochement phase confronts children with the difference between mother's power and their own, between grandiose aspirations and reality, femininity, like masculinity, appears as an ideal, only partly attainable, if not in conflict with affirming one's own desire.

It is also important to repeat that the boy does not need to forgo identification with mother so early unless difficulties in separation lead to an early, defensive repudiation. The child has no sense of mutual exclusivity and does not need to choose between mother and father. As Stoller (1973) pointed out, the boy's preoedipal love for the mother is certainly not heterosexual, it is not, strictly speaking, object love—love for someone different or outside. It is, however, more complementary than identificatory; that is, it is based on interlocking asymmetrical roles that can be reversed. Giver and receiver alternate rather than symmetrically forming "a love of parallels," as Dinesen called her love for Finch-Hatton (Thurman 1981). It is in this sense that mother has traditionally been love object rather than "like subject"—an opposition, as I have emphasized, that need not devolve upon real men and women in the present.

As long as the primary caretaker is the mother—or perhaps even as long as the maternal body is culturally instituted as the essential metaphor of this first relation—this allocation of sameness and difference must initially be the same for both sexes. In this traditional allocation, father has meant the outside object who represents difference. This representation of Difference has been so important, so embedded in the culture, that it usually continues to be effective as an ideal even when a person not defined as father occupies the structural position of "second other."

Let us turn now to the preoedipal, overinclusive phase. What becomes of identificatory love, especially if it is directed toward the sexual other? As we have seen, the positive elaboration of characteristics that may later be yielded to the different other still proceeds through identification with difference. These characteristics depend in part on the parental validation of the identificatory love that informs cross-sex identification. In the preoedipal overinclusive phase, as denoted by Fast (1984), children not only identify with both parents but begin to symbolize genital meanings and assimilate unconsciously the gestural and behavioral vocabulary supplied by the culture to express masculinity and femininity. Now recognizing certain basic distinctions between masculinity and femininity, children continue to try, through bodily mimesis, to imaginatively elaborate both options within themselves. A 30-month-old girl may imitate her older brother's play with action figures in order to assimilate symbolic masculinity, the phallic repertoire of colliding, penetrating, invading, and blocking. A boy of 24 months may insist that he has a vagina, but at 3 years, more aware of external anatomy, he might instead claim to have a baby inside his tummy, elaborating a fantasy of receiving, holding, and expelling. Among the early psychoanalysts, Klein (1928, 1945) most clearly recognized the child's need to identify with and make symbolic use of all the organs and parental capacities, including those fantasized as part of the mother–father interaction.

To the extent that the child imaginatively identifies without yet realizing the impossibility of acquiring certain capacities and organs, envy is not a dominant motive. But gradually the overinclusive period becomes characterized by envy and ongoing protest against increasing realization of gender difference, says Fast (1984). At this point, castration represents for both sexes the loss of the opposite sex capacities and genitals. This protest is not completely symmetrical: for boys the focus is usually on the capacity to bear a baby, whereas for girls the coveted thing is the penis (Fast 1984). But the sexes are parallel in their insistence on being everything, their elaboration of complementarity as opposites held within the self, and their protest against limits.

The oedipal phase, beginning toward the end of the fourth year, might be considered gender differentiation proper, when the complementary opposites are attributed to self and to other, respectively. In other words, the dynamic of renunciation—abandoning hope of fulfilling identificatory love of one parent—might be seen as the road to object love: loving the object as an outside figure who embodies what the self does not, may not, or cannot. But this construction raises an important question about the prevalence of the heterosexual model. Is the radical oedipal separation between love object and like subject equally characteristic of homosexual object choice, or is it a specific feature of heterosexuality? We must ask whether the homosexual positions reflect a simple inversion of the heterosexual: Is the parent of the same nominal gender simply experienced as less the same, or is a different relationship between identificatory and object love formulated? Is not the more complex intertwining of the two tendencies more common than is often supposed?

The delineation I have offered serves primarily to reformulate the notion of how the heterosexual positions are taken up. But it may be safe to say that complementarity becomes the oedipal preoccupation for all children, and the culturally dominant formulation of gender complementarity is internalized as an ideal, however much it may contradict the complexity of the individual's desires and identifications. Complementarity conveys a distance—having rather than being—that carries a possible threat. For to "be" something, to act it in one's own body, is still a crucial mechanism of maintaining closeness. All identifications, especially those that psychoanalysis calls successful, work in this way. By the age of 4, the complementary modality of having—mastery, possession of objects—becomes pervasive, a defense against a barely tolerated loss.

The early oedipal phase (at and just before age 4) is usually more defensive, characterized by a rigid definition of gender complementarity and—as Freud noted of boys but overlooked in girls—by scornful repudiation of the opposite sex. In this phase castration anxiety refers to the loss of one's own genitals, again acknowledged by Freud only for boys. As Mayer (1985) has pointed out, however, the fear of losing one's own genitals is crucial for girls at this point as well and is accompanied by sexual chauvinism, insistence that "everyone must be just like me," fear and repudiation of the other. This chauvinism is characterized by the attitude that, to paraphrase the famous dictum about winning, "What I have is not everything, but it is the *only thing* (worth having)." Freud's theory of phallic monism (Chasseguet-Smirgel 1976) exemplified this dictum perfectly. As Horney (1926) rightly pointed out, Freud's theory corresponds to the thinking of the oedipal boy who believes that girls have "nothing." Envy, feelings of loss, and resentment spur both the repudiation and the idealization of the opposite sex at this point. Sometimes love and longing for the lost other predominate, sometimes rivalry and repudiation.

Conventionally, during the later oedipal phase, the rigid insistence on complementarity and the repudiation of the other are ameliorated (Fast 1984) as the fantasy of object love comes to compensate for narcissistic loss. But oedipal love is both a resolution and a perpetuation of mourning. One cannot yet embody the ideal of femininity or masculinity that mother and father represent, and one cannot yet "possess" the other body in love: one can neither be nor have. In my view, the unaccepted mourning for what one will never *be*—especially the boy's inability to face the loss entailed in not being the mother, even to acknowledge envy of the feminine—has particularly negative repercussions, often more profound and culturally pervasive, if less obvious, than the classically recognized oedipal frustration of not having mother.

Here I want to note an important difference between early identificatory love and later oedipal love identifications. Identificatory love has been wrongly assimilated to the boy's negative Oedipus complex, a linkage that conflates the boy's homoerotic wish to be loved by father as *like* him with the heteroerotic wish to be to father as mother is. These are actually obverse relationships to father. The negative Oedipus, I suggest, represents a movement from identification to object love, paralleling the positive oedipal movement from identification to object love of the opposite sex.[5] However, in the negative oedipal case the boy renounces identification with father, not because of the ineluctable dictates of gender but because of parental impediments to the identificatory paternal bond. In other words, thwarted identificatory love turns into ideal love, a submissive or hostile tie to a powerful, admired father who emasculates the boy rather than confirming his masculinity. This impediment frequently arises when the father is too far outside the mother–child dyad and, prematurely oedipalizing his stance toward his son, is too rivalrous or too afraid of his own sadistic impulses to be tender. This transformation then presents and is often analyzed as a negative oedipal wish for a passive relation with father and falsely conflated with homosexuality.

The "father hunger" shown by sons of absent fathers is primarily a reaction to lack of homoerotic love. In heterosexual men it becomes an impediment to loving women, not simply because there is no role model but because the erotic energy is tied to the frustrated wish for recognition from the father. In cultures dominated by this frustrated father–son erotic, women become valuable not as sources of inner satisfaction but as signifiers of male prowess, as currency in the exchange of power. Frequently, the thwarting of paternal identificatory love pushes the boy to deny his identificatory love of the mother on whom he depends too exclusively, spurring an exaggerated repudiation of femininity.

---

5. Here, too, the question arises as to whether opposite sex means the parent whose nominal gender is different or whether it can be the parent perceived as same. This issue pertains not only to homosexuality. After all, the negative oedipal wish to be loved by father and be like mother is called homosexual, but is a heteroerotic wish. Conversely, the girl's wish to be recognized as a like subject by the father has a strong homoerotic component: sometimes an explicit fantasy of being the son is later expressed in the wish to be the partner to a male homosexual or in a heterosexual love in which she feels she both is one of the boys and loves the boys. In this case, admiring a man is not coded as being feminine, does not mean playing the mirroring role to his phallic power. The real question, as Butler (1990) points out, is whether psychoanalysis leaves room for homosexuality at all—a love that does not mean identifying with the position of opposite sex to the partner.

Then, too, the boy's repudiation of femininity may well represent the next move in a chain that includes the mother's inability to satisfy her identificatory love of her father, which has led her to sacrifice desire and early grandiosity. In her admiration of her son, she unconsciously communicates her feelings as the daughter whose identificatory love of the father became an ideal love of the one she could not be. Perpetuating this ideal love, she projects her desire and grandiosity onto her male child. Thus the boy's gender splitting may be set up before the oedipal, in rapprochement, when an idealized and inaccessible father is paired with a mother who views her son as her ideal masculine self. And so we can reinterpret the sense of Freud's (1933) assertion that a mother's love of her firstborn son was the only unambivalent love. Freud gave the mother a son to love in place of the phallus she could not have. To the mother was granted fulfillment of the wish for identificatory love, not in relation to her father but in ideal love of her son; to the son was given the grandiosity that is mirrored by the mother who renounced it. But Freud's story also bequeathed the son an ideal love—a forever unrequited search for identificatory love of the father who has cast him out as a murderous rival. This may be the great triangle of identificatory love, replayed endlessly in stories of women's submission to and sacrifice for heroes who leave them to follow the quest for the paternal grail, the father's recognition.

The first conclusion I want to draw from the foregoing is that to the degree that the characteristics of the other have been lovingly incorporated through identification in the overinclusive phase, loss can be ameliorated by intimacy; and the sequelae of the oedipal phase can be informed more by other-love than by repudiation/idealization. The acceptance of one's own limits and the ability to love what is different in the other are not compromised by the previous integration of opposite-sex identifications. On the contrary, as Fast suggests, if the individual does not get stuck in the rigid complementarity of the early oedipal phase, the tendency to denigrate what cannot be had may give way to an easier familiarity with opposite-sex characteristics later on.

I diverge from Fast, however, where she insists on the necessity of renouncing what belongs to the other and relinquishing the narcissism of bisexuality. I would rather speculate that elaborating opposite-sex feelings/behavior/attitudes under the umbrella of one's own narcissism persists as a preconscious or unconscious capacity (Aron 1995, Bassin 1994), which comprehends both cross-sex identification and the ability to represent and symbolize the role of the other in sexual relations. For most individuals, this capacity may be a relatively benign form of omnipotence. Aron suggests that it may be more helpful to think of the grandiose, narcissistic aspiration to bisexual completeness as a position that is a source of creativity, as something not to be relinquished but rather to be maintained alongside and modified by the more differentiated positions. Likewise, the wish to attain commonality in the form of identificatory love should alternate with enjoyment of difference in object love. Identification could then be used to ratify sameness and/or to create commonality as a bridge across difference.

The idea that the child renounces the other's prerogatives in the oedipal phase seems to misconstrue gender identity as a final achievement, a cohesive, stable system, rather than an unattainable oedipal ideal with which the self constantly struggles. As Goldner (1991) has pointed out, the relation between the ideal self-representation and actual self-experience is an uneasy tension at best, taxed by rigid and contradictory prescriptions of complementarity. A gendered self-representation is continually destabilized by conflicting mandates and identifications, requiring a capacity for living with contradiction that is in no way culturally supported (Goldner 1991). A psychoanalytic posture requires recognition of these contradictions—the ability, as Harris (1991) has shown, to divine the multiplicity of positions beneath the appearance of singularity in object choice or identifications and to see gender experience as both tenacious and fragile, reified substance and dissolving insubstantial. This posture also means, as Dimen (1991) has argued, deconstructing the reified gender dichotomies and thinking of gender in transitional terms, leaving a world of fixed boundaries with uncrossable borders for a transitional territory in which the conventional opposites create movable walls and pleasurable tension.

The use of a developmental trajectory may seem to imply a telos, and in this case it might be thought that identification is simply the basis for object love, that reaching an oedipal position is the ultimate goal of development, that we need not look any further. Despite my argument for integrating overinclusiveness with complementarity, the alignment of inclusiveness with early narcissism might be misconstrued to privilege later sexual complementarity and object love over early inclusiveness and identificatory love. Such a construction would reflect the pejorative notions about narcissism implicit in some psychoanalytic thinking. Alternatively, the inclusive view could lead to recognizing identificatory love and object love as frequently coincident, rather than as mutually exclusive, and, indeed, could cause mutual exclusivity to appear problematic. From this view follow both a positive revaluing of narcissism and a questioning of heterosexual complementarity as the goal of development.

Thus, as I contended earlier, a developmental view of differentiation need not posit a normative goal of sexual identity, nor must we abandon all empirically based reflections on development to avoid normative positions. The extraction of such positions from notions of development reflects the acceptance of unrelated and unsupportable assumptions: that earlier is more fundamental but later is better (more developed), that development is unilinear, that it is desirable for all conflicts to be resolved and superceded, and that earlier experiences persist like geological layers unchanged by and unalloyed with later symbolic unconscious elaborations. Rather than abandon developmental accounts, psychoanalytic theory needs to decenter its theory of development: later integrations should neither seamlessly subsume nor replace earlier positions but rather refigure them.

If the critique of homogeneous gender development need not foreclose dynamic formulations about the development of gender identifications, it does demand suspicion of theories that assume gender development to be a simple trajectory toward heterosexual complementarity. Even when homosexuality is not directly pathologized, it is presented as a condition that needs to be explained, the object choice whose etiology requires continual and intense investigation. By contrast, as Chodorow (1992) points out, heterosexual object choice is taken for granted, and it is seldom remarked that conventional heterosexuality does not require moving beyond the rigidly organized complementarities of gender polarity. Of course, neither heterosexual nor homosexual relationships inherently guarantee a particular stance toward complementarity or sameness; either may succumb to fixity or play around with convention and previously fixed identities. It is apparent that psychoanalysis as an institution suffers from a significant cultural lag.

Such challenges to oedipal complementarity suggest the need for a reconsideration of the function and meaning of complementarity. What does it mean to posit the integration of the earlier overinclusive position with the later oedipal complementarity in the postoedipal phase? What would it mean to restore, at a higher level of differentiation, capacities that were excluded by oedipal rigidity? I have proposed that object love, which has sometimes been seen as opposed to, exclusive of, or replaced by identification, may also be seen as growing out of identificatory love. But what is the ongoing relationship between object love and identification, what becomes of identificatory love of the opposite sex later in life? Is this a simple proposition—that identification gives way to object love—a kind of reversal of the postulate that object love is replaced by identification in the ego? If not, how to conceptualize the way that identification remains part of love relationships throughout life?

These two sets of questions about the fate of identification and the integration of the overinclusive phase are related. My answer is that sustaining identificatory tendencies alongside object love creates a different kind of complementarity, and a different stance toward oppositional differences. It is possible to distinguish between two forms of complementarity. The earlier oedipal form is a simple opposition, constituted by splitting, projecting the unwanted elements into the other; in that form, what the other has is "nothing." The postoedipal form is constituted by sustaining the tension between contrasting elements so that they remain potentially available rather than forbidden and the oscillation between them can then be pleasurable rather than dangerous (Dimen 1991). Although the rigid form of sexual complementarity may actually utilize a well-elaborated representation of the other's role derived from previous identification, the self repudiates and is threatened by that role as an unwanted part.

As our culture is organized, the child must go through an oedipal period in which complementarity is accomplished by insisting on polarity: mutual exclusivity, black and white, male and female, can and cannot. Using Kohlberg's distinction between conventional and postconventional thinking, we could say that this oedipal polarizing corresponds to conventional thinking about difference, which is appropriate to this stage of children's moral and cognitive development. In Kohlberg's view, postconventional thinking does not develop until adolescence, and this would indeed be the period when we would expect the oedipal recrudescence to resolve with a more differentiated, flexible form of complementarity. In this vein Bassin (1996) has used the terms of genital theory to propose that the phallic phase, with its opposites *have* and *have not*, should give way in adolescence to a true genital phase, in which antithetical elements can be reunited. She proposes that the transcendence of the split unity of gender polarity is expressed through symbol formation, with its transitional bridging function. Unlike projective identification, symbolization reunites the antagonistic component tendencies (Freedman 1980, cited in Bassin 1996)— for instance, active and passive, phallic and containing. Symbolization links rather than prohibits the gratification of both aims, expressing rather than masking the unconscious oscillation between them. The key to this symbolic function is the recuperation of identification with the "missing half" of the complementarity: in symbolization "the familiar is found in the unfamiliar" (Freedman, cited in Bassin 1996).

The familiar can be found by returning to the overinclusive position, in which it was still possible to use the transitional space of communicative play to entertain wishes that reality denies—as when a 3-year-old boy says to his mother, "I have a nipple on my penis, see, and the peepee comes out of the nipple." To pretend that the penis is a breast or that the anus is a vagina need not serve the denial of difference, as theories of perversion have stressed; in response to an earlier version of this essay I have been told of male patients for whom recovery of the fantasy of a vagina resolved unwanted sexual compulsion. Such fantasy play may also serve the symbolic bridging of difference acknowledged and enhance sexual empathy. Development thus requires not a unilinear trajectory away from the overinclusive position but the ability to return without losing the knowledge of difference. The more differentiated postconventional form of symbolic complementarity, which is no longer concrete and projective, requires access to the flexible identificatory capacities of preoedipal life.

This notion of recapturing overinclusive structures of identification and sublimating omnipotence is meant to incorporate the epistemological contribution of contemporary cultural theory, especially feminist theory, by decentering our notion of development and replacing the discourse of identity with the notion of plural identifications. At the same time, this perspective might offer a different kind of developmental and empirical support for contemporary feminist theorizing about gender. The postconventional relation to gender representations need not be seen as a utopian ideal; it is not merely drawn from theoretical speculation but is a material possibility, already visible in the interstices of the gender order. From the perspective of contemporary feminist theory, the problem is that there can be no position outside that order, outside the logic of gender, which constructs masculinity and femininity as binary opposites.

As I have tried to show, the postconventional complementarity, which recognizes the multiplicity and mutuality denied by the oedipal form, does not exist outside the gender system. It reworks its terms, disrupting its binary logic by breaking down and recombining opposites rather than by discovering something wholly different, unrepresented or unrepresentable. It subverts the oedipal complementarity through the leverage of its own negative tension—the impossibility of constituting a complementary system that can exclude all identification with otherness from the self. The postconventional complementarity relies on the psychic capacity to symbolically bridge split oppositions as well as on preoedipal overinclusiveness.

Psychoanalytic theory has, until recently, been unable to think beyond the oedipal level. This fixation is reflected in the prevailing theories that insist on heterosexual complementarity, that equate perversion with homosexuality and "genital whole object relations" with heterosexuality (see Chodorow 1992). The claim that the oedipal achievement of complementarity represents a renunciation of omnipotence and acceptance of limits—being only the one or the other—misses another dimension, the one that gives depth to the delineation of difference. It also serves to conceal the unconscious narcissism of oedipal chauvinism—being the "only thing"—for which Freud's theory of the girl as "little man" *manqué* was exemplary.

The oedipal move that adumbrates the position "I am the one, you are the other," thereby creating the simple form of otherness, is organizing for both sexes. It is overtly hegemonic in the male form but covertly present in its opposite form, female contempt, as Dinnerstein (1976) pointed out. We may choose to speculate that this oedipal move represents a simple reversal of the preoedipal, in which the mother seems to be everything, "generically human" (Chodorow 1979). In any case, the superordinate logic that underlies that move is one of mutual exclusivity, either/or, and it is instituted in the Oedipus complex. This mutual exclusivity is known to us, quite simply, as heterosexual complementarity. In this sense, the joining of heterosexual complementarity and binary opposition (Goldner 1991) in the oedipal moment constitutes "The" sexual Difference.

But the constitution of sexual differences in the multiple sense is not centered around one psychic complex. The reality of sexual differences is far more multifarious than the binary logic of mutual exclusivity allows. The psyche not only unconsciously preserves identifications that have been repudiated, it also expresses them unconsciously or consciously in sexual relations, between parents and children, and between lovers of whatever apparent object choices, imbuing them with far more complexity than this complementarity represents. Oedipal identifications, although pervasive at the level of gender ideals, do not seal off other development, other identifications, even though the theory represents them as doing so; they do not form a seamless, consistent, hegemonic structure that suppresses everything else in the psyche (Goldner 1991). They are, after all, only an organized and powerful set of fantasies.

But for the same reason, no absolute transcendence of the oedipal is possible. Delineating the binary logic of heterosexual complementarity is not equivalent to disavowing or getting rid of oedipal structures. It is no more possible to get rid of the omnipotent aspect of the oedipal position than to get rid of the preoedipal fantasy of omnipotence—or rather, it would be possible only in a wholly omnipotent world, one without loss, envy, and difference. But we can subvert the concealed omnipotence by exposing it, as well as by recognizing another realm of sexual freedom that reworks the oedipal terms. To be sure, this realm depends upon the other face of omnipotence: the overinclusive capacities to transcend reality by means of fantasy, which can be reintegrated in the sexual symbolic of the postoedipal phase.

The tension between the omnipotent wish for transcendence and the affirmation of limits has always found expression in the domains of aesthetic and erotic pleasure. Any effort to destabilize the fixed positions of gender complementarity depends upon the tension between limit and transgression, a limit those positions actually help to frame, a boundary in relation to which symbolic acts achieve their meaning. The knowledge of both nominal gender identification and the oedipal complementarity constitutes a background for the symbolic transgressions of fantasy, for the disruption of complementary oppositions and fixed identities.

The postoedipal complementarity also implies a less definite relation between object love and identification. Freud at one point described identification as the first emotional tie to the object, a way of being related to someone who is there, who is loved and not necessarily lost (1921). He seemingly gave up that idea in favor of identification as an internal process, a precipitate of abandoned, lost, and renounced objects (1923). This supersession, like other moves in oedipal theory, gave away as much as it gained. It probably functioned to turn attention away from identificatory love, the preoedipal period's most important legacy, which contributes to subsequent relationships of love and like. Again, the idea that object love and identification are mutually exclusive is an oedipal product, which neither adequately represents the unconscious relations of desire nor offers a particularly useful basis for bridging the gap between self and other. I see no reason that we cannot be more inclusive and recognize that identificatory love and object love can and do exist simultaneously. Why not see the movements from identification to object love, from object love to identification, as ongoing alternations, often in the same relationship? The unconscious can, as it does with other oppositions, switch and reverse them. The difficulty is to maintain them as tensions rather than breaking them down into split polarities. In postoedipal life object love may include aspects of identificatory love and vice versa. Like difference and sameness, object love and identificatory love constitute a tension that should not be seen as requiring resolution.

Nor are the sides precisely what they have appeared to be within the binary logic of gender complementarity. In that logic of the One and the Other, there is no place for the Both or the Many. If sex and gender as we know them are oriented to the pull of opposing poles, then these poles are not masculinity and femininity. Rather, gender dimorphism itself represents only one pole—its other pole is the polymorphism of all individuals.

REFERENCES

Abelin, E. L. (1980). Triangulation, the role of the father and the origins of core gender identity during the rapprochement subphase. In *Rapprochement*, ed. R. F. Lax, S. Bach, and J. A. Burland, pp. 151–170. New York: Jason Aronson.

Aron, L. (1995). The internalized primal scene. *Psychoanalytic Dialogues* 5:195–237.

Bassin, D. (1996). Beyond the he and she: toward the reconciliation of masculinity and femininity in the postoedipal. *Journal of the American Psychoanalytic Association* 44(suppl.):157–190.

Beebe, B. (1985). Mother–infant mutual influence and precursors of self and object representations. In *Empirical Studies of Psychoanalytic Theories*, vol. 2, ed. J. Masling, pp. 27–48. Hillsdale, NJ: The Analytic Press.

Beebe, B., and Lachmann, F. (1988). The contribution of mother–infant mutual influence to the origins of self and object representations. *Psychoanalytic Psychology* 5:305–337.

Benjamin, J. (1986). The alienation of desire: woman's masochism and ideal love. In *Psychoanalysis and Women: Contemporary Reappraisals*, ed. J. Alpert, pp. 113–138. Hillsdale, NJ: The Analytic Press.

――― (1988). *The Bonds of Love: Psychoanalysis, Feminism, and the Problem of Domination.* New York: Pantheon.

――― (1991). Father and daughter: identification with difference—a contribution to gender heterodoxy. *Psychoanalytic Dialogues* 1:277–299.

Blos, P. (1984). Son and father. *Journal of the American Psychonalytic Association* 32:301–324.

Butler, J. (1990). *Gender Trouble.* New York: Routledge.

Chasseguet-Smirgel, J. (1976). Freud and female sexuality. *International Journal of Psycho-Analysis* 57:275–286.

Chodorow, N. (1979). Gender, relations and difference in psychoanalytic perspective. In *Feminism and Psychoanalytic Theory.* New Haven, CT: Yale University Press, 1989.

――― (1992). Heterosexuality as a compromise formation: reflections on the psychoanalytic theory of sexual development. *Psychoanalysis and Contemporary Thought* 15:267–304.

Coates, S., Friedman, R., and Wolfe, S. (1991). The etiology of boyhood gender disorder. *Psychoanalytic Dialogues* 1:481–524.

Dimen, M. (1991). Deconstructing difference: gender, splitting, and transitional space. *Psychoanalytic Dialogues* 1:335–352.

Dinnerstein, D. (1999). *The Mermaid and The Minotaur.* New York: Other Press.

Fast, I. (1984). *Gender Identity.* Hillsdale, NJ: The Analytic Press.

――― (1990). Aspects of early gender development: toward a reformulation. *Psychoanalytic Psychology* 7(suppl.): 105–118.

Freedman, N. (1980). On splitting and its resolution. *Psychoanalysis and Contemporary Thought* 3:237–266.

Freud, S. (1914). On narcissism: an introduction. *Standard Edition* 14:67–102.

——— (1921). Group psychology and the analysis of the ego. *Standard Edition* 18:67–144.

——— (1923). The ego and the id. *Standard Edition* 19:1–66.

——— (1925). Some psychical consequences of the anatomical distinction between the sexes. *Standard Edition* 19:248–260.

——— (1933). New introductory lectures on psychoanalysis: femininity. *Standard Edition* 22:112–135.

Goldner, V. (1991). Toward a critical relational theory of gender. *Psychoanalytic Dialogues* 1:249–272.

Harris, A. (1991). Gender as contradiction: a discussion of Freud's "The psychogenesis of a case of homosexuality in a woman." *Psychoanalytic Dialogues* 2:197–224.

Horney, K. (1926). The flight from womanhood. In *Feminine Psychology*, pp. 55–70. New York: Norton, 1967.

Klein, M. (1928). Early states of the Oedipus complex. *International Journal of Psycho-Analysis* 9:167–180.

——— (1945). The Oedipus complex in light of early anxieties. In *Contributions to Psycho-Analysis, 1921–1945*. London: Hogarth, 1948.

Lacan, J. (1949). The mirror stage as formative of the function of the I. In *Ecrits: A Selection*. New York: Norton, 1977.

May, R. (1986). Concerning a psychoanalytic view of maleness. *Psychoanalytic Review* 73:175–193.

Mayer, E. (1985). Everybody must be like me: observations on female castration anxiety. *International Journal of Psycho-Analysis* 66:331–348.

Person, E., and Ovesey, L. (1983). Psychoanalytic theories of gender identity. *Journal of the American Academy of Psychoanalysis* 11:203–226.

Roiphe, H., and Galenson, E. (1981). *Infantile Origins of Sexual Identity*. New York: International Universities Press.

Stern, D. (1985). *The Interpersonal World of the Infant*. New York: Basic Books.

Stoller, R. J. (1968). *Sex and Gender*. New York: Jason Aronson.

——— (1973). Facts and fancies: an examination of Freud's concept of bisexuality. In *Women and Analysis*, ed. J. Strouse, pp. 340–363. Boston: G. K. Hall, 1985.

Thurman, J. (1981). *Isak Dinesen: The Life of a Storyteller*. New York: St. Martin's.

Tyson, P. (1986). Male gender identity: early developmental roots. *Psychoanalytic Review* 73:405–425.

9

What Sex Is an Amaryllis?
What Gender Is Lesbian?:
Looking for Something to Hold It All[1,2]

MAGGIE MAGEE AND DIANA C. MILLER

Issues of gender and homosexuality are frequently conflated in contemporary discourse. At the 1995 United Nations Women's Conference in Beijing a quarrel broke out over including even the word *gender* in the conference document, some delegates insisting that gender covers a wide range of meanings, including homosexuality and other permissive lifestyles. In many psychoanalytic discussions homosexuality is the prima facie example of "gender identity disturbance," gender imbalance, or gender deficiency. Gay men are believed to have too much identification with their mothers and/ or too little identification with their fathers; lesbian women are thought to have too much identification with their fathers, and/or too little identification with their mothers. Freud's language in his 1920 "The Psychogenesis of a Case of Homosexuality in a Woman,"

1. We are grateful to Donna Bassin, Adrienne Harris, Virginia Goldner, and Muriel Dimen for their help in untangling organization and conceptual muddles.

2. Originally published in *Gender and Psychoanalysis* 1:139–170. Reprinted with permission from International Universities Press.

expresses several still common assumptions: "She forswore her womanhood and sought another goal for her libido. . . . She changed into a man and took her mother in place of her father as the object of her love" (pp. 157, 158). Joyce McDougall (1989) described "sexual identity formation and its inversions," called homosexuality a "deviation in gender identity," asserted that homosexuals "refuse the sexual role that society attributes to masculine or feminine identity" (p. 206), and saw homosexual object choice distinguishable from heterosexual object choice by its distinctive oedipal dynamics.

> [T]he heterosexual oedipal crisis . . . involves, among other important factors, the wish to possess in the most literal sense of the word the parent of the opposite sex while wishing death upon the same-sex parent. But there is also the homosexual oedipal drama which also implies a double aim, that of *having* exclusive possession of the same-sex parent and that of *being* the parent of the opposite sex. [p. 206]

In this model you can either *be* a woman or you can *desire a woman*. Since to desire a woman is something men and boys are supposed to do, a woman who desires a woman has a gender identity disturbance. Increasingly, critics of various theoretical persuasions and disciplines challenge formulas that split some desires from identifications and inextricably link other desires and identities (Benjamin 1988, 1991, Butler 1990, 1993, Dimen 1982, 1991, Fausto-Sterling 1994, Flax 1990, Garber 1992, Goldner 1991, Harris 1991, Hubbard and Wald 1993, Keller 1985, Laqueur 1990, Longino 1990, Schafer 1974, Sedgwick 1990).

Psychoanalytic developmental models are clumsy tools with which to examine subjectivity. In these models the psyche resembles a heterosexual family album, filled with familiar freeze-frame portraits: baby and mother, child and mother, child and father, mother and father and child. Clinical work, however, reveals psychic experience to be a matter of multiple exposures, the products of fantasy's shaping of memory's distortions of multiple experiences with persons who differ over time. The varying intensity and clarity of these psychic registrations are determined by relational experiences both satisfying and frustrating, by acute traumatic exposures, by affects and intrapsychic conflicts (see Lansky 1989, pp. 27, 38 for a similar photographic metaphor about psychic representation). Genital anatomy is not solely or perhaps even principally the organizer of such amalgamations. Our psyches probably contain multiple and expandable such sets, various aspects of which are called to conscious and unconscious awareness by contextual cues and associated affective states. Virginia Woolf described this psychic situation in *Orlando* (1928).

> "[T]hese selves of which we are built up, one on top of another, as plates are piled on a waiter's hand, have attachments elsewhere, sympathies, little constitutions and rights of their own, call them what you will (and for many of these things there is no name) so that one will only come if it is raining, another in a room with green curtains, another when Mrs. Jones is not there, another if you can promise it a glass of wine—and so on; for everybody can multiply from its own experience the different terms which his different selves have made with him—and some are too wildly ridiculous to be mentioned in print at all. [pp. 201–202]

Psychoanalytic gender theories do not as yet do justice to such textured and contextual experience. In most discussions there are still only a few plates on the psyche/waiter's arm: masculinity or femininity or, at best, that tired old mixed grille, bisexuality. These theories do not help us to appreciate, for instance, how often desires conflict with gender maintenance, (can I be a proper boy in a green room with green curtains?), or how often significant experiences may be gender-free (in a green room with green curtains I might feel serenity or I might feel terror, but little awareness of sex or gender). Instead of capturing the shifting attachments and sympathies that Woolf described, gender and transference discussions often reduce such layered complexities to predictable sets of dramas taking place among archetypal imagoes. As Sedgwick (1990) complains:

> Psychoanalytic theory, if only through the almost astrologically lush plurality of its overlapping taxonomies . . . seemed to promise to introduce a certain becoming amplitude into discussions of what different people are like—only to turn, in its streamlined trajectory across so many institutional boundaries, into the sveltest of metatheoretical disciplines, sleeked down to such elegant operational entities as *the* mother, *the* father, *the* preoedipal, *the* oedipal, *the* other. [p. 24]

Sedgwick's complaint captures a foundational psychoanalytic dichotomy: the division of development into a preoedipal period, dominated by the power and presence of a mother, and an oedipal period, organized around the power and desire of a father. Although there are increasing attempts to include fathers in early developmental schema, these sex-linked divisions support and reinforce sexual polarities in psychoanalytic gender and transference discussions.

CONTRADICTIONS IN PSYCHOANALYTIC
GENDER IDENTITY MODELS

Stoller (1968) challenged Freudian models of development by asserting that sex assignment at birth, combined with conscious and unconscious parental attitudes, led to an unchangeable "core gender identity" established before the child's discovery of the anatomical genital differences. Most psychoanalytic models of sexual development and child observation studies, however, continue to stress the psychological impact of that discovery, although with contradictory, or at least paradoxical, perspectives about the optimal consequences of the discovery. Fast's (1984) differentiation model of gender identity development, itself a formidable challenge to and revision of Freudian theory, sees both boys and girls as "overinclusive in their early experiences, not aware of limitations inherent in being of a particular sex" (p. 19). The developmental task for both boys and girls becomes the management of the sometimes painful awareness of each sex's limitation. Although Fast does not explicitly address homosexuality, her model can easily be used to support the assumption that mature gender identity (heterosexuality) involves choosing an object who has achieved an equally monosexual, and opposite gender identity. McDougall (1989), for instance, describes what happens following the discovery of the anatomical genital difference:

> [T]he genital suddenly becomes an object that can be pointed out and named, and that marks you as belonging ineluctably to one clan only and excluded for ever from the other. . . . Much psychic work is required in order to carry out the task of mourning that will eventually allow the child to accept the narcissistically unacceptable difference and assume its monosexual destiny. [p. 205]

Coexisting (sometimes in the same theorist) alongside the assumption that psychological maturity results in the attainment of a *monosexual identity* is a contradictory psychoanalytic perspective in which optimal gender development (at least in a heterosexual person) derives from the achievement of an internal *mix* of sexual identifications, an achievement believed essential for mature object relationships as well as creativity. From this position McDougall (1989) stresses the "importance of different identifications with *both* parents that essentially structure the sense of sexual identity for all children" (p. 206). Ogden (1987) believes that a monosexual choice can lead to rigid inauthenticity. "[H]ealthy gender identity . . . occurs when one does not have to choose between loving (and identifying with) one's mother and loving (and identifying with) one's father" (p. 496).

Mahler and colleagues (1975) emphasized a father's importance as the first object outside the supposedly "symbiotic" maternal-infant orbit. Actually, Mahler did not include fathers in her observations, and her colleague Abelin (1980) concluded, after his observation of one little boy and his younger sister: "Before rapprochement, the father remains a peripheral, if exciting, object for the girl, tinged with eroticized stranger anxiety. By contrast, he has become the primary attachment object for the boy" (p. 158). Abelin had hypothesized that early triangulation (child/mother/father) set in motion the rapprochement phase. "In this respect, however, I found more than I had bargained for. Although the father emerged so clearly as an object of deep and specific attachment during the first two years of life, so did siblings and other children, grand-parents, and various other familiar adults" (p. 155). But Abelin did not include the significance of this observation in his conclusions. In place of the variety and complexity of object relationships and identifications he had observed, he returned to the developmental schematic of mother/father/child triangulation and maintained that it reflected "an inner blueprint for epigenetic development . . ." (p. 165).

Developmental and gender theories that hold fast to polari-ties, or to triangularities, are uncomfortable with much cross-sex identification. Freud, Greenson (1968), Stoller (1973), Tyson (1986, 1989), and Green (1987) stress the importance of a father for gender identity development in a boy, helping him disidentify with his mother, a process deemed essential in the male child for healthy gender identity, that is, the prevention of homosexuality. In girls, identification with father has most frequently been seen as a defensive regression from love relationship to identification in order to avoid oedipal anxieties, to avoid psychotic merger with mother, or both (Freud 1920, Jones 1927, McDougall 1980, 1989.) Freud does not mention a father in relation to a girl until she dis-covers anatomical sexual difference and, as a consequence, imme-diately enters her Oedipus complex. Leonard's (1966) discussion of the important identification a daughter may make with her fa-ther considered only oedipal fathers. Spieler (1984) used attach-ment theory to review the developmental and clinical literature and believed fathers were neither "first strangers" nor "first others" but were, from the beginning, significant objects of attachment for girls as well as boys. But she did not suggest that identification might result from this relationship. Ogden (1987) describes a transitional relationship essential for a girl's successful entry into the oedipal period: "the little girl falls in love with the (not fully external) mother who is engaged in an unconscious identification with her own father in her internal set of oedipal object relations" (pp. 488–

489). But Ogden's developmental schema still lacks one love relationship that itself might also provide transition to oedipal relationships and make those relationships more or less traumatic, namely,
any early relationship with a father. Although Tessman (1982) believed that a girl's early relationship with her father does have developmental significance, she did not suggest that a young daughter
identifies with her father. On the contrary, the girl uses her father to
represent difference from self and mother. Tessman did, however,
see fathers as the focus of more than oedipal erotic excitement for
daughters. Fathers are also the object of girls' "endeavor excitement,
which begins during the period of individuation. . . . Unlike erotic
excitement, it is not gender linked, but has to do with the anlage
for autonomy, with growing freedom to experiment with one's
skills" (pp. 236–237).

According to Benjamin (1991), however, both boys and girls
want to identify with father. In the developing mind of the rapprochement child, a father

> represents a different kind of object—a subject—who is not so
> much the source of goodness as the mirror of desire. He repre-
> sents a subject who can want and can act . . . to fill those wants.
> The child gains from him not merely direct recognition through
> approval or confirmation, but recognition through symbolic
> identification with this powerful subject who is his or her ideal.
> [p. 283]

Benjamin maintains that a girl's ability to identify with her father
in this capacity to want, and to act, depends to a great extent on a
father's ability to identify with his daughter, on his ability to feel
and to convey, to his daughter as well as to his son, "This little
person is like me."

Benjamin's concept of agency is not sex linked. And the presence of a parent who is male is not necessary for its development,
although Benjamin (1988) describes the problems that result when
a girl has a male parent who is present enough to serve as Idealized Subject of Desire, but emotionally unavailable or unable to
help the girl establish within herself this identification.

SEXUAL POLARITIES IN TRANSFERENCE LITERATURE: WHERE IS THE EARLY PATERNAL TRANSFERENCE?

A review of the literature on transference reveals the sex and gender polarities and the prohibitions against certain identifications it has inherited from developmental narratives. So powerful is the effect of the developmental dichotomy between preoedipal (maternal) and oedipal (paternal) that discussions of transferences to early fathers do not exist in the literature. Even analysts who specifically focus on paternal transferences discuss only transferences to oedipal fathers (Blum 1971, Chasseguet-Smirgel 1984, Kulish 1984). For instance, Karme (1979) believed that male patients found it difficult to establish such a paternal transference with a female analyst because they feared attack by a "phallic" woman. Goldberger and Evans (1985) suggested that relying on the concept of a phallic woman revealed a "limitation" in the "imaginative repertoire" (p. 307) of a woman analyst. But neither Karme nor Goldberger and Evans included a boy's early relationship with his father in their "imaginative repertoire" of transference possibilities. Several of their male patients reported longing to identity with the analyst, the analyst's work, and the analyst's abilities. Karme, as well as Goldberger and Evans, interpreted such longings as evidence of a boy's identification with his mother, failing to imagine that their patients' longings, might also be those Freud (1921) saw as characteristic of a boy's (but apparently not a girl's) loving identification with father.

Karme (1993) and Goldberger and Evans (1993) recently revisited paternal transference with female analysts and male patients, but neither reexamination mentioned the possibility of early father–son transferences. Diamond's (1993) male patient told her at the close of their work: "You are my mirror image—I looked at you and saw myself reflected." Diamond believed "the transference imagoes that this patient so eloquently articulated may be conceptualized as a movement from the preoedipal maternal through the oedipal paternal to the erotic maternal transference" (p. 206). Diamond does not imagine herself in the transference as also an early father, another self-reflection mirror.

Transference discussions of women patients and female therapists generally focus on mother–daughter relationships. Early maternal transference and transferences to an envied oedipal mother are examined. Pregenital erotic maternal transference and countertransference are explored (Wrye and Wells 1994). Paternal transferences are assumed to be toward an oedipal father (Blum and Blum 1986, Kulish 1984, Lester 1990, Meyers 1986, Person 1985). Ogden (1987) describes a particular countertransference impediment in the treatment of female patients by female analysts. "[A]rising from the inadequacy of the transitional oedipal relationship is an inability on the part of the female therapist to engage in a relatively unconflicted identification with her own father in her unconscious set of oedipal object relationships . . ." (p. 494). But Ogden does not suggest that a female therapist must also engage in a relatively unconflicted identification with an other-than-oedipal father.

Bernstein (1991) attributes women's difficulties recognizing paternal transferences to the problem women therapists have in seeing themselves as "penetrating," another oedipal catchword. Meyers (1986) also sees women therapists at risk for missing paternal transference.

> All significant early object relationships are reexperienced in a new version in the transference; all unconscious fantasies are transferred onto the analyst, so that at one time or another the analyst is reacted to as a father, mother, brother or sister, regardless of the actual gender of the analyst. A frequent problem indeed is that this is overlooked. The oedipal father image behind the maternal figure is often missed in the transference with the female analyst. [p. 165]

But Meyers's list of "all significant early object relationships" does not include an early father–daughter relationship or any transference manifestations of such a relationship. Similarly, Person (1985), who described how a woman's erotic oedipal transference could mask an early maternal transference, does not mention the possibility of any early paternal transference in her women patients. Even Lester (1990), who has specifically pointed out the difficulty women analysts have experiencing paternal identifications, discusses only the complexities of the maternal transferences and of the transferences toward oedipal fathers.

But we must heed Sedgwick's warning. Although Benjamin's descriptions of both girls' and boys' desires for an identificatory love relationship with a father early in development may help us find missing aspects of development and may enlarge our imaginative repertoire of transferences, we must avoid creating yet another sveltly elegant portrait for the family album: *the preoedipal father*. We are not interested in adding yet another static archetype to existing developmental dramas. We are interested in examining how polarized sex and gender paradigms in development and transference theories and their attendant prohibitions against, and anxieties about, certain cross-sex identifications impact clinical treatment. In the following clinical illustrations two patients, in their parting gifts and dreams, demonstrate how important cross-sex identifications contributed to their gender and sexual insecurities and to their analyst's clinical confusions.

Richard

The son of socially prominent and narcissistic parents, Richard kept as low a profile as possible. He saw himself as a "worker bee" who toiled for the good of the family. An intellectually gifted and wealthy man, Richard appeared to the world, as he had to the referring physician, as "a shy graduate student who works somehow in his father's business." During treatment Richard moved from existing in a state that he termed "semi-suicide" to a life in which he could more fully claim his feelings, assets, and relationships.

We explored Richard's relationships and identifications as they manifested in transference. Sometimes I (MM) was the grandmother who had cared for him from early infancy. Sometimes I was Richard's mother who managed her anxieties through compulsive neatness. My carpets or couch might get stained with Richard's spills of messy neediness. Richard worried about his extraordinarily highly developed ability and need for attending to others. He identified with a title on my bookshelf, *Dutiful Daughter*. "Am I gay?" he wondered, caught in that gender thicket where nurturing care and attentiveness to feelings=feminine=homosexual male. Richard was initially elated and relieved by his strong sexual desire in his second marriage. But the new potency was soon threatened by his preoccupation with his wife's menstrual periods and by his fear, during sexual intercourse, that she had forgotten to use her diaphragm. He kept a mental calendar of her cycle, and was surprised at my comment that all men did not know the exact state of their wife's menstrual cycle. Finally it became clear that it was not his wife's protection that worried Richard; it was his own. At the height of male potency, and in the intimacy of sexual intercourse, he thought about diaphragms because he was afraid of losing control and "opening" himself.

As Richard became more comfortable with sexual potency and emotional vulnerability, he began to explore new creative enterprises in his business and social worlds. These movements would, in turn, bring new anxieties. And at every step he took away from being an asexual worker bee, he reworked his fears that I (in the transference his oedipal father) would disapprove and threaten: "Don't get too big for your britches."

In the last year of treatment Richard became interested in Robert Bly and the men's movement. He organized a group for fathers and sons at his children's school and an adult drama group in which he could revive some talents given up in his first marriage. He was aware of his positive transference to the leader of his men's group and that he was consciously redoing some steps in his development, namely, forming male friendships, developing his physical potential through sports, and enjoying the admiring attention of women. Although his father died without Richard's having experienced any significant change in their relationship, he cherished his few memories of their closeness.

Richard had never been able to give presents to loved ones at Christmas or other occasions, leaving this task to his secretary. He feared that he had nothing to give, and that what he might offer would arouse the receiver's envious attack. In the last month of treatment he spoke several times of having a parting gift for me. He said he had known for some time what he wanted to give to me. "I just hope I have the courage to do it." In one of his last sessions he brought the gift, a painting of a Native American shaman standing alone against a night sky, his blanket around him, a medicine wand in his hand, a buffalo skull at his feet. His head is uplifted, and his eyes are closed, envisioning other realities. "This figure moves me. He is me. He is you. I hope you aren't upset that it's a man, or that I think of you this way. He is all of us who take this way, who make this journey, this search. This painting was my father's. I knew when he died that I might want to give it to you. It represents for me us, you and me, and what we've been doing together."

Through his gift Richard enabled me to see his most vital internal object relationships, identifications, and transferences. Ogden might see the shaman as a transitional or paradoxical figure, a father-wrapped-in-a-mother blanket, a bridge of identification for a boy as he makes his journey of development. Another image in this symbolic multiple exposure may be Richard's grandmother, whom he lost at nine years, the same number of years he has spent with me. Richard identified the shaman with his father, a longed-for and idealized figure with whom he also wished to identify, a relationship he had also needed in order to find his way and make his journey. The needs and desires for this relationship, which Richard worried that I, like his father, could not see and accept, had provided much of the positive motivation in his treatment. I had recognized his identifications with his mother and grandmother; I had interpreted his expectation of his narcissistic and oedipal's father's attack for his desires and abilities. I had also frequently wondered about my own puzzling lack of envy of this wealthy and powerful man. Instead of envy, I felt a deeply satisfying pleasure in his assets. What was the significance of this countertransference feeling? Sometimes I had assumed my lack of envy must result from his low-profile defense against envious attack, and had made this interpretation. Sometimes, I had assumed that my pleasure in his abilities reflected his wish for an admiring mother, and I had made that interpretation. But like Karme, Goldberger and Evans, and Diamond, I had not been able to imagine myself also as the longed-for admiring *father* of a splendid and admiring son.

Kate's Case

Of her ever busy, constantly-in-motion mother Kate said, "I follow her around like a puppy even now to get her attention." Kate, who seemed indeed often like an out-of-bounds puppy, high-spirited, but "bouncing off the walls," used the analytic relationship to internalize the experience of being "grounded" by a containing object. Kate spoke rarely of her father. She portrayed him as a kind but emotionally inaccessible, somewhat vague figure, usually asleep in front of the TV. Kate saw her brother as "a successful family man," but she believed she and her sister had problems. "My brother just walked in my father's footsteps. My family didn't know what to do with girls." Early in treatment she brought her father a piece of her work and was disappointed with his inability to identify with it. She described the contents of what she called "my case," an "overnight" bag, "train case," or woman's make-up case. She said that her maternal grandmother had had such a case, and had filled it with the medicines for her somatic disorders. Her mother had such a case, filled with the tools of a profession she had been too frightened or conflicted to pursue. "My case has only the odds and ends I've been able to pick up in my few travels."

One particular memory of Kate's illustrates the shattering narcissistic and rapprochement issues that were the focus of much of the analysis. As a young child, she had seen someone eating a soft-boiled egg in its shell. When her mother asked one morning how she wanted her eggs, Kate said she wanted a raw egg. Although her mother told her she would not want to eat a raw egg, Kate, remembering the egg in the shell and not understanding that the egg had been cooked, insisted she did want a raw egg. After several such exchanges, her mother grew impatient: "All right! *Here's* your raw egg!" She shattered the egg shell and dropped its contents onto Kate's plate.

Kate's interpretation of this moment was that she "didn't know the right answer." To protect herself against painful, humiliating shatterings Kate tried to avoid all moments in which she didn't know "the right answer." She searched for gurus, both men and women, who could provide that answer. Kate's fears of making her own choices and expressing her own desires resulted in unsatisfying masochistic passivity and sometimes explosive fury at feeling controlled. She had difficulties with what she called "holding my own," rather than surrendering her desires in her relationship with Margo. To Kate, Margo represented the ability to take pleasure in choosing clothing, make-up, and jewelry, capacities Kate coded as feminine and wished she had more of, as well as the ability to take pleasure in power and competition, capacities Kate gendered as masculine and also wished to make more her own.

Kate worked for several months on a project that she was certain I (MM) would not like and that I would not have chosen to do. She feared that I would "hate" her, that Margo would hate her, that all "feminists" would hate her. She dropped hints about the work that hooked my attention and concern but then refused to discuss her thoughts or feelings further. She had the "ambitendency" (Mahler et al. 1975) of the rapprochement child, the "rapidly alternating desire to push mother away and to cling to her" and "the standing on the threshold" indecision characteristic of the period (p. 96).

Finally Kate and I reached our rapprochement crisis. She brought me a sample of her work, but denied it was "really" her creation, insisting she had only done it to satisfy her male employer. She insisted she felt like a "prostitute" having to do such work for his profit. "Your name is on it. You wanted to do this," I challenged, confused by her ambitendency and frustrated by her disowning her creation.

Instantly I became in the transference the shattering mother who insisted, "You wanted *this* egg. This is what you chose." Feeling misunderstood, hurt, and angry, Kate raged or lay silent in several weeks of sessions. She was sure now that I had never really understood her. She threatened to leave. I interpreted her disappointment that I was not the longed-for guru who could show her how to make a choice that no one would ever disagree with, and her reluctance to acknowledge that her mind and its productions could be different from mine. Kate announced, "I actually feel better now." Shortly after these sessions she set a date for termination.

Although throughout most of the analysis I was occupied with aspects of what I considered maternal transferences, sometimes I would feel, briefly but intensely, that I was a man in the transference, although I could not point to anything that accounted for this feeling. For instance, after a series of sessions in which she addressed her difficulties holding her own with a co-worker, Kate brought me a bouquet of home-grown roses. "These are for you, for these past sessions. You'd be great in business!" Although I sensed that I was a male figure to whom Kate was giving roses, I could not understand why she gave a gift of roses to a man at the moment she felt success in business. What kind of "gender identity confusion" was this?

This moment stood in marked contrast with those in which my sense of being the recipient of male transference projections felt understandable. For instance, while both Kate and her father were undergoing treatments for genital illnesses, psychic surgery and the myth of the Minotaur in the Labyrinth became interwoven metaphors for the analysis. Kate feared that she was like her father and suffered from a "sexual disease." If she liked to have power at work and she loved Margo, did that mean she was too masculine and therefore homosexual? Would "cure" mean she must lose Margo? Kate hated herself for having these confusing thoughts and feared examining them. I was the doctor/analyst/hero/Theseus, equipped with a sword with which I would enter this confusing maze and destroy the monstrous male malignancy inside. Kate was the raging half-bull, half-human Minotaur trapped inside her defensive word mazes and, at the same time, the monster's sister Ariadne, who gave analyst/Theseus the clues to the labyrinth.

As we explored Kate's concerns about her physical disease and her sexual disorder, I gradually realized that she was no longer coming to sessions in the oversized unisex (in other words, men's) clothing that had previously been her style. On my couch now lay a woman whose shapely body had previously been hidden by that camouflage. Kate brought a dream: "I dreamt you gave me a gift. Flute nuts. In a bag. And then you disappeared." Kate was happy about this dream, but had little interest in the flute nuts except to say "they are something you don't usually see in that form. Like cashews in their shells." Although the dream seemed to confirm my countertransference experience of being male, one whose gifts are a phallic flute and nuts in a bag, I did not understand her pleasure in the gift. At the very moment Kate was wishing/fearing psychic surgery to remove some unwanted internal male identifications, she seemed also to be rejoicing in a gift of male genitals. How does a gift of what seems to be male genitals make a woman more comfortable showing off a body she had previously kept hidden? How does a gift of male genitals make a woman feel more comfortable with her sexuality and her sexual choices? Was she wishing/dreaming her way out of penis envy? Were the flute nuts/cashews in shells really seeds in husks or eggs in ovaries?

These moments of receiving flowers or of giving flute nuts were not accompanied by any triangular conflicts. Kate's desire did not seem to be to take mother from father, or father from mother, or did she seem to be complaining that they had one another. And it did not seem that her anxieties about the undeveloped state of her "case" or the "diseased" state of her genitals arose from fears of punishment for oedipal wishes. I could not see her as motivated by a desire for, or envy of, those with a penis; I saw her as more worried that she might have an internal penis which she didn't want. Her wishes for me to help fill her traveling case and her fears of the gynecological/analytic procedures necessary to cure her disease and remove something "abnormal" that had gotten inside suggested fears similar to what Mayer (1985) calls *female castration anxiety*: the fantasized loss of female genitals.

What was the significance of Kate's transformation from unisex/youth to woman, and of my feeling myself to be a pleased, admiring, and admired man in the transference? Did my counter-transference feelings demonstrate Ogden's idea that the oedipal father as love object is first introduced by the transitional figure of the mother-as-father and by the mother's ability to identify with her own oedipal father? Should I understand Kate's lesbian relationship with Margo as a preoedipal defense against heterosexual desires? Did my not making an oedipal paternal transference interpretation collude with such repressed wishes in Kate? Did any of these interpretations fit Kate's case?

Kate had set her termination date for March first. Before she left for a two-week break at Christmas, she gave me a gift she had given me at the beginning of her treatment: an amaryllis bulb. "This is always the perfect gift," she had said on both occasions, expressing an uncharacteristic certainty about her choice. Kate contracted influenza during that Christmas break and was away from sessions for three more weeks. Just as she was about to return, her father died. This left us suddenly with only one month of sessions, the bittersweet culmination of our work. The amaryllis bulb sent up tall green shoots and lovely coral blossoms. In our final weeks together we both watched these graceful symbols of the changes that had taken place in Kate. Watching the transformations of the amaryllis, I found myself musing about the flower as I had about the dream of the flute nuts/cashew seeds. I found I could not settle on the sex of that amaryllis. Out of the round brown bulb a phallic green stem had grown dramatically erect. The amaryllis reminded me of Dylan Thomas's famous identification with flowers: "The force that through the green fuse drives the flower/ drives my blood." The force within the brown bulb had driven through the green phallic fuse of stem, only to transform into vaginal flowers whose petals were spread open, whose erect stamens were pollen-filled. The sexual reproductive anatomy of the amaryllis was vibrantly visible, but even bisexuality seemed a poor description of its arrangements.

Friday of the week before the last week of the analysis Kate brought a dream:

> Two men. One older or bigger. I don't know where they are exactly. There is a frameline at the bottom. Things I can't see. Like I was watching a film. Maybe it's a car or a convertible with the door closed. I couldn't see below the waist. The men are sweaty. There is a leather harness. One says to the other to do something, like 'Hit me.' The other says, 'Okay' But I realize although I thought at first when I looked it was an atmosphere of violence, he wasn't hitting him. He was caressing him. What an odd dream!

"Usually you say something about a dream like this that it's about you and me," Kate prompted. But I was unable to put myself and Kate into the scene as a way of understanding its significance. Kate was asking for a transference interpretation I didn't know how to make.

That weekend, in one of those serendipitous opportunities for analytic learning, still resonating with Kate's dream images, I heard Jessica Benjamin discuss the importance of a girl's identification with her early father. Using Benjamin's (1991) perspective, I thought again about various passages in Kate's analysis. I remembered the difficult weeks before and after she had brought me her work. She had had trouble claiming her own agency and her own choices because of fears about psychological separation. She had not been able to internalize a sense of herself as a person, a Subject, who could want and choose. She and I had explored these disturbances and identifications arising from her relationships with her mother, grandmother, and sisters.

At the same time, however, there were also difficulties associated with her relationship with her father. When she brought her father her work, she felt he could not understand or identify with it. Now I realized how I had also been this father in transference. Since Kate could not feel that she shared agency with her father, she and I had fought over which one of us was the Subject of Desire. She "knew" I did not like such work. Therefore, she experienced my attempts to return agency to her—"This is what *you* wanted. It has *your* name on it"—as her father's rejection. At the same time, since she could not share agency, fathers and employers were felt to demand that she prostitute herself for their pleasure and profit, not her own. As her "feminist" mother, my dislike of the work meant I did not understand or approve of her desire to be loved by the idealized and powerful father; I wanted to keep her from father and his recognition. We had survived the intensities of these overdetermined and sexually split transferences, but Kate was still trying, in the last days of her analysis, to bring to our awareness aspects of an important relationship. One of her attempts had been her Friday dream.

Using Benjamin's perspective, Kate's dream of two male figures, one older, one smaller, could be seen as "A Child is Being Beaten, Revised Edition." Since we can't see "below the waist," at first it seems as if one younger or smaller male is asking to be "hit" by an older, bigger man. There is "an atmosphere of violence." But, it turns out, said Kate, that "he is caressing him." Something has happened to change the "atmosphere of violence" to one of "caress." Kate's wishes to be like her father no longer require harness and punishment. What has happened?

In Benjamin's terms, a loving recognition from a rapprochement father has repaired the humiliation of the wish for mutual identification and removed any need for masochistic ("hit me") solutions to this desire. Kate had attempted to merge herself with idealized gurus because she felt forever other than the Ideal. Merging with an omnipotent object had been necessary because her own capacities to contain anxieties, to calm and self-stabilize, were incomplete. Merging was also necessary because her own capacities to want and to choose were conflicted and incomplete. Over the years Kate had made many comparisons between our ways of working. I had always understood these as arising from maternal identifications. I had thought that her increasing comfort with these identifications had contributed to her increasing confidence about the contents of her "case," that overnight container she needed for her sexual journeys. But Benjamin's concept of an identificatory love relationship with a rapprochement father added another di-

mension of possibilities. It also helped explain the puzzling countertransference experiences of being an admired and admiring male
object. It helped explain the dream in which I gave her a gift of
flute nuts at the time of her most dramatic transformation. "You
gave me the gift and then you disappeared," she had said. A girl
makes a symbolic identification with her idealized father if he is
able to enjoy and encourage that identification. Comfortable with
having internalized this aspect of the Ego Ideal, instead of a defensive, monstrously phallic Minotaur, she can more comfortably display her female body, no longer worried about exposing either
aberrant monstrosity or fragmented "odds and ends."

I had seen Kate's longing for firm containment, and for room
to make her own choices, as longings for a mother-more-attuned,
a mother who herself could sit still and pay attention, able to allow
and support separation and individuation and love for a father.
These were accurate, but not sufficient, transference interpretations.
She and I had also changed "the atmosphere of violence" to one of
"caress" by living out together in transference a longed-for identification with her father.

To the next session, Monday of the last week of her analysis,
Kate brought the following dream:

> I dreamt I was on a bike, racing a car. My mother and my
> little sister were in the car. I thought it was interesting that I
> felt I could go pretty far. Then my bike got hard to pedal. I
> had no first gear. First gear is for starting up. I came to a
> stop. There was an old man in long underwear. I thought of
> my father. We went inside. It was warm inside, poor but
> cozy. I was there for some time. I guess some stuff happened.
> Some movement or something. Then I was in this office. I
> saw my father. I was so happy when I saw him. I said, "Oh,
> look, here's my father." When I said that, he covered up his
> face and pulled away. He said, "Don't do that. Don't say I'm
> here." Because I had pointed him out he was going to
> disappear. I woke up so depressed. I don't know if I've ever
> felt so depressed. I felt so alone. Bereft. I guess it's about my
> father's death. I think he's there and he's not.

The dream narrative contains Kate's depiction of her need for treatment (her vehicle of individuation lacked a gear), what had been helpful in that treatment (a poor but cozy father inside allows movement to happen), and a description of a recent new edition of an old injury (father fearfully denies his presence). This dream was Kate's response to my failure to understand her previous dream of the two men, one smaller, one bigger. She had invited me to make a paternal transference interpretation. My inability to do so replicated for Kate the difficulties she had felt with her father. My response must have felt as if I were covering my face and forbidding her to suggest I was the older man to her younger one. Although through the treatment she had come to think her father was indeed "inside," she had lost him again.

Kate had recently been describing her father's last days. On his deathbed he had told her brother, "You were always the perfect son." Kate had been surprised to hear from her brother that this was the first and only time their father had ever said this, since she had always imagined that her brother and father had had "a perfect father–son relationship." "But," said Kate, "My father was a family man. Beyond what he could say. You felt that." Although as her transference father I had also lacked words, Kate had nevertheless "felt" our mutual pleasure of identification. And we were now, perfect son and father, at my "deathbed," the last week of the analysis. I told Kate that although we had talked much about her feelings toward me as her mother we had not noted enough how she had seen and experienced me as like her father. Kate wept deeply. "That seems so generous of you to say you could be like my father." Her tears expressed her long-standing wish for the recognition from her father that she had always believed her brother, by virtue of his sex, had felt, and her relief with my finally becoming aware of this identification.

Over the next several sessions she eagerly explored the ways I resembled her father for her. "One reason," she said, "that perhaps you as my father have been so in the background here is because, you know, he always was. In the background. It wasn't until he died that I really knew how much he was the anchor, the center around which the family moved. He was still, silent." Kate's anchor metaphor associates a holding environment with her father, a vague yet stable background object in the midst of movement and change.

Then Kate told me about the flowers. "I did tell you about the flowers, didn't I? My father was a gardener; he grew flowers. He had 200 rose bushes. He was always moving them around in the yard. He had all the flower bushes we gave him as children. He planted them in the ground. He had camellias, azaleas, gladioli." She named all her father's flowers. I remembered the romantic roses brought to me when she succeeded in "business," her confidence about giving the amaryllis, always "the perfect gift." Kate had hidden well this love for her father. Even had I been more experienced in looking for paternal transference I would not have thought, without such prompting, to look for a father among the gifts of flowers. The amaryllis had indeed been the perfect gift. Kate "knew" that gift would please because such gifts had always pleased her father, who must have enjoyed and encouraged this aspect of loving identification with him. In her transference gifts of flowers, Kate had conveyed unconflicted pleasure in being able to choose. In my countertransference, I had enjoyed her gifts as well as shared her confusions about gender legitimacies.

On Wednesday Kate said, "You know we've never talked much of babies. You tried once or twice, but I didn't want to. Since my father died, I've wanted to have a baby. I probably won't have one, but the feelings are back. He was such a family man. He loved children, especially babies. When I was 32, I wanted very much to have a baby. [She had never said any of this before.] I had a good job, lots of money, but I had no relationship. When I decided to move, I felt I was making a decision not to have a baby. I knew if I wanted to really succeed in my work, it would be a long time before I had money again, and besides I wanted to be in a relationship. Margo's wanting a baby is stirring all this up again."

Kate's "feelings are back." Now more secure in her own sexuality, partly because she was more comfortable about her identification with her father, the parent who loved children, especially babies, the gardener who nurtured flowers, Kate could feel again her generative desires.

Kate continued, "I had a dream. It had to do with that pin you wore yesterday. The silver pin with the three Indians. You know, silver is not the only precious substance. There is also chocolate."

> I'm in a building. Many floors. There's a party, festive. The woman I had the crush on is there. [This is a reference to a recent dream in which she has a crush on a woman who reminded her of her brother and of me.] The woman says, "I really have to go." She goes downstairs. Should I talk to her? Was she upset or something? I was unsure. There are many steps down, many people. I look for her on all the floors. I never did find her. Some people know where she went; some don't. Some holiday has just passed. There are tables with many chocolate figures, like your pin. Wrapped in silver paper. There's some of Civil War figures. Big ones, small ones, a series in a necklace, cowboys and Indians. The people there say, "You can have as many as you want." It seems they're not charging for them now. They don't seem to mind that I gather so many up. I still feel almost guilty, semi-sneaking. There are these brass letters "K" and "M." M is for you I guess and also for Margo. I take them. And there were other letters. I took a whole bunch. I thought, "Maybe I can spell something out later." I was looking for a box to put this all in. That was the main thing I was doing. For so long it seemed. Looking for something to hold it all."

She was crying deeply as she finished telling the dream. In an early dream Kate had opened a closet door and had been embarrassed to have me see that the closet was filled with chocolate rabbits wrapped in silver foil. Here she was again feeling "semi-sneaking" as she stashed away all the sweet possibilities. But in contrast to the "odds and ends" of her initial overnight case, now she had a plenitude. I said, "There is one very good place to put chocolate." She laughed. "You mean I have to eat them all." I suggested that her dream indicated that she had found, after a long time looking, something to hold it all. She hoped that she herself could now hold inside various precious objects, and that she was aware she was taking away some letters to spell out, in the future, new projects unknown at this time.

LOOKING FOR SOMETHING TO HOLD IT ALL

The various self- and object representations of Kate and Richard illustrate the kinds of complexity that the concrete sexual dichotomies of development, gender, or transference theories have only limited capacity to appreciate. Nevertheless, clinical psychoanalysis does have a singular capacity, as Sedgwick (1990) once hoped, "to introduce a certain becoming amplitude into discussions of what different people are like" (p. 24). Harris (1991) reminded us that "unlinking aim from object and allowing the play of sexual forms and symbolic meanings for bodies, selves, and acts are the radical core of Freud's theory of desire and gender" (p. 201). Musing on the dream of the flute nuts, "something you don't usually see in that form, like cashews in their shells" and watching the "perfect gift" of the amaryllis, the analyst had not been able to settle on a monosexual gender identity for either. She lacked theoretical supports to understand her own associations. Richard's gift was to be able to envision himself and his analyst and their work together in that shaman. He feared that his analyst would be uncomfortable with his vision, and as uncomfortable with cross-sex identifications as he had been.

As we undo the gender splits of much developmental theory we may find that an aptitude for loving mutual identification in every parent is indeed a developmental gift to the child: a shaman's gift of inner vision that helps a boy feel he can grow into a subject of desire instead of an asexual worker, a gift of flute nuts that gives a girl confidence that she, too, is a person equipped with agency. Meanwhile, assumptions of sexually split capacities, desires, and objects restrict men as well as women. These genderings make it difficult for sons to identify comfortably with mothers and other women, for fathers to identify comfortably with daughters, and for girls, women, and those in gay and lesbian relationships all to see themselves as legitimate Subjects of Desire. We are all still looking for something better to hold it all.

REFERENCES

Abelin, E. L. (1980). Triangulation: the role of the father and the origins of core gender identity during the rapprochement subphase. In *Rapprochement*, ed. R. F. Lax, S. Bach, and J. A. Burland, pp. 151–169. New York: Jason Aronson.

Benjamin, J. (1988). *The Bonds of Love*. New York: Pantheon.

——— (1991). Father and daughter: identification with difference—a contribution to gender heterodoxy. *Psychoanalytic Dialogues* 1:277–299.

Bernstein, D. (1991). Gender-specific dangers in the female/female dyad in treatment. *Psychoanalytic Review* 78:37–48.

Blum, H. P. (1971). On the conception and development of the transference neurosis. *Journal of the American Psychoanalytic Association* 19:41–53.

Blum, H. P., and Blum, E. J. (1986). Reflections on transference and countertransference in the treatment of women. In *Between Analyst and Patient*, ed. H. C. Meyers, pp. 177–192. Hillsdale, NJ: The Analytic Press.

Butler, J. (1990). *Gender Trouble: Feminism and the Subversion of Identity*. New York: Routledge.

——— (1993). *Bodies That Matter*. New York: Routledge.

Cath, S. H., Gurwitt, A. R., and Ross, J. M., eds. (1982). *Father and Child: Developmental and Clinical Perspectives*. Boston: Little, Brown.

Chasseguet-Smirgel, J. (1984). The femininity of the analyst in professional practice. *International Journal of Psycho-Analysis* 68:169–178.

Diamond, D. (1993). The paternal transference: a bridge to the erotic oedipal transference. *Psychoanalytic Inquiry* 22:206–225.

Dimen, M. (1982). Seven notes for the reconstruction of sexuality. *Social Text* 6:22–30.

——— (1991). Deconstructing difference: gender, splitting, and transitional space. *Psychoanalytic Dialogues* 1(3):335–353.

Fast, I. (1984). *Gender Identity: A Differentiation Model*. Hillsdale, NJ: The Analytic Press.

Fausto-Sterling, A. (1994). *Myths of Gender: Biological Theories about Women and Men*. New York: Basic Books.

Flax, J. (1990). *Thinking Fragments: Psychoanalysis, Feminism, and Postmodernism in the Contemporary West*. Berkeley: University of California Press.

Freud, S. (1920). The psychogenesis of a case of homosexuality in a woman. *Standard Edition* 18.

——— (1921). Group psychology. *Standard Edition* 18.

Garber, M. (1992). *Vested Interests: Cross Dressing and Cultural Anxiety*. New York: Routledge.

Goldberger, M., and Evans, D. (1985). On transference manifestations in male patients with female analysts. *International Journal of Psycho-Analysis* 66:295–309.

——— (1993). Transferences in male patients with female analysts: an update. *Psychoanalytic Inquiry* 13:173–191.

Goldner, V. (1991). Toward a critical relational theory of gender. *Psychoanalytic Dialogues* 1(3):249–272.

Green, R. (1987). *The "Sissy Boy Syndrome" and the Development of Homosexuality*. New Haven, CT: Yale University Press.

Greenson, R. (1968). Dis-identifying from mother: its special importance for the boy. *International Journal of Psycho-Analysis* 49:370–374.

Harris, A. (1991). Gender as contradiction. *Psychoanalytic Dialogues* 1:197–224.

Hubbard, R., and Wald, E. (1993). *Exploding the Gene Myth*. Boston: Beacon Hill.

Jones, E. (1927). The early development of female sexuality. *International Journal of Psycho-Analysis* 8:459–472.

Karme, L. (1979). The analysis of a male patient by a female analyst: the problem of the negative oedipal transference. *International Journal of Psycho-Analysis* 60:253–261.

——— (1993). Male patients and female analysts: erotic and other psychoanalytic encounters. *Psychoanalytic Inquiry* 13:192–205.

Keller, E. F. (1985). *Reflections on Gender and Science*. New Haven, CT: Yale University Press.

Kulish, N. M. (1984). The effect of the sex of the analyst on transference: a review of the literature. *Bulletin of the Menninger Clinic* 48:95–109.

Lansky, M. R. (1989). The paternal imago. In *Fathers and Their Families*, ed. S. H. Cath, A. Gurwitt, and L. Gunsberg, pp. 27–45. Hillsdale, NJ: The Analytic Press.

Laqueur, T. (1990). *Making Sex: Body and Gender from the Greeks to Freud.* Cambridge, MA: Harvard University Press.

Leonard, M. (1966). Fathers and daughters: the significance of "fathering" in the psychosocial development of the girl. *International Journal of Psycho-Analysis* 47:325–333.

Lester, E. P. (1990). Gender and identity issues in the analytic process. *International Journal of Psycho-Analysis* 71:435–444.

Longino, H. E. (1990). *Science as Social Knowledge: Values and Objectivity in Scientific Inquiry.* Princeton, NJ: Princeton University Press.

Mahler, M. S., Pine, F., and Bergman, A. (1975). *The Psychological Birth of the Human Infant.* New York: Basic Books.

Mayer, E. L. (1985). "Everybody must be just like me": observations on female castration anxiety. *International Journal of Psycho-Analysis* 66:331–348.

McDougall, J. (1980). *Plea for a Measure of Abnormality.* New York: International Universities Press.

——— (1989). The dead father: on early psychic trauma and its relation to disturbance in sexual identity and in creative activity. *International Journal of Psycho-Analysis* 70:205–219.

Meyers, H. (1986). Analytic work by and with women: the complexity and the challenge. In *Between Analyst and Patient*, ed. H. C. Meyers, pp. 159–176. Hillsdale, NJ: The Analytic Press.

Ogden, T. (1987). The transitional oedipal relationship in female development. *International Journal of Psycho-Analysis* 68:485–498.

Person, E. S. (1985). The erotic transference in women and men: differences and consequences. *Journal of the American Academy of Psychoanalysis* 13:159–180.

——— (1986). Women in therapy: therapist gender as a variable. In *Between Analyst and Patient*, ed. H. Meyers, pp. 193–212. Hillsdale, NJ: The Analytic Press.

Schafer, R. (1974). Problems in Freud's psychology of women. *Journal of the American Psychoanalytic Association* 22:459–485.

Sedgwick, E. K. (1990). *Epistemology of the Closet.* Berkeley: University of California Press.

Spieler, S. (1984). Preoedipal girls need fathers. *Psychoanalytic Review* 71:63–80.

Stoller, R. (1968). *Sex and Gender*. New York: Jason Aronson.

Tessman, L. H. (1982). A note on the father's contribution to the daughter's ways of loving and working. In *Father and Child: Developmental and Clinical Perspectives*, ed. S. Cath, A. Gurwitt, and J. M. Ross, pp. 219–238. Boston: Little, Brown.

Tyson, P. (1986). Male gender identity: early developmental roots. *Psychoanalytic Review* 73:405–425.

——— (1989). Infantile sexuality, gender identity, and obstacles to oedipal progression. *Journal of the American Psychoanalytic Association* 37(4):1051–1069.

Woolf, V. (1928). *Orlando*. New York: New American Library, 1960.

Wrye, H., and Wells, J. (1994). *The Narration of Desire: Erotic Transferences and Countertransferences*. Hillsdale, NJ: The Analytic Press.

III

Between Clinic and Culture:
Critical Elaborations

10

Gender as a Personal and Cultural Construction[1]

NANCY J. CHODOROW

> *Crucially, a person is not a text.*
> —Riccardo Steiner
> "Hermeneutics, or Hermes-Mess?"

My view of psychoanalysis, which argues that each of us creates personal emotional meaning throughout life, has implications for both feminist and psychoanalytic understandings of gendered subjectivity and gender identity. Individual psychological meaning combines with cultural meaning to create the experience of meaning in those cultural categories that are important or resonant for us. Here I argue that an individual, personal creation and a projective emotional and fantasy animation of cultural categories create the meaning of gender and gender identity for any individual. Each person's sense of gender is an individual creation, and there are thus many masculinities and femininities. Each person's gender identity is also an inextricable intertwining, virtually a fusion, of personal and cultural meaning. That each person creates her own personal-cultural gender implies an extension of the view that gender cannot be seen apart from culture.

---

1. Originally published in *The Power of Feelings*, pp. 69–91. Reprinted with permission from Yale University Press.

Contemporary feminism has made central a cultural and political analysis and critique of gender and sexuality and has been
rightly wary of universalizing claims about gender and of accounts
that seem to reduce gender to a single defining or characterizing
feature. These two criticisms have especially focused on psychological claims of all sorts. In response, much academic feminist
theory seems to have moved away from psychology (see Mahoney
and Yngvesson 1992). Contemporary feminists see gender as variable, fragmented, contested, destabilized, and contingently constructed, but the feminist view of gender, influenced by Foucault
and other poststructuralist and postmodern thinkers, is almost
unvaryingly linguistic, cultural, and discursive. In turn, language,
culture, and discourse, composing gender meanings in general, are
at base political—generated by power.[2] Feminism recognizes differences, but it defines them politically rather than individually,
in terms of political-social identities like race, class, and sexual
orientation. In this view, meanings are imposed as cultural categories rather than created in contingent, individual ways. According
to this hegemonic feminist viewpoint, cultural order takes prece-
dence over a more nuanced and variable individual personal meaning, and the psyche is entirely linguistic.

In accord with this linguistic and cultural focus, contemporary feminism, when it includes a psychology, tends to draw on
Lacanian theory. As I have argued elsewhere (1989b), both the
Lacanian insistence on the importance of language and the symbolic in the psyche and the argument that development is a move

---

2. I have in mind here the entire corpus of feminist poststructuralism or
postmodernism, making specific citation difficult. Founding texts include Butler (1990) and Scott (1988); Nicholson (1990) is a representative early anthology. In recent writings, Butler (e.g., 1995) has moved toward a more internalist
and psychodynamic view, though she still, finally, seems to claim to privilege
the discursive over the unconscious psychic reality of fantasy. (Layton [1997]
provides an overview of Butler's shifts along with their continuing limits from
the point of view of relational psychoanalysis; see also Butler's response, 1997).
For a critique of the feminist tendency to reduce the cultural-linguistic to the
political, see Bloch (1993).

into culture and not just into a noncultural individuality have been important as general correctives and investigative admonitions for psychoanalysts, and particularly apt in the case of gender. But this Lacanian move, ironically, also polarizes men and women and makes the gender divide absolute. Although subjects can, in the Lacanian view, have different relations to the symbolic and to the gender categories it represents, the symbolic realm itself is reserved exclusively and universally for the phallus and the name of the father; the meaning of the mother, precultural and nonsymbolic, considered again universalistically, is limited to the sphere of the imaginary or the semiotic.

Psychoanalytic understandings of the powers of transference, projection, and introjection run counter to feminist assumptions about the exclusive cultural or political construction of gender and gender meanings. In this chapter, I claim that feminism has eliminated the realm of personal emotional meaning or made it subordinate to and determined by language and power. I suggest that gender cannot be seen as entirely culturally, linguistically, or politically constructed. Whether racial-ethnic, international feminist, linguistic, performative, micropolitical, or based on the analysis of discourse, gender theories that do not consider individual personal emotional and fantasy-related meaning cannot capture fully the meanings that gender has for the subject. They miss an important component of experienced gender meaning and gendered subjectivity.

When I claim that gender is inevitably personal as well as cultural, I mean not only that people create individualized cultural or linguistic versions of meaning by drawing on the cultural or linguistic categories at hand. Rather, perception and the creation of meaning are psychologically constituted. As psychoanalysis documents, people avail themselves of cultural meanings and images, but they experience them emotionally and through fantasy, as well as in particular interpersonal contexts. Emotional meaning, affective tone, and unconscious fantasies that arise from within and are not experienced linguistically interact with and give individual animation and nuance to cultural categories, stories, and language (that is, make them subjectively meaningful). Individuals thereby create new meanings according to their own unique biographies and histories of intrapsychic strategies and practices—meanings that extend beyond and run counter to cultural or linguistic categories.

Neither emotion nor unconscious fantasy is originally linguistic or organized. Initially, unconscious fantasy globally bodies forth aspects of self and other in immediate emotional terms. Articulation of story, characters, and affect in unconscious fantasies can then be more or less highly elaborated, and they can be expressed to some degree in conscious or preconscious fantasy. Unconscious fantasies that are not ostensibly about gender at all may also help psychologically to articulate aspects of gender experience. At the same time, it is certainly the case that aspects of gender identity and unconscious gender fantasy draw on language, cultural stories, and interpersonally transmitted emotional responses, themselves conveyed by people (in the first instance parents and other caregivers) with their own personal-cultural sense of gender.

Gender meanings, as feminism has argued, are certainly indeterminate and contested, but they are indeterminate and contested not only culturally and politically but also as they are shaped and reshaped by an emotional self. Like other processes of psychological creation of meaning, gender identity, gender fantasy, the sense of gender, and the sexual identifications and fantasies that are part of this identity are formed and reformed throughout the life cycle. Senses of self, the tone of individual feelings, and emotionally imbued unconscious fantasies are as constitutive of subjective gender as is language or culture.[3]

---

3. In now-classic articles that bring the insights of feminist postmodernism to the clinical community, Dimen (1991) and Harris (1991) give clinically based accounts compatible with this claim. Dimen describes the intertwining of gender not only with cultural representations but with aspects of self-experience. Harris argues for the complexity, the contextual and varying salience, and the multiple figuration of gender and sexuality in anyone's psyche (see also Goldner [1991], who provides elegant documentation of the paradoxical relational injunctions and cognitive contradictions that create and sustain normal gender as a defense and advocates a psychologically nondichotomous, decentered gender).

My approach aligns itself with other feminist theories that make claims for the potential autonomy and creativity of consciousness. Alison Jaggar (1989) criticizes epistemologies that privilege cognition, value, and reason and artificially divide them from the emotions that are inextricably embedded in them and fuel them. She claims that women, rather than accepting the false divide between emotion and reason, should pay attention to their "outlaw emotions" that can generate political and epistemological critique. Patricia Hill Collins, in *Black Feminist Thought* (1990), asserts the autonomy and individuality of consciousness, although she certainly does not minimize the centrality of relations of domination. Emphasizing that consciousness is created and not determined, she stresses the importance for feminists of bringing constant attention to bear on both the social-cultural-political and the individual creativity of consciousness. She points in particular to two traditional foci of psychoanalytic interest and of psychoanalytic feminist critique—heterosexuality and motherhood—and argues that African-American women's experience of both is created individually as much as imposed through domination: "The same situation can look quite different depending on the consciousness one brings to interpret it. . . . There is always choice, and power to act, no matter how bleak the situation may be" (pp. 227, 237).

Similarly, Gloria Anzaldúa (1990) sounds like an intersubjective psychoanalyst as she describes how the masks that Chicanas or Mexicanas are required to wear "drive a wedge between our intersubjective personhood and the *persona* we present to the world" (p. xv) and how women of color need theories that "will explain how and why we relate to certain people in specific ways, that will reflect what goes on between inner, outer and peripheral 'I' within a person and between the personal 'I' and the collective 'we' of our ethnic communities" (p. xxv). Like Loewald, Schafer, and others who write of reconstructions of past and present, she argues for "acquiring the tools to change the disabling images and memories, to replace them with self-affirming ones, to recreate our pasts and alter them—for the past can be as malleable as the present" (p. xxvii).

Personalized autobiographical accounts by feminists, even those that claim that consciousness is culturally or socially determined, also document how subjectivity, standpoint, and identity on the one hand are situated, contextual, and contested and on the other are actively created psychodynamically, rather than given. Out of many possible examples, I focus here on Pratt (1984) and Mernissi (1994). In "Identity: Skin, Blood, Heart," Minnie Bruce Pratt describes a Southern Christian childhood and identity. Each partially positioning memory and experience and each description of cultural, historical, or social location is infused with grief, pain, joy, anger, uncertainty, fear, and other emotions that particularize that location, memory, and experience for her. Visceral personal experience underlies and creates Pratt's identity. In a key passage, she describes her father's taking her to the top of the courthouse clock tower to look down over the town. She cannot see out as her father can, and she finds herself dominant and subordinate—white and a person whose grandfather was a judge in this court, but small and a girl, someone who would never hold the same position as male citizen or adult. Pratt describes how she consciously rejected her father's (symbolic) position by leaving home and giving up the white Southern identity and hegemonic worldview she was born with. But her gender identity is constructed also by the emotional reaction to that exclusion within inclusion, to the personal meaning of this one encounter (and thousands more) that helped to shape her personal sense of whiteness, middle class–ness, and femininity. Pratt's narrative describes passion and pain: the experienced deadening that accompanied her coming out as a lesbian, as she gave up her children when she left her husband; her fear and terror of isolation; the wrenching distance from black and Jewish women whom she wished to be close to and identified with; her shame at her own ancestors' historical role as slaveholders and appropriators of Native American lands. We feel the emotional animation of these identity categories as Pratt describes everyday walks through her black neighborhood in southeast Washington, DC, and with her we gauge every encounter and reel from those that jar her or go awry.

In her enchanting autobiography *Dreams of Trespass: Memories of a Harem Girlhood*, Fatima Mernissi (1994) likewise conveys the individualized emotional and sensual experience of a specifically gendered culture: the smells and tastes of foods and make-up; the tactile feel of oily jars, fabrics, marble floors; the steam baths; sounds and sights, and how each individual projectively creates and reacts to this culture and his or her gender in specific ways. Mernissi describes the cultural meanings and physical-social organization of different harems, of women in Morocco and in Islamic history, of stories and legends; yet she also makes it clear that the harem, which draws a boundary between male and female, is experienced differently by each of the women and men (or girls and boys) in her account. Each individual has his or her own personality, way of participating, interpretations, ways of escaping emotionally, taking a break, resisting, or retreating, and ways of participating in and appropriating cultural practices.

There are, of course, commonalities. All members of the household agree that they live in a harem (a household that keeps women and girls inside and controlled, not a polygynous family), and some of the women react more similarly to each other than to others. But in each person's integration of culturally gendered forms and in the individual way of playing with them in emotion and fantasy, the component parts are different. Gender here is not simply internalized. Each little step in gender socialization is ruminated upon by the young Mernissi and her boy cousin, and each value is charged, conflictual, and elaborated on in individual and collective stories and plays. Indeed, the emotional charge constitutes the cultural meanings of gender and keeps them alive for all the participants.

Pratt and Mernissi make it clear that one's multifarious cultural and social positioning always includes psychological history—transference and emotionally infused development. As they also make clear, this psychological history, like any history, is not fixed once and for all in early childhood but continually unfolds and changes, lending emotional animation and personal coloring, through current and past relationships and through fantasy, to all aspects of identity—class, nationality, race or ethnicity, and reli-

gion, as well as gender. Mernissi shows how women who hold identical positions in society and are situated in similar ways culturally
can yet have very different psychological experiences of gender. Such
narratives highlight the contribution of individual, personal animation to gender identity. By contrast, feminist suspicion of psychology or of psychology's tendency to universalize precludes
understanding of the role of such personal animation.

To consider our experience of personal meaning in the light
of an individual's inner psychic reality of emotion and fantasy, then,
is to revise and expand our understanding of cultural and linguistic meaning. Insofar as we are talking about individual subjectivity,
cultural meaning does not "precede" individual meaning. From earliest infancy, meaning is emotional as well as cognitive. Creation of
personal meaning and the potential for emotionally resonant experience antedates the acquisition of language. Cognitions, such as
knowing one's gender and having thoughts or experiences of gender, are infused with emotions, fantasies, and personal tonalities.

With this psychoanalytic argument, I am making a universal claim about human subjectivity and its constituent psychodynamic processes, just as a cultural or poststructuralist theorist
might universalize the equally essentialist claim that subjectivity
is linguistically or discursively constituted. For those who draw
on psychoanalysis, the capacity to endow experience with meaning from nonverbal emotion and unconscious fantasy—to create
personal meaning—is an innate human capacity or potentiality
that continues throughout life. Subjectivity creates and re-creates,
merges and separates, fantasy and reality, inner and outer, unconscious and conscious, felt past and felt present, each element
in the pair helping to constitute and give meaning and resonance
to the other. Both in the psychoanalytic and in the cultural approach, we hold in abeyance any universal claim about the content of what is thought or felt: the content of that subjectivity or
process cannot be universalized.

Clinical examples, by persuasively documenting the way in
which emotion and fantasy saturate personal gender, point to the
complexity of individual gender. Examples also illuminate how

people re-create recognizable cultural meanings, personal experience, and their bodies in ways that charge and construct their individual sense of gender—emotionally, often conflictually, through unconscious and conscious fantasy. The meanings I describe are, finally, articulated in language, but as any analyst or patient knows, this language often only approximates the feeling of inner psychic reality. It is a product of interaction between therapist and patient as they work to create a consensual account of an experience that is initially (and throughout) emotional, partially conscious, fragmentary, and marked by disconnected thoughts. The two struggle, that is, to render experience that is not necessarily conscious or linguistic into language.

I believe we can see, from just a few examples of contemporary middle-class white American women—women who are heterosexual in their behavior and their conscious identity—how individual and idiosyncratic a sense of gendered self is. I mention behavior and conscious identity because, especially in the clinical setting, where attention is directed toward such matters, once we explore any person's unconscious fantasy life and multiple sexual and other identifications, nobody has a single sexual orientation. (On heterosexuality, see Chodorow [1994]; on the multiple aspects of sexual identity, see A. Stein [1997].) These few examples that follow give some sense of the multiplicity and variability of individual constructions of gender and indicate some of the axes of definition and emotional castings that different individuals may bring to their own gender construct. They thus both support and challenge contemporary feminism. They document clearly the instability, multiplicity, layering, contradiction, and contestation in constructions of gender, but they also document that this unstable, multiple, layered, contested contradictoriness affects emotional and intrapsychic as well as cultural, linguistic, or discursive meaning. The women I describe range in the nature of their diagnoses and the levels of their psychic functioning. They do not stand out by virtue of their extraordinariness, beyond the fact that all our individual psyches, fantasies, fears, and conflicts are extraordinary. In some cases, the preoccupations these women express are central to what they and I have worked on throughout treatment; in others, they are constructions that are simply noted in passing. Other issues, in which gender is not so salient, are more central for them.

My initial restriction of case examples to women who share certain attributes of sociocultural position strengthens the case for the individual construction of gender. These patients presumably share a similar cultural and social organization of gender: they were primarily taken care of by mothers; they saw fathers as dominant and attractive in culturally recognizable ways (exciting, seductive, cuddly, or domineering); they were not explicitly taught that women were inferior and men superior; they could be said to have followed the Lacanian path developmentally from the imaginary mother–child semiotic realm to the phallic-symbolic world of the father.

Although I draw on female case examples, my point that gendered subjectivity is a melding of personally created idiosyncratic meaning and cultural meaning holds for my male patients (and all men) as well. The particular women I discuss come from a variety of European-American backgrounds. My clinical experience, however, as well as my reading of autobiographical, fictional, and ethnographic literature and feminist and gay-lesbian research and theory, all lead me to conclude that the processes I describe— though not, I emphasize again, the content—of emotion, fantasy, and self-construction characterize nonheterosexual subjectivities and American racial-ethnic subjectivities as well. (The account in Moraga [1986] provides an exemplar of a particularized, emotional, fantasy-imbued construction of a bodily-sexual, gendered, and racial-ethnic subjectivity that is also culturally constituted.) These brief examples are meant only to suggest the personal projective construction of gender: I will not follow the details of change or variation in any one person. I will also not focus on commonalities, although such an approach would be possible. My patients have been conscious of some of the constructions, conflicts, and fantasies I describe for some time; others were previously unconscious and are now recognized; still others did not exist in their current form but were created through our work together.

THE CASE OF J.

For one woman, J., male-female difference is central to the meaning of gender, and an emotion, anger, is one key to gender construction. In the first part of her analysis, she strives constantly to cast me in the image of a father with whom she struggles and to get me to engage in such struggle. She wants to experience a dismissive, condemnatory, accusatory anger toward me that she identifies with her father and with other men. Our interaction is experienced in the form of emotional power struggles, struggles that take on undertones of gender. Alternately, they are between man and woman and between man and man.

J. is terrified of her own anger and is also fearful of mine. Women's anger, as J. tells it, destroys absolutely. There is no surviving it. Mothers can destroy children, and children can destroy mothers. J. worries that her own rage destroyed her mother and that she might destroy me. If she does so, I will not be there for her. By contrast, men's anger is sudden, violent, and explosive, but when it is all over, you are still there. If J. could be a man, she wouldn't have to fear destroying with anger, and she could still express her considera⟩le rage.

For J., then, invulnerable anger is one of the main meanings of masculinity, and her frighteningly destructive anger is a link with femininity. Gender struggles, victory, and defeat animate images of gender difference, and her fantasy particularizes an adolescent daughter's angry struggle with her father. I emphasize the subjective centrality of adolescence here: when we look at individual constructions and animations of gender, different periods may be more or less salient for different people. Stage theories of different varieties draw our attention to potentially important processes for numbers of people, but they do not adequately predict what will be crucial periods in an individual case.[4]

---

4. I have in mind, for instance, Freudian stage theory and Lacanian theory, which categorize gender as an oedipal achievement, and the currently competing second-year genital phase or rapprochement theories, according to which

J. also sometimes constructs gender around a different male-female polarity and desire to give herself masculine attributes. Her preoccupations and fantasies here have their origins in latency, a period in which I have found that gender fantasies and feelings become consolidated for many people. The object-relational origins of these sorts of latency-period gender fantasies are likely to be associated with a brother or with fantasied or perceived maternal or paternal expectations about a brother in comparison to oneself. In her analysis, we discover a previously unconscious fantasy of being forever young—in fact, a young boy. As friends married and had children, J. did not compare herself to them. She realizes that the reason was that she experiences herself as not grown up and not female. Like Peter Pan, she contemptuously dismissed such practices. Having a child would have destroyed the fantasy of being forever young and a boy (heterosexual intercourse also challenges it).

Being a boy has other advantages: you are in a much less vulnerable position than if you are a grown woman or a little girl. "Part of the secret is being a boy: that changes everything. I'm childless and can't decide to settle down with G. because I've chosen not to. It makes it okay to be angry and on edge; that's how boys are. Not only is it okay, but you can't be hurt—a sense that part of myself is male, and powerful. That makes it okay, and there's pride in that, part of my strength. I don't have to be afraid because of that. I'm secretly strong." She remembers exuberant images of power, playing king of the mountain and football with the neighborhood boys.

---

feelings about gender and genitals first become significant in the second year (e.g., Benjamin 1988, Fast 1984, Roiphe and Galenson 1981). At this point, even the timing of what has traditionally been called core gender identity, or what Benjamin (1995) has renamed nominal gender identification—the early cognitive self-labeling that almost everyone develops to refer to being female or male—is in question. Traditionally, it has been seen as developing gradually and consolidating between 18 months and 3 years (see Money and Ehrhardt 1972 and Stoller 1968). For a recent empirical study that queries the relation between the development of genital self-recognition and gender self-definition, see de Marneffe (1997). In her "Commentary" on de Marneffe, Coates (1997) questions the continuing utility of psychoanalytic theories of libidinal phases and developmental lines more generally.

She says, "Boys and men are free; they have more room; they take up more physical space. They don't have to care how they look or dress." Such fantasies serve as a defense against J.'s notion (a notion recognized at different times by different women but often prepubertally) that a woman or girl should grow up and fulfill a powerless, dependent feminine role. Not wanting to grow up, imagining not growing up and time's not moving on, also connect for J. with specific cultural images that have resonance psychologically, especially Peter Pan, but also Tom Sawyer. J. also recalls childhood fantasy identifications with heroic knights who swashbuckled their way to success, rescuing damsels in distress (which she emphatically was not), and she is intrigued with the boy-dressed-as-a-girl-playing-a-boy parts in plays like *As You Like It* and *Twelfth Night*.

At one time, then, J.'s fantasy about gender and power concerns the fantasy of male anger and interpersonal aggression; at another, it concerns comparative strength and the ability to defend oneself. Gender difference also expresses itself in her eyes as boys' and men's ability to not care. In all these cases, central to J.'s gender construction is the sense that femininity is vulnerable in a way that masculinity is not. If she is accosted or threatened sexually or physically, she feels, as a female, that she provoked it because of the badness of female anger (and sexuality). But in the fantasy of being a boy or young man, she has no such feelings.

THE CASE OF B.

Coming straight from meetings with her male employer, B. often arrives late for her hours of analysis. She herself has set up these work meetings to occur just before her hours, and she finds them very hard to leave. Despite having consciously and intentionally sought out analysis, she experiences her sessions as an obligation and an unwanted pull away from the excitement of her relationship with her employer. She compares the obligation to the childhood experience in which she found the weekly good-byes to her father, who was divorced from her mother, painful and difficult. During many of her hours with me she is preoccupied with concerns about her employer. By contrast, she pays little notice to me. Sometimes she dismisses her delay with a perfunctory "Sorry I'm late," but usually she just ignores it. I feel like—and she confirms that I am—taken-for-granted background, a maternal nag who can be kept waiting, who wants only to talk about boring, petty issues like lateness, schedules, and phone numbers. Most of the time, B. feels strongly that what she needs is a powerful man, a perfect, ideal man who will rescue her and make her feel wonderful, rather than rejecting her as she feels her father did. As she puts it (unwittingly borrowing a cultural trope from Patsy Cline), she "falls to pieces" whenever she thinks of an old boyfriend who has rejected the overtures she has made in an effort to get back together.

In contrast to her idealized images of her father and men, her images of her mother and maternal femininity are almost sordid. Her mother, she feels, was weak, unable to care for herself or her children, unable to find good love relationships, unable to keep a nice house. Here, B. compares her father and, alternately, me, with her mother. At these moments, I am not a petty nag, a drag, or a doormat, in implicit or explicit contrast to an exciting man. Rather, in contrast to B.'s pitiful mother, I am seen as good and pure.

The psychological defense B. employs in constructing these conscious and unconscious fantasies of self, other, and gender is that of splitting. All the good parts of the other go to one person— good father/men versus bad mother/women/me; pure me versus impure mother. Splitting also occurs within the self. B. has, as she tells it, good secret wishes that have to be kept secret, because then they will come true. She has to protect these good wishes both from the bad parts of herself, parts that she identifies with her mother, and from me, because I am a woman, and women make things difficult for her. She says, "Recently, my main experiences with women, with my mother, my close friends, are difficult. From childhood, a man could make it all better. Women, my mother, can't give me what I need or long for, to feel desirable."

Yet B. also feels shame and conflict about her dominant gender fantasies. She idealizes masculine rescue but occasionally also idealizes me; she worries, as she puts it, "that all my positive secrets revolve around men." Putting all the good into men and all the bad into women, when she herself is a woman, leaves her identified with her shameful mother. Moreover, she has political objections to her fantasies: they are not the kinds of unconscious fantasies or thoughts that women today wish to discover. They are therefore quite hard to recognize and acknowledge. She says, "I resist that idea—how *could* I think that way?" But she then immediately wonders, "Have I ever admired a woman I worked with?"

B.'s construction of gender has a unique emotional configuration that differs in emphasis from J.'s. B. does not want to be, and does not fantasize herself as, a man. Rather, she emphatically wants to *have* a man. Emotionally, cognitively, and in conscious fantasy she emphasizes heterosexual femininity. B.'s idealization of men revolves around how they can rescue her; for J., men's and boys' seeming self-sufficiency and ability not to care are central. For B., shame and excitement are emotionally central to her gender feelings; for J., anger becomes a defining criterion of gender. In some particulars, these two cases resemble two of three typical patterns of female development described by Freud (1931). B. resembles the girl who rejects her mother and women and develops heterosexual femininity. She desires men sexually, to give her something the mother did not and could not give. J. is the girl who eschews femininity and develops a masculine identification (for Freud, identification with the father). Such an identification may or may not include a behavioral lesbian object choice.[5]

---

5. Freud describes a third pattern, in which the girl gives up sexuality in general as well as the masculine identifications that might lead to achievement in nonsexual spheres. She becomes generally inhibited in gender, sexuality, and sublimations. For discussion of the multiplicity of women in Freud's writings, see Chodorow (1994).

THE CASE OF K.

For K., the most salient aspects of gender are not primarily organized around the male-female polarity. Unlike J., K. is not preoccupied with wanting to have the privileges and attributes of a man;
unlike B., she is not preoccupied with wanting to have a man sexually. As Freud's classic theory would have it, K. organizes her gender with reference to the body—but not in terms of maleness and
femaleness. She organizes bodily gender in terms of the little girl–
mother polarity. K. feels herself to be an inadequate girl with inadequate little genitals—inadequate not in comparison with males, who
possess a penis, but in comparison with grown women with adult
genitals and reproductive capacities. Memories of this inadequacy
come from both early latency and early and middle adolescence.

The dominant feeling-tone of shame in K.'s experience of her
female body extends to and undermines the comparison in her
mother–little girl fantasy, so this fantasy entails its own negation.
In K.'s view, grown women's bodies have their own problems.
Pregnancy and menstruation, for example, give women cramps,
make them weak, sluggish, and heavy, and remind them that they
are tied to uncontrollable bodies. Heterosexual relationships pose
a conflictual solution to this shame, one that generates a further
quandary. Strong, masculine men can help K. appreciate her feminine body and make her feel successfully feminine, but by their
presence they also serve as a reminder of her weakness and the
general shamefulness and weakness of femininity. If she chooses
men whom she perceives as not so masculine, however, so that
she is not so reminded of her own weakness, K. feels inadequate
as a heterosexual feminine woman—and that is shameful in its
own way. A further quandary comes from her identifying herself
consciously as a feminist. As K. puts it, "I hate to think that women
are weak."

For K., gender as a male-female polarity and feminine inadequacy vis-à-vis men are not as intensely experienced as the little
girl–grown woman dichotomy. When these do enter her fantasy

and feelings, they center more on work than on body or sexuality. Being a woman gets tied up with being unable to compete in the work world: "You're too weak, not tough enough to be in that world. Dependent." Work functions, covertly, as a locus for overcoming femininity. K. wants to be "king of the hill," "top man on the totem pole," receiving acknowledgment and recognition as a man, from men, or as a nongendered person (implicitly male) from other nongendered people. But this wish becomes tricky in turn, because wanting recognition is a kind of dependence, and hence feminine and weak.

Because of her fantasy and fear that grown women, tied to their female bodies, are weak and that work success is masculine, for K. competent women are something of an oxymoron. She describes a business meeting with a group of women, and how impressed she was with their competence: "It wasn't a kill-or-be-killed model of interaction, but I'm not committed to it. I'm stuck in the kill-or-be-killed model. I didn't know how to behave in that setting. I'm more comfortable in the other—what I gloss as men, but it's not only men. I know how to handle myself in situations with lots of direct challenges to ideas. It doesn't make me happy, but it's involving. I feel prevented from fitting into a more flattened landscape, one without hierarchy. If it's not up or down, on the way up or on the way down, struggling against being put down, I'll disappear."

There is no emotional or cognitive space in K.'s view for being competent, nonhierarchical, and a woman. Her own professional aspirations and ways of thinking and preferring to interact are, in her view, masculine. She doesn't know how to act otherwise, but such aspirations still create conflicts. She experiences, and gets pleasure from experiencing work in the kill-or-be-killed model, but at the same time she does not like it morally or politically. Moreover, the pleasure is conflictual and shameful. And there is always the fear that she will be found out—found to be not a man but a woman—even worse, not a woman but a little girl, an inadequate woman.

THE CASE OF C.

C. expresses still another construction of gender, another feeling-tone and object of desire. She wants mother, not father; breast, not penis; nurturance, not protective rescue or autonomy. For C., being a woman and being with women elicit thoughts of her mother and feelings of being left out. She experiences a kind of sad neediness, thinking of women's relationships with men. She feels that men have a special ability to bind women to them that women don't have, or that she doesn't have. With women friends, she feels a pervasive sense of wanting more and being angry and sad at not getting it. The problem with being a woman is that, to other women, you are not unique. C. imagines that for me, my women patients are all alike. They all get arbitrary, inconsistent attention, whereas my men patients are unique and prized. She feels excluded and hopeless. So she feels jealousy of men because women favor them, and of other women, who, she assumes, get the same indifferent attention or lack of attention from mother/women that she does.

I do not believe that the tonality of this "left-out-ness" and jealousy is usefully considered oedipal (or "negative-oedipal": for a girl, wanting mother and wanting to get rid of father) or preoedipal (assuming a two-person relationship). The fantasy is triadic, involving mother and father and images of sexuality, but it fuses breast wishes, greed, neediness, feelings of emptiness, perception of one's interchangeability with other women in the eyes of the mother/woman (men's desires are not relevant here), and a sense that feeding and filling are what women offer to men. In this construction of gender, male-female differences are emotionally intertwined with and take the form of sibling concerns. Feelings of empty, needy sadness range across C.'s life and are central to her personal animations and evocations of gender. Clearly, a Kleinian viewpoint, according to which the breast rather than the penis is central to gender difference, and construction of gender is organized around the projected and introjected goodness/plenitude and badness/destructiveness of the breast and self, makes much more sense of C.'s psychology in general and her sense of gender in particular than a classically Freudian understanding does.[6]

All the gender identifications and fantasies I describe are both cultural and personal. A social or cultural critic could claim (and would be partly right) that you do not need a psychology to explain many of these images, fantasies, and gender constructions. It is well documented that men have more power, are allowed to express anger more freely, and take up more space than women, and that women cater to them. It is culturally mandated that women be passive. Women in many cultures and families are expected to give in to and give up to men and not to give to their daughters as they give to their sons and husbands. The views my patients express about these matters come from their particular families and from the culture in general, and we should not minimize this culturally induced inflection of the meanings of masculinity and femininity. It is "realistic" to have these beliefs and thoughts; they are a good analysis of a sexist society. We are less likely to find them gender-reversed either in reconstructions or in transferences. Assessment of the cultural and social setting is also part of my patients' appraisals of and feelings about their situations and psyches.[7]

In these accounts we recognize familiar social as well as cultural patterns—for example, a divorce, an elusive father, and a rejected little girl who thinks everything will be all right if Daddy rescues her. We could consider her, as she considers herself, a victim of family circumstances and gender inequality. Some observers or critics might ask, as she does, how you can have an image

---

6. Klein's suggestive writings on gender (1928, 1945, 1957) have, unfortunately, not been elaborated on by her followers (but see Birksted-Breen 1999, and Chodorow 1999). The direction modern Kleinians have taken in their investigation of the Oedipus complex is not to attend to or problematize gender but instead to look at the generalized child in relation to the (heterosexual) parental couple (see, e.g., Britton 1992).

7. For an especially powerful account of the impact of differential valuation on girls' emotional and fantasied sense of gendered self and sexuality, see Benjamin (1988, 1995).

of a rich, vibrant, fertile mother when your mother is another statistic in the feminization of poverty, Similarly, in a culture that valorizes exciting masculinity, it might be expected that girls and women would idealize men and devalue women. They would turn not to stories like *Peter Pan* and *As You Like It* but to *Cinderella*, *Sleeping Beauty*, and gothic romances, or to Patsy Cline falling to pieces.

Moreover, one theme intersects with all my clinical examples and has been central to the feminist appropriation and critique of psychology. Within the gendered subjectivity that they create, all the women I discuss reflect psychological preoccupation with some aspect of gender inequality. The way in which each person brings masculinity and femininity to life and develops a gender identity imbued with emotion and fantasy includes personal animation not just of difference itself but of differences in value and power. Often but not always, the male-female contrasts are based on male dominance, privilege, or superiority (see R. Stein [1995], however, for a particularly interesting case discussion of a man who emphatically experienced his mother and other women as dominant, privileged, and superior). This prevalent psychological intertwining of sexuality, gender, inequality, and power, all saturated with introjective and projective meaning, demonstrates why it is necessary for psychoanalysts to take both a cultural and a clinical stance.

As these cultural meanings are constructed and reconstructed in personal gender, however, they become entangled with the specifics of individual emotion and fantasy, with aspects of self, and with conscious and unconscious images of gender, fostered by particular families. These personal overtones explain why taking just a cultural stance is not enough either, why an explanation on the basis of cultural values or meanings alone is incomplete. For this reason, we are always walking a fine line when we combine cultural and personal understanding. The existence of gender inequality in both the cultural and social spheres does not explain the range of fantasy interpretations and varieties of emotional shadings with which women confront this inequality. We have only to look at the number of autobiographical and literary accounts by daughters of vibrant, creative mothers who were extremely poor and oppressed to understand that the feminization of poverty alone is not an adequate explanation for a particular woman's sense of powerlessness and neediness.

Furthermore, my patients themselves feel miserable, anxious, and conflicted about their thoughts concerning gender and gender inequality—one woman about her hidden fantasy of being a powerful male and about coveting what she sees as male powers, another about her sad desire for maternal nurturance, another about her scorn for uncompetitive women, another about her desperate need for men, another about her rage at paternal dominance and sadness over her mother, another about her sadness at her father's absence. Their warding off and harboring of these unconscious fantasies have kept them from living as they wish—from having fulfilling relationships and from moving ahead professionally, when such professional achievements interfered with the fantasy of being a boy, with feeling needy and dependent, or with the sense that professional participation threatens to shame them sexually.

A belief that men can be angry, temperamental, or demanding and that women or mothers are powerless is both a social analysis and a powerful motivator of guilt and inhibition, of a need to repair the mother and not to move ahead of her. Guilt and sadness about the mother are particularly prevalent female preoccupations, which are as likely to limit female autonomy, pleasure, and achievement as any cultural mandate. This is so even though unequal gender arrangements and beliefs themselves give rise to conditions in which female autonomy, pleasure, and achievement result in a woman's surpassing her mother. Similarly, shame vis-à-vis men, whether over women's dependence or at being discovered in masculine pursuits, is certainly situated in a cultural context in which such pursuits are coded as masculine in the first place. But this shame is also experienced in itself, inflected with many unconscious fantasies that often stem from a time in development well before such coding could be interpreted. It is a conflict in itself, and it inflects the general sense of self and gender in addition to interacting with specific cultural expectations and meanings.

My examples, then, reflect, indicate, and build on historically situated, cultural, discursive constructions of gender. But none of the women I discuss simply entered the realm of the symbolic or placed themselves within a cultural discourse or unequal society or polity. From birth to the present, all have actively constructed their gender with intense individual feelings and fantasies—of anger, envy, guilt, resentment, shame, wistful desire, rageful entitlement, sadness, jealousy, horror, or disgust—and with characteristic defensive patterns—of guilt, denial, splitting, projection, repression. This personal cast and individual emotional tonality pervade any person's sense of gender.

Feminists have developed fine-tuned theories of discursively constructed, cultural, and political gender. They are sensitive to specifics of history, class, rank, race, or ethnicity and cognizant of the contingent, fragmentary, and ambiguous character of enactments and constructions of gender. But these cannot alone reveal to us how gender is constructed—what these culturally situated practices and discourses mean to the particular person who experiences and constructs gender and a gender identity. The capacities and processes for the creation of personal meaning described by psychoanalysis contribute to gendered subjectivity as do cultural categories and the enactment or creation of social or cultural roles. Clinical work demonstrates that all elements of existence—anatomy, cultural meanings, individual family, economic and political conditions, class, race, socialization practices, and the impact of parents' personality—are refracted and constructed through the projections and introjections and the fantasy creations that give them psychological meaning.[8]

---

8. Rendering to Hegel what is Hegel's I paraphrase and disagree here with Marx's famous claim: "Life is not determined by consciousness, but consciousness by life" (1845–1846, p. 155). This much-quoted claim has become the pretheoretical assumption that underlies the macrodeterminisms of most of sociology, the cultural determinisms of anthropology, the political-cultural determinisms of poststructuralism, and the varieties of feminism that derive from each of these.

REFERENCES

Anzaldúa, G. (1990). *Making Face, Making Soul/Haciendo Caras: Creative and Critical Perspectives by Women of Color*. San Francisco: Aunt Lute.

Bemesderfer, S. (1996). A revised psychoanalytic view of menopause. *Journal of the American Psychoanalytic Association* 44(suppl.):351–369.

Benjamin, J. (1988). *The Bonds of Love: Psychoanalysis, Feminism, and the Problem of Domination*. New York: Pantheon.

——— (1995). *Like Subjects, Love Objects*. New Haven, CT: Yale University Press.

Birksted-Breen, D. (1999). Melanie Klein's "The Oedipus complex in the light of early anxieties." In *Female Sexuality: Contemporary Engagements*, ed. D. Bassin, pp. 281–286. Northvale, NJ: Jason Aronson.

Bloch, R. H. (1993). A culturalist critique of trends in feminist theory. *Contention* 2:79–106.

Britton, R. (1992). Keeping things in mind. In *Clinical Lectures on Klein and Bion*, ed. R. Anderson, pp. 102–113. London: Tavistock.

Butler, J. (1990). *Gender Trouble: Feminism and the Subversion of Identity*. London: Routledge.

——— (1995). Melancholy gender-refused identification. *Psychoanalytic Dialogues* 5:165–180.

——— (1997). Response to Lynne Layton's "The Doer Behind the Deed: Tensions and Intersections Between Butler's Vision of Performativity and Relational Psychoanalysis." *Gender and Psychoanalysis* 2:515–520.

Chodorow, N. (1989a). *Feminism and Psychoanalytic Theory*. New Haven, CT: Yale University Press.

——— (1989b). Psychoanalytic feminism and the psychoanalytic psychology of women. In *Feminism and Psychoanalytic Theory*, pp. 178–198. New Haven, CT: Yale University Press.

——— (1994). *Femininities, Masculinities, Sexualities: Freud and Beyond*. Lexington: University Press of Kentucky.

Coates, S. W. (1997). Is it time to jettison the concept of developmental lines? Commentary on de Marneffe's paper "Bodies and Words." *Gender and Psychoanalysis* 2:35–53.

Collins, P. H. (1990). *Black Feminist Thought: Knowledge, Consciousness, and the Politics of Empowerment*. London: Routledge.

de Marneffe, D. (1997). Bodies and words: a study of young children's genital and gender knowledge. *Gender and Psychoanalysis* 2:3–33.

Dimen, M. (1991). Deconstructing difference: gender, splitting, and transitional space. *Psychoanalytic Dialogues* 1:335–352.

Fast, I. (1984). *Gender Identity: A Differentiation Model*. Hillsdale, NJ: The Analytic Press.

Freud, S. (1931). Female sexuality. *Standard Edition* 21:223–243.

Goldner, V. (1991). Toward a critical relational theory of gender. *Psychoanalytic Dialogues* 1:249–272.

Harris, A. (1991). Gender as contradiction: a discussion of Freud's "The Psychogenesis of a Case of Homosexuality in a Woman." *Psychoanalytic Dialogues* 1:197–224.

Jaggar, A. M. (1989). Love and knowledge: emotion in feminist epistemology. In *Gender/Body/Knowledge: Feminist Reconstructions of Being and Knowing*, ed. A. M. Jaggar and S. R. Bordo, pp. 145–171. New Brunswick, NJ: Rutgers University Press.

Klein, M. (1928). Early stages of the Oedipus conflict. In *Love, Guilt and Reparation, and Other Works*, pp. 186–198. New York: Delta, 1975.

——— (1945). The Oedipus complex in the light of early anxieties. In *Love, Guilt and Reparation, and Other Works*, pp. 370–419. New York: Delta, 1975.

——— (1957). Envy and gratitude. In *Envy and Gratitude and Other Works*, pp. 176–235. New York: Delta, 1975.

Layton, L. (1997). The doer behind the deed. *Gender and Psychoanalysis* 2:131–155.

Mahoney, M., and Yngvesson, B. (1992). The construction of subjectivity and the paradox of resistance: reintegrating feminist anthroplogy and psychology. *Signs* 18:44–73.

Marx, K. (1845–1846). *The German Ideology, Part I*. In *The Marx-Engels Reader*, 2nd ed., ed. R. Tucker, pp. 110–164. New York: Norton, 1978.

Mernissi, F. (1994). *Dreams of Trespass: Tales of a Harem Girlhood*. Reading, MA: Addison-Wesley.

Money, J., and Ehrhardt, A. A. (1972). *Man and Woman, Boy and Girl*. Baltimore: Johns Hopkins University Press.

Moraga, C. (1986). From a long line of vendidas: Chicanas and feminism. In *Feminist Studies—Critical Studies*, ed. T. De Lauretis, pp. 173–190. Madison: University of Wisconsin Press.

Nicholson, L. (1990). *Feminism/Postmodernism*. New York and London: Routledge.

Pratt, M. B. (1984). Identity: skin, blood, heart. In *Yours in Struggle: Three Feminist Perspectives on Anti-Semitism and Racism*, ed. E. Bulkin, M. B. Pratt, and B. Smith, pp. 9–63. Brooklyn, NY: Long Haul Press.

Roiphe, H., and Galenson, E. (1981). *Infantile Origins of Sexual Identity*. New York: International Universities Press.

Scott, J. W. (1988). *Gender and the Politics of History*. New York: Columbia University Press.

Stein, A. (1997). *Sex and Sensibility: Stories of a Lesbian Generation*. Berkeley: University of California Press.

Stein, R. (1995). Analysis of a case of transsexualism. *Psychoanalytic Dialogues* 4:257–289.

Steiner, R. (1995). "Hermeneutics or Hermes-Mess?" *International Journal of Psycho-Analysis* 76:435–445.

Stoller, R. (1968). *Sex and Gender*, vol. 1. New York: Science House.

11

"Being Elsewhere . . .": Women and Psychoanalysis in the Contemporary Arab World[1]

LILIA LABIDI

In recent years there has been a debate in the Arab world concerning psychoanalysis. This debate goes beyond the narrow confines of specialists, it is more in evidence in the Arab west than in the Arab east, and it is more in evidence among women than among men. In addition, other evidence of the great interest of women in these subjects is that, over a similar period, many women have given themselves over to the study of psychology and psychiatry and the feminization of these fields has become a clear trend.[2]

---

1. An early version of this chapter was presented to The Feminist Project of the Harvard Law School Graduate Program in March 1997. I would like to thank the participants for their comments.

2. The Tunisian Faculty of Medicine opened its doors for the first time during the 1960s. Until the 1980s there were only two women section heads in psychiatry, Professors Samia Attia and Saida Doukki, and very few women psychiatrists in private practice. Since then, in both public and private sectors, the feminization of this field has been very rapid. Psychology, where training was interrupted for a period, also shows a strong trend toward feminization. However, for a number of reasons, many of the women students do not reach the

Together with these phenomena, films such as those of Nouri Bouzid, Férid Boughdir and Moufida Tlati, are based on biographical facts, if not their own autobiographies.[3] Theatrical troupes such as those of Fadhel el-Jaibi, Fadhel el-Djaziri, and Raja Ben Ammar present productions drawn from daily life and submit historical events to their artistic and interpretive imagination.[4] Most of these productions also aim to display the processes of individualization and have enjoyed substantial success among the youth. This realism is also present among essayists and testifies to a protest against patriarchal values and the authoritarian political regimes that developed in the young states upon independence. These movements furnish readings that support the work undertaken by thinkers such as Frantz Fanon, Hichem Djaït, Mohamed Arkoun, and Abdallah Laroui, who call for a psychoanalysis of society.

In addition to these groups, there are others that use a religious vocabulary and articulate an identity discourse with regard to modernity, women, and sexuality, coming close to the views of a number of Tunisian psychiatrists who, in an article examining psychiatrists' attitudes toward psychoanalysis, expressed the view

---

doctoral level, a level at which men again become more numerous, just as they are at the professorial level.

It should also be noted that the course of study in psychology does not include the following subjects: women's psychology, adolescent psychology, psychology of the elderly, psychology of the colonized, and psychology of racism.

3. I am selecting here only several examples from a larger group. Nouri Bouzid directed two films drawn from his own personal experience: the first, *The Man of Ashes* (L'homme de cendres), deals with the rape by an employer of a young man apprenticed to him; the second, *Golden Horseshoes* (Sabots en or), revisits his experience in opposition political groups and in prison. Férid Boughdir in *Halfaouine* (*Children of the Terraces*) brings to the screen memories drawn from his childhood in one of the sections of Tunis; the film's theme is the sexual initiation of a young boy from a lower-class milieu. Moufida Tlatli, a Tunisian woman filmmaker, treats the sexual exploitation of women and political repression. Her film was very warmly received both in Tunisia and in other Arab countries.

4. Various theatrical troupes offering new treatments of political and historical themes contribute to a significant debate across the theaters of the region. One thinks of *Ghassalat en-noudar* (*Autumn Rains*) and *Arab*, among many others, which have brought the symptoms of Arab society to the stage.

that "the clients [of psychoanalysis] belong to a specific class and particularly to a clearly determined cultural sphere—here, to that of the West . . . an adherence which leads some psychiatrists to doubt the efficacy of psychoanalysis" because it was conceived "in western society for a western public of Judeo-Christian culture that has nothing to do with our Arab-Muslim reality. Psychoanalysis is a cultural practice that cannot be appropriate for our society" (Lahmar 1990, p. 10). These passages carry stereotypes that we also find in the identity discourse produced in the Arab world by the new intelligentsia that has been trained under systems of mass education, has been cut off from the history of Arab philosophy, and has not been able to participate fully in international debate since the 1970s (Eickelman 1992).

I have chosen to discuss the case of an adolescent girl since, for me, the questions this case evokes are situated at the intersection of modernity and the realism taken up by the artists and essayists of the region, just as did Musil (see Harrison and Wood 1994) and Breton,[5] for whom expressing psychopathology became an aim of their artistic productions. This case will introduce us to symptoms born of the particular situations in which women find themselves and where, when they are unable to find fulfillment, they succumb to illness or seek refuge in tradition, be it the Great or Little Tradition.[6]

This case will show how concepts from Freudian psychoanalysis, as it has been revisited by Lacan, serve, on the one hand, to highlight the new allegiances and the subordinate mechanisms by which the symbolic effects of imposition operate. On the other hand, it will also suggest what needs to be undertaken in order for psychoanalysis in the Arab world to be freed from being what Derrida (1987) calls "hostage to a representation of psychoanalysis that sees it as European, Judeo-Christian, and structured by the apparatus of the colonial state" (p. 331).

---

5. Breton often called hysteria one of the most important discoveries of the nineteenth century.

6. The basic texts of Islam on the one hand and local tradition (proverbs, songs, saint worship, and so forth) on the other.

By exploring the case I refer to as "Being Elsewhere," we will come to appreciate, by means of the adolescent girl Saphia's experience, the effects of uncovering a society's resistance and the degree to which the society does or does not accept Saphia's questioning and doubts, as an individual, as author of her own thinking. Her symptoms reveal the return of a truth—a truth contained in the particular way daughters are received at birth, distinguishing a cultural fact that shapes society at its deepest level, reflected in an ideology that portrays the woman as dangerous because she is able to disturb the religious and political order. This attribution, which still exists today, reveals a civilizational malaise that Saphia expresses to us in all its topicality, as a drama that possesses her and goes beyond her (see Mannoni 1979). This adolescent girl's case epitomizes the impossibility of her situation: the product of society's mishandled conscience, a society that at a particular moment in its history has failed to reflect on the rights of the individual in the face of political and religious powers, even while promulgating a code of personal status that rapidly ran up against the foreseeable limits of reformist thinking.

Reformist thought refers to a movement led by intellectuals and political figures of numerous Arab and Islamic countries who had, by the end of the nineteenth century, called for the modification of structures in the fields of education, administration, military organization, and the condition of women, structures that were taken to be sources of the relative backwardness of the region as compared to the West. That the domains of religion and personality remained untouched is crucial to Saphia's symptom.

Of Egypt, Tunisia, and Jordan, all of which had seen the growth of feminist movements starting at the beginning of the twentieth century, only Tunisia succeeded in adopting, in 1956, a Personal Status Code (Labidi 1984).[7] Under this code, polygamy was out-

---

7. Starting in the 1980s the situation of women in the Arab world improved further, under the influence of both a more highly educated population of women and the actions of the state. In Algeria the mobilization of women against a proposed family code that was favorable to fundamentalist views was an early sign

lawed, divorce became a legal procedure and gave women the opportunity to seek it, women won the right to vote and to hold office, girls gained access to the schools, and sexually mixed schools became mandatory. These developments paralleled the creation of health programs for the protection of maternal and infantile health, including birth control programs, and succeeded in lowering the rates of infant and maternal mortality and restructuring the family. In the domain of work, women acquired the same rights as men.

However, this normative legal framework coexists with a number of inequalities in practice. Among the most significant are the fact that a woman inherits only half of what a man inherits, her testimony is not equal to that of a man's in the courts, and women are extremely underrepresented in the formal political arena. These inequalities continue to structure a societal imaginary culture because it is these distinctions that give order to the symbols.

The images we will deal with here come from the 1980s and the 1990s, and result from the complex confrontation with the West, the ruptures with traditional structures brought on by colonial conquests, a neo-Islam that has been active since the end of the nineteenth century and reactive since the failure of development theories, and what political analysts call the *Naksa* (defeat) following the 1967 war in the Middle East.

THE URGENCY OF SPEAKING

Saphia was 12 years old when she was brought to me, on the advice of her family doctor. She was living with her grandparents and

---

of the civil struggles the country was to witness during the 1990s. In Morocco, at the same time, women gathered more than a million signatures protesting their situation, leading King Hassan II to personally examine their requests and to name four women as members of the next government. In March 1999, Egypt saw its first woman named as an administrative judge after two years of intense debate over this question. Kuwaiti women have not yet succeeded in obtaining the right to vote or to be elected to public office, more than four decades after Tunisian women obtained these rights.

was accompanied by her grandfather, who told me that for the last fifteen days her behavior had been unrecognizable both at school and at home. Everyone around her noticed her strangeness but the teachers at school were the quickest to respond: they wanted to know the reasons for this strangeness, which appeared as an attitude of "being elsewhere, a smile on her lips, a vacant stare." The family was quickly summoned to the school to discuss this behavior. Why did she refuse to participate in class? Why had she chosen to retreat from everything that was happening around her? Saphia was a good student and this behavior was very unlike her.

Saphia said to me, "As usual, on Sundays I go with my maternal grandmother to visit my family who live in the same section of town. Two weeks ago, while I was playing there with my young brother, he got angry, grabbed a scissors, and made as if to kill me while saying, 'Go back home.' I had to use all my strength to take the scissors from him. As I was leaving, I said to my mother, 'You ought to take better care of your son.'"

Her grandfather told me that her parents couldn't leave work and weren't able to come with Saphia to see me. I first saw her mother only several sessions later, and I was never able to see both mother and father at the same session. In the presence of her daughter, Saphia's mother told me the following. As she was giving birth to Saphia, she heard the wishes of her husband, her sisters-in-law, and her mother-in-law that the expected infant be a boy. Immediately after Saphia was born, she was given to her maternal grandmother, after which Saphia's mother refused for a long time to have a second child, fearing the birth of another daughter. She had several abortions, but six years later, when her gynecologist advised her of the risks she ran in having so many abortions, she allowed a new pregnancy to go to term and gave birth to a boy. This is the child who threatened Saphia with the scissors one Sunday, the child whose attack Saphia said she had used all her strength to thwart.

During our interview, the mother's attitude was defensive. She insisted that nothing she had done contradicted her culture and asked me to pay attention only to Saphia's symptoms. Many children live with their grandparents, uncles, or aunts, without that giving rise to any problems, she said. Why should a problem arise in this case? She refused to question her own behavior, saying that if she did so, she would be accused of having feminist views.

"Elsewhere," "a smile on her lips," "a vacant stare": through her symptoms Saphia exhibits a speech that cannot be heard. What is she trying to tell us? What truth are these symptoms expressing? How would she speak of this "elsewhere"? Would she be able to talk about it? Can this trip elsewhere be objectified, and will it teach us what has made the language that she has chosen necessary?

Here I will be joining the itinerary of Saphia and her mother to those of other women, because together they illustrate the relations that are established between the individual and a society in transition. They will shed light on the contradictions that a number of women have confronted when, raised in a traditional environment and benefiting from the advantages of the rule of law in the process of becoming, the difficulties of this transition are not acknowledged as an integral part of modernity.

Gisèle Halimi (1988), the well-known French lawyer of Tunisian origin, relates in her autobiography an experience similar to Saphia's. Halimi was born in Tunisia in 1927, and her father refused to see her until two weeks after her birth, claiming that a daughter was "a package of problems and natural inferiorities." As a lawyer in Paris, she has been involved in some of the most significant events in recent French colonial and postcolonial history. She defended, among others, Jamila Boupacha, an Algerian woman tortured by French colonial authorities in Algeria for her fight against colonialism and she wrote, with Simone de Beauvoir, a book about this Algerian militant (de Beauvoir and Halimi 1962); she defended women arrested for having had abortions and signed the famous Petition of 315, which led to the French law proposed by Simone Veil, guaranteeing women's right to have abortions; during the 1980s she took up the cause of foreign workers in France suffering from racism and, during the Algerian civil war of the 1990s, she called for mobilizing to protect women threatened by religious fundamentalism there. Her most recent actions include mounting a campaign with Marie-Claire Mendès-France and others to save Sarah, a 16-year-old Muslim girl from the Philippines, employed as a houseworker in Abu Dhabi and condemned to death there in September 1995 for having killed her employer while defending herself after he raped her. From all the evidence, Halimi's itinerary is overdetermined: she has succeeded in transforming rejection at birth into a political discourse.

Saphia's mother and Gisèle's father refused, or perhaps were unable, to challenge what society considered to be "natural inferiorities"; whereas the itineraries of Saphia and Gisèle, among many others, show how certain women, in response to the traumatic confrontation with the real, with the necessity of speaking, transform the cruelty of rejection at birth into either a symptom or into cultural and political action.

These two life experiences demonstrate what it costs women to live in a society in transition, passing from a culture founded on shame to one based on a code of personal status, from a culture that constitutes men as superior to one where women and men have equal rights.[8] Both Saphia and Gisèle Halimi, each according to the resources at her disposal, manage to deal with "impossible" situations. If Saphia succeeds in extricating herself from the ideas of persecution that stifle her, her mother chooses instead to tame the superego in order to protect herself from its ferociousness. The work that Saphia undertakes during her sessions with me enables her to cope with her symptoms while still continuing to live with her maternal grandmother. Now an adult, Saphia has married and completed her university studies. But that Sunday afternoon, as an adolescent and attacked by her brother, Saphia was brought to revisit her reception

---

8. Complementary laws to the Tunisian Personal Status Code of 1956 were introduced in 1992. Article 23, which had stipulated that the wife was obliged to respect the prerogatives of the husband and owed him obedience, was abrogated and replaced by the principle of mutual aid between spouses in the management of the household, the education of children, and so on. Also introducing changes were Article 67 where, when custody of the children was awarded to the mother, she was also made their guardian; and Article 153, which provided that the marriage of a girl of 17 years of age freed her from parental supervision.

at birth, a reception that remained unconscious and was later formulated as the question "Do I have the right to be here?"

It is to this question that Gisèle Halimi in Tunisia, Assia Djabbar in Algeria, Nawal Saadawi in Egypt, and others have tried to provide an answer through their writings and struggles to improve the condition of women in the region.[9] They have succeeded in introducing a creativity in which experience is transposed and opens onto a different reality. Saphia gains access to a language that enables her to express herself, the others gain access to creativity, to that in-between space between the subjective and the objective where cultural expression reveals the abject, which Kristeva (1996) defines as "an extremely strong feeling . . . somatic and symbolic . . . [towards] something that disgusts you" (p. 18). Language, the counterphobic object, fulfills in these authors the function of an indispensable know-how that enables them to exorcise the abject. This is also what enabled Saphia, at least at this stage, to cope with her symptoms, inventing what Lacan calls "the play of symbolic articulations."

Saphia's brother continued to display behavior that the family doctor, whom I met several years later, described as "agitated"— impossible on the outside, intolerable on the inside—adding that "he is the one we should have brought to you." However, the brother's behavior still attracted no criticism from those around him.

If we want to understand what makes him impossible/intolerable, we may have recourse to what some of the region's writers tell us (Labidi 1986). Rachid Boujedra (1969) provides a diagnosis of such characters, those who are trapped by the admiration women bestow upon them and who then experience their own self-disgust

---

9. Assia Djabbar has written a number of novels, among which are *Les alouettes naives* (1967), *Les enfants du nouveau monde* (1973), *Femmes d'Alger dans leur appartement* (1980), *L'amour, la fantasia* (1985), and *Loin de médine* (1991).

Nawal Saadawi is an Egyptian psychiatrist known for her political activism and many writings that have gained substantial popularity among Arab youth and intellectuals. These works include essays and fiction, such as *La femme et la sexualité* (1974), *L'homme et la sexualité* (1976), *La femme et les troubles psychiques* (1977), *Deux femmes en une* (1975), *La mort du seul homme sur terre* (1981), and *Journal intime d'une femme médecin* (1988).

and self-aversion. Similarly, Chraibi (1954), Ben Jelloun (1977), and others have tried to bring this not-yet self out of the void and give it a narcissistic significance—"I am disgusting, therefore I am"—thus managing in their works to identify the abject with the absence of the other and with the failure of the desired objects.[10] Novelists from the Maghreb (Morocco, Algeria, and Tunisia) will link the abject to a cold and icy mother who was only a receptacle for needs, and the masculine characters will only reach the oedipal stage by identifying with the aggressor or by fleeing into the borderline state. Through political action, Gisèle Halimi managed to take hold of the abject and to give it a name. In Saphia's case, the abject had invaded her to the point where she became it (see Kristeva 1980, on how individuals contend with the abject, p. 19).

The reading of the abject that Maghrebi novelists and other authors offer is very close to the construction elaborated in the psychoanalytic milieu in Europe. Hichem Djaït (1974), for example, in his study on the Arab-Muslim personality, has talked of the urgency of transforming primary institutions such as marriage and child socialization. Many of these authors spent time in Europe where they were in close contact with intellectual currents permeated by psychoanalytic ideas. The view they provide of psychological development is very close to Freudian theory and does not take into account criticisms put forward by feminist psychoanalysts, nor even those of Lacanians such as Françoise Dolto (1982), who argues that from the beginnings of fetal life, and then in the oral stage, the mother's phallic reference is the same for boys as for girls. "It is only after this stage that things will evolve differently. In one case, there is a centripetal dynamic, in the other a centrifugal one" (p. 194), inducing different developments in the stages that follow. In the girl's case, "When there is only the mother, it [primary

---

10. See R. Boujedra, *La répudiation*; D. Chraibi, *Le passé simple*; and T. Ben Jelloun, *La plus haute des solitudes*. These authors, writing in French, have been the object of much Western academic attention, significantly more than their Arabic-language counterparts.

narcissism] is constructed in a passive dominant attitude of impulses which are active only in language and in action" (p. 194). The boy in similar circumstances may become emotionally disturbed at puberty and may not be able to give a creative satisfaction to his impulses because his desire, repressed, is unable to be either suppressed or sublimated.

THE VIOLENCE OF IDEAS

Many thinkers in the Arab world agree that today the conditions governing the training of the elite, the weakness of cultural infrastructure, the absence of academic debate, and the seemingly ever-increasing political control over individual and political freedoms have discouraged critical thought and the emergence of a self-reflexive elite, putting in ideological difficulty the birth of a new rationality, a new subject. These conditions rapidly promoted a fundamentalist discourse that spread among the new intelligentsia produced by mass education, and that deprived women, youth, people from rural areas, and those on the margins of the cultural resources to support their actions.

During her analysis, Saphia came to recognize what was hidden under a certain kind of normality, and this enabled her to recover an existence as subject. She was able to resolve her symptoms and to see how her speech accommodated to the limits imposed by her mother—limits similar to those of reformist thinking—of not going beyond what the mother considered to be, medically, nothing more than a symptom. Certainly this adaptive attitude will not suffice to transform social reality or to create a subject, a speaking subject (Lacan 1967). We will now locate this symptom parallel to what other women have felt, in order to recover the symbolic dimension of Saphia's language, of Saphia's symptoms.

Among the feminists of the 1930s in Tunisia, several identified this "elsewhere" with living in a fog, the consequence of an oppressive reality in which most women had pregnancies one after another and were unable to limit them, and where some women fell into what regional psychiatry called "exhaustion psychosis." Saphia's other symptoms—"a smile on her lips," "a vacant stare"— lead us to what women say are the female traits highly valued by a society where "words are like silver, but silence is golden." The ideal woman, "beautiful and silent," is a model elaborated by the *oulema* (Islamic scholars) early in Islamic history (see El-Bokhari 1903) and reactivated with great force since the 1970s. In order to comprehend the power and extent of this model, we need to see its repetition in legends, proverbs, and songs that show how the discourse about women is structured, a discourse to which women contribute and which inhabits the popular culture.

Some examples are: "Boys are born with 16 devils and daughters with just one. With each passing year, the girls acquire 16 and the boys lose one." As adults, the boys will become "well-behaved," the girls will become "sorceresses." "To be sterile or the mother of a daughter amounts to the same thing." "A woman who engenders a son cannot be renounced; cursed be the daughter, a shameful result." "The grown-up daughter needs a man or a tomb." Those who give birth to a son sing, "God protect him, he has freed me from those who shut me in a room, he has chased away my enemies." This song refers to the fact that by giving birth to a son and then giving the son to be circumcised, the mother attains full membership in society. For infertile women and those who bear only daughters, exclusion remains their fate. These are the images that structure attitudes concerning sexuality and, as we will see, reappear in ceremonies relating to death (see Labidi 1989 for a more extensive collection).

Sexuality grounded in marriage remains for a number of contemporary intellectuals both a pleasure and a duty, following the strict theological view that makes "physical love between spouses" obligatory (Bouhdiba 1975, p. 110). Basing themselves on texts from the Great Tradition, they emphasize the man's duty to preserve "the virtue of the woman"; and the *keid en-nissa* (an Arabic term referring to women's capacity for cunning retaliation against men) is juxtaposed with the difficulty of satisfying the sexual desire of the woman, revealing simultaneously masculine sexual impotence and women's insatiability.[11] In responding to the husband's sexual needs, the wife protects him from disorder and revolt. It is on the woman's virtue that the man's relation to God depends: if he has a clear head and his mind is open, he can commit himself to prayer and orient himself toward the afterlife. The quality of a woman's morality thus depends on her enabling the man to attain his. The women who are most appreciated are those who laugh little, who rarely speak in a useless way, whose feet are too heavy to wander far from home, who don't disturb their husbands, who stay continually at home while tolerating the absence of their husbands, who have a short tongue and give advice that is God's work. The ideal wife is patient and modest, reserved and demure; she will lead her husband to satisfy the needs of his flesh without revolting against God.

Regarded as dangerous if she abstains from sexual relations, she would in such cases prevent the man, whose meaning in life is to be turned toward the divine will, from reaching this goal; she herself, oriented toward aiding the believer in this direction, may only perform her own religious duties if she is authorized to do so by her husband. This mythical representation collapses as soon as we place ourselves in another frame: in my clinical practice, men and women have spoken of a desire which, with regard to its origins, is the same, whatever the sexual identity of the speaker. But how to communicate knowledge drawn from clinical experience, from intense interpersonal interaction, to a wider public, in a context where exclusion and censorship are the rule?

The funeral ceremony for the unmarried male introduces us to the community's particular representation of the feminine, where the *keid en-nissa* is related to the difficulty women have in taking

---

11. The term *keid en-nissa* is used frequently in Tunisian Arabic as a metaphor for the destructive power of women, seen from the perspective of the dominant patriarchal culture. The Moroccan woman director Farida Benlyazid titled her most recent film *Keid en-nissa* (1999), using the term from a woman's perspective. In the film she shows an adolescent girl, in front of a computer, in conflict with her brother. The girl's mother tells her a story to show her the benefit and confidence that can be gained by utilizing "women's intelligence—*keid en-nissa.*

leave of the deceased and in attaining a state of resignation. Here, the funeral rites are the occasion for reaffirming the union with the mother, a union that had been maintained by ritual practices such as the *rbat* for the young male and by the *tasfih* for the young girl, in both of which the mother takes control of the child's sexuality until marriage.[12] The mother or woman who performs this ritual, or a woman who carries the same name as the woman who performs it, will have to break the effects of these rituals in order to allow the meeting of the bodies on the wedding night (Labidi 1989).

Another element appears in the practices that take place during the funeral ceremony for an unmarried boy (Labidi and Nacef 1993). There are three elements here that work to reactualize the unbroken tie between the mother and her son. They are the position of the deceased when he is brought out of the family home, the cries uttered when the body is transported to the cemetery, and the name he is called when he is put into his grave—three elements that are not found in the funeral ceremonies of adults.

At the time of departure from the family home for the cemetery, the boy's body is brought out head first, evoking the position of the fetus at birth while, at the same time, the women ululate in joy, saying, "He is marrying paradise." The second action is the

---

12. In the *rbat* the boy's mother, three days before his wedding ceremony, ties several knots in his clothing to protect him from impotence, and then unties them before he enters the nuptial chamber. In the *tasfih*, just before puberty, the girl is protected from premarital sexual relations when seven small incisions are made by an older woman in the girl's left knee while she says, "I am a wall, he is a thread," a formula which she will modify to "I am a thread, he is a wall," before entering the nuptial chamber, thus enabling her to perform sexually.

We should note here that if there is a parallel between the rites of the girl and the boy, an important difference remains: the *tasfih* is performed on the young girl prior to adolescence whereas the *rbat* is performed three days before the marriage ceremony. In both cases, the protection is nullified before sexual intercourse. The liberty that young men have for premarital sexual relations does not exist for women. Since 1994, Tunisian law criminalizes "crimes of honor." Reza Afshari (1994) relates how some young virgin girls in Iranian prisons were raped before being executed because in that patriarchal imaginary culture, girls dying as virgins would go straight to paradise.

chant intoned by the young men who transport the body to the cemetery, a chant intoned with a feeling of fury. The chant, "Ya Rahman, Ya Rahim, hada abdak ya Rahim" ("O Most Merciful, Most Munificent, here is your worshipper, O Most Munificent") includes words with the same root as the term for uterus (*rahem* in Arabic). The fury is against death or against "the uterus," which has taken away the young boy before he was able to marry and separate himself from his mother, or because his mother couldn't separate herself from him (Chabbi 1987). Finally, when the deceased is put in the grave, the young man is called, for the first time, by the name of his mother, to remind him of the words he must say when the angels will come to question him. The myth becomes a reality: the victory of the feminine, inscribed in the funeral rite of the unmarried young male, disrupts the political domain.

Taken together, these events express the desire of the mother to remain attached to her son, and affirm that the child who has only one wish—"to return there"—gives expression to a fantasy, fatal for the child. By instituting a ritual that evokes the non-separation of mother and child, the group reinforces the myth according to which the woman is deadly. The funeral rite of the young unmarried male expresses the fury of men against women for engendering disorder, for disturbing the political order (Labidi 1995). By denying her husband sexual relations and thus turning him away from God, the wife upsets the man whose life's meaning is to be turned toward the divine. As mother, she is dangerous to society because she upsets the political order: the young man or young woman who has not been freed from the mother by being reborn in the act of marriage will not have learned to know the mother as other than a vessel for need satisfaction and will be called the "bird of paradise."

This fear, engendered by the feminine, is what returns in Saphia's symptoms, an acting out of what remained unthought within reformist thinking. The *keid en-nissa* engendered by "natural inferiorities" lies at the intersection of representations of desire related to the temporal and the afterlife. The reading of desire developed by the Lacanian school opens up perspectives that distinguish desire from organicity, referring it to its source rather than to its object. Insofar as it is a desire for knowledge, it would be the same for men as for women (Lacan 1967).

The resurgence of such visions in the 1970s and the debates that started to push for changes to the Personal Status Code show how the transformations that began in these post-independence societies were left unconsummated. At the same time, the new means of communication exposed those who accepted them to unsuspected contradictions and difficulties. This leads to the question: Is the "new rationality" put in difficulty ideologically? I suggest that this is the case, and we can see this if we return to the history of ideas during the twentieth century. If we raise this question now it is because it is important for us to know what relationship subjects will have to this new concept of rationality. Two key periods—the 1930s and the 1990s—can help us understand these limits.

Tahar Haddad's work during the 1930s (Haddad 1978), condemning the wretched condition of Tunisian women and the attitudes of a bourgeoisie that continued to maintain the sexual exploitation of women and the political exploitation of men, found no echo. A similar effort, undertaken by the Egyptian writer Taha Hussein (1962) in the literary domain, also was not realized. These two cases illustrate the desire of some critics and historians to transform the culture and to create the foundations for a new symbolic order. Very rapidly, however, their work was interrupted. Haddad died five years after the publication of his book and Hussein had to retract a number of his projects. These incidents, taken together, were the inaugural signs of a murderous century for Arab intellectuals who again and again faced trials or assassinations in recent years in the Arab world.[13] These attacks are the effects of a confrontation between a positive

---

13. Symptomatic of the problem is the following anecdote. On June 13, 1995, in Tunis, I was among those named as having committed "an attack on public morals" ("atteinte à la pudeur") and was called to testify before a judge. This was part of a complaint made against people who had been quoted on the subject of virginity by the Tunisian weekly *Réalités*. The quotation attributed to me was in fact an extract from my book *Cabra Hachma: sexualité et tradition*, which, before its publication in 1989, had been passed by the state censor, as is required of all books appearing in Tunisia.

revaluation of recourse to belief on the one hand and, on the other, what Lacan (1967) presents as the distinctive traits of the modern man, "sure of oneself in one's uncertainties about oneself, that is through the mistrust that one learned long ago to practice as far as the traps of self-esteem are concerned" (p. 517).

In sending her daughter Saphia to the psychoanalyst, the mother calls up an unconscious doubt but, at the same time, she cannot accept the cultural readjustment that such a step presupposes because she herself, her group and/or her society, are not ready or have not been prepared to give support to a "divided subject," to an "I-don't-know-who-I-am" (Milner 1995, p. 40), reactualizing the model that maintains the *keid en-nissa*. The overdetermination in the commitment of Gisèle Halimi and other women to change societal values shows the distance that still exists between the project and the actual experience, a distance that has not been sufficiently thought through. "Being elsewhere," "a smile on her lips," "a vacant stare"—Saphia's symptoms—express the tensions within these societies and what perpetuates the oceanic model in which some would be only too happy to continue to bathe.

This tension still fuels a polemic between a religious vision that claims priority and a philosophical vision founded on truths mastered by the intellect. This tension was at the center of a dispute that opposed Ghazali (1058–1111), whose scholastic vision was primarily theological, to Ibn Sina (980–1037), known in the West as Avicennal, whose vision was predominantly philosophical. Ibn Sina declared that religious law clearly encourages the study of philosophy (the name given to the sciences that were grouped into speculative philosophy [physics, mathematics, and theology] and practical philosophy [ethics, economy, and politics]).[14] Ghazali's position was that the philosophers were infi-

---

14. Ibn Sina was well known as a doctor and philosopher. He opposed the view that the body would be resurrected, a point on which he was attacked by Ghazali. Ghazali wrote two major works against the philosophers: *Intentions of the Philosophers* and *The Incoherence of the Philosophers,* in which he argued against what he saw as impious philosophical conclusions: denials of the creation of the

dels; their reasoning led to impious conclusions such as denial of the resurrection of the body, and he affirmed that reason and ritual did not suffice but that the essential element was worship, the internal means that human consciousness uses in order to approach God. But it also should be noted that an element of Ghazali's position, as Imam, was the need to guide those who, for reasons of education or aptitude, were not able to follow the philosophical path.

Within religious discourse itself, opinions are divided today. In Morocco, Tunisia, Egypt, Kuwait, and elsewhere, we are witnessing a transformation of values. These debates are encouraged by the state and they testify to the efforts these societies are making to reinterpret their heritage. The most frequently discussed themes in this regard are the situation of women, advanced technology as in the case of organ transplants, and the definition of death. The effort to go beyond this dispute has required contemporary thinkers like Mohammed Arkoun (1984) and Abdallah Laroui (1987) to return to the discussion of ethics and freedom, providing cultural support to those who promote social change. If both converge in calling for a psychoanalysis of society, they differ in their approaches to Islam and to politics, with Arkoun arguing for a contextualization of tradition and Laroui arguing for rupture.

The conflict in interpretations concerning the temporal and eternal salvation on the one hand, and between men and women on the other, opens onto the relationships that a society maintains with a mythical imaginary where all change that doesn't fit the mold of an abstract narrative is demonized.[15] With frequent reference to the *keid en-nissa*, we have been able to build a cartography of the

---

world, of the coming end of the world, and of the resurrection of the body. He was deeply immersed in Greek philosophy, and used philosophical reason to place religion at the center of meaning.

15. One symptom of this is that ideas that do not meet with full approval are often labeled with a "foreign," "imported," or "Western" origin. This phenomenon is so dominant that Laroui feels himself obliged to specify in his writings that he is not taking the West as a reference but simply as a point for comparison.

submissions that this mythical imaginary engenders and how such a system continues to propagate fundamental affective disorders.

The cases and situations that I have discussed in the course of this chapter discover psychic formations in this mythical imaginary that constitute the *keid en-nissa* as refuge, as response to an existential anguish. Via Saphia's symptoms we have discovered the repetitions that people display without remembering or recognizing the archetypes and the myths they express. We unite here with the view of Devereux (1939) on social neuroses, when he says that the person who introjects the norms and values of society will also be neurotic and that it isn't the subjects who need to be cared for in these cases but rather the society, arguments that Muhammad Arkoun, Abdallah Laroui, Nawal Saadawi, and Fatima Mernissi, among others, are sensitive to because they themselves call for a psychoanalysis of society which would permit, from their points of view, reinforcing the self/ego.

This approach has the advantage of contributing to the theory of the self as the subject of civilization, as author of its own thoughts—a theory whose birth in the West was in part a product of the widely recognized contributions of great Islamic philosophers such as al-Kindi, Ibn Sina and Ibn Rushd, who transmitted, commented upon, and reinterpreted the Greek heritage. A hypostatized, reinforced ego is what will enable each subject not only to enjoy liberty but also to define him-/herself freely. Hypostatizing the ego is indeed the way Islamic feminists seem to have adopted in order to undertake a reexamination of the religious in the footsteps of the first female figures in Islam, and that secular women have adopted as well in their role as members of social organizations, making themselves the promoters of public life and civil liberty. It is perhaps the differentiation in the places from which these two groups speak and learn that will lead to the emergence of a truth, where the desire referred to its source becomes everyone's desire for knowledge, including women's.

Hypostatizing the ego would amount to what, according to Lacan (1967), the ego's language is reduced to, an "intuitive illumination" (p. 429), provided that the symptom is not taken to be a return of the truth, of a kind of knowledge. The knowledge contained in "being elsewhere, a smile on her lips, a vacant stare" cannot be taken from books of a normative character but only from the language contained in dream and symptom, that is, with the aid of thought and reasoning.

Psychoanalytic concepts applied to Saphia's case have allowed us to see some of the divisions that structure and maintain the Arab social domain. Reformist thought left the sphere of interpersonal relations largely untouched and these remain the privileged arena for the learning of social and psychological conflicts transmitted from one generation to another, and that each time come to refocus on the temporal and on eternal salvation, and on relations between men and women. If we have adopted a Lacanian approach, it is because Lacan's reading of Freudian notions reinscribes them in a modern perspective both with regard to its philosophical references and in divorcing psychoanalysis from what might have reduced it to mere technique. An unrevisited Freudian theory always was subject, within the region, to satisfying the positions of those who wanted to maintain a naturalistic, that is to say a biologically grounded, humanism.

REFERENCES

Afshari, R. (1994). An essay on Islamic cultural relativism in the discourse of human rights. *Human Rights Quarterly* 16:235–276.

Arkoun, M. (1984). *Essais sur la pensée islamique*. Paris: Editions Maisonneuve et Larose.

Bouhdiba, A. (1975). *Sexualité en Islam*. Paris: PUF.

Chabbi, L. (1987). *Repères et archives pour une histoire de la mort en milieu traditionel tunisien*. Tunis: Cahiers des arts et traditions populaires.

de Beauvoir, S., and Halimi, G. (1962). *Jamila Boupacha*. Paris: Gallimard.

Derrida, J. (1987). Géopolitique and the rest of the world. In *Psyche: Invention de l'autre*, pp. 327–344. Paris: Seuil.

Devereux, F. (1939). Maladjustment and social neurosis. *American Sociological Review* 4(6): 844–851.

Djaït, H. (1974). *La personnalité et le devenir arabo-islamique*. Paris: Seuil.

Dolto, F. (1982). *Sexualité féminine*. Paris: Scarabée et Métaillé.

Eickelman, D. (1992). Mass higher education and the religious imagination in contemporary Arab societies. *American Ethnologist* 19(4):634–655.

El-Bokhari. (1903). *Les traditions islamiques*. Paris: Ernest Leroux.

Haddad, T. (1978). *Notre femme, la legislation islamique et la societé*. Tunis: MTE.

Halimi, G. (1988). *Lait de l'oranges*. Paris: Gallimard.

Harrison, C., and Wood, P., eds. (1994). *Art in Theory 1900–1990: An Anthology of Changing Ideas*. Oxford: Blackwell.

Hussein, T. (1962). Fi ash-shiᶜr al-jahiliy (*Pre-Islamic Poetry*). Cairo: Dar al-Maᶜarif.

Kristeva, J. (1980). *Pouvoirs de l'horreur*. Paris: Seuil.

———— (1996). *Julia Kristeva Interviews*. New York: Columbia University Press.

Labidi, L. (1984). Lutte des femmes contre la repression. *IBLA* 2:249–276.

———— (1986). Le passé ou les pouvoirs de l'abject. In *Série Psychologie* (*Psychologie differentielle des sexes*) 3:65–76. Tunis: CERES.

———— (1989). *Çabra Hachma: sexualité et tradition*. Tunis: Dar Ennawras.

———— (1995). Circulation des femmes dans l'espace public-cimitière, carrefour du politique et du religieux dans le monde arrabo-musulman. In *La place des femmes, les enjeux de l'identité et de l'égalité au regard des sciences sociales*, pp. 232–236. Paris: La Découverte.

Labidi, L., and Nacef, T. (1993). *Deuil Impossible*. Tunis: Sahar.

Lacan, J. (1967). *Ecrits*. Paris: Seuil.

Lahmar, A. (1990). Visites chez les médecins de l'âme, du coté de chez Freud. *Tunis Hebdo*, September 24, p. 10.

Laroui, A. (1987). *Islam et midernité*. Paris: La Découverte.

Mannoni, M. (1979). *La théorie comme fiction*. Paris: Seuil.

Milner, J. C. (1995). *L'oeuvre claire: Lacan, la science, la philosophie*. Paris: Seuil.

12

Gendered Subjects, Gendered Agents: Toward an Integration of Postmodern Theory and Relational Analytic Practice[1]

LYNNE LAYTON

In the following pages, I bring postmodern, feminist, and psycho-analytic discourses on gender, agency, and relationship together[2] in what I hope will be a fruitful conversation/confrontation (see Flax 1990). Despite Flax's (1990) work on the topic, most Anglo-American clinicians have not yet come into contact with the difficult ideas and even more difficult languages of postmodern theories. In Anglo-American psychoanalytic feminist circles, a tradition

---

1. Originally published in *Who's That Girl? Who's That Boy?* pp. 1–27. Reprinted with permission from Jason Aronson.

2. While there are several versions of both postmodernism and poststructuralism, and many Lacanians, for example, are sharply critical of those versions thoroughly committed to social constructivism, I have used *postmodernism* as an umbrella term to refer to theories that derive from the work of Foucault, Derrida, and Lacan. I delineate in the text the particular assumptions that have marked these theories as "postmodern" (for example, the decentering of subjectivity), although I am aware that they differ significantly in many of their other basic assumptions. Further, my remarks about Lacanian theory generally refer less to original sources than to their use in Lacanian feminist cultural criticism.

has evolved over the past twenty years that interweaves a focus on gender with the insights of object relations theory, self psychology, infant research, and relational or intersubjective theory. While there are points of intersection between these discussions of gender and those of postmodernists, the different languages and different presuppositions about subjectivity have made it difficult for the two camps to meet in meaningful discussion. Here I explore tensions between the two sets of languages that are generated by the different assumptions about self, other, culture, and identity that structure the theories. I will look at the following interrelated points of tension: (1) the place of culture in the construction of the subject; (2) subjectivity, culture, and the practice of psychoanalysis; (3) the use of the terms *self, individual, ego, subject*; (4) the account of agency; (5) the account of the other and the relation between self and other; (6) the functioning of categories; (7) fluidity and coherence. Differences in the way these are conceived reveal the possibilities and difficulties of incorporating postmodern ideas into clinical work. In describing and critiquing some of the differences between postmodern and relational theories, I define the working assumptions of self, other, and agency that inform my work.

SOURCES OF TENSION BETWEEN RELATIONAL AND POSTMODERN IDENTITIES

The Place of Culture in the Construction of the Subject

When postmodern academics use the word "psychoanalysis," they usually mean the theory of Lacan or Freud. Indices to postmodern psychoanalytic texts rarely contain references to Benjamin, Fairbairn, Guntrip, Kohut, Mitchell, or Winnicott. An often reiterated Lacanian criticism of object relations targets what Lacanians see as a narrow focus on the mother–infant dyad. Such a focus, Lacanians argue, entails a denial of culture, for in Lacanian theory there is no subject before culture enters the scene in the form of the paternal function or third term that wrests the child from a fantasied unity with mother (the imaginary). To avert psychosis, the paternal function enforces the incest taboo and brings the child into the symbolic, the site of difference and lack (Mitchell and Rose 1985). This "castration," which also requires the child to assume one of two gender positions, is the founding moment of Lacanian subjectivity, for it is the entry into language that leads to the inevitable rupture between desire and its fulfillment, between meaning and being. A subject is internally divided, non-coincident with itself; only in fantasy is plenitude possible.

Foucault's (1973, 1979, 1980, 1982) version of postmodernism is a genealogy of the institutions and discourses that produce, construct, and maintain the modern subject, and one of his major contributions has been to clarify how the coming into being of the subject is a process that involves subjection to the power relations that criss-cross these institutions and discourses. Foucault's writings suggest that the modern individual exists as multiple and contradictory positions in discourse. Rather than experiencing cultural coercion as external, this sub-jected subject internalizes a cultural system of surveillance and thus disciplines and punishes his own body, sexuality, and consciousness in what seems like consensus with the dictates of culture.

Judith Butler (1990, 1993), whose work represents one of the most interesting poststructuralist positions on gender and agency, has added that the process of becoming a subject with mind and body is one that dictates what kinds of minds and bodies are speakable, what kinds unspeakable; what parts of the body are sanctioned as erogenous zones, what parts are not; what counts as a gender identity and what does not; and which sexual practices have legitimacy and which do not. Butler (1995) contends that the heterosexual subject is constructed upon a culturally enforced taboo against, and an ungrieved disavowal of, same-sex love. Her contentions go much further than feminist object relations critiques, which, until recently, have had as their subject middle-class white male and female heterosexuals. (Chodorow's recent work [1994] interrogates the "normalcy" of heterosexuality. See O'Connor and Ryan [1993] for a discussion of the long history of psychoanalytic theory's heterosexist assumptions.) Yet, as other critics have pointed out (Abel 1990), Anglo-American relational psychoanalytic theories, which focus not only on intrapsychic processes but on the developing child's caretaking environment, take into account the specificity of the experiencing subject in the context of his/her relationships and thus have the potential to allow one to elaborate individual or group histories in a way postmodern theories, with their universalized schemas of power (Foucault) or the imaginary/symbolic/real (Lacan), or "différence" (Derrida), might not (see Dews 1987).

This tension between individual specificity and cultural processes has been much discussed among clinicians who are also gender theorists. Some Anglo-American relational feminists have argued that postmodernists and clinicians have a hard time communicating because they each address a different level of subjectivity. For example, Jessica Benjamin (1994) has recently pointed out that much of postmodern theory mistakenly equates the subject that is a position in discourse—a construct of multiple and contradictory discourses (for example, "the black middle-class female")—with the psychic self, the conflicted, experiencing self. Frosh (1994), a psychologist and an academic, makes the point four times in the first twelve pages of his book on sexual difference that gender is both a position in discourse, a category of culture to be contested, *and* an intersubjective and intrapsychic element of each individual's sense of self. The question Frosh poses is one that certainly vexes any clinician familiar with postmodern critiques of the gender binary that results from the compulsory assumption of one of two gendered positions: "What can we say or do that might challenge the received wisdom of what is appropriate to being masculine or feminine, whilst also recognising the way people's experiences of themselves are bound up with deeply felt but often implicit notions of what their gender should and does mean?" (p. 1). Chodorow (1995), too, argues that gender is both a cultural and a personal construct, and she implicitly critiques postmodern and other perspectives that undervalue the psychological experience in which one makes idiosyncratic meaning of gender. Her well-taken point is that too few clinicians are aware of the ways that culture constructs gender and too few feminist academics are sensitive to the way gender is constructed and experienced psychologically.

Benjamin, Frosh, and Chodorow underscore an important difference between two levels on which meaning is constructed. If we are to attempt an integration of postmodern and relational theories, however, we have to be clear that these different levels of discourse are not dichotomous: the cultural is psychologically constructed, and the psychological is cultural. The cultural meanings of "black middle-class female" will not exhaust but will be part of the way a girl makes meaning of her gender identity. No part of that identity will be free of culture. But the way a black middle-class girl construes a gender identity at any particular historical moment, the way she puts together the possibilities that circulate in her family and culture, in turn contributes to constructing the set of cultural practices that will define "black middle-class female." Clinicians have a lot to gain from understanding postmodern critiques of the cultural discourses that construct the subject, and postmodernists have a lot to gain from Anglo-American psychoanalytic theory's capacity to capture the specificity, construction, and experience of an individual's inner world and relational negotiations.

Subjectivity, Culture, and the Practice of Psychoanalysis

Like postmodern theories, Anglo-American psychoanalytic theories are also concerned with a general theory of subject formation (which they call developmental theory), and psychoanalytic practice interrogates certain of the discourses and includes at least one of the institutions, the family, that constitute the individual who has come for treatment. But, aside from feminist and Marxist psychoanalytic theory, Anglo-American psychoanalytic theory does not in general have a stake in altering the social status quo and thus does not question the fact that many of its assumptions are uncritically borrowed from the white middle-class dominant culture. For example, the cornerstone of most developmental theory is the heterosexual nuclear family, treated as though it exists in a cultural vacuum. For postmodernists, not only power inequalities between father and mother have to be addressed, but also the assumption that the family ought to *consist* of a father and a mother— or that the family is the best place for a child to grow.

Relational psychoanalytic feminists have deconstructed the Freudian oedipal scenario and pointed to less misogynist directions Freud might have taken in his theorizing (see Sprengnether 1990, 1995), and they have challenged the supposed normality of the monadic individual that is the oedipal scenario's product. Yet, few clinicians or theorists in the Anglo-American tradition of relational theory have talked about the fact that psychoanalysis is one of the many discourses/practices that construct the individual in particular ways (exceptions are usually feminist theorists, e.g., Harris 1995, and Benjamin's [1988] critique of the way psychoanalytic theory has always eliminated the mother's subjectivity). In postmodern discussions, psychoanalysis is not a discourse that helps a subject to discover an identity already presumed to be there. Rather, it is one of the many Western discourses that *produce* identity. Readers familiar with the various two-person psychologies that have been elaborated in recent years will see the connections between postmodern and relational psychoanalytic positions, which also assume that analyst and client co-construct the subjectivities that emerge from the clinical encounter. But relational theories do not generally concern themselves with what postmodern theory insists on as the coercive element of the psychoanalytic enterprise, the fact that psychoanalysis legitimizes some gender identities, sexualities, and ways of being, and delegitimizes others. Nor do non-feminist relational theories show much interest in the cultural strictures that allow some subjectivities to emerge and prohibit others. If we assume that psychoanalytic theories and practices play a constitutive role in producing subjects and theories about subject formation, clinicians need to be more aware than they have been of the kinds of subjects they participate in producing.

Self, Individual, Ego, Subject

A major source of tension between postmodern and relational theories lies in their conflicting definitions of *self*, *individual*, *ego*, and *subject*. Relational theories use *self*, *individual*, and *subject* interchangeably (see Flax 1996, for a critique). Postmodern theories distinguish *subject* from *individual*, *self*, and *ego*, and they tend to assume that *self*, *individual*, and *ego* are equivalent and are essentially narcissistic constructs. Let us look at Lacanian theory as an example. A prime target of the Lacanian theory of subjectivity is American ego psychology, which Lacan accused of having betrayed Freud's most radical discovery—the unconscious. In Lacanian theory, the ego originates in a mis-recognition in the "mirror stage": the baby denies its awareness of its own fragmentation by identifying with its idealized, unified mirror image and by taking this image as exhaustive of its subjectivity. This misrecognition marks the ego as an imaginary structure, a structure built on a fictional coherence. All of the later identifications that make up the ego involve such misrecognitions, and so the ego is constituted by narcissistic fantasies of wholeness and homogeneity that suppress awareness of the subject's heterogeneity and its existential condition of lack. The individual, sustained by the fantasy of indivisibility and conscious control, is the representative of the Lacanian ego. Most postmodern and poststructuralist accounts, psychoanalytic and non-psychoanalytic, share Lacan's understanding of the ego and the individual. As I said earlier, the condition of subjectivity—the incest taboo and the entry into language/the symbolic/culture—is conceived as a loss that splits the subject from himself. The truth of the subject—as distinguished from ego or individual—is that it is split, lacking. A Lacanian clinician, then, as well as a Lacanian critic, figures the cure to the ego's narcissism to be acceptance of the condition of lack.

In relational theories, the self has been defined in a multitude of ways, few of which reduce to the Lacanian view of the ego (indeed, Freud's view of the ego does not reduce to the Lacanian view;

see Whitebook 1995). There is an error, I believe, in the post-modern assumption that the self is equivalent to what feminists and postmodernists have critiqued as the controlling consciousness of bourgeois individualism, the autonomous male subject. The post-modern disdain for the term *individual* seems to result from the postmodern conflation of the bourgeois individual (a self-identical entity that is not relationally formed and claims to be fully conscious) with the individual. While the process of subjectivation (becoming a subject) in Western culture certainly includes the internalization of this dominant version of agency and relatedness, this version does not exhaust even the conscious self. I want to distinguish between *self*, defined as multiple and contradictory and thus akin to Lacan's *subject*, and a *master self* (Fairfield 1996), that is, a self that always suppresses otherness and is pathologically narcissistic.

Versions of subjectivity elaborated by relational analytic theorists do not assume that pathological narcissism is the primary constituent of late-twentieth-century Western identity (see, for example, Benjamin 1988, Bromberg 1996, Mitchell 1988). Relational psychoanalytic theories posit a heterogeneous subject/individual/self who has narcissistic vulnerabilities, but they do not claim, as Lacanians do, that there is a universal structure of subjectivity, a necessary outcome of all people's development (the ego), that is pathologically narcissistic. When pathological narcissism is present, it does not arise from a denial of existential lack but rather from specific familially induced wounds. Clinical work in a relational paradigm suggests that the degree of narcissism that produces oppression and the suppression of otherness is quantitatively greater than and qualitatively different from the degree of narcissism that exists in every psyche. Pathological narcissism and narcissistic vulnerability may exist on a continuum, but the tendency for postmodern theories to equate the two may make it difficult for clinicians to incorporate postmodern theories into their work.

In distinction from postmodern theories, I use the terms *subject*, *self*, and *individual* interchangeably, reserving the term *pathological narcissism* to describe the inability to experience an other as a separate subject and to describe the suppression of heterogeneity both within the subject and between subjects. In distinction from relational theories, which tend to focus on pathological narcissism as an individual rather than a cultural problem, I follow those feminist relational theorists who have argued that dominant versions of femininity and masculinity are marked by pathological narcissism.

The Account of Agency

Because subjection to cultural forces is so central to subject formation in postmodern theories and so absent in relational theories, another source of tension between the two sets of theories concerns the way they conceptualize agency. Diverse theorists who draw on Lacan to critique the cultural status quo struggle to bridge the gap between what, in Lacanian theory, seem to be two different levels of subject formation and two different kinds of agency. In Lacan (1977), the components of originary subject formation— the mirror stage that inaugurates the narcissistic ego, the splitting of subjectivity that results from language acquisition, the compulsory assumption of one of two gendered positions—are set forth as universal, ahistorical processes. Because of this, it is no easy task to bring them into relation with contingent and historical processes of development, such as those that produce racial or class identities or those that produce narcissistic wounds, such as parental or cultural slights. In Lacanian culture criticism (see, for example, Mulvey 1975, Silverman 1996), one finds that wounds produced by parental pathology or cultural pathologies such as racism and sexism are often explained in the final instance as a defense against acknowledging the original wound: fragmentation in language, the inevitable rift between desire and its fulfillment. From a relational analytic perspective, this explanation itself appears as a rationalization that calls on existential necessity to circumvent the pain of acknowledging our dependence on loved ones and the hurt caused by them.

The early processes of Lacanian subject formation figure the subject as sub-jected to cultural systems. Culture and language alienate the subject in the expectations and desires of the other, which exist even before a baby is born. It is not at all clear how later processes would escape that same problematic, since Lacan asserts that all imaginary ego identifications are made on the model of the mirror stage; that is, they are all narcissistic in that they reduce heterogeneity and lack to coherence and unity. The agency of the ego, then, is located in subjects' capacity to deny their essential lack or fragmentation by identifying as whole and unitary. But what does the agency of the subject look like? Lacanian theorists who want to challenge the status quo have found this agency difficult to derive.

Smith (1988), who has attempted this task, distinguishes between the individual, the subject, and the agent in his reading of Lacanian theory. Although in a footnote Smith recognizes two origins of *subject* (p. 164), one from political theory that focuses on subjection to the state, church, and other hegemonic discursive formations, and one from German philosophy that focuses on the capacity for autonomous critique of authority, he chooses to define *subject* only by the former and to reserve the term *agent* for the latter. He defines the subject as a colligation of seamless subject positions (such as race, gender, and class) provided by family and culture and (mis)recognized by the individual as positions to which s/he belongs.[3] Smith discovers agency in the contradictions and disturbances created in the "subject/individual" by the multiplicity of different subject positions imposed by the culture. Agency is defined as resistance to ideology. However, Smith does not challenge the Lacanian assumption that these subject positions, like originary ego formation, occur on the model of pathological nar-

---

3. See Althusser's (1971) notion of interpellation, where the person is hailed by the culture as, for example, a gendered individual, and recognizes himherself as the person who is hailed. How much choice this person has in recognizing or not recognizing the self in the cultural position offered is a subject of debate among those drawn to Althusser (see Morley 1980).

cissism (for challenges to Lacan's assumption, see Flax 1990; for a critique of Lacan that takes a different direction from mine but which also seeks a way out of narcissism, see Whitebook 1995). Because I challenge this assumption, I prefer to preserve the two origins of *subject* and not reduce the subject to internally coherent subject positions (see de Lauretis 1986). The contemporary subject internalizes more than one version of agency and relatedness, each of which is embedded in particular relational matrices. Conflict arises not from the collision of subject positions, nor from the fact that some of these subject positions are more pleasurable than others (a remnant, in Smith's work, of the influence of Freud's pleasure principle), but rather from the fact that internalizations are products of numerous conflicting relationships, relationships with different degrees of power to approve or disapprove, to give or withhold love.[4] The multiple versions of agency and relatedness that we internalize are not equally powerful contenders for self-acceptance or expression because they are also subject to cultural proscriptions or cultural approval.

Anglo-American relational theory/practice focuses almost exclusively on the contingent processes of development. The capacity for agency, presumed to exist from birth (Stern 1985), is first observed in the infant's multiple ways of relating (for a critique of Stern, see Cushman 1991). In this view, agency takes shape in relationships, in various kinds of mutual encounters with early care-

---

4. My work, in its focus on the relational core of gender identity, owes a great debt to Goldner's (1991) article, "Toward a Critical Relational Theory of Gender," which brilliantly draws on systems theory, feminist theory, and deconstruction to elaborate the construction, experience, and consequences of the masculine/feminine binary. Goldner argues that "since gender develops in and through relationships with gendered others, especially parents and siblings, its meaning and dynamics must be located, minimally, in a three- or four-person psychology that can make room for the interplay between different minds, each with an independent center of gravity" (p. 262). Goldner's critical relational theory of gender focuses on how "personhood, gender identity, and relationship structures develop together, coevolving and codetermining each other" (pp. 261–262). Along with Flax (1990), Goldner is one of the very few publishing U.S. clinicians who has made the integration of postmodernism and object relations theory her project.

taking others.[5] In some of these encounters, agency is identified when infants match the other's affect and behavior or get the other to match theirs. In other encounters, agency is identified when infants resist the other's call to match affect and behavior. It is also identified in infants' attempts to repair a disruption in mutuality. There is little focus on subjectivity as sub-jection in these theories, except in cases where, for example, a narcissistic parent might demand the infant's subjection. The relational school's account of the development of agency does not necessarily conflict with postmodern theories and might provide these theories with more specificity (indeed, there are potential intersections between Stern's theory and Butler's use of performativity). But non-feminist relational theorists tend to omit the cultural context in which agency develops, and this omission obscures the questions postmodernists and feminist relational theorists ask about agency: What cultural functions does agency serve? Why assume only one kind of agency? What versions of agency are allowed to develop and what versions are not? (An important feminist debate on agency takes place in Benhabib 1995.)

Clinicians and developmental theorists of the relational school tend not to differentiate between the kinds of interactions that produce individuals and the kinds that reproduce them. Relational theorists thus presume that individuals might become less conflicted, might find more satisfying ways of relating, might feel less self-hatred, and might come to appreciate their own complexity and fluidity, but they tend not to wonder whether agency, affect, and relatedness themselves take shape in a particular cultural field

---

5. A difference between Smith's position and mine might be seen in the examples of agency each of us would highlight. Smith's model of someone who comes close to incarnating a subject who mediates between being sub-jected and agentic is Roland Barthes. He champions Barthes for constantly undermining his unitariness in relation to his objects (e.g., photos). I would turn instead to Pratt (1984), who constantly undermines her unitariness by interrogating her history in relation to that of others—men, blacks, Indians, lesbians (see Martin and Mohanty 1986).

that makes some versions acceptable and others not. In the worst case, this tendency not to wonder produces the individual who reproduces the cultural status quo—which should *not*, to my mind, be the project of psychoanalysis.

The different views of agency again highlight the tension between the postmodern focus on the cultural determination of subjectivity and the relational focus on the microprocesses of mutuality. An integration of the two might ponder the cultural constraints on the ways, for example, female parents and male babies, male clinicians and female clients talk, play, regulate affect, display affect, and so forth, thereby generating particular kinds of agencies.

The Account of the Other and the Relation between Self and Other

Yet another source of tension between postmodern theories of subject formation and relational analytic theories, one that follows from the above, is the conceptualization of the other and of self–other relations. In most postmodern theories of subjectivation, the other—in the guise of culture, language, and family—is figured as coercive. In Lacan, paternal law wrests the child from a narcissistic fusion with the mother and brings him into the realm of the symbolic. Lacanian theory is called intersubjective by its proponents because the subject is constituted by intersubjectively shared, culturally determined linguistic structures that speak the subject. Those in the Anglo-American psychoanalytic tradition of intersubjective theory, however, will likely not recognize this usage of *intersubjective*, for in Anglo-American theory the term means that the subject's development and his/her desire are mutually negotiated with caregivers from birth, with the child's needs and desires exerting their own independent influence. Winnicott's (1974) "potential" or "transitional" space, a space created between mother and child, is where internal and external, difference and sameness, are continuously negotiated (see Benjamin 1995, Pizer 1992). In relational theories, the attainment of language is not seen to be motivated solely by compensation for loss, nor is language primarily used to cover over lack, as it is in Lacanian culture criticism (with roots in Freud's [1920] discussion of the *fort/da* game). Rather, in the relational school, language acquisition and use are equally motivated by the pleasures of attunement, creative play, a non-defensive liberation from dependence and helplessness (here again we must note the influence of Loewald 1980 and Winnicott 1974). Indeed, relational theories, unlike Lacanian theory, do not envision subject formation as motored solely by loss and the mastery of loss. Rather, the pain of loss and the pleasures of attachment are equally determinant. For instance, Benjamin (1988) roots the capacity both for intimacy and for erotic love in early parent–child moments of mutual attunement. And Winnicott (1965) writes that the capacity to be alone grows not from mastery of the loss of the other but from persisting attachments to the other. (Winnicott has been egregiously caricatured by postmodern gender theorists.)

These differences in conceptualizing the relation between self and other bear directly on the relation between client and therapist in clinical work. Both postmodern and relational theorists would want the therapy relationship to make new versions of subjectivity and intersubjectivity possible. But they might have different ways of figuring the stance the therapist ought to take to accomplish this. The assumption of relational theory is that agency is structured by the quality of attachments (see Lyons-Ruth 1991). New kinds of attachments open the client to new ways of being a subject, so the presence and subjectivity of the therapist, the kind of relationship therapist and client forge, are stressed in relational theory. It is in relational negotiation, for example, that narcissism is confronted. Attachment is not the starting point of postmodern theories. Lacanian theory assumes that clients will place the analyst in the position of the one who knows, a position the analyst must refuse in order to enable the client to come to know his own desire and to know that he is lacking. The analyst's stance, then, does offer a different kind of attachment (one that refuses imaginary projections), but by the end of analysis the attachment to the analyst should not be constitutive of the client's desire.

Barratt (1993), an analyst who acknowledges a debt to Derrida, claims that the postmodern core of psychoanalysis is free associa- tion. Interpretations of any kind, on the other hand, are modernist attempts to re-establish the client within an identitarian logic and so encourage adaptation to the social status quo. Free association, curative in itself, is "a process that works against the fixities, priori- ties, certainties of every act of interpretive establishment" (pp. 14– 15). In Barratt's version of postmodern analysis, the analyst's role is far less constitutive of the process than it is in contemporary rela- tional theories. Ironically, Lacan's and Barratt's postmodern psycho- analytic therapies rely on what seem to be modernist one-person clinical models, while most relational therapies rely on what seem to be postmodernist two-person models (Aron 1990).

The Functioning of Categories

Related to many of the above tensions is the tension between post- modern discussions of cultural categories like *masculine* and *femi- nine*, and the place of such categories in clinical practice. Derrida's (1976, 1978) work focuses attention on the structural relation to each other of binary pairs of categories such as speech/writing or conscious/unconscious. His writings take aim at the binary logic at the core of Western metaphysics. Derrida contends that the wish to avoid uncertainty, to lay claim to a universal truth that would be the foundation of all we know (be that truth appealed to in the name of God, class struggle, evolution, or core gender identity) is a wish that produces rigid binaries in hierarchic relation. While clinicians have long been aware that black-and-white thinking characterizes such self-disorders as borderline and narcissistic, Derrida alerts us to the constricted black-and-white nature of Western thought in general, and thought is where ideology and power differentials operate.

What about masculinity and femininity? Until fairly recently I would guess that most people, including myself, thought they knew exactly what they were talking about when they evoked these categories; the pages of most psychoanalytic journals still suggest that a lot of people are clear about what masculinity and femininity mean.[6] In everyday language and in mainstream ideologies of all disciplines, including psychoanalysis, masculinity and femininity are presented as mutually exclusive opposites. But they are neither opposite nor are they equally valued: one member of any binary pair, in this case masculinity, is always in a superior cultural position to the other. Derrideans show the way in which masculinity and femininity actually co-construct each other and have meaning only in their relation. Maintaining the categories as mutually exclusive binaries keeps the hierarchical relationship intact. The dominant strand of "difference feminism," which informs much mainstream psychoanalytic writing on gender, argues that women's self structure, ways of knowing, ways of making moral decisions, and ways of using language are different from and as valuable as men's (see the work of Belenky et al. 1987, Gilligan 1982, Miller et al. 1991, Tannen 1990). A deconstructive politics, on the contrary, leads rather to an uncovering of the constitutive connection between men's and women's "ways," and opens the door to other gender/sex possibilities beyond male and female.

In most poststructuralist theories, categories like the master self and the coercive other are also oppressive because they impose unity on heterogeneity. This is one very important way that categories operate—but not the only way. Certainly femininity and masculinity are often evoked defensively to suppress heterogeneity (see May 1986; cf. Thompson's [1995] discussion of clients' defensive use of race). Sexual difference can be used ideologically to obscure the relevance of other categories; for example, see

---

6. Chodorow (1989) differentiates "psychoanalytic feminists," among whom she includes herself, from contemporary psychoanalysts who write about women and femininity, particularly about the way that femininity is constructed from female anatomy. Included in her discussion of the latter are Kestenberg 1968, Mayer 1985, and Tyson 1982. These defenders of primary femininity elaborate on early work by Horney (1924, 1926).

Williamson's (1986) discussion of the way advertisements encourage men of all classes to bond in their domination over women, using gender difference to cover over potentially more explosive class differences. But another function of categories is to facilitate provisional unities that have the potential to transform both the individual and culture. I am thinking of the civil rights, the feminist, and the gay and lesbian movements (see Hacking's [1986] interesting position that categories and the kinds of persons they cover emerge historically at the same time). It is this facilitative function that poses a challenge to proponents of postmodern theories.

Gender categories, then, can be facilitating. In clinical work, therapists and clients grope for new categories to provide points of identification as they deconstruct the old ones that constrict possibility. Let us look more closely at the difficulties that postmodern views of categories pose for clinical work.

Fluidity and Coherence

In the history of social movements, a central tension arose as theorists and activists sought to respect the histories of particular identities—gay, lesbian, female—yet simultaneously pointed to ways that those identities were not discrete, were co-constructed by what they excluded. This is a version of the problem of the category discussed above. Some postmodern feminists, Butler included, have found it difficult to defend their deconstruction of gender identity while maintaining an allegiance to women's political struggles. Here lies one of the main tensions between postmodernists and their critics. On one side are those who defend identity politics. On the postmodern side are those who find identity a necessarily oppressive and narcissistic construct, one, as we have said, that imposes coherence on multiplicity, that necessarily makes normative inclusions and exclusions. The debate often becomes quite complicated, especially when a group attacks an identity position as exclusionary and thereby in effect constitutes a new identity category. This occurred, for example, when feminists of color began to challenge the white subject of white feminism (see hooks 1981, Moraga and Anzaldúa 1983, and Smith 1984). Their position seems to be that the identity of feminists of color is a decentered, multiple identity that does not impose coherence, that embraces non-identity, and is thus a model for feminist subjectivity (note that some early feminist theory made this claim for women in general, e.g., Rabine 1988).

Butler (1992) has proposed a way to sustain allegiance to feminism while contesting the category *women* with her notion of "rifting," a way of both elaborating a "we" and letting it be open to what it necessarily excludes, which will continuously change the nature of the "we." This "double gesture," however, cannot work as a way to hold identity politics and postmodern politics in tension if each subject making up the "we," as well as the "we" itself, is seen to be exhausted by narcissism. Butler makes a similar point in *Gender Trouble* (1990) when she speaks of coalition politics. If the people in a coalition do not recognize that their own identities are made up of repudiations of the identities of others in the coalition, the group cannot work. I read this as saying that it can only work if the subjects involved are capable of taking the position of the other, of respecting both difference and likeness. But where Butler seems to see narcissism as endemic to identity, I think that identities need not be mere defenses against difference (see Weir 1996 for a different argument toward the same conclusion).

A very important tension between postmodern and relational theories of identity concerns the dispute over whether or not there is anything about identity that is "core." Many Anglo-American psychoanalytic feminists accept Stoller's (1976a,b, 1985) idea that a core gender identity, that is, the conviction established by 18 months that one is either male or female, is essential to subject formation. In recent work Jessica Benjamin (1995, 1996) has begun referring to this as nominal gender identity. With this switch in terminology, she wishes to maintain the idea that children know by 18 months that they are either male or female; at the same time, she wants to integrate cognitive findings (e.g., Fast

1984) that make it clear that these categories are at first empty of meaning.[7]

The division into male and female is something I would guess few clinicians ever question. Yet such a binary "conviction" is precisely the kind of thing that a poststructuralist such as Judith Butler will challenge. She will want to establish the genealogy of this division and will ultimately want to replace it with other possibilities that she considers less homophobic. For she believes that the division into male and female is not a necessary but a culturally contingent decision, one that guarantees compulsory heterosexuality.

Butler's is a most important project. Yet clinicians meet with people who have at least in part been culturally produced to replicate the status quo. When these people do not replicate it, they usually find themselves in great pain, because they are not met with love and approval. And they want clinicians to make them "normal," they want to fit in. Indeed, clinicians find that those who do not have a conviction of being either male or female do not usually enjoy the fluid identity that postmodernists hold out as ideal but instead often hate themselves and are riddled with shame. A fluid identity is a desirable outcome, but clinical work suggests that fluidity is an accomplishment, not a given—and that achieving it may presuppose the experience of a core gender identity.

The tension between the way gender conflicts are conveyed to a clinician and the way gender is discussed in postmodern theory is my concern. Much of the difficulty postmodernism poses for clinicians arises because postmodernists radically question the very categories that structure what most of us call our "identity," cate-

---

7. Note the recent study by de Marneffe (1997) that shows that one's sense of gender is not necessarily based on one's bodily experience: children know what genital they have by 24 months but only later know that having it means they are male or female. When looking at anatomically correct dolls with no other gender-identifying features, they know which doll has genitals like their own and know which gender they are, but they don't know which doll is a boy and which a girl. De Marneffe argues that the fluidity between body representation and gender representation continues through life.

gories that anchor us psychologically and relationally: male and female, black and white, straight and gay. Indeed, there is a radical schism between postmodern celebrations of identity fluidity and what most people find it like to live an embodied, raced, and gendered life in contemporary America (see Hennessy 1995). Deconstructive theory and politics argue persuasively that the consequences of maintaining such dichotomous categories can be oppressive both intrapsychically and intersubjectively, but the contemporary uses of deconstructive theory and politics consistently ignore or underestimate the difficult work of extricating oneself from reified binaries.

Postmodernists charge that notions of a "core" are essentialist, that they fix identity in a way that denies cultural construction and emancipatory practices. But feminist relational theorists' conception of a "core" does not in fact assume the kind of unity postmodernists abhor, the kind that silences otherness (see Abel 1990, Flax 1990, Rivera 1989). In the relational paradigm, *core* does not mean *innate*, nor does it imply a true self. And it is not incompatible with cultural construction. Perhaps the relational and postmodern camps have been falsely polarized (see Brennan 1989, Fraser 1995). But "core" does imply something internal that recognizably persists even while it may continuously and subtly alter, and there are real differences between theorists for whom a constructed interior relational world motivates behavior and those, like Butler (1990), for whom interiority is an appearance, an effect of discourse.

Because of what they see in practice, clinicians versed in psychoanalytic theories of self disorder and fragmentation find themselves uncomfortable with the celebrations of fragmentation and fluidity put forth in some popular versions of postmodern theory (for example, Haraway's [1985] cyborg subjectivity). Because of what they see in practice, psychoanalytic relational theorists assert that gender and other identity elements are culturally constructed pieces of an internal relational world that both evolves and is relatively coherent and stable (Glass 1993). It is this stance for coherence, I believe, that most garners the contempt of postmodernists for relational theorists.

CONCLUSION

Given these important differences, can we conceptualize a notion of the subject that is informed both by the postmodern emphasis on the general constituents of subject formation and by the Anglo-American emphasis on its specific, individual relational constituents? Can we find a way to theorize both the coercive and the non-coercive moments of subject formation? I maintain that "the subject" is both a position in discourse (sub-jected to the multiple and contradictory discourses of culture, including family) and a multiple and contradictory being whose negotiation of early relationships will shape the meaning that these discourses take on and so shape the discourses themselves. Of course, it is the nature of this being that is in question: A precultural true self, à la Winnicott? Fully constituted by discourse, à la Butler?[8]

I define the self/subject/individual as neither a true self nor fully determined by existent discursive positions but rather as a continuously evolving negotiator between relationally constructed

---

8. In feminist circles, debates are ongoing about whether the subject is fully constituted by discourse, and about how something new might be generated from what is culturally determined (see Adelson 1993). Judith Butler's position in her introduction to *Bodies that Matter* (1993) is at one end of the continuum: material reality is always already discursive. Newness is generated from the fact that meaning always exceeds the linguistic categories that try to fix meaning. Another view is propounded by Frankenberg (1993), who seems to equate discourse not with language but with dominant ideology and argues that a person can get a distance from discourse and evaluate it from another place. Frankenberg sees the discursive and the material dimensions of the category she investigates, whiteness, as connected but distinct. The connection generates experience: "Discursive repertoires may reinforce, contradict, conceal, explain, or 'explain away' the materiality or the history of a given situation" (p. 2).

multiple and contradictory internal and external worlds. We are both subject to these worlds and create them as we engage in current relations with intimates, groups, and the social environment. We are born into families with their own histories and ways of mediating culture, and so we immediately engage in particular patterns of relating. The way those patterns are internalized is conditioned by the accidents of gender, race, and class and by the power differentials that structure them at a given historical moment (see Collins 1994). It is also conditioned by the bodies and temperaments of individuals and those with whom they come in contact. The meanings these bodies, temperaments, and other individual identity elements take on are not outside of culture; they *are* culture. Neither are they reducible to already existing discursive positions, because neither the individual nor the discursive level is static. Rather they are mutually negotiated and renegotiated. Subjects idiosyncratically make meaning of, identify with, disidentify with, take up parts of, or modify these positions in accord with ongoing relational experience.

The fluidity inherent in subjectivity does not originate in the fluidity of the language that speaks the subject, as poststructuralists would have it. Rather, the fluidity of the subject and of the meaning subjects make results from the internalized multiple and contradictory relational patterns that both constitute the subject and are negotiated by the subject. And the stability of these patterns as they repeat over time accounts for the subject's coherence. This stability in itself has coercive and non-coercive moments: coercive in that the relational patterns will inevitably be informed by gender inequality and other cultural and familial constraints, non-coercive in that the stability of internalized attachments can be the very thing that opens one to creative and emancipatory possibilities. Postmodern theories suggest that oppression and hierarchies of all kinds are created and sustained by defenses against uncertainty or against existential lack. My assumption here is that they are created and sustained by defenses against relationally inflicted pain, that binaries in hierarchic relation are the sequelae of trauma, and that the capacity to go beyond binaries is a developmental achievement. To investigate relational patterns in their cultural context, we need the insights of both postmodern and relational theories.

REFERENCES

Abel, E. (1990). Race, class, and psychoanalysis? Opening questions. In *Conflicts in Feminism*, ed. M. Hirsch and E. F. Keller, pp. 184–204. New York and London: Routledge.

Adelson, L. (1993). *Making Bodies, Making History*. Lincoln: University of Nebraska Press.

Althusser, L. (1971). Ideology and ideological state apparatuses (notes towards an investigation). In *Lenin and Philosophy and Other Essays*, trans. B. Brewster, pp. 127–186. New York and London: Monthly Review Press.

Aron, L. (1990). One-person and two-person psychologies and the method of psychoanalysis. *Psychoanalytic Psychology* 7:475–485.

Barratt, B. (1993). *Psychoanalysis and the Postmodern Impulse*. Baltimore, MD: Johns Hopkins University Press.

Belenky, M., Clichy, B., Goldberger, N., and Tarule, J. (1987). *Women's Ways of Knowing*. New York: Basic Books.

Benhabib, S. (1995). Feminism and postmodernism: an uneasy alliance. In *Feminist Contentions*, ed. S. Benhabib, J. Butler, D. Cornell, and N. Fraser, pp. 17–34. New York: Routledge.

Benjamin, J. (1988). The *Bonds of Love*. New York: Pantheon.

———— (1994). The shadow of the other (subject). *Constellations* 1:231–254.

———— (1995). *Like Subjects. Love Objects. Essays on Recognition and Sexual Difference*. New Haven, CT: Yale University Press.

———— (1996). In defense of gender ambiguity. *Gender and Psychoanalysis* 1:27–43.

Brennan, T. (1989). Introduction. In *Between Feminism and Psychoanalysis*, ed. T. Brennan, pp. 1–23. New York and London: Routledge.

Bromberg, P. (1996). Standing in the spaces: the multiplicity of self and the psychoanalytic relationship. *Contemporary Psychoanalysis* 32: 509–536.

Butler, J. (1990). *Gender Trouble: Feminism and the Subversion of Identity*. New York and London: Routledge.

———— (1992). Contingent foundations: feminism and the question of "postmodernism." In *Feminists Theorize the Political*, ed. J. Butler and J. W. Scott, pp. 3–21. New York and London: Routledge.

———— (1993). *Bodies that Matter*. New York and London: Routledge.

———— (1995). Melancholy gender-refused identification. *Psychoanalytic Dialogues* 5:165–180.

Chodorow, N. (1989). *Feminism and Psychoanalytic Theory*. New Haven, CT: Yale University Press.

———— (1994). *Femininities, Masculinities, Sexualities: Freud and Beyond*. Lexington: University Press of Kentucky.

———— (1995). Gender as a personal and cultural construction. *Signs* 20:516–544.

Collins, P. H. (1994). Shifting the center: race, class, and feminist theorizing about motherhood. In *Representations of Motherhood*, ed. D. Bassin, M. Honey, and M. Kaplan, pp. 56–74. New Haven, CT: Yale University Press.

Cushman, P. (1991). Ideology obscured: political uses of the self in Daniel Stern's infant. *American Psychologist* 46:206–219.

De Lauretis, T., ed. (1986). Feminist studies/critical studies: issues, terms, and contexts. In *Feminist Studies/Critical Studies*, pp. 1–19. Bloomington: University of Indiana Press.

de Marneffe, D. (1997). Bodies and words: a study of young children's genital and gender knowledge. *Gender and Psychoanalysis* 2(1):3–33.

Derrida, J. (1976). *Of Grammatology*, trans. G. Spivak. Baltimore, MD: Johns Hopkins University Press.

———— (1978). *Writing and Difference*, trans. A. Bass. Chicago: University of Chicago Press.

Dews, P. (1987). *Logics of Disintegration*. London and New York: Verso.

Fairfield, S. (1996). *On deconstruction, psychoanalysis, and the master self*. Unpublished manuscript.

Fast, I. (1984). *Gender Identity. A Differentiation Model*. Hillsdale, NJ: The Analytic Press.

Flax, J. (1990). *Thinking Fragments. Psychoanalysis, Feminism, and Postmodernism in the Contemporary West*. Berkeley: University of California Press.

———— (1996). Taking multiplicity seriously: some implications for psychoanalytic theorizing and practice. *Contemporary Psychoanalysis* 32:577–593.

Foucault, M. (1973). *Madness and Civilization: A History of Insanity in the Age of Reason*, trans. R. Howard. New York: Vintage.

———— (1979). *Discipline and Punish: The Birth of the Prison*, trans. A. Sheridan. New York: Vintage.

———— (1980). *The History of Sexuality*, Vol. 1, trans. R. Hurley. New York: Vintage.

———— (1982). The subject and power. *Critical Inquiry* 8:777–795.

Frankenberg, R. (1993). *White Women, Race Matters: The Social Construction of Whiteness*. Minneapolis: University of Minnesota Press.

Fraser, N. (1995). False antitheses: a response to Seyla Benhabib and Judith Butler. In *Feminist Contentions*, ed. S. Benhabib, J. Butler, D. Cornell, and N. Fraser, pp. 59–74. New York: Routledge.

Freud, S. (1920). Beyond the pleasure principle. *Standard Edition* 18:3–64.

Frosh, S. (1994). *Sexual Difference: Masculinity and Psychoanalysis*. New York and London: Routledge.

Gilligan, C. (1982). *In a Different Voice. Psychological Theory and Women's Development*. Cambridge, MA: Harvard University Press.

Glass, J. M. (1993). *Shattered Selves: Multiple Personality in a Postmodern World*. Ithaca, NY: Cornell University Press.

Goldner, V. (1991). Toward a critical relational theory of gender. *Psychoanalytic Dialogues* 1:249–272.

Hacking, I. (1986). Making up people. In *Reconstructing Individualism: Autonomy, Individuality and the Self in Western Thought*, ed. T. C. Heller, M. Sosna, and D. Willberry, pp. 222–236. Stanford, CA: Stanford University Press.

Haraway, D. (1985). A manifesto for cyborgs: science, technology, and socialist feminism in the 1980s. *Socialist Review* 15:65–107.

Harris, A. (1995). *Animated conversations: embodying and engendering analytic discourse*. Paper presented at the meeting of Division 39, American Psychological Association, Santa Monica, CA, April.

Hennessy, R. (1995). Queer visibility in commodity culture. In *Social Postmodernism. Beyond Identity Politics*, ed. L. Nicholson and S. Seidman, pp.142–183. Cambridge: Cambridge University Press.

hooks, b. (1981). *Ain't I a Woman: Black Women and Feminism*. Boston: South End Press.

Horney, K. (1924). On the genesis of the castration complex in women. *International Journal of Psycho-Analysis* 5:50–65.

———— (1926). The flight from womanhood. *International Journal of Psycho-Analysis* 7:324–339.

Kestenberg, J. (1968). Outside and inside, male and female. *Journal of the American Psychoanalytic Association* 16:457–520.

Lacan, J. (1977). *Ecrits*. London: Tavistock.

Loewald, H. (1980). *Papers on Psychoanalysis*. New Haven, CT: Yale University Press.

Lyons-Ruth, K. (1991). Rapprochement or approchement: Mahler's theory reconsidered from the vantage point of recent research on early attachment relationships. *Psychoanalytic Psychology* 8:1–23.

Martin, B., and Mohanty, C. (1986). Feminist politics: What's home got to do with it? In *Feminist Studies/Critical Studies*, ed. T. de Lauretis, pp. 191–212. Bloomington: Indiana University Press.

May, R. (1986). Concerning a psychoanalytic view of maleness. *Psychoanalytic Review* 73(4):175–193.

Mayer, E. L. (1985). "Everybody must be just like me": observations on female castration anxiety. *International Journal of Psycho-Analysis* 66:331–347.

Miller, J. B., Jordan, J., Kaplan, A., et al. (1991). *Women's Growth in Connection*, New York: Guilford.

Mitchell, J., and Rose, J. (1985). Introductions I and II. In J. Lacan, *Feminine Sexuality*, ed. J. Mitchell and J. Rose, pp. 1–57. New York: Norton.

Mitchell, S. A. (1988). *Relational Concepts in Psychoanalysis*. Cambridge, MA: Harvard University Press.

Moraga, C., and Anzaldúa, G., eds. (1983). *This Bridge Called My Back: Writings by Radical Women of Color*. New York: Kitchen Table.

Morley, D. (1980). Texts, readers, subjects. In *Culture, Media, Language: Working Papers in Cultural Studies, 1972–9*, ed. S. Hall, D. Hobson, A. Lowe, and P. Willis, pp. 163–173. London: Hutchinson.

Mulvey, L. (1975). Visual pleasure and narrative cinema. *Screen* 16:6–18.

O'Connor, N., and Ryan, J. (1993). *Wild Desires and Mistaken Identities: Lesbianism and Psychoanalysis*. London: Virago.

Pizer, S. (1992). The negotiation of paradox in the analytic patient. *Psychoanalytic Dialogues* 2:215–240.

Pratt, M. B. (1984). Identity: skin blood heart. In *Yours in Struggle: Three Feminist Perspectives on Anti-Semitism and Racism*, ed. E. Bulkin, M. B. Pratt, and B. Smith, pp. 11–63. Brooklyn, NY: Long Haul.

Rabine, L. W. (1988). A feminist politics of non-identity. *Feminist Studies* 14:11–31.

Rivera, M. (1989). Linking the psychological and the social: feminism, poststructuralism, and multiple personality. *Dissociation* 2:24–31.

Silverman, K. (1996). *The Threshold of the Visible World*. New York and London: Routledge.

Smith, B., ed. (1984). *Home Girls: A Black Feminist Anthology*. New York: Kitchen Table.

Smith, P. (1988). *Discerning the Subject*. Minneapolis: University of Minnesota Press.

Sprengnether, M. (1990). *The Spectral Mother*. Ithaca, NY: Cornell University Press.

—— (1995). Reading Freud's life. *American Imago* 52:9–54.

Stern, D. N. (1985). *The Interpersonal World of the Infant*. New York: Basic Books.

Stoller, R. (1976a). *Sex and Gender. Vol. 2: The Transsexual Experiment*. New York: Jason Aronson.

—— (1976b). Primary femininity. In *Female Psychology*, ed. H. P. Blum, pp. 59–78. New York: International Universities Press.

—— (1985). *Presentations of Gender*. New Haven, CT: Yale University Press.

Tannen, D. (1990). *You Just Don't Understand. Women and Men in Conversation*. New York: Morrow.

Thompson, C. L. (1995). Self-definition by opposition: a consequence of minority status. *Psychoanalytic Psychology* 12:533–545.

Tyson, P. (1982). A developmental line of gender identity, gender role, and choice of love object. *Journal of the American Psychoanalytic Association* 30:61–86.

Weir, A. (1996). *Sacrificial Logics*. New York and London: Routledge.

Whitebook, J. (1992). Reflections on the autonomous individual and the decentered subject. *American Imago* 49:97–116.

—— (1995). *Perversion and Utopia: A Study in Psychoanalysis and Critical Theory*. Cambridge, MA, and London: M.I.T. Press.

Williamson, J. (1986). Woman is an island: femininity and colonization. In *Studies in Entertainment: Critical Approaches to Mass Culture*, ed. T. Modleski, pp. 99–118. Bloomington: Indiana University Press.

Winnicott, D. W. (1965). The capacity to be alone. In *The Maturational Processes and the Facilitating Environment*, pp. 29–36. Madison, CT: International Universities Press.

—— (1974). *Playing and Reality*. London: Tavistock.

13

Race in Psychoanalytic Space

KIMBERLYN LEARY[*]

For some time, discussions of difference have been the bellwether of interdisciplinary work in the humanities and in psychological theory. Most psychoanalytic theorists have considered difference from the perspective of gender and sexuality. Other forums for inquiring into difference—for example, the impact of race and ethnicity on psychological life—have attracted less psychoanalytic attention. Although our understanding of how interior life may be gendered in subtle and complex ways has expanded, psychoanalysis has typically confined itself to a view of human experience that does not take racial and ethnic identity into account. As a result, the psychology of people of color has in crucial ways remained outside of analytic purview.

Psychoanalysis, in contrast, has tended to view itself as offering universal accounts of human experience. Until recently, most

*Originally published in *Gender and Psychoanalysis* 2:157–172. Reprinted with permission from International Universities Press.

psychoanalytic models have assumed—without conflict—that the psychology of those who were white, male and economically well off was also "universal." Feminist critiques have powerfully illustrated the way in which such presumptions reinforced hierarchies of power that marginalized women's experience in the consulting room and the society at large.

I believe that the reticence of psychoanalytic theory to speak more specifically to issues of race and ethnicity is a result of a number of factors. Psychoanalytic silence about race is not so dissimilar to the widespread discomfort that exists in this country whenever talk about race surfaces. Toni Morrison (1992) has called the United States a "racialized" society. The very existence of this country is intertwined with the politics and psychology of immigration, integration, and the assimilation of its diverse peoples. In contemporary America—and for that matter, in different forms across much of the world—talk about race brings about a range of reactions, from affiliation to apprehension. What we are—and, by extension, what we call ourselves—establishes conditions of safety or disrupts them. The stakes in this regard are extraordinarily high. As we know from the ongoing crises in Bosnia and Rwanda, racial and ethnic distinctions may cost people their lives.

At the same time, it is inaccurate to suggest that psychoanalysis had distanced itself entirely from considering the role that race and ethnicity play in mental life and clinical practice. There is a small body of psychoanalytic writing in North America on clinical issues in the treatment of minority patients (usually African-American) and an even smaller collection of papers by analysts of color concerning the impact a racialized analyst may have on the treatment process (e.g., Calnek 1970, Curry 1964, Fisher 1971, Holmes 1992, Jones and Thorne 1987, Kennedy 1952, Myers 1977, Perez-Foster et al. 1996, Schacter and Butts 1968, and Thompson 1995).

Even when the wider analytic literature conceded to encountering the particularities of human experience connected to race (e.g., the psychic scars associated with racial discrimination), the bias toward universal theory remains. Even a designation like the "culturally different patient" prevalent in more contemporary writing bears this same stamp. The therapist (who, statistically speaking, is likely to be white) becomes the standard against which a patient of color in understood to be "different." Further, most of the time, apart from the discussions of the white analyst's potential racism, the white analyst's race is effectively dissociated from clinical inquiry. Race and ethnicity tended to be treated as being only the providence of patients and therapists of color. This, in my view, results in a truncated conversation about race in the consulting room.

Contemporary analytic writing on race is considerably more sophisticated (see Perez-Foster et al. 1996 as an example). Holmes (1992), among others, suggests that clinical attention directed to the realities and fantasies of race may provide a critical point of contact with the patient's transferences, conflicts, and resistances. In line with Dimen's (1991) formulations about gender, race may be viewed as a code in which problems about the self are inscribed. Similarly, self-experience may also be shaped through one's cultural experience of race. To the extent that patient and therapist are free to negotiate racial meanings within the treatment dyad and those within each participant, the meaning of race can encompass far more than the social realities to which therapist and patient remain bound, in and out of the consulting room (cf. Leary 1995).

While this is a perspective that clearly admits of more relational complexity than earlier formulations, other problems remain. For example, when race is treated as a code to be deciphered in the analytic exchange it is also appropriated to secure additional disciplinary turf for psychoanalysis. Race becomes limited to another medium for psychoanalytic exploration. This can be problematic for those who contend that their difference endures. As an example, when an African-American cultural practice is translated into the psychoanalytic lexicon (when, for example, a patient's report of the closeness of her extended family is given a psychoanalytic meaning, however benign), there is a risk that those practices may lose their status as independent centers of identity in their own right. In this regard, Collins (1990) notes that "oppressed people are frequently placed in the situation of being listened to only if we frame our ideas in the language that is familiar to and comfortable to the dominant group" (p. xiii). This may be one of the reasons psychoanalysis has been greeted with caution—if not dismissed outright as irrelevant—by those advancing agendas for social change within African-American communities.

Despite the Eurocentric origins of psychoanalysis, I think there are many points of contact between analytic discourses and those concerned with African-American psychological life. Ironically, many African Americans write with a sensibility that is akin to many analytic values. Collins (1990) notes that real change occurs in the private, personal space of individual consciousness. Others argue that true liberation rests on the ability to reclaim subjectivity and the freedom to desire openly (Collins 1990, hooks and West 1991). Thus, the estrangement between psychoanalysis and African-American communities, while critically important, may not be as complete as many would conclude.

Racial discourses, like gender dialogues, offer an extended meditation on distinction and differentiation. Talk about race and ethnicity invites us to reconsider how difference exists as both a material fact in the world and as a rhetorical device to advance or suspend particular human aims.

The introduction of postmodern critiques into psychoanalytic conceptualizations has been especially fruitful for many gender theorists. The postmodern invitation to include multiple perspectives and its bedrock suspicion of any theorizing invoking universalistic or essentialist conclusions about human subjectivity has permitted more complicated understandings of sexual and gender experience than traditional psychoanalytic approaches had allowed.

From this vantage point, for example, psychoanalytic authors have challenged the notion that gender conforms to an essence or disposition (Dimen 1991) and have instead argued that one's sense of masculinity and femininity may be better understood as a set of relations constructed, accomplished, or otherwise performed. In suggesting that we become gendered not by what we are but by absorbing the contrast between masculinity and femininity, Dimen (1991) positions gender in transitional space. Gender is located in creative tension rather than limiting itself to one position or the other. May (1986), Goldner (1991), Shapiro (1993), and Butler (1995) are among those arguing that an internally consistent sense of gender identity is neither possible nor desirable. In order to maintain a stable sense of masculinity or femininity a person is required to disavow and sequester aspects of the self that are defined as belonging to the gendered other (Shapiro 1993). Aron (1995) indicates that destabilizing traditional notions of gender identity can allow for an acceptance and celebration of multiplicities.

Thus, contemporary analysts have usefully appropriated postmodern critiques to further the study of gender and sexuality. The aim of these proposals is to problematize dichotomous gender categories and reconfigure gender as a set of relational negotiations always in creative flux. Butler (1995) extends this idea further in her suggestion that "it may only be by risking the *incoherence* of identity that connection is possible" (p. 179).

To what extent do postmodern critiques open up our understanding of racial identity? In which ways are gender and race comparable? Is it equally useful for one's experience of race to remain in creative flux and even be "incoherent"? Or are alternative formulations about race necessary in order to be clinically effective with patients of color?

In general, theorizing directed at African-American subjectivity has greeted postmodern inquiry ambivalently. In an issue of the *Black Scholar* devoted to critical theory, a number of theorists addressed the relevance of postmodernism for African-American scholarship. Some argued for the concept of an essentialist racial identity and what we might term "an authoritative blackness." Other critics, more sympathetically inclined toward postmodern ideals, opposed the notion that race constitutes any kind of genuine category. Critics on both sides, however, concluded that race is and should have a foundational status in contemporary theory.

Theorists who advocate the claim to racial identity argue that having a racialized body puts constraints on the types of narratives that can be told about African Americans. Specifically, they suggest that African-American identity is anchored in the particular histories endured because of a black body—namely, slavery, racial abuse, and the struggle against maltreatment. To these theorists, whatever else it references, being black means that one is a member of a minority group historically despised by the majority culture. Racial injustice in this sense extends beyond the rhetorical and philosophical abstraction (Mitchell 1993). In this sense, narratives pertaining to African-American subjectivity are not elastic and cannot be retold differently.

In articulating an essential black identity in this way, these critics link blackness to specific experiences, especially the suffering imposed by racial injustice, past and potential. "Identity politics" (Sampson 1993) can be understood to place black concerns at the very center of attention and to aim to build a black consensus to push for social change. Racial identity is understood to be both a response to racism and a means to combat it by forcing a collision between the dominant culture and the cultures of its minority members.

The tension between cultures can be illustrated, for example, in the differing understandings that many blacks and whites have about what constitutes relief from racism. For many whites, the absence of racism is signaled by "not noticing color" and viewing "people as individuals." Those advocating identity politics suggest that creative responses to racism can occur only when color and race are seen and acknowledged, especially in terms of inequalities in the political-economic system (Peck 1994). Stressing the reality of difference is part of a strategy to persuade dominant groups to review their practices and relinquish privilege.

Postmodern critics writing about race counter by noting that particular constructions of race are made in accord with prerogatives to gain or consolidate power. They are not intrinsically real. Their only reality resides in their utility for particular purposes. Further, these narratives can and do shift when power is redistributed.

Arguing from a position similar to that taken by May, Dimen, Butler, and others, these theorists suggest that racial categories— like gender categories—are not in any way natural. This claim is also supported by human genetics. Simply put, the variation *within* racial groups is greater than the variation *between* racial groups.

Race is not a valid marker of difference. Accordingly, there is nothing obvious about the construct of African-American identity.

Collins (1990) offers one deconstruction of racial identity. Deploying a postmodern critique, she notes that even as the call for racial solidarity has been an effective strategy for black politics, it has the disadvantage of promoting exclusionary practices within African-American communities. It has the practical impact of authenticating some blacks as *really* black and disenfranchising others who fail to meet its constraints. Smith (1993), also sympathetic to postmodern approaches, suggests that claims to racial identity are not even necessary for black political action as there are perfectly legitimate political, social, and cultural reasons why blacks might choose to align with the majority of black people.

Despite their disavowal of race as an essentialist construct, these same theorists maintain that race does speak to something real beyond abstraction. Cornel West (1993) writes that "race matters" in material ways in the United States as all people with black skin and African phenotype are subject to potential racial abuse. Although blackness has no intrinsic meaning outside of a system of race-conscious people and practices, in the United States it references an undeniable history of struggle. In this way, race functions as what Werner (1993) calls an effective fact. Smith (1993) captures a similar sentiment: "theoretically race is an indefensible category; practically it is an inescapable aspect of social life" (p. 76). Although potentially open to a variety of narrative possibilities, race also has a factual status not amenable to revision.

Thus, theorists who begin with very different assumptions about racial categories converge on the view that racial discourse speaks to something foundational all the same. In advocating this view, these authors speak to a notion of difference that, in their eyes, is "really real" (Greene 1993). The radical openness to uncertainty so central to postmodern gender theory gives way to a view that with respect to race we cannot afford to let the certainty of some things slip. Although racial deliberations may be what West (1993) terms "a vulgar form of reasoning," he suggests that it would be equally amoral to refrain from employing them.

I believe that in taking the position that racial difference is "really real," these theorists remain within a conceptual tension like that employed by Dimen, Aron, and Butler with respect to gender. Their formulations admit of postmodern multiplicity but are also constrained by the exigencies of the real world, especially as it acts on real bodies. These theorists then operate at the intersection of a conceptual tension in which race is understood to be simultaneously a positivistic fact and a postmodern construction.

In this way, race, like gender, exists in transitional space. It is located in the tensions among biological distinction, sociocultural fact, and future possibilities—a tension that may be difficult to sustain in either social or clinical life. The collapse of transitional space may be seen whenever racial or gender experience becomes either reified or wholly indeterminate.

When race is treated as a fact, it is assumed to speak for itself and its more complicated, idiosyncratic meanings are excluded from meaningful consideration. Transitional space is also compromised when therapists or patients render racial identity ambiguous and indeterminate. Race comes to refer to everything and so speaks to nothing in particular (Chodorow 1995). The analyst or theorist may gain the potential advantage of uncertainty and multiplicity but it is purchased at the cost of failing to appreciate the distinctive struggles faced by African Americans whose racial difference makes for real world difficulties.

It is clear that the more useful clinical stance lies in sustaining the conceptual tension located between these positions. To do so requires the understanding that race speaks to the exigencies of a difference that is beyond trope. In this sense, race effectively functions as a fact even as it needs to be permitted to vary in each clinical dyad as a narrative possibility with meanings unique to the pair. In the clinical example to follow, I will explore some of the problems of sustaining this transitional space in practice and the factors that may lead to its collapse.

Ms. B., a single, African-American woman and a student in a professional school, sought treatment at a university clinic. It was understood at the outset that she would be leaving town at the end of the academic year and that her treatment would be of limited duration. Ms. B. was an attractive, dark-skinned woman with a winning smile. Though some forty pounds overweight, she maintained that she was comfortable with being heavy. Her hair was shaped into a distinctive style and she often wore extremely stylish and vividly colored clothing. As a result, Ms. B. regularly drew attention to herself even as she viewed this attention as an unwelcome intrusion.

As is the practice at our clinic, Ms. B. first met with a consulting therapist to whom she said that she sought therapy because she felt isolated in her program. Specifcally, she felt that she had no one she could talk to. She mentioned other worries about her academic progress and difficulties sustaining romantic relationships, but the focus of her distress was her felt sense of loneliness.

Ms. B. and the consulting therapist came to frame Ms. B.'s concerns in racialized terms, linked to her experience of being a minority person in a majority environment. Ms. B. appeared to endorse this assessment. The consulting therapist noted that Ms. B. mentioned a well-publicized incident of racial conflict at the university that felt "personal" to the patient. During one session, the patient compared herself with Anita Hill, mentioning the difficulty African-American women have when they try to speak their minds. Ms. B. also mentioned her discomfort with some white friends who she believed might not protect her from being captured "if an edict were passed reinstating slavery." Ms. B. also found fault with her African-American peers who she found "clueless" about racial problems.

The consulting therapist was also aware that Ms. B.'s story was a complicated one: although Ms. B. complained about being at sea in an unfamiliar environment (her prestigious professional school), she had grown up in a family of considerable means, had attended private school, and had enjoyed a successful tenure at an Ivy League university. In fact, her move to her current university meant that she was again in a quite familiar circumstance.

The consulting therapist and her senior colleagues decided that the patient's treatment needs would best be served by assignment to an African-American therapist. The decision was made even though the patient did not independently indicate a preference for a therapist of color and appeared ambivalent when the option was presented to her. The consultant put it this way in her report: "At no time in the session was [Ms. B.] able to say that she would prefer one race of therapist over another." The consultant appeared to assume that Ms. B. was inhibiting herself from expressing a desire for an African-American therapist. In retrospect, it seems to me to be as likely that the patient did not feel free to decline the offer to see a black clinician. In any case, she consented to the assignment, saying to the consultant, "You're the expert. You do what you think is best."

Ms. B.'s referral for therapy to me was further contextualized by her agreement to participate in our clinic's research program when this option was raised with her by the consultant. Ms. B. happened to come to the clinic when I as a staff member was expected to see a research case. Thus, Ms. B.'s treatment was distinguished—as it is perhaps for all patients—by her accommodation to our clinic's manifold requests and the needs of the clinicians involved. In this way, the institutional setting in which the therapy took place became an important backdrop to the treatment and our involvement with one another.

Ms. B. greeted her transfer to me with amused detachment that came to be her signature for the tenure of her treatment. In early sessions, she explained that her feelings of alienation were a consequence of bureaucratic structures of the university that failed "to take individual circumstances into account." In time, Ms. B. and I connected this idea to her lifelong complaint that her personal needs were ignored in her family because her younger brother was developmentally disabled and had absorbed much of her parents' attention and resources. Later, it seemed to me that Ms. B.'s reproach might have been directed at the clinic, reflecting her ambivalent feelings about being specifically assigned to an African-American therapist when she had made no such request herself.

Ms. B. was able to use the early part of her therapy to articulate some of her feelings about her family. This included her sense of being underprotected by her parents from the danger of her brother's unpredictable and violent rages and her subsequent identification with him by becoming for a time physically provocative with her grade school classmates. Because her parents were consumed with caring for a disabled child, Ms. B. struggled with accepting the fact that her feelings of deprivation and neglect were legitimate.

Gradually, I became aware that although Ms. B. was manifestly cooperative (coming on time and always completing research questionnaires) and appeared engaged and able to speak freely, the sessions often seemed to lack depth. After some weeks, I had the nagging sensation that while I knew many facts about Ms. B.'s life, I didn't know very much about *her* and the specifics of her take on the events she described.

I wondered if this might be connected to Ms. B.'s feelings about seeing a therapist of color, which she had so far not mentioned. When I raised this subject with her, Ms. B. responded with an exaggerated sense of gratitude that did not seem altogether genuine to me. She said she was grateful to see me because she was sure she could not speak with a white doctor. At the same time, as the sessions continued in the same vein as before, I also felt that Ms. B. was having trouble conveying to her African-American therapist very much of what was on her mind. It was true that we had established a dialogue—Ms. B. talked fluidly during her sessions and appeared to listen to what I had to say—but I continued to feel that the sessions were constrained in subtle ways. Despite her disclaimer, it seemed that Ms. B. was in the position again of feeling that she had no one with whom she could speak about her experience.

In considering this quality of the treatment work, I think that Ms. B.'s assignment to an African-American therapist—and the assumption that she would be more comfortable with this arrangement—became a significant obstacle to her developing a more tenable treatment alliance and limited the therapy's usefulness to her. I believe the difficulty we experienced in forming a more genuine connection was due to a number of factors. Through her associations, my sense was that the clinic's decision to assign her to a therapist of color when she had not made such a request echoed the backstage maneuvering that characterized her parents' management of her disabled brother. For example, Ms. B.'s parents referred to her brother's problems euphemistically and refused to acknowledge directly his considerable limitations. Rather than treatment offering her a new relational experience, her therapy had quite unwittingly enacted the very circumstances that were instrumental in her seeking help.

In considering the treatment assignment, I believe that the consulting therapist's recommendation of an African-American therapist in this case—and, of course, my willingness to go along with this—was a result of race being treated as though it were a fact that spoke for itself. Ms. B.'s early communications had, after all, indicated her distrust of *both* blacks and whites. The referral to a black therapist rested on the assumption that the patient's problems with blacks were less of a problem than her difficulties with whites. There was also the expectation—initially unchallenged by each of us—that I would as a matter of course be "black" in some manner that would be useful to Ms. B. In permitting myself to be pressed into service in this way, I believe I came across to Ms. B. as "clueless" as she found the other African-American students in her program.

Thus, the circumstances under which Ms. B. entered treatment constrained the establishment of transitional space. Race was treated by the clinic, the therapist, and by the patient herself as a static and reified fact. "Blackness" was assumed to be authoritative in such a way that it needed no further elaboration. In this respect, I think that my initial efforts to draw attention to this assumption by asking the patient about her feelings about being assigned to a black therapist did little to open up the conversation. My question treated race as though it were something we were free to discuss openly when the treatment assignment had already demonstrated that in important ways it was not.

A significant shift in the therapy occurred when I raised with Ms. B. my continuing sense that it was important to her to keep a feeling of distance between us. Conversation about blacks who think differently from one another opened up via Ms. B.'s criticism of African-American professors at her undergraduate college whose racial views did not fit comfortably with those of black student organizations on campus. Ms. B. then permitted herself to explore some of her thoughts about me. She and I, in fact, shared a number of experiences in common of which she was well aware, although she did not know specific details of my life. Both of us were, for example, professionally educated or in the process of becoming so, just as we were both African-Americans who had chosen to affiliate ourselves with academic institutions that were largely white. However, the similarities between us were not the focus of Ms. B.'s attention. Instead, she conveyed her feeling that we were very different from one another. At first, and tentatively, she speculated that I was a black who did not put black concerns first. Since Ms. B. did not know what my particular racial views were, she also entertained thoughts of the converse—that I might be politically radical in a way that surpassed herself. Ms. B. appeared less concerned about testing the plausibility of her ideas and more interested in their impact on me. She thought it likely that I would find her ideas about race objectionable. I believe Ms. B. was working in this way to find a means to create for herself a needed sense of us as different and distinct from one another. This I conveyed to her.

As I reflected on Ms. B.'s experience of our blackness, I thought that she was also establishing the multiple meanings that being black had for her. While her blackness existed as something in and of itself and was an essential part of her self-identity, race was also important as a quality of difference. One aspect of her racial identity was that of being a person of color in the many white settings in which she had lived, worked, and studied. Blackness, therefore, existed as something that was counterpoised with whiteness, and that made her stand out. I thought this was particularly important in the context of Ms. B.'s. felt sense of alienation in her family and her wish to be noticed. It was this aspect of her racial identity that was interrupted for Ms. B. when she was unilaterally assigned to a therapist of color.

I think that Ms. B. developed a keener sense of herself when she could differentiate us more clearly. This highlights another aspect of racialized experience. At some times, and for some persons, the meaning of race occurs in conjunction with a sense of needed sameness, shared ideas, and mutual recognition. On other occasions, race may be experienced primarily in the context of experiencing a sense of oneself as dissimilar and distinct. Although this idea is speculative, it is possible that Ms. B. might have found greater freedom to express herself with a white therapist with whom racial contrasts and hence self-experience could be more easily established.

Following our open acknowledgment of a barrier—despite the assumption of sameness that our blackness might not be comparable—Ms. B. began to speak in a manner that seemed more personal. She talked, albeit still in a limited way, about the many difficulties she had encountered in her relationships with the African-American men she had chosen as her romantic partners. She disclosed for the first time details of her adolescent sexual activity to which she turned in part to compensate for the lack of attention from her parents. Ms. B. was assaulted during one of these encounters with a much older boy, and was nearly raped. She had told no one about this incident because she feared that her already overburdened parents would only blame her. Ms. B. also talked about the emotional abuse she had received from other boyfriends. During the therapy, she learned that her current boyfriend had been cheating on her and had been dishonest in other ways. Her unhappiness with these relationships had led her to consider dating white men. Near the end of the therapy, Ms. B. mentioned her feelings of attraction for a white man in her program. She was ambivalent about her interest in this man and alluded to her belief that this would only bring humiliation, given her expectation that he would not find her attractive. Our exploration of these issues and themes was limited by the short duration of the therapy and by Ms. B.'s concern that her feelings about both black and white men would bring the same censure from other African Americans (including the therapist) that Ms. B. would herself confer on others for similar feelings.

By termination, Ms. B. was able to clarify—again to a limited degree—the anger and distrust that permeated her relationships with African-American men and that we recognized she had introduced in the consultation when she had compared herself to Anita Hill. Hill, of course, was not believed when she accused an African-American man of sexual misconduct just as Ms. B. expected to receive censure rather than understanding from her parents when she was assaulted. We also connected Ms. B.'s ambivalence about black men with its historical antecedents, including her struggles with her anger and guilt toward both her brother and the attempted rape. These issues—and the patient's conflicted turn to white men for relational relief—were the ones about which Ms. B. felt she had no one to talk with openly.

As this clinical illustration shows, the "reality" of race can easily exert a countervailing pressure on patient and therapist that can collapse the sense of possibility necessary for a dynamic psychotherapy to flourish. Although not evident here, it is also the case that an exclusive focus on the metaphoric meanings of race could also foreclose important areas of exploration by obscuring the impact of real world discrimination and injustice. Effective psychoanalytic treatment results when patient and therapist can inhabit the space in between (Dimen 1991).

For Ms. B., the recommendation that her needs would be better served by an African-American therapist when she made no such request herself and the treating therapist's assent to this arrangement with the clinic had the practical result of establishing race as something that was non-negotiable in the treatment space. The institutional context of the clinic in which we met conferred sameness upon us. The racial background of patient and therapist was treated by the clinic as well as the patient and the therapist as though it only reflected abiding commonality, creating a dilemma for the patient, who seemed to need to feel different from the therapist. Without this sense of needed difference, Ms. B. and I found it difficult to genuinely connect. When we became able to explore, even to a limited degree, Ms. B.'s view that blackness might be experienced differently by each of us, a point of contrast could appear. Rather than being only the same, Ms. B. and I also had the freedom to be different. In those moments in which this tension could be sustained, patient and therapist were able to encounter one another with more depth than was otherwise possible.

REFERENCES

Aron, L. (1995). The internalized primal scene. *Psychoanalytic Dialogues* 5(2):195–238.

Butler, J. (1995). Melancholy gender-refused identifications. *Psychoanalytic Dialogues* 5(2):165–180.

Calnek, M. (1970). Racial factors in the counter-transference. *American Journal of Psychiatry* 135:1084–1096.

Chodorow, N. (1995). Multiplicities and uncertainities of gender. *Psychoanalytic Dialogues* 5(2):291–300.

Collins, P. (1990). *Black Feminist Thought.* New York: Routledge.

Curry, A. (1964). Myth, transference and the black psychotherapist. *Psychoanalytic Review* 51:7–14.

Dimen, M. (1991). Deconstructing difference: gender, splitting, and transitional space. *Psychoanalytic Dialogues* 1(3):335–352.

Fisher, N. (1971). An inter-racial analysis: transference and countertransference. *Journal of the American Psychoanalytic Association* 19:736–745.

Goldner, V. (1991). Towards a critical theory of gender. *Psychoanalytic Dialogues* 1(3):249–272.

Greene, B. (1993). Psychotherapy with African-American women: integrating feminist and psychodynamic models. *Journal of Training and Practice in Professional Practice* 7(1):49–66.

Holmes, D. (1992). Race and transference in psychoanalysis and psychotherapy. *International Journal of Psycho-Analysis* 73(1):1–12.

hooks, b., and West, C. (1991). *Breaking Bread: Insurgent Black Intellectual Life.* Boston: South End Press.

Jones, E., and Thorne, A. (1987). Rediscovery of the subject: intercultural approaches to clinical assessment. *Journal of Consulting and Clinical Psychology* 55(4):488–495.

Kennedy, J. (1952). Problems posed in the analysis of Negro patients. *Psychiatry* 15:313–327.

Leary, K. (1995). Interpreting in the dark: race and ethnicity in psychoanalytic psychotherapy. *Psychoanalytic Psychology* 12(1):127–140.

May, R. (1986). Concerning a psychoanalytic view of maleness. *Psychoanalytic Review* 73:179–194.

Mitchell, C. (1993). "Multiculturalism": the coded redescription of race in contemporary educational discourse. *Black Scholar* 23(3, 4):71–74.

Morrison, T. (1992). *Playing in the Dark: Whiteness and the Literary Imagination.* Cambridge, MA: Harvard University Press.

Myers, W. (1977). The significance of the colors black and white in the dreams of white and black patients. *Journal of the American Psychoanalytic Association* 25:163–181.

Peck, J. (1994). Talk about racism: framing a popular discourse of race on Oprah Winfrey. *Cultural Critique* 27:89–126.

Perez-Foster, R. M., Moskowitz, M., and Javier, R. (1996). *Reaching Across Boundaries of Culture and Class: Widening the Scope of Psychotherapy.* Northvale, NJ: Jason Aronson.

Sampson, E. (1993). Identity politics. *American Psychologist* 48(12):1210–1218.

Schacter, J., and Butts, H. (1968). Transference and countertransference. *Journal of the American Psychoanalytic Association* 16:792–808.

Shapiro, S. (1993). Gender role stereotype and clinical process. *Psychoanalytic Dialogues* 3(3):371–388.

Smith, D. (1993). Let our people go. *Black Scholar* 23(3, 4):74–76.

Sterba, R. (1947). Some psychological factors in Negro race hatred. *Psychoanalysis and the Social Sciences* 1:411–427.

Thompson, C. (1995). Self definition by opposition: a consequence of minority status. *Psychoanalytic Psychology* 12:533–546.

Werner, C. (1993). On the possibility of a committed postmodernism: a response to Jon Michael Spencer. *Black Scholar* 23(3, 4):78–80.

West, C. (1993). *Race Matters.* Boston: Beacon.

14

Linking the Psychological and the Social: Feminism, Poststructuralism, and Multiple Personality[1,2]

MARGO RIVERA

The issue of multiple personality is embedded in the issue of child abuse, particularly the sexual abuse of little girls. Two independent studies drawing their cohorts from individuals in treatment with a wide variety of mental health practitioners found that nine out of ten of the people with multiple personality seen in clinical settings are women (Putnam et al. 1986, Ross et al. 1989). Ninety-seven percent of individuals with multiple personality have a documented history of child abuse, usually severe and prolonged, and in the majority of the cases this included childhood sexual abuse, usually incest (Putnam et al. 1986).

There is a growing literature that explores various aspects of the etiology, phenomenology, and treatment of multiple personal-

---

1. Originally published in *Dissociation* 2(1):24–31. Reprinted with permission from *Dissociation*.

2. *Editor's note*: Dr. Rivera has decided against using precise diagnostic terminology (e.g., multiple personality disorder, now termed "dissociative identity disorder") because she is addressing broader philosophic and social issues rather than clinical concerns alone.

ity. Two landmark contributions have been edited volumes of essays by innovators in this field (Braun 1986, Kluft 1985). This literature addresses such questions as: How does multiple personality develop within an individual? In what ways is this internal organization different from and similar to psychological and physiological processes in individuals who are not divided in the same way? What methods are effective in treating individuals with multiple personality? This work has opened up an understanding of a phenomenon that had previously been ignored, distorted, or sensationalized by clinicians and the general public alike. There is a growing awareness among the helping professions that multiple personality is not rare at all (Braun 1984, Coons 1986) and that it can be treated effectively (Kluft 1984, 1986). Many individuals who are suffering from the effects of severe dissociation are now, for the first time, able to get help.

However, though there has been a significant increase in knowledge and understanding about the phenomenon of multiple personality, it has thus far been seen almost entirely in a psychological light. Multiple personality has been framed as a mental health issue, and its investigation remains largely the purview of the professions focused on the treatment of individual pathology, mainly psychiatry and psychology. Though multiple personality is intimately connected with the issue of incest, it has not been raised as a social and political issue in the way that the sexual abuse of children has been in the past ten years.

This chapter explores the issue of multiple personality from a feminist perspective, using some basic concepts of poststructuralism to elucidate this viewpoint. A social as well as a cognitive and psychodynamic understanding of multiple personality is necessary in order to place it in its historical context (Rivera 1988a). This broader conceputalization of the problem is important if we are to succeed not only in helping suffering individuals deal with the consequences of their childhood abuse, but in pointing to the roots of the oppression these individuals experience, and therefore addressing the issue of prevention.

CHILD SEXUAL ABUSE AS A FEMINIST ISSUE

The issues of incest and child sexual abuse were brought into public awareness by the women's movement of the 1970s and early '80s (Armstrong 1978, 1983, Butler 1978, Herman 1981, Herman and Hirschman 1977, Rush 1974, 1977, 1980). Social action programs responding to the needs of rape victims uncovered childhood histories of sexual abuse in large numbers of victims (Butler 1978). Some of the silence about the widespread sexual exploitation of children in our society began to be lifted, and some of the cultural myths that surrounded the issue—for example, that incest is rare (one case in a million in the general population according to the 1975 edition of the *Comprehensive Textbook of Psychiatry* [Freedman et al. 1974]) and that children frequently lie about being sexually abused by adults—began to be challenged.

Feminist theorists and clinicians who address the issue view violence against women and children not simply as a manifestation of the sickness of individual abusers or pathological family systems, but as an inevitable consequence of the inferior social and economic status of women and children and social structures in which male power over women and children is institutionally integrated (Rush 1980). In response to the findings of her large, random sample, retrospective study of adult women in the general population, Russell (1986) found that thirty-eight percent of them had experienced sexual abuse before they were 18 years old, and sixteen percent of them were victims of incestuous abuse. Ninety-five percent of the perpetrators were male, and only five percent of the incidents were ever reported to the police. As a result of her data, Russell concluded that two of the major—and most neglected—causal factors in the occurrence of extrafamilial and intrafamilial child sexual abuse are the way males are socialized to behave sexually and the power structure within which they act out this sexuality.

It was in 1980, when I began to work almost exclusively with children who were victims of sexual abuse and their families, that

I had my first solid realization about sexual politics. The families I worked with had many differences—different racial, ethnic, and cultural backgrounds; different levels of education; different economic status. What they had in common was that the physical and sexual abuse of children by adults and of women and children by men were central issues in almost all of these families, in their past and in their present. As part of trying to understand what I was seeing, I began to read everything I could find about sexual abuse and violence against women and children. The feminist literature in this area made the most sense to me, and I started to frame the suffering I was seeing in broader terms than individual and psychological circumstances. It was also in this context that I met the first woman I recognized as having developed multiple personality as a result of long-term sadistic abuse in childhood.

The multiple personality literature (though there was not very much to read on this subject yet) helped me put a clinical framework around what I was experiencing with this woman and others whom I began to work with. Consequently, after a volatile beginning, I was able to work more deliberately and planfully.

My experiences with the women I was seeing who had multiple and highly dissociated personality states were also giving new meaning to the feminist literature I was reading, and my growing feminist perspective. It became increasingly clear to me that multiple personality and the abuse that precipitates it is not only a personal problem for the women who suffer from it, but is also a manifestation of the oppressive power relations between adults/children and men/women that are endemic in a patriarchal culture. I began to see multiple personality, one of the most severe personal consequences of child sexual abuse, as a feminist issue as well as a psychiatric concern.

Much of the multiple personality and the feminist literature made sense to me, reflected accurately my own perceptions, and, what is more, was pragmatically helpful in my encounters with my clients. The only trouble was that everything I was learning from one type of literature seemed to contradict everything else I was learning from others. The multiple personality literature, mostly

written up to this point by a few doctors, with one notable exception all men, never addressed politics or social oppression at all,
and the feminist literature about violence against women declaimed
the medical model of understanding women's abuse as one of the
foremost ongoing oppressors of women. I learned a great deal from
both of these sources that helped me offer the individuals with
multiple personality compassionate and informed help. But they
did not fit with each other at all.

I found that the same struggle the women with multiple personality were going through in therapy, I was encountering in trying to put my thoughts together about multiple personality. A
plethora of voices—inside my head and outside—were talking to
me about this issue. Both feminist theory and the scientific literature about multiple personality seemed to illuminate certain aspects of the condition, and each seemed to me to be crucial to a
full understanding of multiple personality as it is lived out in a western patriarchal culture. But the medical profession talked in the
language of disorder and pathology; popular literature labeled the
experience exotic, weird, and wonderful; and feminists would
sometimes discount the specificity of the experience, protesting,
"But aren't we all multiples after all?"

Because such a large percentage of individuals with multiple
personality are women and because the issues I address here relate
most obviously to the experience of women in our society, I shall
use the female generic (she, her) in this chapter. This does not indicate any denial on my part of the experience of the many men who
suffer from multiple personality. A social analysis of multiple personality as it is manifested in men in a patriarchal society would be
likely to have many similarities and some significant differences from
one that relates largely to women. But that is a project for the future.

POSTSTRUCTURALISM AND MULTIPLICITY

In order to make some links between these two perspectives, the
social emphasis of feminist theory and the psychological perspec-

tive of the scientific literature, it is useful to look at a third per-spective about multiplicity, that of poststructuralism. The litera-ture of poststructuralism does not directly address the issue of multiple personality. Rather, it questions the very existence of non-multiple unitary identity.

Many influences have helped constitute current poststruc-turalist theory. One of the most fundamental (though often unac-knowledged) of these was the development of quantum theory by physicists in the first three decades of the twentieth century. Quan-tum theory (Bohr 1958, Heisenberg 1971) replaced the determin-ism of classical Newtonian physics (with its basic principle that material creation moves in a way that can be predicted with abso-lute accuracy and is independent of human will and purpose) with the notion of randomness at the foundation of natural processes. This does not mean that knowledge is impossible but that it is rela-tive, a matter of probability distributions, the correlating of ran-dom sequences. The symbol of the universe evolved from that of Newton's clock to one of a game of dice or a pinball machine (Pagels 1982). From the point of view of quantum theory, Bohr (1958) declares that the task of physics is not to find out how Nature is, but rather to discover what we can say about Nature.

At the same time that these revolutions in physics were tak-ing place, the science of structural linguistics was evolving, and poststructuralist theory is derived more immediately and con-sciously from this new field, which came to be called semiotics. Semiotics is a metaphysics of symbols that is based on the premise that reality is not knowable except through its representations in language, its signs. The basic insight of poststructuralism was first taken from the structural linguistics of Ferdinand de Saussure (1974) in which he challenged the modernist assumption that knowledge (which is always framed in language) reflects a real-ity that is outside itself, that is, that we can study objects. Saussurean structural linguistics posits a pre-given fixed structuring of lan-guage, prior to its actualization in speech or writing. Language, for Saussure, is a chain of signs, an abstract system. This struc-ture, far from reflecting some sort of natural world outside its domain, itself constitutes social reality for human beings (Weedon 1987).

This notion of universal structures that construct our social reality was taken up in a number of different areas. The psychoanalyst Lacan (1975) applied the principles of structuralist semiotics to the work of Freud, pointing to universal social structures that guarantee psychosexual development along certain lines. The anthropologist Lévi-Strauss (1963) developed a structuralist theory of human society in which the incest taboo and the exchange (as property) of women by men are the universal principles that underlie the functioning of all societies. These notions of fixed and universal meanings were central to the structuralism that poststructuralism grew out of and transformed.

The term *poststructuralism* is applied to a range of philosophical positions, some very different from others. Foucault's (1972, 1981, 1982) theory of discourse and power, Derrida's (1976) critique of the notion that language is a tool for expressing something beyond itself, and the French feminist challenge to white male definitions of identity and self (Cixous 1986, Irigaray 1985a,b, Kristeva 1986) all represent streams of poststructuralism. What they all have in common is a radical critique of the humanist notion of the coherent, essentially rational individual who is the author of her own meanings and the agent of her own productions. They also profess an abandonment of the belief in an essential unique individual identity. Poststructuralism deconstructs the object that psychology takes as pre-given: the human subject. It insists that forms of subjectivity are produced historically in a field of power relations. The notion of the individual has no meaning outside the socially and historically specific practices which constitute her (Henriques et al. 1984).

A modernist philosophy of science views the human being as the center and agent of all social production, including knowledge. This humanist perspective defines the self as essentially coherent and rational. Mistakes in socialization, conflicting and confusing stimuli, sometimes cause glitches in the smooth and predictable running of the machinery, and these need to be set right through appropriate intervention. We are all imbued to a large extent with this view of the world and ourselves as orderly and knowable entities.

However, though this is a comforting view, we live in a time when the modernist faith in a science that claims to study objects and claims the knowledge derived as an object is under attack and indeed has been effectively undermined. A poststructuralist philosophy, rather than attempting to map the contours of nature and to grasp the object of study, attempts to study constructions of knowledge, using a language of verbs rather than nouns. Within the field of psychology this contemporary movement to challenge the nature of knowledge has been called the social constructionist movement. Social constructionism views the role of psychology as exploring the processes by which people come to account for their lives in the world, rather than describing and explaining those people and that world (Gergen 1985).

Poststructuralism posits language as the place where our identities and our social organizations are constructed, defined, and contested. The basic insight that poststructuralism draws from semiotics is that language, far from reflecting the "natural" world or social reality, constitutes these realities for us. Different discourses are competing ways of giving meaning to the world and of organizing social institutions and practices, offering the individual a range of modes of subjectivity (Weedon 1987).

Poststructuralist theory offers an explanation of why changing conceptualizations in psychiatry and psychology often have more to do with shifting relations of power than they do with scientific advance. The decline of interest in the concept of dissociation and in hypnosis as a treatment technique in the early twentieth century, for example, reflects patterns of social history that kept multiple personality almost entirely unacknowledged and untreated for the better part of a century after Pierre Janet (1889) and Morton Prince (1906) both offered groundbreaking explanations and treatment paradigms for dealing with the phenomenon. Freud discounted this important work, and with the growing ascendance of psychoanalysis as the theory and technique of prestige, both the concept of dissociation and the diagnosis of multiple personality fell into disrepute. There were two significant contributions to the decline in professional interest in hypnosis and multiple personality (Ellenberger 1970): Freud's positing of *repression* rather than Janet's notion of dissociation as identifying the mechanism by which information becomes inaccessible to conscious recollection, and Bleuler's introduction of the term schizophrenia (and stating that multiple personality is a form of schizophrenia).

In the Middle Ages and the Renaissance, when the discourse of religion was the most powerful force in Western culture, women who displayed multiple personality would have been considered under the power of the devil, and they would have been punished, usually burned for their sinfulness. Twentieth-century ideology frames that practice as ignorant and barbaric. We call *multiple personality disorder* a *mental health problem*. Within the contemporary Western discourse of psychiatry, the notion of multiple personality disorder refers to a mental abnormality that demands psychiatric intervention. It contains, therefore, all the conceptualizations and social practices that relate to the framing of the phenomenon in this way. In other cultures and at other times, *speaking in tongues* was interpreted as a sign of spiritual insight and giftedness. The individual who can take on different voices and personae at different times was considered an adept, and she experienced herself and played a particular role in society concomitant with that definition. Isadore (1986) explores some of the varying discourses that exist around dissociation in different cultures and the roles and functions they play in the maintenance of societal norms and functions within those cultures.

Poststructuralist theory addresses an individual's experience by showing where it comes from and how it relates to material social practices and the power relations that structure them. It addresses issues such as desires, meanings, and the relationship of socially and historically constructed desires and meanings to the development of identity and social practices (Henriques et al. 1984). Poststructuralists do not deny the complexity of the often unconscious forces that contribute to the construction of the individual—indeed, one important stream of the poststructuralist movement emerged from within psychoanalysis in France (Irigaray 1985a,b, Kristeva 1986, Lacan 1975)—but they emphasize the reconstruction of our culture in the life history of every new member of the human race (Mitchell 1974).

POSTSTRUCTURALISM AND MULTIPLE PERSONALITY

The phenomenon of multiple personality is a vivid illustration of poststructuralism in action. Following the poststructuralist emphasis on the production of forms of subjectivity through social apparatus, we can look at the construction of the alter personalities of an individual with multiple personality as an example of the continual production and reproduction of specific social positionings and practices. Each personality state identifies with a particular position according to the role that that personality state learned to play as part of the individual's overall survival strategy. We can learn a great deal about both the individual and the culture by watching the interplay among personalities.

In my experience working with women who experience multiple personality, it is very common for their vulnerable child personalities and their seductive and/or compliant personalities to be female and their aggressive protector personalities to be male. Other therapists have also found this to be the case, though there has been no research so far on the subject (Kluft, personal communication 1987). The experience of these alter personalities as they fight with each other for status, power, and influence over the individual and her behavior is powerfully illustrative of the social construction of masculinity and femininity in our society.

Also, the range of positions offered to the states in which the individual perceives herself as female are illuminative. Within one woman, for example, a particular alter often identifies with the position of woman as sexual object for the use of men, another identifies with the position of woman as emotionally vulnerable and invested in creating and nurturing personal relationships with others, and yet another with the position of woman as self-sacrificing and masochistic. Each of these roles enables her to respond adaptively as a child in a situation of threat and sexual assault. These roles, as they are incorporated into the increasingly consolidated identities of the alter personalities as the little girl grows into womanhood, are developed in an idiosyncratic way in response to her particular circumstances. They also represent the extremes of stereotypical self-identification that are central to the constitution of femininity as it is lived by all women in a patriarchal society.

The interactions of these personalities are a play in which social processes can be viewed with more clarity than is usually possible. For every personality who identifies with one position (the compliant little girl, for example) there is often another personality who ferociously resists that position (the anti-social boy). Thus, both social control and resistance to that control can be clearly seen in the life of the individual with multiple personality. The dynamic of power and powerlessness inheres in the differences between personalities and in the shifts from one to another, depending on the circumstances and their responses to those circumstances at any given moment. Each alter personality also illustrates within itself aspects of both social regulation and resistance to that regulation (for example, the woman who sees her duty as servicing men sexually may keep a razor blade handy, and she may occasionally use it on an unsuspecting customer), and they all influence each other. Thus, in the life of a woman with multiple personality at the florid stage of her condition, we have an unusual opportunity to watch personal identity as it continues to be constructed and reconstructed with the social context of the individual and within the larger social order.

In witnessing and participating in the therapeutic journey of a woman with multiple personality, the notion of identity undergoes a shift. The search for identity does not appear to be a digging for an essential self, the *true self* of the object relations psychoanalysts (Winnicott 1965) that is hidden beneath protective layers of socialization. What emerges is a multiple, shifting, and often self-contradictory identity made up of heterogeneous and heteronomous representations of personal experiences of gender, race, class, religion, and culture (deLauretis 1986).

I have found many powerful and telling insights in this work on the deconstruction of identity that are useful for understanding the phenomenon of multiple personality. It opens up for study the complex relations of power and domination—such as the widespread devaluation and oppression of children and women—that structure our world as an area of exploration when looking for the causes of multiple personality, rather than simply focusing on the immediate causal factors of child abuse, seen as a consequence of individual or family pathology. It emphasizes the reality that individuals construct their identities in relation to their social positionings that are intimately related to variables such as race, class, gender, and religion, rather than responding to oppression by developing symptoms that can be seen and addressed in an ahistorical and universal way. It points to the important similarities between the contradictory personalities and positionings within the individual who uses her dissociative capacities to create an array of clearly distinguishable personalities and the rest of us who are capable of pretending to a unified, non-contradictory identity and denying our complex locations amid different positions of power and desire. It challenges simple notions of *fusion* and *integration* as a togetherness that dissolves all contradictions, and it problematizes our psychological and cultural construction of categories such as gender, sexual identity, and sexual orientation. Each of these areas merits exploration, but for the purposes of this chapter, let me address just one of the issues in a little more detail: notions of fusion and integration.

COMING TOGETHER: FUSION AND INTEGRATION

Notions of *fusion* and *integration* are pivotal in the literature about multiple personality. They are often juxtaposed to concepts such as identity problems and fragmentation, the latter being the problems and the former the solution, the goal of the therapeutic process. Multiple personality is, above all, a severe and chronic phenomenon of dissociation, of dividedness. There has been a great deal of discussion about the relative merits of integration as a goal of the clinical treatment of multiple personality, with some practitioners and some individuals with multiple personality opting for functional dividedness with negotiated cooperation among alters. However, most experienced therapists have found, empirically, that those individuals who did not move toward integration and continued throughout treatment to guard their separations jealously were much more likely to lapse into their earlier state of dysfunctional dividedness and acute suffering (Kluft 1986). Consequently, moving in the direction of replacing dividedness with unity, and learning other ways of coping with stress than dissociating, are usually among the long-term goals of therapy.

In the lexicon of poststructuralism, concepts such as a unified self and a well-defined individual identity are not only not viewed as ideals but are considered to be dangerous ideological fictions used to erase the awareness of differences within and between human beings. The notion of a self constructed throughout a lifetime of multiple positionings and practices elaborated by poststructuralism is used to undermine the concept of a nonproblematic individual identity. It poses a challenge to both the epistemological basis of mainstream psychology and psychiatry and the practices of social control that often emerge from them (Henriques et al. 1984).

Is there any way to combine clinical notions of integration as a therapeutic goal with the poststructuralist challenge? At first glance, these perspectives, as they relate to the notion of integration, appear polarized, perhaps even irreconcilable. Placing them side by side raises important questions for therapists working with people who have multiple personality. What are we suggesting when we talk about integration as the goal of therapy? Are we fostering the creation of someone who will fit in better, who will not always be torn by conflicting voices and desires? Someone who is complacent in the knowledge she has constructed about who she is and her place in the world? Someone who can suppress the awareness of the terrible contradictions we live with every day in a racist, sexist, classist society? Whether these notions are inherently contradictory depends on what it is we mean when we use terms like *integration*. Given the challenge to the notion of a unified, non-contradictory individual identity or self that conforms with social expectations that poststructuralism properly raises, is there any way of talking about integration, fusion, or unification as regards the phenomenon of multiple personality without falling into a trap of creating the illusion of a stable, non-problematic notion of identity that lends itself to manipulation and social control? Is the concept of integration a useful one at all?

I think so. Effective therapy demands that the person with multiple personality attempt to hold different and sometimes contradictory emotional states and points of view that have been encapsulated in the alter personality states in one central consciousness. We can talk about the erosion of dissociative barriers to a central consciousness that can handle the contradictions of the different voices and different desires within one person in a way that offers a functional and useful definition of integration, and I think we need this kind of vocabulary when we are talking about the therapeutic process. This definition of integration prescribes, not the silencing of different voices with different points of view, but the growing ability to call all those voices "I," to disidentify with any one of them as the whole story, and to recognize that the construction of personal identity is a complex continuing affair in which we are inscribed in culture in myriad contradictory ways.

With this framework, the goal of treatment is not to stop this continuous process of the construction of identity but to open it up to examination, so that, in eroding the dissociative barriers between the personality states with their often contradictory positions, the individual who has had relatively little control over her personalities can reflect upon the power relations that constitute her and the society in which she must live and work. This opening up of previously hidden, disguised, and inaccessible areas offers her not unlimited freedom, but an opportunity to choose from a wider range of options and to produce new meanings for herself that are less rigidly constrained by the power relations of her past. It offers her more maneuverability among the power structures that frame all our lives.

For example, a woman who develops an array of personality states, some of which she subjectively experiences as male and others of which she experiences as female, does not necessarily, through the process of integration, relax into a comfortably and stereotypically feminine sense of her identity as a woman as our society defines woman. The claims of the different personalities to be different genders offer us a unique opportunity to explore an area that is often taken for granted: the social construction of the notion of gender in our society and the way in which it shapes our lives (Rivera 1988b).

A poststructuralist perspective expands the notion of gender beyond its concrete manifestation in the different physical reproductive organs of women and men and points to the reality that the notion of "natural" sexual difference functions in our culture to mask, on the grounds of incontrovertible facts of nature, the social opposition of men and women (Wittig 1982). By examining the various ways different cultures, subcultural groups, and individuals in different contexts within the same culture understand gender, the referents for the terms *woman* and *man* are obscured (Gergen 1985). Possibilities are opened up that destabilize and reframe the question of gender differences.

The polarization of man and woman that is a result of differential socialization in a patriarchal culture is not a natural process. The relationship of human beings to their sexed bodies is not a simple instinctual one, as it is in most mammals. Men and women must struggle to fit themselves into the proper gender positionings that the laws of society demand, and the outcome of this struggle is never secure. The notion of a pre-existent sexual difference that secures sexual identity for both sexes is a myth (Mitchell and Rose 1982), and the position that there is a natural, essential sexuality that predates the child's insertion into the process of her or his socialization blinds us to the more complex and problematic nature of sexuality and gender difference that is central to the individual's difficult insertion into culture.

Opening up an awareness of the social construction of categories such as male and female as they are applied to human beings offers a wider scope for the integrated individual with multiple personality so that integration need not involve a simple solution to her conflicts regarding gender identity. The failure to slip easily into cultural roles and relationships lies at the heart of a rich psychic life, and a woman who has integrated dissociated personality states into one central consciousness need not pretend that this is not so. Her state of struggling consciously with what it means to be a woman in our society can be an example of what Freud declared to be the situation of all women—they do not assume their femininity without a struggle and only at great cost (Freud 1924, 1931). The range of healthy and happy outcomes of this struggle is wider for a woman who has acknowledged a variety of contradictory impulses and desires in terms of her gender identity than Freud might have dreamed possible.

It is not the multiplicity that the individual with multiple personality experiences that is problematic but the defensive dissociation and the consequent limited awareness and ability to act on that awareness. Jane Flax (1987), a feminist psychoanalytic psychotherapist, notes that, though she recognizes the contribution poststructuralist writers have made in deconstructing the artifacts of white male concepts of self, they are naive and unaware of their own privileged cohesion when they call for a decentered self. They tend to confuse all possible forms of self with the unitary, mentalist, de-eroticized, masterful, and oppositional selves they rightfully criticize. Flax (1987) argues that it is important for women to retrieve repressed aspects of the self and to hold them in their consciousness together, rather than abandon any claim to agential identity and cohesiveness. She suggests that, though it is important to be skeptical toward the humanist myth of the rational unitary individual, it behooves us to be suspicious as well about voices that may be urging us to submit to our limitations as the essence of our nature. Flax asks the question, "Is our only choice a masculine, overly differentiated, unitary self or no self at all?" (p. 106).

She answers the question with another question: "Without remembered selves, how can we act?" (pp. 106–107).

So, the vocabulary of *integration, fusion*, and *personality unification* proves necessary. However, it is also important to recognize the dangers involved in any such discourse and to be aware of the pitfalls of taking for granted that we know just what integration is or to assume that it is more than it is. Integration—or consciousness-raising—does not accomplish itself by replacing old discourses with new, unproblematic ones. It is accomplished as a result of the contradictions in our old positions, desires, and practices mingling and dialoguing with the contradictions in our new ones (Hollway 1984) with more flexible tools for constructing consciousness.

CONCLUSION

Poststructuralist philosophy points to the similarities between individuals who elaborate multiple personality as an outcome of child abuse and others who, although they do not use the radical dissociative defenses individuals with multiple personality do, also construct their identities in a field of power relations, both personal and political, in multiple and contradictory ways. This perspective can aid us in seeing multiple personality more clearly and consistently, not as a strange and exotic phenomenon, a clinical oddity, but as one of the many manifestations of alternative forms of consciousness on the continuum of the personal human responses both to our immediate, intimate environment that affects our growth and development and also to the wider social and historical context that has a no less powerful, although often less obvious, impact on determining who we become as persons.

Integrating psychological understandings of multiple personality with social and political ones is helpful in a number of ways: philosophically, clinically, and practically. That maxim of feminist praxis, *the personal is political*, can be an effective principle in the therapy of individuals with multiple personality. Much of the rage and fear and confusion in the woman with multiple personality is a direct result of social oppression, both in her childhood and in her present-day life. One of the consequences of placing her experiences within a larger framework is that an individual can begin to take her history less personally at the same time as she is personally reclaiming that history. This can be a liberating answer to the perennial question of the abused child—why me? What is there about me that causes the people who are supposed to care for me to hate me and hurt me? In combination with recovering her own past, a woman can come to understand that it was *not* just her, that she shares her oppression with other women, and to some extent, with all women. This, then, usually eases considerably the shame that pervades her sense of herself (Rivera 1987).

Framing multiple personality as a social and political issue as well as a psychological problem for the individuals who suffer from it not only enhances the healing process for traumatized individuals, but also opens up a wider field for investigation and intervention beyond the treatment of those who have already suffered from severe abuse. The critical issue of prevention of the abuse of children must be linked to an accurate and full understanding of the multileveled causes of this crime. In order to effect change in the high prevalence rates, prevention strategies must be directed to as many levels of the problem as possible. So far, much of the emphasis in prevention programs has been on the individual child and family, and little work has been done on the relationship among social norms, structures, and practices (such as child pornography and the sexualization of children in the media) and the prevalence of child abuse (Finkelhor 1984). The cultural configuration of societies that have high levels of child abuse and sequelae such as multiple personality is an area that needs further scholarly exploration similar to some of the research that has been carried out regarding rape (Sanday 1981).

Multiple personality is a rich clinical phenomenon. It offers valuable potential for studying the psychophysiologic makeup of the human being (Putnam 1984). Its exploration provides a unique learning experience for both researchers and clinicians. The depth, complexity, and volatility of its treatment present a challenge to even the most experienced practitioner. But it is essential to remember that multiple personality is, above all, a vulnerable child's response to abuse and terrorization and the adult's ongoing incorporation of these defensive adaptations into her life in ways that often result in a great deal of suffering. Ultimately, taking into consideration the social and political aspects of the issue of multiple personality is important because it expands our capacity to address this suffering on many levels in the broadest and most effective way.

REFERENCES

Armstrong, L. (1979). *Kiss Daddy Goodnight*. New York: Hawthorn.

——— (1983). *The Home Front: Notes from the Family War Zone*. New York: McGraw-Hill.

Bohr, N. (1958). *Atomic Physics and Human Knowledge*. New York: Wiley.

Braun, B. (1984). Foreword: symposium on multiple personality. *Psychiatric Clinics of North America* 7:1–2.

———, ed. (1986). *Treatment of Multiple Personality Disorder*. Washington, DC: American Psychiatric Press.

Butler, S. (1978). *Conspiracy of Silence: The Trauma of Incest*. San Francisco: New Glide Publications.

Cixous, H. (1986). Sorties. In *The Newly Born Woman*, ed. H. Cixous and C. Clement. Minneapolis: University of Minnesota Press.

Coons, P. (1986). The prevalence of multiple personality disorder. *Newsletter of the International Society for the Study of Multiple Personality and Dissociation* 4:1–7.

deLauretis, T. (1986). Feminist studies, critical studies: issues, terms, and contexts. In *Feminist Studies, Critical Studies*. Bloomington: University of Indiana Press.

Derrida, J. (1976). *Of Grammatology*. Baltimore, MD: Johns Hopkins University Press.

Ellenberger, H. (1970). *The Discovery of the Unconscious*. New York: Basic Books.

Finkelhor, D. (1984). *Child Sexual Abuse: New Theory and Research*. New York: The Free Press.

Flax, J. (1987). Remembering the selves: Is the repressed gendered? *Michigan Quarterly Review* 16:92–110.

Foucault, M. (1972). *Madness and Civilization: A History of Insanity in the Age of Reason*. New York: Vintage.

——— (1981). *The History of Sexuality. Vol. 1: An Introduction*. Harmondsworth, UK: Pelican.

——— (1982). The subject and power. *Critical Inquiry* 8:777–789.

Freedman, A., Kaplan, H., and Sadock, B., eds. (1975). *Comprehensive Textbook of Psychiatry*, 2nd ed. Baltimore, MD: Williams & Wilkins.

Freud, S. (1931). Female sexuality. *Standard Edition* 21.

Gergen, K. (1985). The social constructionist movement in modern psychology. *American Psychologist* 40:266–275.

Heisenberg, W. (1971). *Physics and Beyond*. New York: Harper & Row.

Henriques, J., Hollway, W., Urwin, C., et al. (1984). *Changing the Subject: Social Regulation and Subjectivity*. London: Methuen.

Herman, J. (1981). *Father–Daughter Incest*. Cambridge, MA: Harvard University Press.

Herman, J., and Hirschman, I. (1977). Father–daughter incest. *Signs* 2:1–22.

Hollway, W. (1984). Gender differences and the production of subjectivity. In *Changing the Subject: Social Regulation and Subjectivity*, ed. J. Henriques, W. Hollway, C. Urwin, et al. London: Methuen.

Irigaray, L. (1985a). *Speculum of the Other Woman*. Ithaca, NY: Cornell University Press.

——— (1985b). *This Sex Which Is Not One*. Ithaca, NY: Cornell University Press.

Isadore, S. (1986). *The role and function of dissociative reactions in society*. Paper presented at the Third International Conference on Multiple Personality Dissociative States. Abstract published in *Dissociative Disorders* 1986. Chicago: Rush-Presbyterian St. Luke's Medical Center, September.

Janet, P. (1889). *L'Automatisme psychologique*. Paris: Alcan.

Kluft, R. (1986). Personality unification in multiple personality disorder: a follow-up study. In *Treatment of Multiple Personality Disorder*, ed. B. Braun. Washington, DC: American Psychiatric Press.

———, ed. (1985). *Childhood Antecedents of Multiple Personality Disorder*. Washington, DC: American Psychiatric Press.

Kristeva, J. (1986). *The Kristeva Reader*. Oxford, UK: Blackwell.

Lacan, J. (1975). *Le seminaire livre. XX: Encore*. Paris: Editions du Seuil.

Lévi-Strauss, C. (1963). *Structural Anthropology*. New York: Basic Books.

Mitchell, J., and Rose, J., eds. (1982). *Feminine Sexuality: Jacques Lacan and the École Freudienne.* New York: Pantheon.

Mitchell, L. (1974). *Psychoanalysis and Feminism: Freud, Reich, Laing and Women.* New York: Norton.

Pagels, H. (1982). *The Cosmic Codes; Quantum Physics as the Language of Nature.* New York: Simon & Schuster.

Prince, M. (1906). *The Dissociation of a Personality.* New York: Longmans, Green.

Putnam, F. W. (1984). The psychophysiologic investigation of multiple personality disorder. *Psychiatric Clinics of North America* 7:31–39.

Putnam, F. W., Gurott, J., Silverman, E., et al. (1986). The clinical phenomenon of multiple personality disorder: 100 recent cases. *Journal of Clinical Psychiatry* 47:285–293.

Rivera, M. (1987). Multiple personality: an outcome of child abuse. *Canadian Women Studies: Les Cahiers de la Femme* 8(4):18–22.

―――― (1988a). *All of them speak: feminism, poststructuralism and multiple personality.* Ph.D. dissertation. University of Toronto, Ontario, Canada.

―――― (1988b). Am I a boy or a girl? Multiple personality as a window on gender differences. *Resources for Feminist Research / Documentation sur la Recherche Feministe* 17(2):41–46.

Ross, C., Norton, G., and Wozney, K. (1989). Multiple personality disorder: an analysis of 236 cases. *Canadian Journal of Psychiatry.*

Rush, F. (1974). The sexual abuse of children: a feminist point of view. In *Rape: The First Sourcebook for Women,* ed. N. Connell and C. Wilson. New York: New American Library.

―――― (1977). The Freudian cover-up. *Chrysalis* 1:31–45.

―――― (1980). *The Best-Kept Secret: Sexual Abuse of Children.* New York: McGraw-Hill.

Russell, D. (1986). *The Secret Trauma: Incest in the Lives of Girls and Women.* New York: Basic Books.

Sanday, P. (1981). The socio-cultural of rape: a cross-cultural study. *Journal of Social Issues* 37:5–27.

Saussure, F. de (1974). *A Course in General Linguistics.* London: Fontana.

Weedon, C. (1997). *Feminist Practice and Poststructuralist Theory.* Oxford, UK: Blackwell.

Winnicott, D. (1965). *The Maturational Processes and the Facilitating Environment.* New York: International Universities Press.

Wittig, M. (1982). The category of sex. *Feminist Issues* 2:103–111.

Index